Every Inch a **A NEW LIGHT SIX PAIGE**

Fred O. Paige

THE GRAHAM GLASS CO
STRENGTH
BLOWN UPSIDE DOWN
EVANSVILLE. IND.

PAIGE-DETROIT
PD
DETROIT - MICHIGAN

GRAHAM BROTHERS
TRUCK - BUILDER

JEWETT

J. B. Graham.

JEWETT

A Thrifty Six JEWETT *Built by Paige*

PAIGE
The Standard of Value and Quality

CKS

Paige-Detroit

G-Boy

GRAHAM

The Graham Legacy:
Graham-Paige to 1932

Michael E. Keller

Best Wish

Turner Publishing Company
Publishers of America's History
P.O. Box 3101
Paducah, Kentucky 42002-3101

Co-published by Turner Publishing Company
and Mark A. Thompson, Associate
Publisher

Author: Michael E. Keller
Pre-Press work by M. T. Publishing
Company, Inc.
Graphic Designer: Elizabeth A. Dennis

Library of Congress Catalog
Card No. 98-75193

ISBN: 1-56311-470-4

Printed in the United States of America

Limited Edition of 1000 copies of which this
book is number ___454___

A Graham-Paige motor car – an enduring source of pride.

Contents

Dedication

Dedicated to my family for its unwavering support.

Psalm 143:5

Acknowledgments

My research into the Graham legacy has been profoundly enriched
by the gracious help of the following individuals:
Karen England
Richard Lythgoe
Jeff Gillis
Jerry Viste
Beth Sillars
G. R. Brigham
Bob Greene
D. J. Kava
Bill Whorrall
Walter O. MacIlvain
Dean Snellgrove
Michael Lamm
Agatha Pierce Kraft
Robert C. Graham, Jr.
David Graham
Karl Zahm

Foreword

Graham-Paige Motors Corporation lives again in the pages of *The Graham Legacy: Graham-Paige To 1932*. Michael E. Keller's factual account is based upon his thorough research, giving a clear picture of the formation and operations of this former Dearborn, Michigan, automaker. Keller addresses the myriad of Graham Brothers' trucks, Paige, Graham-Paige and Graham automobile types and provides a full recounting of these vehicles' mechanical and styling details. In addition, the book incorporates the history of the three Graham brothers (Joseph, Robert and Ray) who rose from near anonymity to positions of prominence in such diverse fields as farming and glass manufacturing to the production of trucks and fine automobiles. This blending of historical, personal, business and technical aspects result in an informative and thoroughly interesting read.

In keeping with Graham-Paige Motors Corporation's motto—"To Sell Well is to Serve Well"— the Graham brothers sought to foster the same measure of integrity, honor and loyalty in their employees and dealers as they adhered to since childhood. The development of those values, rarely stressed in modern corporate America, was the cornerstone upon which the Graham brothers built their business. Keller explores the extent to which the company-sponsored "Graham-Paige Legion" pursued those virtues in its management, manufacture, promotion and sales.

Michael Keller is eminently qualified to write *The Graham Legacy* given his long and intense interest in all aspects of Graham-Paige Motors Corporation. Not only has he been involved with the Graham Owners Club-International for over 20 years (serving as president for two terms), but he also owns two Graham-Paige automobiles. Keller's personal archive of original resource data is large and inclusive: comprised of factory sales literature, magazine advertisements, internal corporate documents, photographs, service manuals, sales bulletins, data books, and other materials. He has also amassed hundreds of clippings from contemporary industry trade publications, which provide a comprehensive overview of virtually every facet of the Graham brothers' companies. The *Graham-Legacy* is enhanced by Keller's invaluable personal interviews with the Graham brothers' relatives, former employees and original owners of company-built vehicles.

The Graham Legacy: Graham-Paige To 1932 by Michael E. Keller is the most definitive work ever written on the history of the antecedents, principals and products of Graham-Paige Motors, Incorporated.

Karl S. Zahm

Preface

They were Captains of Industry. It was a time in American history when successful industrialists were held in high esteem.

Visitors to Detroit in January of 1929 were exposed to the city's typically frigid winter weather conditions. But to the more than 3,000 men in attendance at the cavernous Masonic Temple Auditorium on the evening of the 3rd, the weather was inconsequential. After all, this was the Motor City, a place from which much of America's prosperity emanated and this was the second annual dealers' meeting for one of the fastest-growing concerns in the motor car industry. Expectations were high.

Many of the men had been in New York City less than a year before when this company presented its first offerings to the public. That first meeting of dealers and stockholders had not only been a spirited success, but an indicator this was one concern which was not only going to produce a quality product but also do business in a first class manner. Sports luminaries Knute Rockne and Gene Tunney were guest speakers at that initial meeting held at the prestigious Hotel Roosevelt. One newspaper described that dealers' luncheon as one which "set a new standard for impressiveness and effectiveness." The new automobiles immediately met with favorable public and industry reaction.

The 12 months following the initial introduction were a period of tremendous growth. The manufacturing plant had more than doubled in size and demand was far ahead of what the company could produce. In 1928 the firm produced and sold more automobiles during its initial year than any other firm in the industry.

Considering the profits accrued during that year, there was no need to go to extra lengths to encourage dealers to attend this second annual meeting. But the firm did so in a historic manner. This company had provided a "speaking film" encouraging the major distributors and dealers to attend. This was the very first time the motion picture medium had been used in the motor car industry. It was a presentation done with style and class. The film was narrated by Lionel Atwill, one of the nation's foremost actors, and the incidental music was provided by the great Roxy Theater Orchestra.

The principals of this new firm invited dealers, salesmen, and stockholders to visit the plant to see the newly enlarged facility, to hear of even loftier goals for the immediate future, and to enjoy an impressive evening program dedicated to success.

That film and the program easily fueled the dealers' enthusiasm with reports on the record-level production during those first 12 months, the parallel growth of European and other foreign markets, and the formation of an ever-expanding dealers' organization called the "Legion." The historic talkie ended with the Legion March, the anthem penned for this new dealers' organization by Arthur Pryor, eminent American musician and composer.

The film noted that following the meeting and program, tours of the manufacturing facility, new engineering building, and recently completed test track on Lonyo Road would be conducted. There was much to look forward to, but it was the program on that cold winter's evening at the Masonic Auditorium which would be in everyone's memory for years to come.

The program was titled "Four Speeds Forward," an obvious reference to one of the motor car's engineering features. The theme of the program was Chivalry, and appropriate medieval features were employed throughout. The evening was produced by John Murray Anderson, a name well known for his many successes on Broadway. The evening's presentation included dialogue, choral and orchestral pieces, ballet, and a unique animal act. Tyrone Power, distinguished actor, portrayed "The Spirit of the Legion" with the assistance of a cast of over 260. Scenic design was provided by the Metropolitan Opera House of New York City, and the dance portions were presented by the New York Ballet Company. A chorus of over 100 voices accompanied the Detroit Symphony for the musical portions. The four-act presentation included themes of courage, loyalty, integrity, and unity of purpose; themes that the advertising department would employ in portraying the company's business creed. The portion concerned with courage displayed the skills of the famous animal trainer Clyde Beatty, supported by twenty-six lions and tigers. Official congratulations and hopes of continued future success were extended by Michigan Governor Fred W. Green. News reports gave notice this program was the most opulent dealers' meeting in Detroit history.

The hosts of this sales convention were three brothers. As a business team, they had over two decades of manufacturing successes in businesses both large and small, related and unrelated to the automobile industry. In a quiet and dignified manner Joseph Bolden Graham, Ray Austin Graham, and Robert Cabel Graham observed the evening's events. Having achieved many previous business goals, their loftiest dream had come true—they had produced a successful motor car bearing their name. The Graham-Paige automobile was well on its way to becoming known in America and abroad as a quality car, backed by a successful management team, one giving value for investment.

The following pages tell the story of the Graham-Paige Motors Corporation to 1932. The genesis of the three brothers as a management team is examined, with the trucks and automobiles they produced highlighted. But just as important, it is the story of the Graham family. In contrast to many other marques, Graham trucks and automobiles were a family undertaking, from beginning to end. This is a story of which the Graham family can be justifiably proud.

Michael E. Keller
Appleton, Wisconsin
September, 1998

Antecedents

Antecedents

There is no doubt that James Graham felt confident and quite satisfied with his life when he affixed his signature to the document placed in front of him on February 6, 1797. After all, he was 25 years old, considered by all to be a success in his chosen profession and was recently engaged to one of the most attractive and socially desirable young women in town. Having left his native Delaware upon reaching his majority, Graham had sought his livelihood, as most young men did in those pioneer years, by tilling the soil. Honest hard work, coupled with his Scottish background, served him well and he prospered, enough so that William Mitchell, one of the more affluent businessmen in Bourbon County, Kentucky, not only promised his daughter Jean's hand in marriage but also guaranteed their union in the form of a $50 marriage bond.

Three sons were born to Pennsylvania natives William and Mary (nee Wilcox) Mitchell, but Jean[1] was the only daughter to survive to adulthood. Her parents had emigrated to what is now known as Paris, Kentucky, in about 1782, shortly after the Battle of Blue Licks. The need for a qualified tanner in the rapidly developing area had drawn the Mitchell family to Kentucky, and William quickly gained a reputation for quality work. Good business sense and a strong work ethic provided the Mitchell family with the respect and the rewards associated with a successful business.

The parents of Jean Mitchell approved of young James Graham not only because of his ability to support their daughter, but also because he shared their strict Scottish-Presbyterian religious beliefs. Jean Mitchell's grandparents had emigrated from Scotland to America, via the north of Ireland, and although they fully embraced the American spirit, they did not abandon the beliefs of the "Old Scotch Church."

William Mitchell's faith in young James Graham was well placed. The next year the marriage was consummated and a homestead established. The eagerly awaited and proudly announced news of Jean's first pregnancy was made known in early 1799. Tragically, James and Jean were to know grief early in their marriage. Their first born died the day of its birth, December 1, 1799. In 1800 their first daughter was born. James and Jean's wish to have a large family was granted, and over the next nineteen years their daughter was joined by nine siblings.

History does not record why James and Jean Graham elected to leave Paris, Kentucky, in 1826. It may have been the reports that Jean's brother, James, relayed to the entire Mitchell clan concerning the opportunities and good life to be found in Indiana.[2] Perhaps a man with a large family and limited land at hand heeded the call to seek the promises of the American frontier. Regardless of what prompted their

Dated February 6, 1797, this marriage bond was signed by James Graham (Grayham) and William Mitchell (Mitchel). James Graham was legally indebted in the amount of $50.

Thomas Bolden Graham (1806-1885) and Margaret Hyatt Graham (1827-1853), paternal grandparents of Joseph, Robert, and Ray Graham.

move, James and Jean were to make Daviess County, Indiana, their home. It was to prove a propitious decision. James' success as a farmer continued, and although several of his older children remained in Kentucky, southern Indiana was to become the home of future generations of Grahams. One of the children to make the move with his parents was Thomas Bolden Graham. Born in 1806, Thomas was to become a prominent citizen of not only Daviess County, but the state of Indiana.

Family tradition made its impression on Thomas, and he chose a profession related to leather, just as his grandfather had done many years before. Thomas learned the saddler's trade while in Kentucky, apprenticing under his uncle, Thomas Mitchell. As his grandfather had earlier profited by fulfilling a need in a frontier, Thomas filled a related need in a newer frontier. His business prospered, allowing him to expand into related areas of business. Soon he was recognized as the most successful general merchandiser in the area. At different times of his business life he was associated with other pioneers of the area, notably Elisha Hyatt, Col. John Van Trees[3], and John Fairchild.

Historical accounts described Thomas "as self-made and successful man, and [has] aided much in the progress of the county." The United States Census of 1860 lists not only his family, but also notes that as a merchant he had holdings in real estate valued at $40,000 and personal property of over $25,000. His political principles and ideals were those of the Republican Party, but his character and standing in the community and state were never tainted by political scheming.

Thomas' personal life was marked by tragedy: his first wife, Lydia McCormick, and his second wife, Charlotte Foote, died young. There were no children. His par-

ents died only four days apart in 1838. But in 1847, at the age of 41, Thomas married Margaret Hyatt, daughter of an early pioneer of Daviess County, Thomas Hyatt. This happy union produced seven children. Once again a strong work ethic, coupled with the opportunities afforded by the American frontier, provided the Graham family not only the security of a happy hearth but also the respect of the community. Again, it also was the basis for the achievements for the following generation; of the seven children born to Margaret and Thomas Graham, Ziba Foote Graham was to become the patriarch of the family's industrial legacy.

Originally part of the Northwest Territory, Daviess County, Indiana is nestled between the east and west forks of the White River.[4] When Indiana was granted statehood in 1816, most areas of the state were the domain of trappers, Indians, and hardy settlers intent on turning the massive forests into productive farm land. Most accounts of the county's history record one William Ballow as the first white settler in the region, arriving at the Sugar Creek Hill area in 1801.[5]

Daviess County became the nineteenth Indiana county formed from the former territorial land, and in February of 1817 the small village of Liverpool was named the county seat. The name of the county was in recognition of Captain Joseph H. Daveiss, a war hero who fell at the Battle of Tippecanoe.[6]

The perils that presented themselves to the early inhabitants were not confined to the land itself, evidenced by the fact that these years saw the erection of at least ten timber and wooden forts to provide safe haven from the Indians in the area. For the most part the Indians and the settlers had friendly relations, but fighting did occur and deaths were recorded in each camp. Nonetheless, this wilderness area to which James Graham saw fit to bring his family in 1826 was blessed with natural riches. Many others came to take advantage of that same opportunity. The area's population increased steadily, as all of Indiana was being settled. Agriculture, of course, was the first and foremost industry in those first few decades of the century, but by mid-century the announcement of the Wabash and Erie Canal development in the area fueled speculation the area might become a transportation center. At least partially, this was realized, but not because of the canal.

The railroads had commenced their movement to the far reaches of the western frontier, and this expansion could only but help the developing economy and industries of southern Indiana. It wasn't until a road crew for the new Ohio and Mississippi Railroad discovered a vein of bituminous coal in Daviess County did anyone realize the entire county sat atop a vast resource of the valuable ore. Of course, the railroads needed coal dearly and the area became important in the railroad magnates' plans to proceed even further west. Indiana's fast-developing agricultural economy paralleled railroad development, and took full advantage of it. The bounties reaped from the fertile farmlands could now be shipped efficiently to large markets. From simple beginnings, the entire State of Indiana had shed its frontier status and was truly a robust, developing state.

From 1826 forward, generation after generation of Grahams helped fuel the development of Daviess County. It was during this dynamic period that Margaret Graham presented to her husband a baby son, Ziba Foote Graham.

The 121 acres of Daviess County which James Graham originally purchased upon arriving in 1826 increased considerably with the passing years. When the business and personal success of father and son allowed, they added acreage to the

Antecedents

family's holdings. The combined success of retail merchandising, livestock dealing, and the ever prosperous family farm gave Thomas and Margaret Graham the opportunity to raise their children in a manner rather removed from what they themselves had experienced.

Born on August 30, 1853, in Washington, Indiana,[7] Ziba Graham was the fifth child born to Margaret and Thomas, their second son. It was obvious from the start that Ziba enjoyed his agricultural background, and easily took to the family business. Staying with his parents until his marriage to Margaret Agnes Cabel[8] in 1877, the partnership of father and son was a benefit to both. Through their combined efforts even more acreage was added to the Graham family holdings. Margaret Cabel was an ideal helpmeet, and her family's passionate faith in Roman Catholicism redirected the Graham family's religious foundation.[9]

Ziba became head of the family farm and businesses upon his father's death on May 18, 1885. A biography printed the next year indicated that he owned over 1,440 acres of fine farming land, with over 1,000 acres under cultivation. He actively pursued the profitable trade of livestock dealer while continuing to manage the farming interests of the family. Just as his father did, he supported and took an active interest in the Republican Party but never desired elected office. The same biographical sketch called him a "prosperous and wide-awake young farmer."

By all standards, the manner in which Ziba operated his farms and businesses was enviable. Not only had his efforts provided a good life for Margaret, but his standing in the community of Washington was one of which to be proud. He was successful, popular, and his word was good as gold. Newspaper accounts describe him as independent, self-reliant, and prudent, but not afraid to act when the need arose. He encouraged those around him to assume responsibility, and treated all he employed with respect.

With Graham Farms operating successfully, Ziba Graham was able to enter other fields. Although he was known as a man of caution and as not one to act impulsively, he did not hesitate to act upon his business instincts.

As the city of Washington grew in the later decades of the nineteenth century, it was obvious to him that as the citizens of his hometown became more sophisticated, more services would need to be provided to them. Ziba's financial abilities allowed him first to investigate and then to invest in a number of local businesses and utilities.

The city of Washington had been served by horse-drawn street cars since 1887. In that year, James C. Lavelle established a seven-day-a-week service to the small community and its utility was well received. When it appeared the business might be available for sale, Ziba initiated negotiations with Mr. Lavelle. Outright purchase was completed by 1890. Within a short time it was obvious to Washingtonians the operation of a horse-powered transit system was not exactly what Ziba had in mind for the future.

At about the same time, purchase of the power plant in Washington was being negotiated by Ziba Graham. The generating plant's location on East Main Street made it a logical place for the street car barns when he electrified the line in 1892. With the electrification of the company, the Ziba F. Graham Railway Company was formed. The small town considered this to be quite a civic asset and embraced the service enthusiastically.

Riding the success of this new enterprise, Ziba made a decision after the turn of the century to upgrade the services offered on the 2.7 mile system. Six new street cars of the latest design were purchased. Half the units would be winter, or enclosed, cars and the remainder would be open sided, or summer, cars. More importantly, four of the six would be "Safety Cars."[10] Named so primarily because of the powerful air braking system used, these deluxe cars also featured modern headlights, destination signs, and comfortable leather seats.[11] This pioneering transit system was the source of no small amount of pride in the city of Washington. The line was further enhanced when Ziba Graham donated land to establish Oak Grove Park. This park, complete with benches, tables, and bandstand donated by Ziba, was situated beyond the newly opened B & O Railroad shops, and gave city dwellers a destination distinct from work or business.

Employing the same sensible business acumen that allowed the street cars to be ultimately successful, the generating plant—aided greatly by the city's industrial and residential growth—proved to be successful also.

But Ziba Graham's idea of success was not entirely built on the accumulation of dollars. Both the generating plant and the street car line were points of pride for the city. With that community pride in mind, he deeded the well-managed and dependable generating plant to the city at an extremely reasonable rate in 1909.[12]

With the same benevolent motive, the Ziba F. Graham Railway Company was deeded to the city of Washington following World War I.[13] It, too, was offered to the city at a bargain rate.

Perhaps it was that sense of community which allowed this rather wealthy man to be known simply as "Zibe" to his hosts of friends. Described as unobtrusive and modest to the point of reticence, he had the courage to be himself at all times. He never

Ziba Foote Graham (1853-1927) and Margaret Cabel Graham (1856-1944), parents of the three Graham brothers.

Antecedents

forgot his pioneer beginnings and well knew the importance of family and hard work. Although he had acquired the means to live a life of relative luxury, he did not. An often heard quote was indicative of his nature: "A man is rich whose wants are few."[14]

Although the successes of Ziba Graham's career are easily recalled, there were also disappointments. In a progressive effort to make farm work less dependent on the physical labors of farmers such as himself, he experimented with the development of a machine to replace the ubiquitous draft horse. Although he was certainly not the first, Ziba Graham was a pioneer in the development of an agricultural steam tractor. In the late 1800s a prototype tractor was developed in the shops of the Graham farms with the hopes a practical machine could be successfully manufactured and sold. Like many other tractor pioneers, Ziba learned the nature of steam power, at least in that period of its evolution, required a considerable chamber and means to transmit that power. Although a great deal of time and effort went into its development, the prototype proved to be much too heavy to use in the fields[15] and was nearly impossible to steer. The project was dropped after the one prototype was built.

In later years Ziba Graham did not hesitate to enter other fields of endeavor when he was convinced it was prudent. The Graham family had already developed a long history of efforts toward improving the quality of life for both family and community. The lessons of previous generations had not been lost on Ziba Foote Graham. Nor would they be lost on his children.

Margaret and Ziba Graham were blessed with three sons. As men, they too would have disappointments and less than successful business enterprises during their long careers. But their successes would go far beyond what their parents had ever dreamed for them. These successes would not be limited to Daviess County or even the State of Indiana. The Graham name would be well known throughout the United States and the world.

One of the "Safety Cars" purchased by the Ziba F. Graham Railway Company in 1901. Acquired in St. Louis for $5,000 each, four of these enclosed cars served the city. There were also a pair of open or "summer" cars operated by the railway.

Antecedents

Chapter One
End Notes

[1] At least one reference cites "Jane" rather than Jean, but the overwhelming majority of references record Jean as the proper given name.

[2] Over 42,000 pioneers moved to Indiana in 1816, the year of statehood for the former territory. The majority of these new citizens came from Kentucky and North Carolina. The passage of two new federal laws prompted this immigration. Because of a faulty and inequitable system of deeding land in Kentucky at the time, there were a multitude of conflicts over claims, deeds, and property ownership. The Land Ordinance of 1785 mandated that the federal government survey land prior to selling it to pioneers (originally, one mile squares). This effectively reduced conflicts. Especially important to religious pioneers was the fact that the Northwest Ordinance of 1787 forbade the practice of slavery. A notable Kentucky family which moved from Kentucky to Spencer County, Indiana, was that of Thomas Lincoln. The father of our 16th President was among those thousands who thought Indiana would be the land of promise.

[3] In addition to being an early pioneer settler and businessman, Mr. Van Trees also became the Daviess County Clerk. It was Mr. Van Trees who gave the oath to one Abraham Lincoln, attorney, when he was in Washington, Indiana, in the interest of a client.

[4] The Northwest Ordinance of 1787 was adopted by the United States Congress, thus creating the Northwest Territory. Present-day Ohio, Indiana, Illinois, Michigan, Wisconsin, and part of Minnesota were under territorial government until statehood was eventually granted to the individual states.

[5] Disagreement has arisen on this point among historians. There is some evidence that Eli Hawkins came from South Carolina in 1806, settling in Maysville. Mr. Ballow is thought to have arrived sometime later, according to this source. Regardless, official records show that the first deed registered in the county was issued to Mr. Hawkins in 1806.

[6] The states of Kentucky, Missouri, and Illinois have also named counties after this fallen war hero.

Joseph Hamilton Daveiss was born on March 4, 1774 in Bedford County, Virginia, to Joseph and Jean Daveiss. At the age of five, Daveiss moved with his parents to the recently settled area of Danville, Kentucky, were he was taught at home by his mother. Daveiss' early education included a frontier grammar school and tutoring by a local physician. This tutoring prematurely ended when the death of a brother and sister required him to return home and help on the family farm. However, agriculture was not to be his calling. Following his eighteenth birthday he joined a company of militia, raised by Major Adair, which were to protect the forts north of the Ohio River and to provide safe transportation for white settlers.

Upon fulfilling his obligations, Daveiss returned to his home and undertook the study of law. Proving to be a "most laborious and indefatigable student," he opened his law office in June of 1795 and began his climb to becoming one of most celebrated, respected, and requested lawyers in the area. In 1801, Daveiss became the first "western states" lawyer to argue a case before the United States Supreme Court. In 1803 he married Anne Marshall, the sister of the Chief Justice of the United States. His reputation grew and, under the auspices of the United States Government, he was asked to prosecute Aaron Burr for treason in that famous trial.

Upon earning the rank of Colonel, Daveiss joined the army of General William Henry Harrison (the future 9th President of the United States) in the campaign against the Indians on the Wabash (River). On November 7, 1811 shortly after receiving the commission of Major, he led a charge against the Indians, and fell mortally wounded.

Daviess County, Kentucky, was created by an act of the state legislature on January 14, 1815. A careless clerk misspelled the name, transposing the "e" and "i" on the official act. In 1817 the Kentucky legislature passed an act correcting the error, but Daviess County has officially been misspelled ever since. The error was continued in the other states also, excepting Illinois where the county is officially known as Jo Daviess County.

[7] After the village of Liverpool was chosen as the county seat, its name was changed to Washington.

[8] The Cabel family was a prominent one in Daviess County. Joseph (Josef) Cabel was the father of Margaret Cabel. Born in Shasburg, Germany, in 1817, Cabel came to the United States in 1839 settling first in New Orleans. He came to Indiana by boat, landing in Evansville and then walking to Washington where he began his long association with the Kaufmann family.

Joseph Cabel was initially employed by George Kaufmann at his hotel located at East Third Street and Main Street. Kaufmann eventually became his father-in-law, in addition to being father of his future partner. At the turn of the century, the family had the means to donate choice real estate to the city, creating Cabel Park. This park was later used to accommodate the Carnegie Library. Both are landmarks in Washington.

Joseph Cabel was also known for his coal mining interests. The profits from the coal business were sufficient enough that in 1892 he established a "Smokeless Fuel Factory." This plant produced "manufactured" gas from the refracting of coal. A local journalist called it "The Wonder of the Age."

[9] There is some uncertainty about the root of the Graham family's fervent Catholic faith. It is generally believed that Margaret Cabel's enthusiastic belief in the church of Rome was the genesis of the Graham family's subsequent denominational direction. However, not all Graham family members were Catholic. For example Ray Graham's wife, Eugenia "Gene" Bruce Winston, was a lifelong Episcopalian. There are no indications that this caused any serious problems in the family. Agatha Pierce Kraft, the granddaughter of Ray Graham and student of Graham genealogy, believes the Graham family's association with Roman Catholicism began with Margaret McFerran, who married Thomas Hyatt on May 17, 1807. Kraft also submits that the Graham family Catholicism may be traced from earlier Hyatt ancestors, but this cannot be substantiated.

[10] The Safety Cars were purchased from the National Safety Car and Equipment Company of St. Louis.

[11] The other two cars were standard versions with friction brakes. This required the winding of a brass crank at the control station in front of the car to stop them.

[12] Ziba Graham sold the electric plant to the city of Washington on January 9, 1909, for the sum of $83,291. Due to growing electrical demand, the plant was moved from the West Main Street site to the East Side Park area in 1921.

[13] The Ziba F. Graham Railway was deeded to the city on November 24, 1923, for the benevolent sum of $15,000. The acceptance of the deed by the city made it the first municipally owned and operated street car line in the state of Indiana. The system served the city until October 31, 1935.

[14] Although Ziba Graham owned the first automobile in Washington, (a Model R Ford) he never learned to drive. During his years in active farm management, he was known to keep a stable of fast ponies available to get to the fields. In his later years he was chauffeured in one of several seven-passenger Pierce-Arrow touring cars.

One of Ziba's more prominent friends was Carl Fisher, a fellow Hoosier and developer of the Indianapolis Motor Speedway, the Lincoln Highway, and Miami Beach. Ziba bought a home in Biscayne Bay and wintered there, near the home of Fisher.

[15] One publication described the tractor as "gigantic" in its proportions. Manufacturing directories prior to World War I illustrate that many tractors which were put into at least limited production weighed well in excess of several tons. The tractor industry did not develop and evolve nearly as quickly as the automobile industry in this country.

The Graham brothers enjoy a friendly game of marbles with their mother, 1892. (Courtesy of Willard Library)

Three Brothers

Three Brothers

The years following the Civil War saw Indiana's economy diversify dramatically. No longer simply agricultural, this expanded economy allowed the state and its people to develop far beyond what could have been imagined by James Graham in the early part of the century. The nation was racing headlong to a new century, full of optimism, with a belief that America was going to lead the way for all nations to follow. By 1882, America was strong and growing stronger, developed, and yet becoming more and more sophisticated.

The Graham family had been very much a part of that development, and now, in the fifth year of their marriage, Ziba and Margaret would be part of that growth also. The birth of Joseph Bolden Graham on September 12, 1882, was a prayer answered.

Margaret and Ziba's firstborn was cause for much joy in the entire Graham clan. Both mother and infant were healthy, and the birth of a name bearer was looked upon favorably. The continuation of the Graham lineage seemed to be assured with the birth of this son, and the parents of this infant looked forward to raising him in the Graham manner. Ziba's business interests would allow him to be a good provider and Joseph's future appeared to be filled with much promise. There would be no lack of love for the little boy in this household, nor attention from his grandparents and other relatives. He would also be given all the tools needed to achieve the prosperity to which earlier Graham men had aspired.

Joseph's parents were again blessed three years later when a brother, Robert Cabel Graham, joined the family on August 21, 1885. Again, both mother and child were healthy, and the birth of another boy was looked upon as a special blessing.

In 1887, the birth of Ray Austin Graham on May 28 fulfilled the wishes of both his parents and his older brothers. Ziba could now share his prosperity with not only his spouse but also a trio of sons who could carry on the family business and tradition.

Early in their childhood the Graham boys exhibited much diversity in character. Each was very much Graham in his makeup, but also very much different in his mien. The household at 7 East Walnut Street[1] was to be one full of life and vitality.

Joseph was the "serious" boy in the trio, and even at an early age exhibited an inclination toward those things in which he would eventually excel. Following the example of his father, Joseph was eager to observe his father at work, and tried to get involved whenever possible. That interest never abated and during his adolescence it was obvious he would rather be helping his father in some way than attending the elementary school in Washington. The Graham work ethic was not lost on Joseph, nor was his parents' insistence he attend school dutifully, even though it may have been reluctantly. His father's work never failed to fascinate him, and he emulated the elder Graham whenever possible. Friends recalled many years later that Joseph was a young businessman, earning money on his own before his eighth birthday.

This initiative was encouraged not only by his parents but also his grandparents. Joseph's maternal grandfather was a partner in the firm of Cabel and Kaufmann, one of the early department stores in nearby Evansville. As a general retailer and grocer for the area, Cabel and Kaufmann was the clearinghouse for the local poultry producers. Each and every Saturday found young Joseph in the basement of that store in Evansville counting hundreds of dozens of eggs. He wanted to be involved, he wanted to learn what he could, and—not incidentally—he wanted to earn the wage involved.

A formal portrait, 1889. (l. to r.) Robert, Joseph, and Ray. (Courtesy of Willard Library)

Having reached the grand age of nine years old, Joseph came up with the idea he would fare much better if he were to enter the coal business rather than continue his education.[2] He was convinced the coal industry would be not only more interesting but also much more profitable than either attending Washington Elementary School or tallying poultry products. Only quick paternal action prevented him from boarding a train bound for Louisville, Kentucky, where he intended to find work in a coal company office. Foiled in that grand dream, Joseph then channeled all his efforts

Three buildings housed the Cabel and Kauffman Department Store in 1880. As a youth, Joseph Graham's first gainful employment involved counting eggs in the basement of the corner building. (Courtesy of Robert C. Graham, Jr.)

Joseph Cabel (1817-1902) and Mary Kauffman Cabel (d. 1859), maternal grandparents of the Graham brothers.

into persuading his parents he should be allowed to become a coal miner in one of the Daviess County mines which his grandfather Cabel operated. That idea was also squelched by a loving father who had other ideas regarding his son's childhood.

Those plans included elementary school in Washington, followed by matriculation in the Jasper Academy of Indiana. Attendance at St. Meinrad's school followed. Although he retained his desire and urge to be gainfully employed during those years, his education continued and he graduated from Christian Brothers College in St. Louis.

Robert's personality grew in a direction quite distinct from that of his elder brothers. Robert Graham was most often described in those years as the "bookworm" of the family, and was often chided in his youth as "always having his nose in a book." Robert too attended elementary school in Washington, and in contrast to his brother, reveled in it. Where Joseph had the ideas and projects of an enterprising young businessman, Robert had an entirely different perspective. A published recollection years later declared

> *...what his elder brother exerted in practical force toward his ends, Robert expended gaining theories. And he continue[d] this bent through his childhood and into manhood.*

Encouraged by his parents to further his formal education to at least the level of his elder brother, Robert initially chose to attend St. Mary's College in Kansas, and later Cornell University. However, Fordham University in New York City was the institution from which he was to obtain his degree in chemistry. Robert confided to his children many years later he had not even considered that famous institution, but during a short stop over in Gotham he was immediately attracted to "the bright lights of the city." Robert transferred immediately to that prestigious New York university.

Ray Graham was a duplicate of neither Joseph nor Robert. With Joseph described as serious and Robert characterized as the theorist, Ray's family and peers described him as friendly, outgoing, and mechanically minded. It was with a wink they also added he was blessed with a sometimes mischievous nature. He was "a bundle of energy, always doing something." Blessed with an innate ability to think in practical and mechanical terms, Ray came to be known as the inventor and handyman of the three Graham boys.

Ray Graham's penchant for inventing and improving upon things was exhibited rather early, paralleling his brother Joseph's desire to gain employment. Prosperity for Ziba Graham had allowed him to surround his family with a fine home in Washington, and the trappings of relative wealth. One of Ray's favorite toys was a miniature steam engine. At seven years of age he conceived the idea that if he disconnected the oil heater which generated the steam for this toy engine, he could attach the engine directly to the radiator used to heat the Graham home. This greatly increased the amount of steam at his command. The success resulting from this "invention" instilled an even greater desire to continue this sort of activity.

No doubt spurred on by his business-minded older brother, nine-year-old Ray established a pot-mending business in the Graham neighborhood. With a cast-off anvil and minimal adult supervision, he did commendable repair jobs. During this period, no household within walking distance was free from solicitation for pots and pans with holes. Just as Joseph and Robert had been, Ray was encouraged by his

Three Brothers

All three Graham boys attended Washington Elementary School. This photograph was taken in 1885.

father to continue and develop these adolescent projects. Later, acting upon a perceived need of his father, Ray's next business venture involved supplying horseshoes to the family stable. The shoes were no doubt used for recreation rather than practical purposes, but the effort was pleasing to his parents and was an indicator of his energetic personality.

Like his brothers, Ray enjoyed being with his father during non-school hours. At an early age the boy decided his talents would serve him well in a life of agriculture. To say the very least, this pleased his father. St. Simon's Academy in Washington provided his prep education and, like his brother, he attended St. Mary's College in Kansas. In 1908 he took a degree in agriculture from the University of Illinois.

If anything defined the younger years of the Graham brothers it would be that at a very early age they acquired their parents' sense of family. They developed a closeness to one another which would serve them their entire lives. A peer commented many years later when the Graham Brothers name was world renowned, that in their childhood, when you saw one Graham brother you generally would also see the other two. The three acted as one. Of course, they all had individual interests and strengths, and they all pursued them to the fullest, both in adolescence and manhood. However, at an early age, the three were already known as the Graham Brothers.

An early example of this kinship, partnership, and cooperation was seen in 1898. The then current fad for boys in their early teens was the construction and sale of bird, or pigeon, houses. The three commandeered one of their father's old street cars, and established the first Graham factory. All three took part in the manufacture and sale of these birdhouses, and the results were encouraging. The Graham brothers enjoyed working together as well as playing together.

Although it was not a pleasant thought to Margaret and Ziba Graham, the boys' parents realized each would eventually leave the pleasant household of his youth and, with the educations provided, begin their individual careers. They were comforted by the fact in a few short years the boys would also be beginning their own families, and continuing the Graham name. With university degrees in three distinct fields, the young men would undoubtedly follow widely divergent paths in life.

The Graham boys had been taught well the value of hard work and effort. Ziba's successes were not handed to him, nor would any success to which his sons aspired. All three boys realized there were no guarantees of prosperity in the world, even though they would have the full support of their parents.

A young man intent upon entering the business world could have no better resource than a father with practical business experience. Over the years Ziba Graham had used the resources generated from his agricultural success to invest in the ventures of others. In addition to Graham Farms, investments included those of other Daviess County companies and businesses. Ziba's standing in the business community and the community at large allowed him to invest wisely and for the most part successfully. A prudent man, these investments were local and in businesses of which he had some knowledge, allowing him to monitor and follow his investments as closely as need be.

Located 16 miles east of Washington in Loogootee, Indiana,[3] the Lythgoe Bottle Company was Ziba's first such investment outside of Daviess County. The firm was owned by Charles Lythgoe, a native of Liverpool, England, who ran away to sea in his youth, rejoined his emigrated father in Scotland in early adulthood, and then came to the United States to seek his fortune.[4] Following in the footsteps of his father, Lythgoe was a practitioner of the ancient art of glass blowing. While the discovery of coal in the 1850s in Daviess County opened up new and prosperous

East Main Street from Third Street, Washington, Indiana, 1900.

Three Brothers

Charles Lythgoe (inset) founded Lythgoe Glass in Loogootee, Indiana. This letterhead illustrates the glass house during his tenure. Commonly used throughout the industry, the disclaimer reads, "All orders subject to stoppage by strikes, fire, or other unavoidable accidents." (Courtesy of Martin County Historical Society)

Three Brothers

avenues of industry in that locale, the discovery of natural gas deposits in the area of Loogootee around the turn of the century enhanced industry there. Charles Lythgoe had purchased the Caledonia Bottle Company and with no little pride in his abilities, renamed the firm the Lythgoe Bottle Company. However, even with the advantageous resource of almost unlimited and cheap fuel, the prospects of developing a thriving industry from the tedious, slow, and labor-intensive art of glass blowing was bleak. It was the rather constant demand for the firm's product which kept it extant, not because of any innovative business plans formulated by Charles Lythgoe.[5]

Eager to begin his business career, Joseph engaged the advice of his father concerning his possible involvement in the glass bottle business. Granted, it was not at all connected with Graham Farms, and it wasn't really what Ziba and Margaret had in mind for their firstborn, but Joseph's father thought enough of the firm to invest money in it earlier, so he could hardly dismiss it out of hand. Father and son investigated further.

Ziba made no secret of his reservations concerning the entry of his son into such an industry. Joseph Graham was an optimistic and energetic young man, and could see a profitable future in this small rural firm. With teenage enthusiasm, Joseph elected to go into the glass business.

Fresh out of Fordham University with a degree in chemistry, it seemed unlikely Robert Graham would find himself on the family farm or in a small rural glass factory. This, however, would be exactly the case. Following Robert's graduation from Fordham University, a call went out from Joseph to join him in this new business. A position with the glass firm in Loogootee was eagerly accepted.

Ray Graham acknowledged the resources available to his eldest brother would naturally be available to him as well. His degree in agriculture from the University of Illinois was ideal for his professed desire to join his father on the family farm. In short order Ray was to make an impressive impact. He quickly became known as the "scientific farmer" of Graham Farms. Many of the new concepts he learned at

Illinois and implemented on the family farm were quite distinct from standard and traditional farm practices of his father; however, they were fully embraced when they almost immediately began to show increased productivity. As Graham family tradition dictated, Ray became instrumental in sharing this information with the farmers in the area, providing schools and demonstrations on the family's holdings. Ray Graham enjoyed being a farmer, especially on a modern, productive, and profitable farm which he now co-managed with his father.

Fully involved with all facets of the grange, Ray also saw a need for improvement in the farm machinery of the day. Continually involved in projects beyond the ken of planting and harvesting, he put special emphasis on a project concerning the development of a truck conversion. This project involved creating a functional one-ton farm truck from a Ford automobile. Development of this concept was involved and time consuming, and many prototypes were developed before anything near a usable unit was ready for practical testing. Ray took particular pride in the unit and continually improved upon it.

* * * * * * *

Much to their parents' surprise and pleasure, it appeared all three boys would return to Indiana and remain close to Washington. Moreover, they were pleased to learn the brides of their sons would all be from local, and very much respected families.

Nell Sefrit became Mrs. Joseph Graham on July 18, 1907, and Eugenia "Gene" Bruce Winston became the bride of Ray Graham on April 18, 1911. Bertha Hack, daughter of a prominent brewer in Vincennes, became the wife of Robert Graham on May 16, 1911, in that city.

It was with no lack of parental pride that Ziba and Margaret Graham acknowledged their three hardworking and energetic sons had entered manhood, and the continuation of the Graham family legacy was assured.

Chapter Two
End Notes

1. The home has been razed.

2. The symbiotic relationship between the railroads and the fledgling coal industry in southern Indiana flourished after the accidental discovery of rich veins of soft coal at mid-century. In 1898 over 5,000 tons of bituminous coal were mined in Daviess County, much of it coming from small independent firms similar to the one his grandfather Cabel operated. The veins of coal were fairly easily worked in that glaciation, primarily the First Illinoisian Ice Sheet, allowed the coal to be fairly close to the surface. By 1940 over 200 tons of coal were mined in the area daily.

3. The Township of Loogootee was plotted by Thomas Gootee on April 4, 1853, and chartered in 1866. With a name this unusual, one would think the origin would be well-documented. This is not the case. At least one historian contends it was derived from the combination of the engineer who surveyed the right of way for the railroad (Lowe), and the original plotter. Others claim that the township was originally called Waterloo, only to have the township supervisors learn

at a later date that designation was already in use. Supposedly the last syllable of Waterloo was added to (Thomas) Gootee. Others believe that two settlers, DeGrootee and DeLoo, were the basis for the unusual name.

4. Charles Lythgoe was born in 1858, son of Richard Lythgoe, the first glass blower in the family. Prior to coming to Loogootee, Charles had established a factory in Bowling Green, Ohio, which specialized in flint glass bottles.

5. Charles Lythgoe was known as "Uncle Charlie" by his employees and friends. While aboard seagoing ships during his youth he developed his skills at the game of checkers, and was considered a world class player. At one tournament in Canton, Ohio, President McKinley was an opponent.

The Evansville plant of Graham Glass, circa 1912.

CHAPTER THREE

Graham Glass

When Ziba Graham first invested in the fortunes of Charles Lythgoe's bottle company, little did he realize that one day he and his family would control its destiny.[1] Banking, real estate, and other investment interests had always been secondary to the management of Graham Farms. When Joseph inquired as to the nature and condition of the former Caledonia Bottle Works, the advice of his father was that of a minority stockholder.

Ziba had invested in Charles Lythgoe's business venture, but was not any part of its day-to-day functioning. When it became obvious Joseph truly wanted to become involved in the glass bottle business, Ziba invested more heavily in the company, and was able to become its president in 1901. The first order of business was to install his son as secretary and treasurer[2] of the firm, while retaining John W. Young as vice-president and plant manager. As always, he supported his son to the fullest, but this was to be Joseph's challenge, not his. The transition was fairly smooth, although John Holland replaced Young in 1902 and W. F. Modes replaced him the following year.

Although Ziba Graham never did develop a desire to become involved in a business as remote from his strengths in farm management as that of bottle manufacturing, he did all he could to encourage and help his eldest son in his strong desire to do so. Ziba was indeed the president of the company, and his son was installed as an officer, but this teenager had much to learn. The very beginning was a most trying time. Before any thought of improvements to the company could be planned and acted upon, its very survival needed to be assured; something neither guaranteed nor easy. But Joseph was an energetic and optimistic young business-man, and relished the challenge.

The production of glass bottles in America was an industry with roots in the earliest years of European colonization in North America. Eight Dutch and Polish glass blowers were members of Captain John Smith's English Expedition of 1608 and they built their first crude furnace on an island in the James River in Virginia during the summer of that year.

The technology of glass blowing evolved slowly and by the end of the nineteenth century, glass bottles were basically produced in the same manner as in colonial days. A "shop" system was employed in which one small glass furnace or pot was tended by several (usually five or six) men and boys. The division of labor included gatherers, mold boys, carry-out boys, and, of course, the skilled blower. Molten glass was forced, by sheer lung power, into the metal molds.

When Ziba Graham became president of the Lythgoe Bottle Company, the most valuable asset of the firm was not its furnaces nor its buildings. Undoubtedly it was the glassblowers, strong-lunged artists who painstakingly produced each individual bottle. Of course, mass production was simply out of the question because of the labor intensive nature of the product. But it was the insight of nineteen-year-old Joseph Graham which gave him the courage to pursue such an enterprise. He had big plans for this marginal bottle producer.

The first year at Lythgoe Bottle Company was arduous indeed, and the second was not any easier. The bulk of responsibility fell on the shoulders of Joseph, and he found himself being involved in much more than bookkeeping and office duties. His father's position as president was truly titular and Joseph was put in a position of making the company a success or seeing it fail. The first order of business was to insure the firm's tenuous existence.

Not assured of even the basics, Joseph found himself scouring the countryside for broken glass, bottles, windows, and any other glass product which could be melted down. Years later Joseph described how he really ran the company "on a shoestring" for the first few years. Published accounts relate that many failures and disappointments greeted him during those start-up years, and how friends suggested it would be better for him to quit the enterprise than continue to work so hard and long for so few rewards. Joining his father on their prosperous family farm would be much easier, these friends explained, and the almost certain failure of the glass company could easily be put in the past. That, of course, was not the nature of a Graham, and Joseph persevered.

By 1905 the company was on steady enough financial footing that its outright purchase by Ziba and Joseph Graham was justified.[3] Upon purchase, the name of the seventy-five employee firm was changed to Southern Indiana Glass Company. Modernization and progressive business practices during the preceding four years garnered not only business stability and local notice but also long-distance respect; the firm was found to be worthy as the site of at least one glass blowers' convention;[4] no small achievement when you consider the perilous condition of the firm when Joseph took over its management. Having bought the firm (with his father), Joseph was able to not only oversee its successful day-to-day operation, but also to plan for a successful future.

Perhaps Joseph's most important move after acquiring complete control was the installation of a battery of "Johnny Bull" bottle blowing machines.

Even before the start of the century there were American bottle makers who had been experimenting with bottle blowing machines. The advantages of a machine over the lungs of a single man and several boys was obvious. But the early machines were primitive and sometimes production was even slower than with the handcrafted type of bottle. Because of the wide neck of fruit jars, the first machines were designed solely for the manufacture of that type container. Many companies patented their own machines, most notable of these being F. C. Ball; Ball-Bingham; Blue;

Southern Indiana Glass Works, Loogootee, as it appeared directly after Joseph Graham took control in 1901.

Bridgewater & Haley; Buttler; Dilworth; Good; Power; Pyle; and Scott. These early fruit jar machines were basically offshoots of the Arbogast machine patented in 1882. The principle involved in these types of jar-blowing machines was the "press and blow." In this design, a gob of molten glass was positioned at the mouth of the mold, and a plunger forced the glass into the mold to accomplish the outside finish. Compressed air then accomplished the "blowing" of the inside finish. The Arbogast machine allowed these jars to be produced much more quickly, and the services of the glass blowers were no longer required. As one might imagine, the elimination of the blowers' services was not taken lightly and the fruit jar industry found itself involved in much labor unrest and strikes.[5]

These pioneering machines had several drawbacks, one of which was the need for a skilled "gatherer" to measure the precise amount of glass to be brought into each mold. In 1903 Homer Brooke, of the Brooke Mold Making Company, patented a device to be used for just such a purpose. With the use of these devices, the machines became semi-automatic.

Just prior to the turn of the century, work also began on machines which utilized a quite different principle. Michael J. Owens, an employee of the Libbey Glass Company of Toledo, Ohio, was working on a fundamentally different machine. Basically, it utilized suction to draw the pre-measured glass into the mold. This "bicycle pump" system was very workable also and in December of 1899 he applied for a patent on the system.

The developments in Europe of bottle-blowing machines, those capable of narrow necks, were further advanced than their American counterparts in those early years. For that reason a number of domestic manufacturers began the production of

This is the Graham Automatic Bottle-Making Machine shown at the National Bottlers' Convention this week.

The eight-armed Graham Automatic Bottle Making Machine. This photo illustrates the revolutionary machine as it was displayed at the National Bottlers Convention in 1913.

similar machines, licensed under, and based on, the Ashley machine from Great Britain. The Johnny Bull machines, also known as the "English" or "United" machines (built by Pierpont-Morgan), were what Joseph felt he needed to transform the sleepy little bottle manufacturer into a profitable concern. One can imagine the tension created in the work force upon their installation. These machines made for radical changes in the operation of the bottle plant, but under Joseph's skilled direction and management the company was able to make this major transition with a minimum of problems. Over the years the Graham family had acquired a well-deserved reputation for treating their employees on the Graham farm fairly. This policy helped immeasurably during this time of radical change at the glass house.

Another important step toward stability and success in the bottle industry was the purchase of the Loogootee Sand Glass Company in 1906. With this needed commodity assured, the company could couple its already stable management and work force with the availability of cheap local natural gas to enable it to grow far beyond the limitations of the original Lythgoe operation.

In 1907, upon the suggestion of Robert Graham—the manufacturer's newest employee—the name of the corporation was changed again, this time to the Graham Glass Company. The firm's name now truly reflected what had been fact for some time.

These early "Johnny Bull" bottle-blowing machines were real pioneers in their field and speeded production, but at best could be described as cumbersome. Joseph immediately began an in-house program to improve upon them, and by 1907 had a Graham-built version in operation.[6] The improvements were many, but the primary advancements involved feeding the machine. The use of only two tables for hand-gather and hand-transfer of the bottles was a tremendous labor-saving move. This consolidation of functions made the efficiency of the machines impressive. Although the Graham-built machine was still semi-automatic, the only skilled workers required were hand gatherers. Further development on the feeder function allowed the Graham machine to be considered the best in the industry by 1912.

The primary steps had been taken to make the former Lythgoe Bottle Company a successful, robust, and growing enterprise.

With this growth came changes in responsibility and direction. At his brothers' behest, Ray Graham joined the Graham Glass Company in 1908 as secretary and manager. No doubt he played a major part in the development of the Graham version of the semi-automatic bottle-blowing machine. He also continued with his duties as co-manager of the Graham Farms. In 1910 Joseph became manager and treasurer, and brother Robert joined the firm as vice-president.[7] Robert was almost immediately dispatched to Oklahoma to establish the Graham Glass Company plant in Okmulgee, and later an ancillary furnace in Checotah.

The Graham brothers had been joined in a business enterprise as adults for the first time. From that day in 1910 when Robert joined forces with his brothers at Graham Glass, they would be business partners for the rest of their lives.

Just as Joseph was the driving force of the Graham family's entry into the glass bottle business, he was also the family member who took the firm from a simple local company to a major player in the glass bottle industry. One of the first steps in achieving this goal was to obtain large orders from outside the Loogootee area. After many sessions of spirited negotiations, a contract was secured with Thomas Taggert, owner of the Pluto Water Company of West Baden, Indiana.[8] Taggert's company was the major supplier of bottled water in Indiana and this new contract consumed a considerable portion of the new capacity of the Loogootee plant. Winning this significant contract proved to be a springboard to other similar contracts. Joseph Graham's dream for the bottle company was beginning to become a reality.

Already the Graham brothers team had staked out further business moves. Joseph continued to work on improving the currently used Graham bottle blowing-machines, and in 1913 proudly displayed the Graham Automatic Bottle Machine at a national industry convention. The incidence of broken bottles—although greater in the days of individually blown bottles—continued to plague the industry well into the automated machine era. Because of the manner in which the bottles were produced, the shoulders of glass bottles were inherently weak and easily broken. This weakness was due to the fact that when the glass flowed into the machine's molds, the curves of the shoulders retained less glass than the straight portions. It was a perplexing problem for all bottle manufacturers, not only the Grahams. Although he was certainly not the first, Joseph Graham became one of the first to successfully develop, patent, and put into use a bottle manufacturing machine that blew the bottles upside down, causing the glass to flow toward the shoulders and thus strengthening them. A further sophistication involved the reversing of the mold's position once the neck and shoulders were formed. The Graham "turn-over" design was one of the best devised and received much national trade attention.

S. Padgett, "Slip" Neridifer, and Louis Frank "gathering" the finished product from a Graham Glass Machine at Loogootee during the second decade of the century.

Baseball was an exceedingly popular spectator sport in and around Loogootee during the first two decades of the century. When the Grahams assumed control of Southern Indiana Glass they began sponsoring corporate teams. This photo shows the Graham Colts during the 1914 season.

Graham Glass

In order to call even more attention to this revolutionary development, the logo and trademark of the Graham Glass Company was changed from a simple block lettering of the firm's name to a capital "G" with an upside-down bottle running through it and the legend "STRENGTH" embossed on the bottle. "Blown Upside Down" tagged the logo. The theme of the strength in the Graham-produced bottles was advertised extensively, and the company proudly guaranteed less than 1% breakage upon first filling. This was a first for the industry and one well received. Bottlers were invited to send for a free sample of a Graham-made bottle so they could break it, examine the uniform thickness of the pieces, and see directly the quality of the product.

The famous "Blown Upside Down" trademark of the Graham Glass Company was used extensively not only in this country but also in Mexico and South America.

Graham Glass also developed a fire polish for the finish of the bottle's lip and neck, proving to be one of the most progressive techniques in the industry. This development was widely hailed by the bottling industry in that it made for easier sealing (the cork was not cut by seams) and the neck was stronger. This sophistication in its product made the name Graham synonymous with quality throughout the industry.

It was obvious early on to Joseph, after expanding the original Loogootee plant several times, the facilities in that city would be inadequate for what he envisioned for the business. In 1912, the June issue of the *National Bottlers Gazette* announced

the former Citizen's Glass Company plant in Evansville, Indiana, would be modernized and reopened on September 1st of that year under the ownership of the Graham Glass Company. Although the plant did not actually commence production until October 13, when presented to the public it was shown to be capable of producing narrow mouth water, beer, soda, drug, and chemical bottles, in addition to pressed ware. Equipped with a full battery of the new Graham Automatic Bottle Blowing Machines, the production capacity of this plant dwarfed the original Loogootee plant, which remained in use.[9]

The new Graham Glass plant in Evansville employed 150 men the first day of production. Two nine-hour shifts were able to produce 1,000 gross of various bottles per day. The quality of Graham bottles gained quite a reputation for the firm, and orders streamed in from far and wide. With the parallel success of the two plants organized by Robert in Oklahoma, the Graham brothers found themselves involved in a most successful undertaking.

By the end of the year, orders continued to exceed plant capacity and the decision was made to expand the Evansville plant yet again. Plans were made for another kiln to be constructed and more Graham Automatic Bottle Machines installed. These expanded operations called for the employment of an additional 150 men, and promised to double the capacity of only a year before. When the new buildings were put into operation, the plant on North Kentucky Avenue and Canal Street was operated with three shifts, twenty-four hours a day. The investment of the company during its first eighteen months in Evansville exceeded $500,000.[10]

The reputation the Graham Glass Company had earned for value and quality in its bottles did not go unnoticed. Trade advertising was done on a national level. It wasn't long before contracts from the Coca-Cola company of Atlanta, Georgia, and a multitude of its franchises throughout the South were being fulfilled regularly. Over the years it had become evident to glass manufacturers the silica sand of the Midwest was superior to the sand of the deep South for glass manufacturing. In fact, Graham Glass had grown to the point that its own Loogootee source was inadequate for current needs and much of the sand used in the expanded production of the

Prior to full automation, working in a glass house was a laborious, tedious and dirty job. Profit margins were slim for the owners because of the labor-intensive nature of manufacture. Regardless, the Grahams enjoyed good relations with their employees by paying fair wages and treating all with respect. The employees at Loogootee, Indiana, proudly gathered for this company photo in 1910.

Downtown Evansville, 1913. (Courtesy of Willard Library)

Graham Glass works came from a gigantic deposit located in Ottawa, Illinois. Contracts from many more southern companies were obtained as Graham quality became even better known. Eventually, Graham Glass became the largest supplier to Coca-Cola bottlers in the nation.

With gross sales increasing at a rather rapid rate, Joseph was able to advertise even more widely. The capital "G" with the inverted bottle trademark was an effective tool, and almost all trade advertising featured illustrations of the uniform wall thickness of Graham bottles.[11]

In late 1915 the Evansville factory produced more soda, beer, ginger ale, and general purpose bottles than any other single plant in the United States. Plans were made to again double the Evansville plant footage and remodel the facility with all new equipment and machinery. Over three and a half acres of buildings would attempt to meet the demand for Graham glass products. Much of the increased capacity was intended to meet the demand of Mexican and South American bottlers.[12]

The two plants in Oklahoma were experiencing similar success, if on a smaller scale. The Grahams had been encouraged to take advantage of the plentiful natural gas reserves and glass sand deposits in Oklahoma by Dr. L. S. Skelton, an early developer of natural gas and industrial concerns. In addition to convincing the Grahams the area's natural resources were more than adequate for initial production and future expansion, Dr. Skelton was also able to obtain tax advantages and a $20,000 bonus raised from locals eager for more industry.

The local press proudly announced that Graham Glass of Oklahoma, Incorporated,[13] was to be located on the east side of Okmulgee in the New Lake Park Addition. The nearly new buildings[14] were singularly suitable for the Grahams' needs and in little time the crew of management and employees brought from Indiana had most all aspects in order.[15] Fires were to be kindled on September 1, 1911, and full operation would commence on September 15.[16] A satellite plant was established in Checotah, and was soon afterward also producing Graham bottles.[17]

Due to the leadership of Joseph and the hard work of all three Graham brothers, the little glass company a few miles from their place of birth had become a huge, four-plant, international business concern.

Just as Joseph Graham was able to successfully develop a small bottle firm into a successful international firm, Michael Owens was following a parallel course in the flat sheet glass business. By the time the Grahams were able to take credit for owning the world's largest and most efficient bottle plant, Owens and his partner, Edward Drummond Libbey, were able to make the same claim in a related field of glass manufacturing.[18] In the spring of 1916 Owens and Libbey had joined forces to create the Libbey-Owens Sheet Glass Company of Toledo,[19] making their combined plants the leaders in that specialized area of flat glass manufacturing.

The employees of Graham Glass in Okmulgee, Oklahoma, circa 1912.

Graham Glass

The Grahams' success had not gone unnoticed. In that same year, Michael Owens dispatched one of his key aides, John D. Biggers, to learn more of the famous Graham Automatic Bottle Blowing machines and the prospering business the Grahams had built in Indiana.[20]

The Graham machines fascinated Biggers and Owens because the Graham machines had been developed to operate on a flow rather than the more common suction principle. Of more import was the fact the Graham machine principle developed the forming and gathering processes[21] far beyond any other bottling machine. It appeared to the glass magnates the Graham machine was on the verge of being a breakthrough development. The machines held out the promise they could be further developed to become truly automatic.

Owens-Illinois Glass Company Board minutes for December 2, 1915, record negotiations carried on by E. D. Libbey and Michael Owens with the Graham brothers to purchase the patents pertaining to the Graham Bottle Machine were unsuccessful.

Biggers subsequently reported on the potential of the modern, high-capacity plant, the solid and loyal work force, and the first-rate management, Owens and Libbey were convinced they should acquire the Graham business in its entirety. Owens and Libbey tendered offers for the Evansville and Loogootee plants, and for partial interests in the two Oklahoma plants.[22] Included in the offer was a desire to have the Grahams continue in the management of the four plants.

After much soul searching, the three equal partners agreed to sell the Graham Glass Company to the Libbey-Owens Sheet Glass Company in 1916.[23] The firm was to retain the Graham name and to operate as before the sale.[24]

Historians have many times questioned the rationale of the sale of Graham Glass to Libbey-Owens. Graham Glass was a firm which appeared to have good prospects of becoming even more lucrative. Perhaps the offer was simply too good to refuse. The success of the Libbey-Owens firm had afforded them capital to purchase not only Graham Glass, but also the prominent American Bottle Company, the Charles Boldt Bottle Company, and a number of lesser bottling firms. Joseph, Robert, and Ray Graham may have seen already in 1916 that huge consortiums would be taking over the ever-expanding industry, leaving little room for the independent producer.

Selling their namesake glass concerns turned out to be a wise choice indeed. Although few could have predicted the passage of the Volstead Act three years later, the federal law would have a devastating effect on the glass bottle industry. Authored by John Andrew Volstead, a previously obscure Minnesota politician, the Volstead Act of 1919[25] ushered in that era of American history known as Prohibition. Immediately—and drastically— the demand for the staple of the factories in Evansville, Loogootee, Okmulgee, and Checotah was reduced. In a newspaper interview more than two decades later, Joseph Graham recalled the time. He said,

...in southern Indiana we had four bottle factories and were manufacturing

Graham Glass secured large contracts with a plethora of Coca-Cola distributors. This advertisement appeared in the February 14, 1914, issue of Coca-Cola Bottler magazine. The strength and breakage issue were addressed with the line "It's the soda [bottle] with the strength of a syphon."

more than 1000 gross of beer bottles every 24 hours. Then along came Volstead and [we] were practically out of a job.

This quote was, of course, a bit of exaggeration in that the brothers—especially Ray—were to be involved in the glass industry for many years to come. However, with less and less of the daily involvement (and decision making) in their former company, coupled with the sizable capital realized from the sale of their lucrative business, the three brothers were able to explore other avenues of business. Joseph, Ray, and Robert Graham did exactly that, with enthusiasm.[26]

Chapter Three
End Notes

[1] The original investors in the stock company organized by Charles Lythgoe included Patrick B. Larkin, William Houghton, Noah Moser, M. J. Carnahan, Joseph Abraham, James Hall, John Sproull, Ziba Graham, and Charles Lythgoe. The company was chartered on April 25, 1901.

Charles Lythgoe died on February 4, 1912. While sailing from Seattle to San Francisco on a business trip, he contracted pneumonia and died after a short time in a San Francisco hospital.

[2] Some references indicate that Joseph's first job with the company was that of bookkeeper.

[3] Local historian Robert Greene reports some confusion concerning the dates attached to the Loogootee glass companies. There are oral histories from the former employees and Loogootinians which indicate the Caledonia Glass Works continued to exist as late as 1902 as an adjunct to the Lythgoe concern, producing prescription and medicine bottles. A local hardware store's ledger indicates a billing to the Southern Indiana Glass Company which appears to be dated 1903. There are also reports by local old-timers that Lythgoe Glass preceded Caledonia Glass, but these reports are unsubstantiated.

[4] Three other glass companies were in Loogootee at the time. The discovery of natural gas in 1899 had prompted the founding of Loogootee Glass (60 employees), the Phoenix Window Glass Company, and the New Caledonia Glass Works (50 employees), in addition to the Graham concern. By 1915 all but Graham had gone out of business.

[5] The Grahams were proud of their relationship with employees. The glass industry of the day involved hard and dirty work, with a prevalence toward strikes. Graham was never struck. A contemporary historian, U. W. Wolter, recorded that,
"the [labor-management relationship] was productive...the likes of which were seldom seen. It [Graham Glass] had the reputation of having the most democratic relationship to be found anywhere in the U.S. It moved along day in and day out as one big happy family. It was one of the things it became noted for throughout the nation. There was much personal contact between owners and workmen, from spare boy up to president."

It was during this time that Joseph Graham became known as "JB" to all his employees. Nicknames were prevalent and "the only time men saw or heard their real names was on their pay packets."

[6] The machine was developed under license from the Louis Proeger Company.

[7] It is curious to note that just a few months prior to joining his brothers in the glass business, Robert Graham had plans of entering the automobile industry. A short article in the Loogootee Times indicated:
"Robert Graham left for Chicago Wednesday afternoon to attend the national automobile show. He has taken the agency for Regal and Packard machines for Martin and Daviess Counties and will have a demonstrating car here as soon as the roads and weather are in condition to give proper display. Mr. Graham is also contemplating the building of a garage at Loogootee in the early spring."

[8] Mr. Taggert was a successful businessman whose interests were not limited to bottling water. In addition to the two bottled water plants (a considerable plant was later constructed in French Lick, Indiana), he also successfully operated the prestigious French Lick Hotel and was elected mayor of that city four times. Local legend has it that when the famous Chicago gangster Al Capone entered the circular drive to the hotel in the twenties, Taggert personally confronted him and denied him a room. He later explained that Capone's presence would make the other guests "uncomfortable." Angered, Capone reportedly moved to the resort down the road where he hence frequently stayed.

Pluto Water has become world famous since the twenties for its medicinal qualities. Because of the high sulphur content the drink was used for its laxative effect, despite its strong odor. The tag line in Pluto advertising was, "If Nature won't, Pluto will." Sales of Taggert's medicinal solution topped $1,000,000 per year during the 1920s.

[9] Bottles produced in Loogootee carried a "model" or order number on the bottom edge followed by a suffix such as LP, LS, or LG (e.g. 513 LS). Bottles produced at the Evansville plant employed a similar coding system. The model or order number was followed with the letters EG and the date (year), e.g. 2736 EG-29. The last two digits indicate the year of the original order (2736 EG-29 would refer to Evansville, 1929), not necessarily the date of manufacture.

The most famous, and collectible, type of Graham-produced bottle is the "Christmas Coke" bottle. These six-ounce bottles carry the familiar Coca-Cola logo beneath which is noted: TRADE MARK REGISTERED BOTTLE PAT'D DECEMBER 25, 1923.

[10] The huge Graham Glass plant was to serve Evansville well for many years after the end of the Graham association. When Libbey-Owens ceased production of bottles in the plant, Joseph Graham was instrumental in arranging for Servel, Inc., to purchase the existing building. Servel occupied the plant for more than 20 years, producing ice machines, refrigerators, and other products. For many of those years Servel was Evansville's largest employer. Occupants of the building since that time have included a number of firms, including Sign Crafters, Incorporated. This firm is notable in that for nearly two decades it was the sole producer of the "Golden Arches" for McDonald's restaurants. The plant still stands.

[11] For a short period of time the offices of the Sales Department were headquartered in the Majestic Building in downtown Indianapolis, Indiana.

[12] A commentary at the time recorded that Graham Glass advertised in all "civilized countries."

[13] Residents of Okmulgee referred to the plant as "the Graham bottle factory."

[14] The building was erected the prior year for the former Pine Glass Company.

[15] About twenty employees were sent to Oklahoma to set up production there. Jacob Keck was day foreman, Otto Ketchum was night foreman, and Howard Robinson was chief machinist, with the remainder to be clerical and machine crew. Four Graham-designed bottle-making machines were put in service. The output of the two Oklahoma plants was specifically intended to serve the needs of the bottle trade in Texas and Oklahoma.

[16] Actual production, however, did not begin until October 20. Jacob Keck served as superintendent of the operation even after the Grahams had sold the company. In 1924 that position was taken over by former night foreman Otto Ketchum, serving until the plant closed in 1928. At that time the plant's bottle-making equipment was shipped to the Owens-Illinois plant in Ladoga, Indiana.

[17] The area was well served by the railroads, in that Ball Brothers (fruit and jelly jars); Baker Brothers; Southwestern Sheet Glass Company; Interstate Glass Company; and other glass concerns were located in the same area. As late as 1936 almost 500 men were employed in the Okmulgee area in the glass industry. More than 640 railroad cars of glass sand were used annually by the various firms.

[18] Association of the Libbey name with the glass industry extends to 1870 when William L. Libbey became the sales manager for the New England Glass Company of Cambridge, Massachusetts. His son, Edward Drummond Libbey, became a clerk at that company in 1874, and a decade later the two Libbeys were partners in ownership of the company. In 1883 the elder Libbey died. A few years later Edward renamed the company the Libbey Glass Company and moved the operation to Toledo, Ohio, to take advantage of the abundant natural gas supplies found there. It was in that city that inventor Michael Owens met Edward Libbey. A short time after their initial meeting Owens became the manager of the Libbey Glass Company and began their lifelong partnership.

[19] Toledo, Ohio, went on to become the glass capital of the world. Edward Drummond Libbey established his first glass company in Toledo in 1888 (Libbey Glass Company). Ten years later the Edward Ford Plate Glass Company began production there. Michael Owens invented his version of the semi-automatic bottle-blowing machine for tumblers in 1901, and formed the Owens Bottle Machine Company. When Owens' company merged with the Illinois Glass Company, the Owens-Illinois Glass Company came into being. This company currently produces glass tableware and a variety of non-glass products. Libbey Glass is an operating unit of Owens-Illinois.

In the 1920s Owens founded the Libbey Owens Sheet Glass Company. When this company merged with the Edward Ford Plate Glass Company, the Libbey-Owens-Ford Company (LOF) was formed. This company currently manufactures flat glass, primarily to automobile manufacturers and the construction trade.

When Owens-Illinois and Corning Glass Works merged, the Owens-Corning Fiberglass Company was formed. When the 1955 merger between Glass Fibers, Incorporated, and the L-O-F Fiberglass Division was completed, it was purchased by Johns-Manville Fiberglass, Incorporated, (now the Manville Corporation). Owens-Corning produces fiberglass and other glass-related products.

[20] Biggers went on to become an internationally known and respected businessman. Loyal to the Grahams he became the head of Graham-Paige International Corporation for the firm's first two years. In addition to serving as president of Libbey-Owens-Ford from its formation in 1930 until 1953 (then becoming board chairman, and later chief executive officer until his retirement in 1960), Biggers served on many corporate boards, as diverse as railroading to automobile manufacturing to banking, in addition to glass manufacturing firms. He was also very much involved in community affairs and served the federal government in numerous capacities. Most notably, Biggers—a Republican—was asked

by President Franklin Roosevelt—a Democrat—to initiate the very first United States Census.

[21] It did not go unnoticed by these executives that the much simpler eight-arm Graham machine cost $8,000 to $9,000 and the more complex fifteen-arm Owens machine ranged between $35,000 to $40,000. Also, the Graham machine was much more adaptable to smaller runs of specialized bottles.

[22] The offer was tendered and held to despite the fact that near disaster struck on August 11, 1916. That night a "terrific" wind storm swept through Evansville, doing serious damage when one of the smokestacks at Graham Glass was toppled. The stack crashed through the roof of the building which housed the amber glass furnace. The building was entirely destroyed, with an estimated loss of $35,000. Summer shutdown for repairs and maintenance had been planned to be in effect the next week and there were fewer than the maximum number of employees in the building. This contributed to the miracle that no life was lost, and that those at the plant were able to stop the spread of the fire.

[23] Negotiations for the purchase of the company—ostensibly to obtain the bottle machine patents—were successful. The sale was finalized on June 28, 1916. Purchase price was $650,000. Cash was exchanged in the amount of $185,000, in addition to 3,000 shares of preferred stock in Owens Bottle Company ($105 each) and 2,000 shares of common stock in Owens Bottle Company ($75 each).

It was a prudent purchase for Libbey and Owens in that not only did they purchase the patents, Evansville and Loogootee plants and the continued services of the Grahams, they also purchased controlling interests in Graham Glass of Oklahoma. Combined with the purchase of the American Bottle Company, Owens and Libbey immediately became major "players" in the nation's bottle industry.

The promise that the Graham machine held out for becoming truly automatic, however, did not come to fruition. Over $490,000 was spent on research and development to make the machine automatic, eliminate crinkles in the necks, and other inherent drawbacks. But these problems were never overcome. Eventually more sophisticated and efficient machines were developed by the industry and the Graham machine became obsolete.

[24] In 1919 the Owens Bottle Company merged with the Illinois Glass Company to form the Owens-Illinois Glass Company. Production ceased at the plant prior to World War Two.

Owens-Illinois Glass Company continues to be one of the three major glass manufacturers in Toledo, Ohio. All three companies (Owens-Illinois, Libbey-Owens-Ford, and Owens-

Corning) are separate entities yet are the result of efforts by three glass industry pioneers.

Edward Drummond Libbey came to Toledo in 1888 to operate the Libbey Glass Company. Edward Ford founded the Edward Ford Plate Glass Company there a decade later. In 1901 Michael Owens formed the Owens Bottle Machine Company.

The Owens Bottle Machine Company later merged with the Illinois Glass Company to form the present day Owens-Illinois Glass Company. Libbey Glass exists today as an operating unit of Owens-Illinois.

Michael Owens established the Libbey Owens Sheet Glass Company after the success of his bottle-making machine company. It was later merged with Ford's company to become Libbey-Owens-Ford Company. Ray Graham was a major factor in this merger, owing to his important holdings in the Libbey-Owens Securities Corporation.

Owens-Illinois and Corning Glass Works merged and formed the Owens-Corning Fiberglass Company. In the 1950s Glass Fibers, Incorporated, merged with the Libbey-Owens-Ford Fiberglass Division to create Johns-Manville Fiberglass, Incorporated. It is known today as the Manville Corporation.

[25] Volstead was a Republican who represented Minnesota from 1903 until 1923. The formal name of the legislation which ushered in Prohibition was "The National Prohibition Act of 1919." The law created the 18th Amendment, and was passed by Congress over the veto of President Woodrow Wilson.

Prior to the passage of what was to become known as the Volstead Act, John Andrew Volstead was known primarily for his work with drainage and homestead issues and his authoring the "Farmers Co-Operative Marketing Act." Interestingly, Volstead was not opposed to all drinking. While he did not oppose moderate drinking, he was very much opposed to the operation of saloons.

[26] Joseph Graham continued to serve as president of Graham Glass until 1924. During his tenure many changes were made regarding organization and manufacture. The Checotah, Oklahoma, plant was sold to the Illinois Glass Company in 1923 and subsequently, under the auspices of then Graham Glass president J. M. Lents, sold to the Liberty Glass Company in 1927. The Okmulgee plant had its ownership shifted from Graham Glass of Oklahoma to Graham Glass of Evansville, and later to the Owens Bottle Company. Closed in 1929, the buildings were used as a warehouse and then razed a year later when the land was sold. The Loogootee plant was closed in 1926. Nineteen thirty-two was the last year glass was produced at the Evansville plant. The buildings were razed and the property sold to the Servel Company in 1939.

Graham Glass

Final chassis and cab assembly at the Stringtown Road plant, Evansville. (Courtesy of Willard Library)

30

Graham Brothers Tractors And Trucks

CHAPTER FOUR

Graham Brothers
Tractors And Trucks

With the desire to use the capital and experience gained from Graham Glass as a basis for future business endeavors, the Graham brothers again paused to consider what industry would be best suited for their talents. This time the decision was to be made by four successful and experienced businessmen, not a father and a teenage son.

Substantial funds were available due to the sale of the glass company and the Grahams had the luxury of making a studied, logical, and practical approach to the question. Of course, the decision was made in a business-like manner and not a great deal of time was needed to come to a consensus and act upon it.

Although Joseph, Robert, and Ray Graham had been active in the world of business for less than a decade at the time of the sale of Graham Glass in 1916, their father had already had a long and successful career. Contributing to his sons' successful debut in the marketplace was Ziba's unwavering support. Upon his passing in 1927, business associates and family friends alike commented how Ziba treated his sons as associates rather as offspring.

Confident that the correct decision had been made, and even more confident that his three sons would carry on in an admirable manner, Ziba elected to retire upon the sale of Graham Glass to Libbey-Owens.[1] His well-earned retirement promised to be comfortable not only financially, but also in the sense that the Graham tradition would continue.

The decision to enter an industry distinctly different from bottles began a new era for the Graham family. Although the three would be entering a new business arena, it was clear the management team of Joseph, Robert, and Ray Graham was now that of the Graham Brothers.

The involvement of the Grahams in glass manufacturing had not by any means ended; in fact, it would continue for many years. Because of the successful management and excellent production record in Evansville, part of the sale agreement was that the brothers would remain in their capacity as officers of the firm. Since the beginning, Graham Glass had been associated with quality products and Michael Owens wanted to continue that reputation. Upon the insistence of Owens, Joseph remained as president of the subsidiary for eight years after the sale. But the Graham family was not made up of single-minded men. There were, and would always be, multiple concerns to command their attention. As a new entity, they were eager to begin another business.

Joseph's entry into the glass industry was one initially advised against because of the lack of any family member's familiarity with the field. As we have seen, this obstacle was overcome following a great deal of effort, and the business was made more than successful. This objection could not be made concerning the brothers' next business decision. It was a rational step, one very much in keeping with the abilities, experiences, and interests of the three young men.

Shortly after his association with the Lythgoe Bottle Company, Joseph began a project at home in his "spare" time. Spurred by reports in the press concerning the development of horseless carriages in other parts of the country, he used the facilities in the back of his father's electric power plant to build the first automobile to be seen in the city of Washington, Indiana. He used the body and springs from his family's horse-drawn runabout as a base, and developed a one-cylinder vehicle which garnered nearly as much attention on Washington's streets as when the first Baltimore and Ohio steam engine puffed into town a half century earlier. This vehicle was truly a "horseless carriage." It used bicycle wheels, a tiller for steering (right hand drive), a single seat, and a "one lung" marine engine mounted directly over the axle. It was quite a novelty for the city. Completed in 1904, the vehicle was similar to a multitude of other rather crude machines built in back rooms and workshops during the first decade of the century. Joseph was one of scores of energetic and mechanically inclined young men who built a single automobile during that era. This automobile served Joseph's immediate and personal purposes and was not intended for any manufactural aim.[2]

As a man intimately involved in the day-to-day operation of a substantial business, Joseph (and his brothers, later) had first-hand knowledge of the vehicles of the day. Joseph is said to have owned the first (purchased) automobile in Loogootee.[3] Even though the majority of all Graham bottle deliveries were large and handled by rail cars, all three businessmen were familiar with the fleet of trucks Graham Glass employed in local deliveries.[4] As Graham Glass prospered, all three brothers were able to afford and maintain their own automobiles.

By the turn of the century, an agricultural revolution had affected almost all farmers in the United States, especially those in the Midwest. Tilling the soil had always been labor-intensive, and success had come not only from good management but, just as importantly, from healthy horses and a strong back. Initially an automotive development, the improvement of the internal combustion engine opened up many avenues of opportunity for those who attempted to mechanize the workings of a modern farm. No longer were those innovators restricted to the limited abilities of a draft horse nor the disadvantages of a portable steam engine.

Having transformed the Graham Farms into a productive, scientific, and even more profitable endeavor than his father had known, Ray Graham directed his energies into other agriculturally related fields. The mechanization of the modern farm, coupled with other "scientific" methods, promised to make a typical farm even more productive and efficient. Ray Graham wasted no time in investigating these methods and devices, implementing them and improving them whenever possible. Just as his father was described decades earlier, Ray could have been reported to be "a prosperous and wide-awake young farmer."

Whereas Ziba Graham and many contemporaries had produced unwieldy, and ultimately unsuccessful, steam tractors prior to the turn of the century, others had been busy developing smaller, much more maneuverable gasoline-powered units. One such firm was the Hercules Tractor Company of Evansville, Indiana.

Originally named the Hercules Buggy Company, the firm was established in Evansville in 1903 under the leadership of William H. McCurdy.[5] Mr. McCurdy had amassed a considerable fortune in Cincinnati providing horse-drawn buggy bodies to Sears, Roebuck, and Company, and owned quite a number of shares in that firm. With both Sears and McCurdy keenly interested in the new horseless carriages suddenly appearing throughout the nation, they consummated a deal

Sears highwheeler bodies were crafted in this plant prior to the manufacture of the Hercules Tractor.

This 1908 Hercules Buggy Company flyer featured a "H-24 Special" runabout and extolled buyers to request their forthcoming catalog.

which would have McCurdy provide Evansville-built bodies for the Sears Motor Buggy assembled in Chicago. This business association continued until 1911 when Sears ceased production of its highwheeler.[6]

The huge Hercules plant was located along the Southern Railroad tracks at Morton Avenue, and was an important aspect of Evansville's manufacturing base.[7] When the production of highwheeler bodies was discontinued, the firm began the development and production of one of the nation's first successful farm tractors.

Graham Farms was a progressive farm and one of Hercules' first customers in the area. As the largest farm in the area, Hercules tractors and those of other manufacturers were given a thorough testing. It was during these early years that Ray Graham became more than a good customer of the firm. His association with Hercules evolved quickly and he soon was one of their star salesmen. It was an association which benefitted both parties.

Ray's sales record was enviable, and the job not only allowed Graham Farms to keep abreast of the latest developments in tractor evolution, it also opened his eyes to the growing need for efficient motorized farm equipment.

Earlier, Ray Graham had seen a need on Graham Farms for an inexpensive and lightweight motor truck to serve intermediate hauling needs. It appeared obvious to him that if Graham Farms had this need, so would many of the neighboring farms. His travels around the Midwest on behalf of Hercules confirmed this belief.

As the "inventor" of the brothers, Ray began to spend his free hours devising a special rear axle which, when combined with a spliced (or telescoping) framing system, could be used with the ubiquitous Ford Model T to become a one-ton stake or express truck. The end design was simple and the conversion was easily accomplished by the local mechanics of the day.

Graham Brothers Tractors And Trucks

Such a conversion had presented many elemental engineering problems, but it was that type of challenge which Ray Graham relished. The unit met with the immediate favor of neighboring farmers, and early on Ray's eyes twinkled with the thought that some day the conversions could be mass-produced and marketed. Of course, helping make Graham Glass a successful enterprise was the major goal of all the brothers, but each had outside projects.

Ray's experience with the tractors encouraged him to study tractor design and construction. The Hercules tractors were some of the best available, but Ray's nature did not allow him to believe they were as good as they could be.[8]

In 1910 the Graham Farms was the first farm operation south of the Indiana wheat country to use four-cylinder internal combustion engine farm tractors. Graham Farms was now large enough to experiment with virtually all the newest agricultural machinery available. Hercules and other makes of tractors were used in the fields alongside an array of various makers' planters, threshers, and cultivators. While Ray was developing and perfecting the truck conversion unit, he also spent considerable time designing what he thought to be a "better" tractor than that currently available.

In 1915 Ray settled on a basic tractor design and worked diligently to bring his ideas to reality. The prototype was to be a four-cylinder, three-plow tractor for use on an average-size farm. Although the Graham Farms were to continue to grow and in a few years became the largest farm in the state, Ray always had in mind what the multitude of small operators would want and need. The agricultural "schools" he organized and presented to local farmers, in addition to his interest in moderately-sized trucks and average-sized tractors only highlighted how the Graham family tradition was directed toward community good. As the largest and most profitable farm in the state, it would have been easy to keep all their methods to themselves and ignore the well-being of their neighbors and competitors.

This was not the Graham way.

Realizing that the tractor project would be much more complex than the truck conversion concept, Ray intensified his efforts in that direction and began to engage engineers and designers to help him.

The Grahams were three confident businessmen when they decided in 1916 to enter the truck conversion and farm tractor industry. The study they made of the field promised that a quality product at a reasonable price would appeal to the typical farmer. The potential for such products in midwestern agricultural economy and, indeed nationally, was just as appealing as the glass industry had promised to be more than a decade before.

Within months, production of the truck conversion units began in Evansville, Indiana, under a factory sign which simply read: Graham Brothers, Inc. Production of Graham Brothers tractors would commence as soon as the prototype was made marketable.

When the Graham brothers elected to go into the truck conversion and tractor business, it was in Evansville, not Washington, Indiana, where they began the endeavor. Although they loved the small town of Washington and always considered it "home," they chose Evansville as the site to debut their new enterprise. There were a number of reasons for this decision, all based on business principles rather than emotion.

Evansville, Indiana, located about 75 miles southwest of the Grahams' home town, was situated near the site of an old Indian village on the Ohio River. Early in the nineteenth century large tracts of land in the area were purchased from the government by General Robert M. Evans, a member of the Indiana Territorial Legislature, and Hugh McGary. Hoping to make the village a trading center for the entire area, the two men attempted to encourage settlement. The area held many natural resources, not the least of which was its location. Its proximity to the mighty Ohio River played a big part in acquiring its future moniker, "The Gateway to the South." Although the settlement became the seat of Vanderburgh County in 1817, and was chartered as a village in 1819, steamboats had come to Evansville as early as 1811.

Also known as the "Crescent City" because of the terracing of the city on the bend in the river, Evansville quickly became a hub for all manner of transportation, especially river traffic. In 1834 investors announced that the city was to be the southern terminus of the proposed Wabash and Erie Canal, promising to make the city even more of a transportation hub.[9] The city continued healthy growth until the cancellation of the project a few years later and the hard economic crash of 1847. There were several years of difficult times for Evansville but, with slow and steady growth, it regained its stature as the largest and most robust city in the area.

Evansville was originally an Irish and English/Scottish settlement, but political unrest in Germany in the 1840s brought many Teutonic immigrants to the area. The character of the work force and the ethnic make-up of the population was changed forever. With the emergence of the railroads in Indiana and beyond, coupled with the already established river trade, the city was able to use its stable work force to become a manufacturing center as well. By 1850 the population of Evansville was over 11,000.

Abundant natural resources also were a factor in the development of the city as a manufacturing center. Coal, gas, and oil were available in the area and vast forests of hardwood trees surrounded the populated areas. By 1900, the well-diversified economy supported 38 furniture factories within the city limits.

A contributing factor in Evansville's growth as a manufacturing center was the fact that it was the only "big" city in the area. Neither Washington nor Loogootee were able to support the scale of business being done there, including that of Graham Glass. Surely neither city, nor any other in southern Indiana, would be able to support such a heavy duty business as truck conversions and tractor manufacturing.

Evansville also already had a history in regard to vehicle and automobile manufacturing. Prior to the turn of the century, a few motorized buggies, built by Evansville native Willis M. Copeland and designed after those of the Apperson brothers of Kokomo, Indiana, were scaring the horses on the city streets. Copeland also built the first manufactured automobile in the city. His factory at Fifth and Locust Streets, a former lumber mill, produced the chain-driven Zentmobile[10] in 1903.[11] In a few years Copeland had put into use a new transmission system and, teaming with Mayor Charles Heilman and Otto and Charles Hartmetz, established the Evansville Automobile Company. The first car produced by the new firm was called the Simplicity and was priced at $1700.00 FOB. By 1909 the model had been redesigned and renamed the Traveler, available at the same price.[12]

Numerous other companies, dealing with full and complete buggies, such as Hercules, had called Evansville home, as had a number of other firms which had

Graham Brothers Tractors And Trucks

FACTORY SCENES AT GRAHAM BROTHERS, INC., EVANSVILLE, IND.

LARGEST MANUFACTURERS OF COMPLETE TRUCK-BUILDERS

These scenes from a 1917 catalog depict the Graham Brothers factory at Fourth and Main Streets in Evansville, Indiana.
Mild winters allowed the storage of frame components out-of-doors year around, as shown in the center photo.

been founded to supply body and hardware parts, custom bodies, and other components. The city had been the home of the Grahams' success in the glass industry and they were confident it could also be the home of a successful truck conversion and tractor industry.

The task at hand was twofold: establish a suitable manufacturing plant and hire a skilled work force. These two goals were rather easily and quickly achieved. It was determined that the manufacturing plant was to be a recently vacated, three-story brick and concrete building at Fourth and Main Streets. Although not built with truck or truck component manufacturing in mind, it was large enough for the Grahams' assembly needs. It was of fairly modern construction, featured extensive grounds for stock storage, and was served by the local railways. The structure did not require a multitude of changes to make it functional, but those necessary were almost immediately accomplished. In regard to labor, the brothers' reputation for fairness with their glass workers and the Graham Farm employees was well known

in the area. Skilled workers were eager to apply at the new Graham Brothers factory, knowing they would be treated and paid fairly.

The background which made Evansville a manufacturing center for other like products served the Grahams well. That these two integral parts of manufacturing were so easily developed was no fluke. It had been only a few years prior when the Graham brothers had brought a small glass-making concern to the city, and now it was a major employer and taxpayer. When the Graham Glass sell-out was accomplished, the Grahams were successful in keeping the glass manufacturing plant in their adopted hometown. These points were not lost on the local political and financial leaders, and they were eager to help the brothers in this new endeavor, thereby helping their city's overall economy.

Prior to these rapid developments, much work had been done to ensure they had a marketable product. Ray Graham's experience gained by traveling for Hercules had convinced him that the majority of farms in the Midwest had an actual

Graham Brothers Tractors And Trucks

need for a light duty truck. He also had the foresight to develop his product around the ubiquitous Model T Ford automobile. By 1916 the inexpensive Model T had proved its toughness, economy, and versatility to legions of farmers.[13] To convince the typical farmer that a modification of that already famous automobile would provide him with a tough, economical, and versatile light truck was not difficult at all. The first print advertising issued by the new Graham firm did indeed emphasize that "Ford parts and repairs are cheap, and at every town and crossroads are mechanics who understand the Ford thoroughly." The new company also made a point of advertising in the Ford Accessories section of trade and farm journals.

Convinced of the need for such a product, Ray Graham was determined to produce a quality unit. Trials of his prototypes in and around Graham Farms proved the goal had been achieved.

But to ensure his unit would be practical, durable, well-engineered, and suitable for manufacture, Ray Graham brought in a team of engineers headed by George W. Dunham. A well-known engineer, Mr. Dunham had begun his already illustrious career in Cleveland as chief engineer of the American Motor Carriage Company. From this pioneer automotive firm he moved to the Olds Motor Works in a designing capacity, and then was involved with the very beginnings of the Hudson Motor Car Company. He later was the first president of the fledgling Society of Automotive Engineers (SAE).[14] Mr. Dunham's duties at Graham Brothers, Inc., were to include the "perfecting" of the truck conversion unit, and the developing of the prototype Graham tractor to the same end.

As with the Graham glass products, the truck conversion was to be of the highest quality. As an assembled unit, the best components were used. Axles and springs were provided by Hess, Bock roller bearings were utilized, Cullman provided the special sprockets, and Prudden was the source of the heavy, best grade hickory wheels. After the installation of the Graham unit, the truck had a wheel base of 125 inches, was driven by a double chain (one on each rear wheel), and had a 2,000-pound carrying capacity. The foot brake was on the original Ford transmission and the emergency brake functioned from the large cast iron brake drum on the rear wheels. An additional measure of the well-thought-out engineering design was the fact that the tread of the rear wheels remained standard—56 inches.

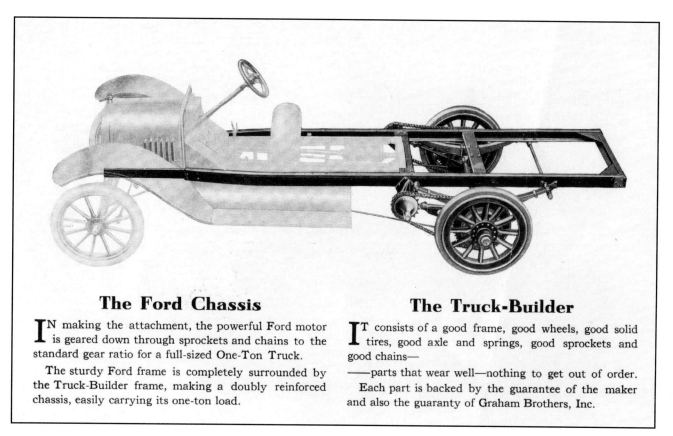

The Ford Chassis

IN making the attachment, the powerful Ford motor is geared down through sprockets and chains to the standard gear ratio for a full-sized One-Ton Truck.

The sturdy Ford frame is completely surrounded by the Truck-Builder frame, making a doubly reinforced chassis, easily carrying its one-ton load.

The Truck-Builder

IT consists of a good frame, good wheels, good solid tires, good axle and springs, good sprockets and good chains—

——parts that wear well—nothing to get out of order.

Each part is backed by the guarantee of the maker and also the guaranty of Graham Brothers, Inc.

From a 1917 catalog.

Perhaps the facet of the Graham unit which most exemplifies its superior engineering was the in-house designed acorn sprocket drum. To quote the brochure,

> We are able to mount our sprocket drum on the Ford Axle without disassembling the Ford rear system, and putting in a shorter axle. We take the dust cap off of the end of the Ford housing. As you probably know, the part of the housing over which this dust cap fits, is a machined surface. Our sprocket drum is machined to fit over this housing, leaving about 1/16" clearance. The drum does not touch this part of the housing unless there is an undue strain put on the Ford axle. When this happens the axle springs lightly, allowing the drum to come over against this machined surface of the housing, and absolutely eliminates the danger of bending the Ford axle. This means a great deal from the service standpoint.

To be sure, there were other somewhat similar products being offered at the time.[15] The Grahams chose to differentiate their product from the others not only by its inherent quality, but by its completeness. That difference was proudly pointed out in their initial advertising brochure:

> The big thing that has been lacking until now in converting a Ford into large delivery use has been the inability to obtain the complete job—ready for actual work.

Conversion units were available from others, but the Graham changeover was complete with not only the split frame unit but also a cab and either a stake or express body for the "new" truck. It was quite a departure from the norm. The brochure also made it clear not only were the mechanical aspects easily accomplished by a local mechanic, but the cab and body were,

> ..easily and quickly attached. No special tools are needed. Especial attention is directed to the modern cab construction, fully protecting the driver and representing the last word in quality, comfort, and convenience.[16]

To ensure the customer received a first rate cab and body with a perfect fit, each unit was assembled at the factory prior to being knocked down and crated for shipment. Quality and completeness were to be the Graham trademark again.

Sales in 1916 surpassed anything the Grahams expected. Granted, the quality of the "Graham Brothers One-Ton Truck Unit" was unsurpassed, and there was a definite need for the product. But the success of the sales department was due not in small part to the price. For only $350.00 F.O.B. Evansville, a farmer could use his used Ford chassis and have a functional "new" truck. This proved to be a tremendous value and was seen as such by multitudes of farmers. Locally, and then in an ever-expanding radius, the royal blue conversions with straw colored striping were becoming more and more common.

The number of dealers who were now jobbing their "One Ton Truck Units" was rapidly expanding and it became evident within months their product was not to be one restricted to regional acceptance. As sales mounted the brothers looked forward to expanding the new business as much as possible.

The initial offering to the rural trade included a stake body or express body as standard. It was felt that these two simple styles would meet the demands of the majority of purchasers. But there were requests, almost from the beginning, for other, more specialized bodies. Within a year the offerings increased from these original two styles to 11, making the market for their product even larger. It was not only the farmers they now targeted, but any businessman who had light hauling requirements.[17] When it was apparent that the idea of a "complete" truck conversion was one popular with the rural and small business trade, the Grahams' immediately developed it further.

By mid-1917 the Graham Brothers had renamed their product the "Graham Brothers All-3 Truck Attachment." The logo was changed from simple block letters to a cursive logo with the words "unit-cab-body" enclosed within the tail of the "3." Market influences also dictated a new selling price of $385.00. The increased sales also allowed advertising to now appear in the automotive and truck trade journals, with full and multi-page ads. No longer would the Graham product be included only in the Ford Accessories section. The base of customers also became national with the establishment of sales branches in New York, Chicago, and Dallas.

Robert Graham graduated from Fordham with a chemistry degree in 1906 fully cognizant that the career of a research chemist was not to be his legacy. He enjoyed his college days and his time in New York city, but had no problem in returning to a family-operated business back in Indiana. Hands-on experience at both Graham Glass and Graham Farms showed the area of sales is what stimulated him and brought out the best in him. Although his eldest brother was the president and plant manager of Graham Glass when he joined the firm, it was Robert who eventually took on the mantle of primary salesman. Now, the truck attachment business was an endeavor in which he could relish and excel. The role of salesman, in each Graham enterprise, was one which he was to enjoy for the rest of his life.[18]

With the sales department and the plant working at capacity, George Dunham and the engineering department at Graham Brothers, Inc., was also hard at work. Improvements to the unit included the use of a Torbensen internal gear drive axle on all units, greatly improving the strength and durability of the resulting vehicle. Perhaps more important in the eyes of the customer was the decision to expand the application of the conversion principle to non-Ford products. Development work early in 1917 allowed the brothers to advertise, later in the year, the use of the conversion on almost any type of automobile chassis. Now re-named the "Graham Brothers Truck Builder," the unit was advertised as usable on Dodge Brothers,

Cadillac, Buick, Hudson, White, Reo, Maxwell, Chevrolet, Apperson, Stutz, Haynes, Hupmobile, Marmon, Oakland, Packard, Reo, Overland, Chalmers, Locomobile, Premier, Cole, White, Kissel, Mitchell, Pierce-Arrow, Lozier, King, Cadillac, Velie, Auburn, Premier, Ford, and "many other good motor cars." Catalog advertising now featured these other makes in their illustrations, as well as the standard Ford. Needless to say, this increased the potential market considerably. The Graham brothers' logo now read: "Graham Brothers Truck Builder and a Motor Car Make a Complete Truck."

In 1914 the Grahams were building their glass business into a major undertaking and were no more interested in the news of European political unrest than any other local businessmen. Although the assassination of the direct heir to the thrones of Austria and Hungary on June 28th of that year was unsettling to all of America, the isolationism dominant at that time was enough to keep such matters distant, especially for those involved in primarily domestic businesses. However, by the time the Grahams had introduced the Truck Builder not only had the nature of their business interests changed but so too had the attitude of the American people in regard to the war now raging in Europe.

On April 6, 1917, the United States issued a formal declaration and the country was immediately thrown into the First World War. International isolationism was a thing of the past, and everyone's lives changed dramatically. Almost immediately the government began the transition to war readiness, both in manpower and materiels.

At first glance one would think this would have impeded the production of Truck Builders at the Evansville plant, especially with the government's massive and prompt need for steel. The opposite proved to be the case. During the nineteen months of the war, Graham advertising stressed the wisdom and patriotism of converting used automobile chassis into usable trucks. "Turning existing power plants into trucks" was looked upon now as not only economical but also as serving the nation's best interests. It was the Grahams' good fortune to be able to assist in the war effort and at the same time advance their business concerns.

With the ability to use chassis other than Ford, the Graham Brothers Truck Builder was now able to expand in capacity as well. Although there was much to be done in the engineering department and modifications needed to be made during actual manufacture, the use of chassis from heavier cars allowed the Grahams to offer 1 1/2, 2, 2 1/2, and 3-ton conversions, in addition to the original one-ton offering. These developments did nothing but increase dramatically the potential and sales of the Graham unit. By late 1917 the Graham Brothers, Inc., plant in Evansville was the world's largest manufacturer of complete truck attachments.

The Graham brothers were not simply successful businessmen, they were also very busy men. Not only were they the officers in this unexpectedly prosperous truck unit enterprise, but they were active in the affairs of Graham Glass (Joseph was still president), and they operated the largest farm in the State of Indiana.

As busy as the engineering department was with the many makes now coupled to the conversion unit and the increasing tonnage inherent, the department was also very much involved in the development of the Graham Brothers Tractor. George Dunham was personally involved and was very much aware of the Grahams' desire to bring the farm tractor into production as soon as possible. The brothers were determined to make the tractor as big a success as the Truck Builder.

The Truck-Builder and a Lozier Motor Car

The Truck-Builder and an Overland Motor Car

The Truck-Builder (with semi-trailer) and a Ford Motor Car

The Truck-Builder and a Case Motor Car

The Truck-Builder is proving beyond question that good used power plants contain thousands of miles of truck service.

When built into trucks they are making amazing records of faithful service everywhere.

On the opposite page is given a list of well-known makes of motor cars that are being applied to meet the demands of light and heavy trucking.

Equally adaptable to Apperson, Auburn, Buick, Cadillac, Case, Chalmers, Chandler, Chevrolet, Cole, Dodge Brothers, Dort, Ford, Garford, Grant, Haynes, Hudson, Hupmobile, King, Kissel, Locomobile, Lozier, Marmon, Maxwell, Mercer, Mitchell, Moon, National, Oakland, Oldsmobile, Overland, Paige, Peerless, Pierce-Arrow, Premier, Reo, Stearns, Stevens-Duryea, Stutz, Thomas Flyer, Velie, White, Winton and other cars.

The Truck-Builder and a Buick Motor Car

The Truck-Builder and a Chevrolet Motor Car

The Truck-Builder and a Reo Motor Car

The Truck-Builder and a Ford Motor Car

The Truck-Builder and an Oldsmobile

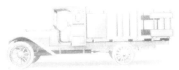

The Truck-Builder and a Premier Motor Car

By the end of the war, development of even higher tonnage conversions had been in the works for months. Graham Truck Builders were now available for over 50 makes of automobiles. "Traction Truck Builders" of three- and five-ton were now available on Ford, Dodge, and several other makes. These units featured fifth wheel, semi-trailer, and full trailer[19] equipment and proved to be as successful as the original units. "Special Truck Builders" were available for Dodge and Ford Cars.[20]

Far removed from the original offers of only a stake or express body, the factory now advertised to "manufacturers, wholesalers, retail merchants, farmers, expressmen, and contractors." Special bodies and cabs had been designed for "each particular need."[21] The Grahams were not shy in pointing out that such nationally known firms as Bell Telephone, Coca-Cola, United Cigar Stores, and Standard Aircraft Corporation used their units.

As successful as the Truck Builder had become, the Graham brothers were becoming aware of the fact that it was indeed an interim product and, with the conclusion of the war, competition would become much more pronounced. It would not come from other conversion unit manufacturers, but rather from large automobile manufacturers who would see the advantages of producing their own light duty trucks. This was done by a number of manufacturers prior to the war, but when it was noticed that the market niche of the Graham Brothers was expanding at such an impressive scale it would only be time before the major manufacturers of automobiles would look at it and the profits available. As automobile manufacturers became more sophisticated with their products, so too did their customers become more demanding. It was evident to the Grahams that this also would be the case in the truck market, and the time was fast passing for farmers and small businessmen to be satisfied with a chain-driven Model T with a top speed of 12-20 miles per hour.

The Grahams' response to this evident and expected change in the market was twofold. By early 1919, development of the Graham Brothers farm tractor was progressing at a steady, if not rapid, rate, and the brothers' dreams of an entirely new Graham Brothers truck were being studied and developed.

On March 12, 1919 a coterie of twenty Evansville businessmen and politicians met for a noon luncheon at the McCurdy Hotel, invited by the Graham brothers. Ray Graham acted as spokesman for his brothers at this rather short meeting. He was not to speak of the glass manufacturing plant bearing the family name, nor was he to address them about the current invested capital of $875,000[22] in Graham Brothers, Incorporated. He had called them together to discuss the status of Graham Brothers Tractor, its financing, and the proposed new factory. It was no secret in Evansville that following Ray's association with the Hercules Tractor Factory[23] he had begun serious development of his own version of a farm tractor.

Ray Graham's talk began with a discussion of the tractors on the current market and the technicalities of their design. The testing done on Graham Farms over the years was discussed as well as Ray's initial design which began development in 1915. The association of George Dunham and also J. F. Loop (another designer associated with major automobile manufacturers) in 1916 was noted and development was detailed. In addition to testing on the Graham Farms, the prototypes had been tested on the farm lands of Senator Bourne at Mobile, Alabama, and at farms where various soil conditions were present. The design problems with the recently recalled Hercules tractors and other various makes were discussed, as were how these influences were taken into consideration when the Graham prototypes were developed.

Roy Criswell, one of three test drivers for Graham Brothers Truck Corporation, with a prototype Graham Brothers tractor in 1916. Extensive field testing of prototypes was accomplished at the Graham Farms and on other farms with distinctly different soil conditions.

Ray Graham was confident the current design was the best available, although it was quite distinct in design and appearance from the standard designs. He explained:

> Due to the wearing of parts exposed to dirt and dust, [our] machine [is] designed with all parts enclosed and running in oil. A high grade four cylinder motor [was] developed and the transmission [is] entirely enclosed.

A patent filed by George Dunham in 1917 (assigned to the Graham Brothers, Incorporated) indicated the four-cylinder engine was a unit featuring an overhead camshaft. Another patent assigned to the Graham Brothers that year included a unique tractor stabilizing bar. The new tractor was to be of three-plow design.

Just as Ray Graham and his brothers were confident of the design, they were confident the financial and political elite of Evansville would back their plans for a tractor plant which would now also serve as their proposed truck manufacturing plant. Their faith was confirmed when over $500,000 was subscribed within one-half hour.

The Graham Brothers tractor on display at the Centennial Exposition and Central States Tractor Show at Bosse Field, Evansville, 1919. The banner reads, "This Is Power Farming." (Courtesy of Willard Library)

The shortage of tractors in Europe before and during the war prompted government leaders to prevail upon Ford's resources to alleviate the crisis. Although the first year of Fordson tractor manufacture totaled only 254 units, by the end of 1919 56,987 units were produced and the next year saw that total increased by over 10,000 units. The fact Henry Ford was becoming active in the tractor industry was very much in the brothers' minds. The Grahams paused to re-evaluate the (now) rapidly changing tractor market. The three brothers had not been successful in two distinct lines of industry by ignoring the prevailing business climate.

By 1919 Ford's success with the Model T had made him fabulously wealthy and powerful. It would have been less than prudent for the Grahams to compete head-to-head with a like product in a limited market place. Development of prototypes continued and Dunham and company continued to work on a design, but manufacture of a production unit was delayed. In 1919, a "perfected" design was displayed at the Centennial Exposition and Central States Tractor Show at Bosse Field, Evansville. Design work continued into January 1920, with two additional tractor designs patented and assigned to the Grahams; the most notable of these being one which featured a starting crank which passed through most of the length of the tractor, permitting it to be started from the rear. Despite all these efforts, production of the Graham Brothers Tractor never materialized. Ford had all but captured the market.

Even though World War I lasted less than two years after the United States became involved, it had a profound effect on not only the politics and culture of the nation, but also on how the country did business. In addition to the lessons of history, the nation learned that the trucking industry had proven its industrial and commercial utility. The medium- and heavy-duty truck were the machines which would

Plans for the new plant were well in hand when the local media announced the factory would be erected by August 1 and it would employ over 100 additional men. Of the most modern construction, the building would be of concrete foundations, brick walls with upper side walls of continuous steel sash, and structural steel trusses. With floor space of over 20,000 square feet, it was planned that about 1,000 trucks and tractors could be produced the first year. Backers in the Grahams' corner included S. I. May, President of the Evansville Chamber of Commerce, and Benjamin Bosse, Mayor of Evansville.

It was announced the truck conversion corporation would be absorbed by this new entity and that the capital stock for the corporation would exceed $1,000,000.

Enthusiasm ran rampant for this new endeavor and the entire city of Evansville expected another healthy economic boost from the Grahams. However, the caution and conservative business principles inherited from their father were still evident and heeded by the sons.

The Grahams were not the only business leaders to profit from the war shortages in agricultural machinery. There were quite a number of manufacturers[24] during these years who had produced kits, similar in principle to the Grahams' own Truck Builder, for converting Model T Fords to usable light-weight farm tractors. Coupled with the already established tractor manufacturers, there was indeed competition. Also, the agricultural background of one Henry Ford had prompted him to begin experimentation of a feasible farm tractor as early as 1906.[25]

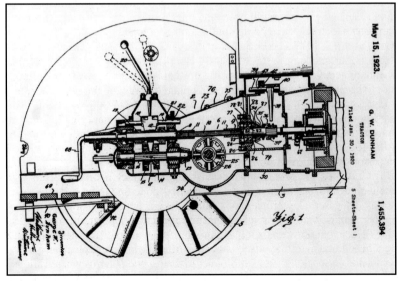

This patent drawing, one of many pertaining to the prototype Graham Brothers tractor being developed by George W. Dunhill, detailed an innovative rear cranking mechanism.

distribute both the raw materials and finished products for America's anticipated post-war prosperity. Already, demands for improved highways were being heard in Washington, D. C., and many state capitals. To an alert businessman, it was obvious the future of the market would not be in light-duty conversions. That product was an end in itself. Chain-driven conversions made from automobile chassis would soon be hopelessly out of date in a market poised for maturation.

Of course, the Grahams had already proven themselves sharp businessmen. By becoming the world's largest truck conversion manufacturer during the three prior years, they not only became prosperous but also garnered a great deal of practical knowledge concerning the automobile and truck industry. It was no great surprise when the three brothers announced late in 1919 that they would be erecting a new manufacturing plant which would produce Graham Brothers Trucks. A new era was to begin for the long successful Graham family: that first truck was to be only the first of many tens of thousands which would proudly wear the Graham Brothers nameplate.

Those basic requirements which presented themselves when they planned for tractor manufacture were again easily dispatched. The reputation of the Graham Brothers' name was enough to insure the venture had solid backing and support. When the call went out for even larger numbers of skilled laborers, Evansville's population of over 85,000—swelled by returning veterans—was equal to the muster. This time a new, even larger plant was planned and construction began almost immediately after the announcement.

Aided by the same Evansville financial, political, and civic leaders who raised the money for the initial plant, the plans for a new Graham Brothers Truck plant were developed and acted upon. This new plant, to compliment the existing building at Fourth and Main Streets, was erected in record time in the outlying "Beltline" district at Stringtown Road and Maxwell. Considered state-of-the art at the time of erection, the plant was built with the best fireproof materials, utilized the ultra-modern saw tooth roof design, and was well-served by railroads.[26] The plant was designed to be unitized, with each of the (eventually) thirteen units being 90 feet wide and 240 feet long. This new manufacturing complex was the largest one-story industrial structure in Evansville.

Shown while under construction, this building was the first of 13 units to comprise the Stringtown Road plant of Graham Brothers, Inc. It is important to note the erection sign declares this site as the future home of Graham Brothers Trucks & Tractors. (Courtesy of Willard Library)

The office building of Graham Brothers Trucks in Evansville. The huge state-of-the-art truck plant was directly behind this headquarters.

Under the progressive guidance of George Dunham, the Graham engineering staff had been working on the design for a completely new 1 1/2-ton truck. The need for an appropriate truck on the family farm continued to be real, the Graham brothers thought, thus the initial example was geared for agricultural purposes. This entry into the fast-growing truck manufacturing industry was to be an "assembled" vehicle. That is, it would be assembled from the best proprietary products available. Even though the cabs, bodies, and other major components of the 130-inch wheelbase[27] truck would be created in the Graham Brothers truck plant, mechanical items such as engines, transmissions, and chassis parts would be obtained from major independent manufacturers who supplied the trade from stock. For example, these first trucks were powered by either Ford, Continental, Rutenber, Weideley, or Dodge engines.[28] An improved Torbensen internal gear drive was used, as were Disteel pressed steel disc wheels, Monarch governors, Stromberg carburetors, and other well-known components.

Three versions of the wildly successful Graham Brothers Speed Truck.

To distinguish this new offering from its competition, the Graham brothers again made good use of not only the engineering department but also the sales department. This new truck was to be known simply as the "Graham Brothers Speed Truck." Print advertising explained two definite tendencies current in the selection of motor truck equipment: first, "a turn from 'light delivery' to trucks of real capacity", and, "the acceptance of truck cord pneumatic tires as the ultimate truck economy." It was further explained that the ultimate truck would be one which combined the strength of a full-size truck with the speed of a light-duty truck. (By modern standards this truck could not be considered in any manner a truck of speedy qualities, but when it was announced this truck would carry a full ton-and-a-half load safely and efficiently at 22 miles per hour, it was considered just that.) By offering the truck-buying public a vehicle perceived to fill their most urgent needs, the Grahams insured their success.

Four-cylinder engines, rated at 22.5 horsepower, were used from each of the manufacturers (3 3/4 x 5, cast enblock). The 133-inch wheelbase chassis featured a three-point flexible spring suspension which was said to eliminate strains on the crank case, and cooling was achieved by a thermo-syphon system. Ignition and

A prototype Speed Truck chassis is put through its paces in the Evansville countryside by Roy Criswell, test driver for Graham Brothers.

The logo used by the Graham brothers during the manufacture of the Speed truck was unique in what it represented. The emblem contained a shield showing three shells at the horizontals. The shells represent Coquille St. Jacques, the symbol of St. James the Apostle and Fisherman. The shells were used as drinking vessels by pilgrims to the Holy Land and here represent the Roman Catholic faith of the brothers.

Rolling chassis for Graham Brothers Speed Trucks are united with engine, radiator, and steering assemblies in this department at the Stringtown Road plant at Evansville.

One corner of the supply rooms at the Stringtown Road truck plant. The men at the benches are assembling magnetos.

Graham Brothers Tractors And Trucks

lighting were supplied by an Eisemann high tension magneto/generator set, and the Fuller clutches were multiple-plate dry-disc units. The pneumatic tires were mounted on disc wheels, 36 x 6 in the rear and 35 x 5 in the front. From the beginning the Graham Brothers trucks were sold with "a complete line of body and cab equipment...covering practically all hauling requirements." The chassis sold for a reasonable $2295. For an additional $200 a choice of four body styles were made available.[29]

When it became obvious to the three brothers that the Dodge powerplants and transmissions were developing a reputation to rival the best of the other available engines, a higher percentage of Dodge components were used in this new Speed Truck. It was not long before large orders were placed for components through Hartmetz Brothers Motors, the Evansville Dodge dealer.

The Graham brothers' reputation for quality and value had again preceded them. Sales in late 1919 through 1920 were at an unprecedented level. At once the plant was at full capacity to meet the ever-increasing demand. Sales were surprising-even to the optimistic brothers themselves. One contemporary commentary described their entry into the truck marketplace as "an overnight success."

As this phenomenon was unfolding, the brothers not only concerned themselves with coordinating factory capacity, developing distribution and dealer systems, and other day-to-day business details. They at once began the large-scale implementation of a policy which had served them well in the recent past. They would offer trucks to the industry which would serve almost every need.

"A Body For Every Line of Business" was the tag line which accompanied each piece of new advertising. Delivery trucks, dump trucks, postal delivery trucks, fire trucks, bottling company trucks, and furniture delivery trucks were made available, in addition to the standard stake-bodied truck. As before, this policy served them well. Sales of the Graham Brothers Truck increased monthly, and new body styles were added as quickly.

In 1920 the introduction of the "Speed Bus" was announced to the trade journals. The first of many bus styles marketed, this initial offering was an eighteen-passenger model. As described in the May issue of the Commercial Car Journal, the Speed Bus,

> ...is built like a street car; spring cushioned seats, well up-
> holstered; door lever operated from the driver's seat; drop win-
> dows; electric dome lights and signal buttons; wheel housings
> and swell sides provide a roomy interior.

As was the Speed Truck, the Speed Bus was looked upon as a good sturdy vehicle and a great value. Many municipalities and school districts became satisfied customers.

At the same time the Grahams began to experience unparalleled success with the Speed Truck and Speed Bus, other important developments and changes were unfolding in another sphere of the vehicle manufacturing industry.

By 1920 the name Dodge was well known throughout the nation. The two Dodge brothers, John and Horace, earned an enviable reputation during the first two decades of the century. Associated with a number of automobile-related manufactur-

Speed Truck dealers within 500 miles of the Evansville plant were able to "driveaway" the product, alleviating the expense (and sometimes, delays) involved with rail delivery. These two stake trucks were in transit to the Mooney-Mueller-Ward Company, a wholesale florist in Indianapolis. The company encouraged these driveaways to help reduce the on-site inventory of already sold vehicles.

ing ventures, most notably Henry Ford, they had a solid big business background. When they began production of an automobile bearing their name in 1914,[30] the Dodges' product and reputation allowed them immediate success. The first full year of production saw the brothers build and sell over 45,000 automobiles, earning them the third position amongst the largest producers of automobiles in the world. Tallies at the end of the 1920 model year showed Dodge Brothers as the second-best selling automobile in the world. The Dodge brothers were rich, successful, healthy, and in the prime of life.

The Dodge brothers and their thriving automobile concern also survived the horror and economic effects of "the war to end all wars." World War I lasted little more than a year and a half, but its effects were profound. In addition to changing world politics and American culture and business forever, it took the lives of 34,000 Americans on the battlefield. Manpower and material shortages challenged all manufacturers, and scores of companies failed to survive. By assisting in the war effort, prudent use of resources on hand, and managerial expertise, Dodge Brothers was able to remain profitable and prosperous throughout the conflict.

Tragically, an even more destructive adversary attacked the nation, and indeed the world, following World War I. Many historians feel the confluence of service men—European, American, and African—in northern France at the end of the war provided the environment for this formidable killer. In a matter of months the Influenza Epidemic of 1918 took nearly half a million American lives. Crowded troop ships returning to home ports, poor sanitation, and a lack of medical services available to the public contributed to the eventual pandemic. "Spanish" influenza was responsible for over 22 million deaths worldwide in late 1918. The intensity and speed at which the disease advanced shocked the entire nation.[31] One leading scientist was quoted in 1919,

> *Never before had there been a catastrophe at once so sudden, so devastating, and so universal. It is the greatest failure of medical science ever.*

Fortunately, the pandemic was as short lived as it was deadly. For those who survived the ravages of infection, life quickly returned to normal. Although there were minor waves of influenza in the following months and years, nothing like the Influenza Epidemic of 1918 was again experienced.

Armistice was a symbolic starting afresh in public life, government, and business. With the formal end of hostilities, the Dodge brothers looked forward to renewed enthusiasm in manufacturing their automobiles and the public's consumption of new models.

It was not to be. Tragedy stuck the Dodge family in January of 1920. While attending the National Automobile Show in New York City, Horace was suddenly stricken with a serious bout of influenza. While attending to his brother, John became ill with the same disease and unexpectedly died. His still weakened and grieving brother, Horace, then lost his battle with the flu and succumbed in December.[32]

Confusion and problems followed. The Dodge widows were in no position to take over their husbands' responsibilities and definite succession arrangements had not been considered by these robust men beforehand. Following a three month-shutdown, it was decided the company was to be headed by Frederick J. Haynes. Mr. Haynes was a longtime employee and associate, first working with the burly brothers in their bicycle shop in Canada in 1900.[33] Rising through the corporate ranks, he was both a vice president of the Dodge Brothers firm and also general manager for a num-

In 1921, Frederick J. Haynes negotiated an agreement which brought together the Graham brothers and Dodge Brothers, Inc. It was an association which would prove to benefit both firms tremendously.

ber of years. When the great Dodge Hamtramck factory was built, John Dodge had personally selected Haynes to be superintendent. The brothers' deaths brought Haynes to the top of a company now in dire straits.

If the death of the founders was not enough to severely challenge the abilities of the new corporate head, the much anticipated post-war boom also failed to materialize. In fact, a short but severe recession was to hit the entire country within a year of his assuming the presidency. For three months following Horace's death the entire work force at Dodge Brothers was not asked to report to work. Upon the resumption of production, only a fraction of those previously manning the lines were called back. Total full-time employment went from a high of over 22,000 to less than 4,000. It was a difficult time, and one fraught with concerns of the automaker's viability.

The recession almost immediately knocked scores of marginal, under-financed, and poorly administered automobile companies from the scene—large and small alike.[34] But the confidence placed in Haynes by the Dodge family was well-earned. His administrative abilities were excellent, and the economic storm was weathered. Within months the factory was at, or near, normal levels of production. Even after all the distractions, changes, and economic woes of the year were played out, Dodge Brothers was able to produce over 81,000 vehicles. Only two other firms in the nation sold more automobiles in 1920.

When the Grahams began production of the Speed Truck, ordering of engines and transmissions was done locally. When the upper management of Dodge noticed the increasingly large number of components going to a relatively small town in Indiana, they investigated. In short order the engines and transmissions (and in many cases the chassis themselves) which were shipped to Vanderburgh County were accompanied by representatives of Frederick J. Haynes.

Arrangements were made for a series of meetings between the Graham brothers and the president of Dodge.

Until 1917, the manufacturing aim of Dodge was entirely concentrated on automobiles. In February of that year, design engineers began experimenting with commercial bodies which could be fitted to their passenger cars. On October 25, after months of development and secret testing, production of a half-ton screen-side commercial vehicle commenced. Quite simply, this "new" offering was the standard 114-inch wheelbase passenger car chassis with a light commercial body attached. The engine, transmission, cooling components, wheels and front sheet metal were identical to the sedans and coupes being produced in the same factory. Deliveries of this 2600-pound vehicle to dealers began in November of 1917. From its introduction, Dodge management advised its dealerships this was not a Dodge truck, but a Dodge commercial car, intended for light hauling. Production of these newly introduced vehicles was jump-started by an order from the U.S. Army Signal, Ordnance, and Quartermaster Corps. Readying itself for the demands of World War I, the Government ordered 9,352 screenside Dodges.[35]

Just as heavy-duty trucks had proved their worth during war effort, the light-duty commercial cars had also earned their niche. Dodge continued to produce these screenside commercial cars basically unchanged until 1922.[36] They were moderately successful and, since there was no disruption on the automobile assembly line, they were an easy model addition for the firm.

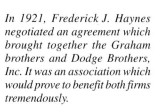

Graham Brothers Tractors And Trucks

When Haynes took over the Dodge firm, he realized he needed to act decisively and boldly to insure the company's survival. Having lost both founders of the corporation in less than a year, this Cornell graduate and only son of a lawyer desperately needed to retain the employee loyalty the Dodge brothers had earned.[37] On the day he was elected president—January 11th, 1921—two million dollars in employee bonuses were announced. Putting the majority of the workers back on the job was a high priority and he did all he could to accomplish that with due haste. He also realized that to prosper the corporation needed to expand its sales base.

Leadership and corporate progress for Haynes was going to be much more of a challenge for him than it was for the Dodge brothers. Even though he had a vision of what needed to be done, he now had an entirely profit-minded board of directors to deal with, in addition to two strong-willed widows. But major changes were made: the basic wheel base of the Dodge automobiles was lengthened to 116 inches, an attractive new coupe was added to the basic line, and Budd/Michelin disc wheels were now being utilized. The high and boxy bodies with cathedral rear windows were replaced with more stylish designs and interiors. With the nation's economy beginning to pick up, sales of Dodge-built automobiles were starting to skyrocket again.

Although sales of the half-ton commercial car were satisfactory, it was the wish of President Haynes to add a truck line to the Dodge offerings. The meetings with the Graham brothers had proved promising and the reports of their product and manufacturing facilities showed strength in all areas. Their product was one with which the Dodge people could proudly associate.

The end result of these meetings was an agreement, announced in April of 1921, which appeared to benefit both parties. The Dodge organization would henceforth sell and service Graham Brothers trucks worldwide through their extensive dealer system. This was a tremendous asset for the successful but comparatively small Graham enterprise. By association with the well-known and respected Dodge Brothers, their product was now to be promoted not only nationally, but internationally. Rather than being accomplished by years of intense corporate effort, this sales advantage was made reality by simple pen stokes. Since a great many of the current Graham Speed Trucks were utilizing Dodge components, the transition to using Dodge components entirely was not difficult.

As appealing as this looked to the Grahams, it was even more so for Haynes. With absolutely no investment, the Dodge line now offered a complete heavy truck line with a multitude of specialized models. The assembly lines for the popular coupes, sedans, and touring cars were not disrupted for even an instant when Graham Brothers trucks became available under the Dodge Brothers banner.

Although in the strictest sense the Grahams' efforts were still independent and controlled entirely by the Graham brothers, advertising from that point described Graham Brothers trucks as "Sold by Dodge Brothers Dealers Everywhere."

Almost immediately the capacity at the Stringtown Road plant in Evansville was inadequate. Advertising by Dodge touted Graham quality ("The fact that Dodge Brothers do not hesitate to associate their name with this truck means that it has fully measured up to the most exacting requirements"), and enhanced sales. With the resources of the Dodge engineering departments available, small improvements began to be evident in the ever expanding number of models available. Concentrat-ing on the ton and ton and a half chassis, the rear pneumatic cord tires were of larger and heavier dimensions, the sheet metal was becoming more and more sophisticated, and the power plant was becoming more powerful.

When the Grahams decided another plant would best serve this increasing demand, it was not hard to determine where it would be located. Although the Evansville plant had been expanded several times, the Grahams decided a new plant with sufficient labor, materials, and transportation should be located in Detroit. With the help of Dodge management, a dedicated search was made of available business properties and in short order the former home of the Denby Truck Company,[38] a nearly new 13,000-square-foot building located at 1222 Meldrum Avenue, was purchased in early 1922. The Evansville plant continued its overtime pace producing bodies and most components; this Michigan plant was intended for assembly only.

Full advantage was taken of the fact that the Dodge produced engines and components were near at hand. The ready availability of labor allowed this new Graham Brothers Truck plant to get on line quickly. In the partial year of production since the signing on with Dodge Brothers, 1,086 trucks were sold by Graham. During 1922, the first full year since the agreement with Dodge, a full 313% increase in sales was realized.[39]

One of the reasons for the Grahams' success prior to the association with Dodge was the standardization of chassis design and the interchangeability of body styles. Each of the 1921 Graham Brothers trucks,[40] for example, had a basic chassis weight (with cab) of 4,245 pounds and was powered by the powerful Dodge 212.3 cubic inch four-cylinder engine. There was a plethora of body styles, however.

With each succeeding month there was an expanding line of specialized bodies available for specific businesses. This made their product, already acknowledged nationwide for its quality, even more appealing to the prospective truck purchaser. The association with Dodge also strengthened the areas of engineering and design. Frames on the 1922 trucks (now with a 140-inch wheelbase) were strengthened, with parallel side rails now extending from the front of the body to the rear. Increases in the strength of components of the drive shaft (including the propeller shaft and its mounting), heavier and sturdier sheet steel fenders, standardized running boards, wider and more heavy duty brakes, and additional spare tire mountings were soon implemented. Paralleling the demands of the consumer in the automotive trade, the consumers in the trucking industry were demanding more style and comfort also. Graham obliged them. The same Marshall springs used by most automobile manufacturers would shortly be employed in the seat cushions of Graham trucks. The overall appearance of the truck was considered and the design improved. An early advertising folder stressed these considered designs as "an appearance which is really valuable to the owner as it reflects the character of his business."

Graham Brothers Tractors And Trucks

The trucking industry was indeed maturing, and the Graham brothers were at the forefront.

Not unimportantly, the Graham enterprise remained independent during this rapid increase of production and sales. Although the Grahams were affiliated with Dodge as closely as possible, the truck manufacturing firm was a separate entity entirely.[42] To insure that independence, a new Michigan holding corporation was established. In 1922 Graham Brothers, Incorporated, was created, with Joseph Graham as president and his brothers as principal officers.

With its association with Dodge, the Grahams reached a level of success only dreamed of while laying the foundations of a solid business in the glass industry in Loogootee. It is important to note that, throughout, all three brothers remained community-minded, modest, and humble.

The glass factory in Loogootee had been kept open as long as possible, and when inefficiency forced its closing, most men were transferred to the Evansville plant. When Joseph and Nell Graham left to tend to affairs in Detroit,[43] they did not forget Evansville. Always a civic booster of their adopted "hometown," a final parting gift to the city was the erection of a building to house the Babies Milk Fund Association. For several years the Grahams had provided meeting rooms for the association's weekly clinics, and this gift underscored their interest in Evansville's well-being. The building was also to be used as a community center. A newspaper editorial wishing Joseph well in Michigan noted this was only one of his many "helps to the community" and that he was always "in the vanguard of community affairs, not a follower".

When Ray Graham's success took him far beyond the limits of Evansville, he, too, continued his longtime support of the city. There had been much involvement in community affairs on his part prior to his move to Detroit. An active outdoorsman, Ray was instrumental in creating hunting and trap shooting clubs in Evansville and the Recreation Gun Club in Washington. He was also a pioneer in the community's aviation history.

With his mechanical bent, the development of early flying machines became one of Ray's many interests. In 1917 several planes were purchased,[44] which led to the establishment of Evansville's first airport, Graham Field. Constructed on land leased from fellow enthusiast Victor Baumgart, Graham Field was located on the northeast corner of Division Street and Green River Road and operated until late 1919.[45] Graham Field was not to be long lived, however. That fall an extremely powerful tornado swept through Evansville, destroying the existing hangers and eleven planes. At that point, the operation of Evansville's first airport was taken over by the municipality.[46]

Robert Graham was also active in the communities of Washington and Evansville, in ways almost entirely different from his brothers. An avid fisherman, he helped boost involvement in that pastime for children, was a member of the Washington (Indiana) Club, the lodge of the BPOE (Elks), and the Knights of Columbus. Even more so than his brothers, many of his community contributions were of a more private nature, and he avoided publicity as much as possible.

The diverse nature of the three brothers was evident in almost all areas, but their ability to work together as a team—forged from almost two decades of business partnership—was evident to all who dealt with them.

Model 3 School Bus

Furnished in 1½ Ton Capacity Only

Seating Capacity

16 Adults and Operator   20 to 28 School Children and Operator

The Model 3 School Bus is designed primarily to meet all the requirements of urban and rural school transportation, though it has often been used for passenger transportation as well. One long seat runs the full length of each side, and both the seat and seat back are comfortably upholstered. In addition to many other advantages, this bus incorporates the following outstanding points which every School Board or individual operator must consider: Quality, Dependability and Safety; Prompt Service at a Reasonable Cost and Moderate Initial Cost.

Model 2 C and 2 L Passenger Bus

Furnished in 1½ Ton Capacity Only

Model 2 C, Cross Seat Type   Model 2 L, Lengthwise Seat Type

Capacity: 16 Adults and Operator

This bus, with either cross or lengthwise seats upholstered in rattan, street car type advertising racks, electric signaling and lighting equipment, is meeting with ever increasing favor in all sections. It is proving that its low operating costs, flexible and dependable service and moderate initial cost, make it more profitable in most services than the larger capacity types. An extremely important advantage is the fact that this type of bus permits rush hour additions of reserve busses without a tremendous increase in overhead.

Two examples of the myriad of bus designs offered to the nation's school boards, municipal and corporate customers by Graham Brothers.

The truck plant on Meldrum Avenue in Detroit was originally intended to supplement the production of Evansville, which continued to manufacture a myriad of Graham Brothers truck models at full capacity.[47] As production and sales continued to increase, so did the Grahams' attempt to make a truck applicable to all business needs. Maintaining the status quo in regard to their offerings was not the Grahams' aim. Advertising brochures presenting the basic body styles to prospective truck buyers stated,

> *Contrary to the general practice, Graham Brothers, from the beginning, have given the closest study to users' requirements and have built standard bodies for every important line of business. This fact has enabled the buyer to obtain his truck complete without the delay, inconvenience and extra cost of negotiating with body builders.*

The one-ton and one and one-half ton truck trucks produced were said to supply 80% of all business needs. Since the production of the very first Graham Brothers truck, pneumatic tires were used exclusively (something very much taken for granted today, but important to those using the rapidly improving roads of the day to earn a living). If a buyer's business needs did not fall within the noted 80%, Graham Brothers were proud to announce,

> *...if the user's requirements are of a special nature, they can be met with dispatch,...the Evansville factories are equipped to build special bodies for any purpose.*

With the growing number of body styles and chassis available, a nomenclature was developed which described the models and chassis by letter (chassis) and number (body). For example, a typical catalog description read: Truck with Model 4 cab and model 21 stake body/furnished in one-ton (chassis B) and one and one-half ton (chassis C) capacity. One fully illustrated catalog proudly listed over 400 specific businesses which Graham trucks would serve admirably.

When Joe Graham moved to Detroit, his brother Robert remained in Evansville to manage production at the original plant and headquarters. Even at full capacity, it became evident at year's end the Meldrum plant would not be able to keep pace with the increased demand. All across the nation, dealers were clamoring for more Graham Brothers trucks.

In 1922 the former plant of the King Motor Car Company[48] on Conant Avenue was purchased. Surely, the Grahams thought, production from this new 60,000-square-foot facility would meet demand. The plant appeared, at least at the outset, to be just what was needed to meet that goal. But appearances were deceiving: even the Graham brothers had not anticipated how popular their highly touted and much advertised trucks would become. To each party, the Grahams' association with Dodge had been even more advantageous than hoped. Dodge management was extremely pleased with the quality of "their" new heavy truck line, and it had not detracted from their automobile capacity in the least. During 1922, models were being exported around the globe, with a substantial number being shipped as far as New

A view of a spraying booth at the Graham Brothers plant in Evansville, Indiana.

Zealand. The Grahams had, in just a short time, increased their production at a rate previously unseen in the industry. Additions of 36,000 square feet and 50,000 square feet to the Conant Avenue assembly plant the next year helped meet demand, but not entirely. In 1924, the Graham factories produced almost 11,000 trucks.[49] From 1923 to 1925, school bus sales trebled. Graham Brothers Trucks experienced an increase of nearly 1,000% in less than four years.

With their advertising emphasizing the multitude of truck models and styles available,[50] sales of the Graham Brothers trucks were compounded. The Graham Brothers name was now well known throughout the entire nation and in those many foreign countries which Dodge Brothers distributed their automobiles. Full color and multi-page ads were appearing in both trade publications and general circulation magazines, especially the *Saturday Evening Post*. Total production by 1925 was increased more than 60% over the already imposing 1924 totals. The new plant on Conant Avenue, thought to be adequate for the needs of the foreseeable future, was almost immediately inadequate. The principals of Graham Brothers, Incorporated, again began to look for an alternative site which would fulfill their ever-increasing production needs. That alternative was to be an additional truck manufacturing plant on Lynch Road in Detroit.[51]

When the Grahams elected to establish an additional assembly plant on Lynch Road in 1924, they again decided to use an existing building. Originally erected by John Dodge in 1917, the 600 foot by 800 foot plant had housed one of the many contributions the Dodges made to the war effort. The $10 million building was built specifically to produce the special, hand-tooled recoil mechanisms for the French 155 mm guns used by the Allies in Europe.[52] Built in a scant four months during the frigid winter of 1917, the building and its output were in response to the government's direct call to produce the sophisticated devices in quantity. Used in a limited basis since Armistice, the 11-acre site and plant were exactly what the Grahams needed to respond to the challenge of ever-increasing sales.

A lesson the Grahams learned early in their industrial careers was the importance of excellence in engineering. Engaged prior to the production of their first truck, Louis Thoms had been the Grahams' chief engineer from the beginning. A University of Michigan graduate who earned top honors in Mechanical Engineering, Thoms was hired away from the Advance Rumley Truck Company of Chicago. He is credited with helping the Grahams design the first Speed Truck. As a longtime employee, he was considered an important part of the management team.

Another notable name from the engineering ranks of Graham Brothers was Malcolm Lougheed. Just as Louis Thoms found the progressive engineering attitude of the Grahams appealing, so did Lougheed. In 1921 he headed a team developing better braking systems for motor vehicles. The system he developed and perfected, "Lockheed Internal Expanding Hydraulic Brakes", became available on Graham Brothers Trucks in 1921. "Lockheed" brakes became the standard of the industry in a few short years.[53]

When sales of Graham Brothers trucks began to geometrically increase, several trends were noticed. Sales were strong throughout the country. However, the popularity of the trucks seemed to be especially strong in the far western states, most notably agricultural California. One would imagine the primary volume dealer in that state would be found in one of the major metropolitan areas, but that was not the case. The largest dealer was also a distributor, located in the relatively small community of Stockton, east of Oakland. Mr. E. Allen Test was the Dodge Brothers and Graham Brothers dealer in that community of 55,000, a successful businessman who had an optimistic view of what the Graham Brothers organization might someday become. To Mr. Test it was obvious the Grahams were indeed fulfilling the needs of many businessmen and particularly the rural trade in his state.

The same success the Grahams enjoyed nationally, Mr. Test enjoyed locally. It was with a view to the future and an unshakable faith in both the Graham brothers' product and his city's resources that he approached Joseph Graham in late 1921. It was Test's opinion that when the inevitable satellite manufacturing sites were considered, Stockton would be an ideal candidate. When approached, the Grahams believed the Evansville and subsequent Detroit sites would be more than adequate for years to come. Mr. Test was politely received, but little serious consideration was given. However, Mr. Test persevered, and over the next two years kept that option alive through many telephone calls and conversations with the brothers. When the sales of trucks in California began to climb appreciably,[54] he succeeded in having both Joseph and Robert Graham visit Stockton during their business trips to the West Coast. Favorably impressed, Joseph Graham cautiously agreed that should a plant be needed on the Pacific Rim, Stockton would indeed be considered.

The Graham Brothers truck plant on Lynch Road. Erected by John Dodge during the World War, it originally housed machinery to produce firing mechanisms for French cannons.

Graham Brothers Tractors And Trucks

E. Allen Test, the man primarily responsible for bringing production of Graham Brothers trucks to Stockton, California, in 1925. (Courtesy of Bank of Stockton Archives, Stockton, California)

A decision was made in the fall of 1924. In that year well over 1,000 Graham Brothers[55] trucks were sold in California alone, with comparable sales in neighboring states. The persistence of Mr. Test was coupled with the boosterism and assistance of the local Chamber of Commerce, spearheaded by Mr. A. C. Oullahan. Mr. Oullahan made several trips to Michigan to convince the Grahams that Stockton was an ideal location for expansion, and brought with him the enthusiasm of the entire business community.[56] Several properties were available at the time which would suit the needs of a heavy equipment manufacturer, more than adequate supplies of skilled laborers were available, and the city was well supplied with railroad lines. At that time the community was also actively engaged in a campaign to have the federal government undertake a "Deep Water" project which would afford Stockton direct access to the Pacific.[57] Secretary of Commerce Herbert C. Hoover had recently visited the city and recommended at the hearing in Washington, D. C., that the project be approved. Approval for this dredging project was announced at the same time a final decision was being prepared by the Grahams. It was Stockton's goal to entice other automobile and truck manufacturers to the area, making it the "Detroit of the West."[58]

In the first week of December 1924, a news release was issued by Joseph B. Graham announcing the establishment of a manufacturing plant in Stockton. The timing seemed ideal and, again, it appeared to be a business deal which would benefit all parties.

The Grahams would be purchasing the facilities of the former J. M. Kroyer Motors Company, a thirty-acre site located on Cherokee Lane, just outside the city limits. Kroyer, manufacturer of the Wizard tractor, erected the on-site building in 1921, and then transferred ownership to the Los Angeles Lumber Company, from which the Grahams purchased it.[59] The almost new manufacturing site was 442 feet long and 90 feet wide, with nearly 40,000-square-feet of usable floor space. The offices of this new Graham Brothers plant were located on the north side of the building and a concrete shipping platform ran the entire length of the building. The facility appeared to be ideal for the manufacture of trucks.[60]

The press in Detroit and Stockton announced that newly named plant manager Robert A. Houston would be leaving Detroit immediately with a skeleton crew to begin work preparing the site for manufacture, with January 15 as the target date. It was, however, February 17, 1925, before the initial machinery and men arrived.[61] It was projected that 60 local men would be employed to organize the building and be trained in the Graham manner of manufacture.[62] Projections were made that well over 100 men would be employed by the plant when at full production.

The efficiency and talents of the organization and Mr. Houston were evident when production at the site began in earnest a few short months later. The formal opening and dedication of the plant was on Thursday and Friday, June 18 and 19th, 1925. Held in conjunction with a West Coast Dodge Brothers dealers meeting,[63] the gala event featured a downtown parade, a dealer "drive away" of the first 150 trucks produced,[64] a celebratory banquet at the local Masonic Hall, guided tours of the new plant for the public and press, and presentations by Ray C. Graham and A. T. Waterfall, vice-president of Dodge Brothers, Inc.[65]

Production was ten trucks a day the first week, but increased almost immediately. Production totals for the final six months of 1925 at Stockton showed 1,298 trucks built.[66] When the Graham Brothers became the world's largest independent producer of trucks during the next year with 37,463 units sold, more than 4,000 of those came from Stockton alone. When Mr. A. T. Waterfall spoke on that summer

The Wizard tractor, Model 20-35, a product of the J. M. Kroyer Motors Company, was manufactured for only a short time in Stockton prior to the sale of the plant to the Graham brothers. (Courtesy of San Joaquin County Historical Museum)

Graham Brothers Tractors And Trucks

The very first Graham Brothers truck manufactured in California in front of the Stockton plant prior to opening day ceremonies. (Courtesy of Holt-Atherton, Dept. of Special Collections, University of Pacific)

distances involved, Canadian-based vehicles were generally more expensive per unit and cost more to produce. Also, since their products were already well known, American manufacturers were able to engage the most successful dealers. This was due to the fact that the American industrialists were realizing the value of having a worldwide market. Since Canada was a part of the far-flung British Empire, any vehicles made in that country could enter any part of the Empire at a much-reduced rate in regard to tariffs. Too, the 45% import tariff which the United States (originally) imposed on Canadian-built vehicles was met with only a 35% tariff for American-built vehicles.

In March of 1925, all Dodge Brothers/Graham Brothers print advertising had a base line which read "Graham Brothers-Evansville-DETROIT-Stockton-Graham Brothers (Canada) Unlimited, Toronto, Ontario-A Division of Dodge Brothers, Incorporated."

The Toronto Graham Brothers assembly plant was located on Dufferin Street, and was a full-scale factory.[69] The trucks were virtually identical to their American cousins, excepting the radiator badge: the circular brass emblem replaced the inscription "Graham Brothers-Detroit" with "Graham Brothers-Canada." The plant remained in production at full capacity during the lifetime of Graham Brothers trucks. Exports from this Canadian plant were shipped as far as Australia, South Africa, Britain, Brazil, Siam, and Morocco.

night in California in 1925, he announced to an eager audience he had no doubts it wouldn't be long before the existing plant would be inadequate to fill the needs of Graham Brothers' customers. This, of course, was very much welcomed by the listeners and was heavily emphasized in the local press. It was not, however, simply self serving and expected rhetoric: In the spring of 1927 construction began on a $150,000 addition to the plant, almost doubling its size.[67]

The success the Stockton plant enjoyed was incentive enough for the Grahams to investigate other satellite assembly plant sites. One of the locations which eventually did become a Graham Brothers truck plant would make the truck maker an international firm.

Even though Canada did have a fairly healthy industry in regard to domestic trucks,[68] Canadian truck manufacturers—as well as their native automobile industry—labored under several distinct disadvantages. Beginning with pioneer automobiles, American vehicles were popular with Canadians and sold well. Advertising and media coverage of American companies, their current models, road races, and the industry in general was popular in the mass circulation magazines and newspapers. Because of the less dense population (thus less voluminous sales) and greater

It had become obvious to everyone involved in the truck manufacturing industry the Grahams were producing a quality product, the product was fulfilling the needs of the consumer, and the company had become handsomely profitable.[70] This was more than obvious to F. J. Haynes. Continuing to administer Dodge Brothers, Inc., in the same aggressive manner as in the recent past, Haynes decided the Graham Brothers organization should officially become part of the world's third largest automobile maker. A deal was struck, predicated upon the purchase of 49% of the existing stock, making the Graham Brothers a divi-

Graham Brothers Tractors And Trucks

sion of Dodge Brothers, Inc. Over $3 million was realized by the Grahams from the sale of this block of stock, with a like figure placed on options the Dodge organization exercised on other Graham-held stock.

On October 6th of 1924, the following statement was released to the motoring press:

> In 1921 Dodge Brothers became the exclusive marketing organization for Graham Brothers trucks. Since that time these trucks have demonstrated that they possess the merit required of a product associated with the Dodge Brothers name. Dodge Brothers confidence in Graham Brothers, as well as the product, has prompted the action that has brought about a closer union between the two organizations.. Although Graham Brothers will be known and operated as a division of Dodge Brothers, it will continue as a separate unit, maintaining its own organization and individual identity.

So the general public understood this also, full color multi-page ads were placed in the *Saturday Evening Post* and other large circulation magazines. From this point, each advertisement published included not only the phrase "Sold and Serviced by Dodge Dealers Everywhere" but also "A Division of Dodge Brothers."

Again, it was a business deal which appeared to benefit both parties from the start. Dodge now had a heavy truck division, complete with consumer confidence, fully equipped plants, expert management on site, and a history of profitability. For the Grahams, they had proved their mettle in a highly competitive industry and, with this sale, had become wealthy men. Ultimate control of the division was also still in their hands. Being modest and energetic young men, it was decided these considerable earnings be invested in something which would further their industrial pursuits. Much of the money acquired was invested in additional shares of Dodge Brothers, Incorporated, stock. The Grahams now were involved in the affairs of not only the new division of Dodge named for them, but with this reinvestment in Dodge stock, they were among the largest investors in that huge corporation.

Sitting on the Board of Directors, they were involved in automobile and truck manufacturing decisions at the highest level. It was a position they were comfortable with, as two decades of industrial and manufacturing background had prepared them for just such an achievement. Working with their friend Frederick Haynes on a much closer basis than previously, they presented their ideas and visions for the manufacturing giant. The future of the company in which they had so heavily invested was another in a long series of invigorating business challenges.

Involvement in a business which generated almost $217 million of sales in 1924 was, however, not the sort of challenge in which the Dodge widows reveled. Since the Dodge brothers' deaths in 1920, it had become evident the two surviving sons of John and Horace[71] were neither capable nor interested in carrying on their fathers' business. The Dodge widows, too, had wearied of troublesome business details, and sensed it would be easier and more profitable to simply sell the company.

Nineteen-twenty four had turned out to be a very lucrative year for the truck and automobile manufacturer. Dodge Brothers stock had steadily climbed for quite some time and it proved to be an excellent time to offer the corporation for sale. It is reported that Mathilda Dodge (John's second wife) contacted Henry Ford personally for advice, and to give him first refusal. That is exactly what he did. Rumors were being circulated that a conglomerate made up of Packard, Hudson, Briggs, and Dodge would be formed to battle General Motors in the sales arena. In fact, that manufacturing colossus did tender an offer of $124,650,000. It was also rumored that J. P. Morgan had submitted a bid sheet. These and other less believable reports were prevalent after it became common knowledge that the Dodge women wished to sell.

When the sale was finalized in March of 1925, the Dodge widows were on the receiving end of the largest single cash transaction ever to take place in the United States. Since the death of the Dodge brothers in 1920, the value of the family-held stock had increased an incredible $90 million. When the Dodge widows learned they would be paying an additional $12 million apiece in taxes on the $146 million transaction, they reacted accordingly. Yet, they were the wealthiest widows in the nation, quite possibly the world.

The most amazing facet of the sale was not the large numbers involved in the cash sale—the company was honestly valued at that amount—but the purchase was made by a company quite removed from the automobile and truck industry. The winning bid was tendered by Dillon, Read & Company, a Wall Street investment firm. As expected, the sellers in this transaction were interested only in the total amount of funds to be realized, but the officers and management of Dodge Brothers, Incorporated, were duly concerned about the new owners. Clarence Dillon and his firm had virtually no experience in managing a major automobile manufacturer.

This concern, and the ultimate motives involved in the purchase, became more than evident in the months and years following the purchase. Dillon immediately proceeded to initiate a major reorganization of the company's finances. A syndicate

One corner of the wood fabrication unit at the Evansville plant. All cab and body units were produced in Indiana, supplying both the Evansville and Detroit assembly lines.

Graham Brothers Tractors And Trucks

of investment bankers throughout the nation was created and authorized to present a new stock offering. With the good name and reputation of the Dodge brothers, it was not surprising that sales of this new issue quickly totaled $160 million. Not known at the time by most investors, however, was the fact that complete and absolute control of the company was retained by Dillon, Read & Company by their purchase of virtually all of the voting stock. Fourteen millon dollars of profit were realized by this unethical maneuver. Since the laws of the day did not prevent such a tactic, outrage of public sentiment was the only new stockholder recourse. This was not how the Dodge brothers and the Graham brothers had done business in the past.

E. G. Wilmer, a banker with no experience in the motor car industry, was named chairman of the board of Dodge Brothers in November of 1926.

Not withstanding the initial public reaction, Haynes and company proceeded. Programs of expansion were initiated and a very respectable 265,000 automobiles were sold.[72] In short order, a major decision was reached in regard to the Graham brothers and the Graham Truck Division. The remaining 51% of Graham Brothers stock was purchased, and the truck manufacturer became a wholly owned subsidiary of the parent company. The purchase price of that controlling block of stock totalled approximately $13 million. The Grahams had become even wealthier.

In November of 1925, a management reorganization was effected which radically changed the face of the company. The steady hand of Frederick Haynes, the man who "saved" the company after the deaths of the founders and increased its value by $90 million in little more than five years, was relieved of his responsibilities.[73] He was replaced by a banker, E. G. Wilmer. Mr. Wilmer was quite successful in the financial world, but paralleling Clarence Dillon, had no experience whatever in the automotive world.[74]

Attempting to fill the void created by Haynes' departure, the Graham brothers were appointed to the top functional positions in the company. Ray Graham became general manager and vice-president of Dodge Brothers, while Joseph became vice-president in charge of manufacturing, and Robert became vice-president in charge of sales. These were positions of prestige, respect, and influence. The Graham brothers had built their success on years of hard work, intelligent business decisions, and respect for their employees. Those policies had taken them to the level of America's business elite.

Although they worked diligently in those positions and Dodge automobiles were again selling well under their direction, it was clear the philosophies of the bankers were taking precedence over those of experienced manufacturers. Foregoing the proven and substantial Budd steel bodies, less expensive and less durable wood and steel bodies of the Fisher Body Company[75] were utilized in construction of the new coach. The Dodge brothers' philosophy which dictated that success could be found in the low price field by offering Ford-like prices on an appreciably better car, was abandoned. Other cost-cutting methods were employed in materials and manufacture without a corresponding cost reduction in price. These changes were not lost on the automobile-buying public. Nor by the journalists of the day: *Fortune* magazine declared,

> *The trend of the new management [is] obvious and it [is] also obviously wrong. Dodge owners [have fallen] into a state of confusion. Dodge dealers [are beginning] to wail at a sales policy which [is] not the policy they [know].*

It was obvious to the Grahams—and anyone else who was following the developments in Detroit—the purchase of Dodge was solely a short-term money-making ploy by the investment bankers. There was little interest by the bankers in the long-term success or survival of the company. It was a situation which the three brothers found more than a little disconcerting. It was also a situation over which they had little control. In relatively little time a business decision was made, again with cool heads, free from sentimentality. To further their business aims and continue their business challenges, not to mention the preservation of their high ideals in business conduct (both in regard to their customers and employees), the three brothers elected to leave the positions which had so recently become available to them. Sale of their stock in Dodge would leave them with an enviable amount of capital, and the ability to re-enter the business world under their own terms. In April of 1926, Joseph, Ray, and Robert Graham resigned from their positions at Dodge Brothers, Incorporated, and began to liquidate their stock holdings.[76] Over two decades of hard work and dedication had brought the brother team to the highest levels of American business. They had been at the helm of one of the world's largest automobile makers for less than six months, but when they left they were confident they had made the correct and proper decision. Just as they had done when they sold their interests in their namesake glass company.

Even with the withdrawal of the founders of Graham Brothers trucks, the success story of the truck line did not end. As a wholly owned subsidiary of Dodge, the Graham Brothers trucks continued to meet the needs of their customers. Sales of Graham Brothers trucks in 1926 totaled 37,463 units, establishing another sales record for the Division. At this point Graham Brothers became the world's largest exclusive truck manufacturer in the world.

Continuing to offer custom body building abilities at the Evansville plant, the standard line of models from each plant consisted of 17 basic truck chassis (with the usual myriad of body styles available) in addition to four basic bus styles (including school buses). Early in the year Graham Brothers took over production of all Dodge Brothers commercial cars, now carrying the Graham nameplate. Wheelbases ranged

Graham Brothers Tractors And Trucks

When this photo was taken in Detroit in 1925, the Graham brothers were three of the largest stockholders in Dodge Brothers, Incorporated. (Courtesy of Robert C. Graham, Jr.)

from 116 inches to 162 inches with capacities of one, one and a half, and two tons for the standard offerings. Regardless of the difficulties being experienced by Dodge from the tarnished public image of the new owners,[77] Graham sales not only kept pace, but exceeded production capacity. Production at the four Graham Brothers plants was nearly 1,500 vehicles per day early in the year, but a full 2,000 per day was needed. In February of that year, an $8 million expansion of the Detroit plant was announced and construction began immediately.

The reputation the Grahams garnered in Evansville, the truck-buying public, and their employees were not ignored by the current Dodge Brothers management. Shortly after the Grahams' departure, President E. G. Wilmer visited Evansville and stated:

> *My associates and myself intend to continue to carry out the many projects envisioned by the Graham brothers of your city, while they were with the organization. The Graham brothers have always been held in high esteem by the Dodge organization and the Dillon-Read Company. Their ideas still live in the manner in which the business is expanding. The entire Dodge organization appreciates the splendid opportunity offered in Evansville to the growing industry.*

Since the first "Model A" in 1919, experimentation of new models and designs had become a hallmark of Graham Brothers, Inc. In 1923, an experimental "hog nose" design was test driven in and about the rural roads surrounding Evansville,[78] one of many designs which never reached production status. When the main office of the engineering department was later moved to the Lynch Road plant in 1924, a test track was built (a 3/8-mile oval with high-banked turns and 20-foot-wide straightaways) to enhance and expand the tests involved and to avoid the busy Detroit streets. A final inspection building measuring 80 feet by 320 feet was also erected at the sight. The engineering facilities and test drivers were seldom idle.

Two notable models developed during the Graham brothers tenure at Dodge did come to production directly after their departure. Both are important and interesting: one because of its uniqueness, and the other because of its tremendous popularity.

Beginning in 1919, a huge number of custom-and sometimes unusual-trucks were built. The February 15, 1926, issue of *Commercial Car Journal* announced what was considered to be the most unusual vehicle ever produced in the Graham Brothers plants. The available line of buses was expanded[79] with the addition of a double-deck model, powered by a combination gas-electric power source. The Continental six-cylinder engine[80] was mounted traditionally on this non-traditional vehicle, with two electric motors directly attached to the rear wheels through individual drive shafts. The wheelbase of the 60-passenger bus (28 on the lower deck and 32 above) was a gargantuan 234 inches. The bus was created in cooperation with Westinghouse, who supplied the air braking system. Limited demand and inherent design problems with the dual power sources kept the huge bus from going into mass production. It did, however, exemplify the Graham Brothers dedication to engineering challenges and the quest for new markets.

Limited production, however, was not the case for the "G-Boy", introduced that same spring. Almost immediately this new design found many eager and satisfied buyers. The medium duty, one-ton design was available on a 126-inch wheelbase with the standard Dodge four-cylinder engine redesigned for additional power and speed.[81] In an effort to make the truck look more like a heavy-duty truck and less like a truck built on an automobile chassis, the front axle was moved four inches backward and 20-inch cast steel wheels were utilized. Styling was not overlooked. The cabs now featured a new configuration, a single belt molding,[82] a two-piece windshield,[83] and a sloping cab roof. The truck-buying public was favorably impressed. Supplementing the imposing number of body styles already available, the G-Boy began to break all records for a single Graham Brothers model. Calendar year shipments of G-Boy models totalled 16,992. Much advertising done by the now wholly owned Graham Brothers Division of Dodge was directed toward prospective G-Boy buyers. The dark blue truck with the gold pin striping and cream colored wheels[84] was their individual sales leader, and was continued in 1927 with few changes.

As had been done in previous years, every body which was carried by a Graham Brothers truck was manufactured in Evansville, and shipped to the assembly plants. Proudly noted on trade advertising was the claim that the plant in Evansville was "...the most modern plant of its kind in America." While involved with the high level business dealings in Detroit, the Grahams had not forgotten the people of Evansville. When the officials at Dodge had suggested that in the best interests of efficiency and economy the body plant should be relocated to Detroit, the Grahams responded by announcing—only months prior to their departure—a general expansion of the Evansville plant and the acquisition of the Evansville Band Mill Company on Morgan Avenue.[85] The best interests of the people of Evansville was very much on their minds when the Grahams left the Dodge Brothers organization.

In 1927, Graham Brothers also introduced a new light-duty vehicle. This 3/4-ton panel truck was one which also found an immediate market and sold extremely well. Similar in design to the original screen side and panel commercial car available as a Dodge product, it nonetheless exhibited attractive Graham styling and impressive mechanics. As a complimentary offering in the same sales niche, Graham Brothers also introduced the smallest vehicle ever offered by the division. The Fast Four panel truck was a 108-inch inch wheel base commercial car, powered by the same Fast Four engine used in the like named passenger automobiles.[86] It was considered by the company a half-ton commercial vehicle.

Over 56,000 Graham Brothers trucks were purchased worldwide in 1927.

Several important changes were made in 1928 by the management of Dodge Brothers regarding Graham trucks. The venerable four-cylinder engine which had powered nearly all but the earliest Graham trucks since 1920 had been retired. All Graham-badged vehicles now were powered by the new six-cylinder engine developed for the Dodge Victory Six automobile.[87] A full line of trucks was available. Models now ranged from the half-ton commercial car to the two-and-one-half-ton, long wheelbase, heavy-duty trucks.[88] Styling was again updated to reflect customers' desires.

* * * * * * *

Graham Brothers Tractors And Trucks

Dillon, Read & Company had profited immensely from the purchase of Dodge Brothers, Inc., and from subsequent reorganizations and stock offerings. By the spring of 1928, it was made known Dodge Brothers, Incorporated, would be available at a "reasonable" price. Again, rumors ran rampant in the Motor City, but in the end it was a confident Walter C. Chrysler who signed on the dotted line. After several decades of success in the automotive field, most impressively with Buick and General Motors, Chrysler had introduced his namesake vehicle in January of 1924 to immediate success. It was, however, Chrysler's opinion that an automobile manufacturer would be ultimately successful only if he also had a firm foundation in the low price field. Lacking the considerable funds needed to enter this low price market—expensive by the virtue of the need to erect new foundries, new stamping plants, new assembly plants, and establishing a dealer network—Chrysler elected to purchase the assets of Dodge from Dillon, Read & Company. The purchase price was $225 million.[89]

During 1928, advertising for Graham Brothers trucks carried the tag line, "Built By Truck Division of Dodge Brothers."[90] Excepting the name of the vehicle, any association with the Grahams was excluded. On January 2, 1929, officials of the Chrysler Corporation issued a statement to the press announcing that the Graham name was being dropped from truck production. From that point on, the corporation headed by Walter Chrysler would be building Dodge Brothers trucks.[91]

The last Graham Brothers truck had been built and the trio were now spectators in regard to the production of motor vehicles. However, the Graham brothers were not by any means retired from the industry.

Graham Brothers (**G-Boy**) Stake Truck
BODY MODEL 554—CAB MODEL 205—CHASSIS MODEL BC
Capacity 1-Ton

Stake Body Model 554 is designed for Chassis Model BC (G-BOY). It has a loading space 94″ long by 66½″ wide.

For use with 1½-ton Chassis Models CB and MBM, Body Model 221 is furnished; it has a loading space 108″ by 66½″; Body Model 222 with a loading space 144″ by 66½″ is also available for 1½-ton Chassis Models FB and LBM.

Stake sections of all Stake Bodies are fitted around the edge of platform and are held in place by positive locks. Front side sections are made solid for use as sign boards and are equipped with guide strips on the inside to hold a full panel front endgate. Stake pockets of the inside type are set into edge of platform and are protected by a steel guard rail.

The Cab, on these models, is built as a separate unit and is furnished with full-length doors. (Description of cab, page 32.)

Painting: Body and Cab are painted with Graham Brothers standard dark blue lacquer with gold striping; wheels, light cream; hood, fenders and splash shields are finished with baked enamel.

Available in a great many functional styles, the Graham Brothers G-Boy was to become the most famous Graham Brothers truck of all time.

Chapter Four
End Notes

[1] Ziba Graham continued to hold the corporate title of President, but his sons operated the business day to day and were the functional officers of the company.

[2] In 1976 a publication by the Indiana Historical Board (Indianapolis) indicated that an automobile was indeed later produced in Washington. Besides the fact that the Brown was produced by the Brown Motor Car Company in 1910, little is known of this Washington-produced vehicle. It has also been reported by historians that the Hambrick was manufactured in 1908 in Washington, as was the Washington from 1908-11.

[3] The make of the automobile is lost to history.

[4] In addition to large orders from the Coca-Cola headquarters in Atlanta, Georgia, many deliveries were made to the Evansville Coca-Cola bottler after Coke's satellite began operations there in 1904.

[5] Mr. McCurdy was later to become Mayor McCurdy, Col. McCurdy, and owner of the McCurdy Hotel. The Sears automobile was not the last connection Mr. McCurdy had with the industry. Following World War I one example of an electric vehicle was produced, and in 1922 the McCurdy automobile appeared. According to the *Standard Catalog of American Cars, 1805-1942*: The McCurdy "represented not so much a corporate venture as the whim of McCurdy's son, Lynn McCurdy. While attending the 1920 Indianapolis Auto Show, young McCurdy had been impressed with a new prototype shown there, called the Gale Four, designed by Garde Gale. Gale was unable to secure financing for production, and consequently the Gale Four evolved into the McCurdy Six (Continental engine), with the announcement made in December of 1921 that Hercules would enter the automobile field early in 1922. Garde Gale became the general sales manager of the new automobile department at the Hercules Corporation. Bodies for the McCurdy were built in the company's shops, the engine and chassis parts arrived from various accessory manufacturers in the field. The wheel base was 127 inches (one source indicates 126 inches). The exact number of McCurdy's built is in dispute. One reference indicates five begun and only two completed. Another source (a former employee) recalled seven built, with five of these experimen-

tal, and two cars sold. The two cars which are definitely known to have been built were purchased (for $2500 apiece) by executives of the Hercules Corporation. They are also known to have provided a good many problems."

[6] The last Sears automobile offered to the public was shown in the 1912 catalog, and is properly titled a 1912 model. However, production ceased in 1911. Approximately 500 Sears automobiles with Hercules bodies were produced. One example, a Model J Business Runabout, is currently on display at the Evansville (Indiana) Museum.

[7] The factory covered over 31 acres. In 1921 Hercules set a production record of 84,000 buggies and carriages, 40,000 truck and commercial car bodies, and 62,000 gas engines. The Hercules sales organization was not only domestic in scope, but also international with agencies in Canada, Mexico, Central and South America, and Europe. Sales in 1920 topped $20,000,000. The Graham brothers were major stockholders in the firm.

[8] The Hercules firm continued to prosper after Ray Graham left its employ. They were to later job the Graham Brothers truck conversions and later still to construct special wooden bodies for automobiles. Hercules advertising in 1918 boasted of the availability of over 40 body styles built especially for the Ford automobiles chassis, and a number of bodies for one-ton trucks. Later yet, the Pontiac Motor Division of General Motors and the Packard Motor Company contracted with Hercules to produce a number of "woody" bodies well into the 1940's. A Hercules "woody" is highly prized today by collectors, even more so than the contemporary Cantrell-built "woody."

Joseph Graham later served as president of the company. Under his tenure the company continued to build bodies for Graham Brothers trucks, Ford automobiles, and Chevrolet automobiles. He also initiated the production of Servel refrigerators in the huge plant when the body building business waned, paralleling W. C. Durant's involvement with Frigidaire. Hercules exists today as the Hercules Manufacturing Corporation of Henderson, Kentucky.

[9] The canal system failed mainly because of the competition offered by the rapidly expanding railroad system. The Wabash and Erie Canal, patterned after the successful Erie Canal, was ultimately a failure.

[10] Named after his mechanic and co-designer, Shuyler Zent. A prototype, named the Single Center (or Centre), was their initial effort.

[11] Other automotive endeavors begun in Evansville during this era included: the Windsor in 1906, the Worth in 1907, the Evansville 1907-1909, the Fellwock 1907-1908, the

Copeland 1907-1909, the Evansville 1907-1909, the Hercules Electric in 1919, and the McCurdy in 1922.

[12] Because of the vehicle's inability to operate well in the rain, the resulting bad publicity forced the company out of the automobile industry by 1912.

[13] Although never repeated in any other advertising literature, the first brochure touted "Ford efficiency, Ford simplicity, Ford economy." When the price was increased to $385 the revision of the piece included the same text.

[14] George Dunham went on to a long and illustrious career as a designer following his tenure at Graham Brothers. He is known today not only for his truck and automobile designs, but also for his work in unrelated fields. Mr. Dunham held patents for the modern spin dry washing machine, and also the common push type lawn sweeper.

[15] One example was the unit produced by the E & W Manufacturing Company of Milwaukee, Wisconsin. A similar product to the Graham unit, the E & W conversion also utilized Dodge components which created 1 1/2 and 2 ton trucks with a 140" wheelbase. Others included the "Fitzall" (a product of the Hudford Company of Chicago, Illinois), the "Tonford" (a product of the William H. Jahns Company of Los Angeles), the "Maxfer-Ton-Truck-Maker" (a product of the Maxfer Truck Company of Chicago, Illinois), the "Ralston" (a product of the Ralston Iron Works, San Francisco, California), the "Tonsmore" (a product of the Charles Albert Smith Company of Windsor, Ontario, Canada), the "Form-A-Truck" (a product of the Smith Form-A-Truck Company of Seattle, Washington), and the "Tonhustler" (a product of the Harold G. Stiles Company of Chicago, Illinois).

[16] The 1916 idea of comfort and full protection differed a bit from the modern interpretation of the phrase. The first Graham One-Ton Truck Unit was shown with a cab featuring side and back windows with rolled-up fabric curtains (no glass), no windshield, no doors, nor anything besides the roof to keep out the elements.

[17] These styles included: open express body, no flare boards; stock rack with stake body platform; double box body and stake body platform; full panel body; specially designed body for bottler's use; extension rack only for express body; canopy top on 22 inch panels, box seat included; open express body, flare boards; canopy top with flare boards; canopy top only for express body; and stake body.

[18] The 1910 Indiana Census records Robert Graham as a "commercial traveler." He was to have that title for the rest of his life.

[19] The full trailer had a two-ton capacity.

Graham Brothers Tractors And Trucks

[20] Market pressures and the war effort conspired to raise the prices on the units, but they were still excellent values. By March of 1918, the price of a basic Truck Builder (for Ford) with a stake or express body was $400. The same unit for Dodge automobiles was $575, and a Universal Truck Builder was $585, complete. Conversion units without the cab or body were now also available, and priced accordingly.

[21] Other body builders recognized the quality of the Graham unit and used them in their custom work. For example, the Hoover Body Company of York, Pennsylvania, successfully marketed a bank body (armored car) using a Dodge Brothers chassis and a Graham Truck Builder.

[22] Half a million dollars in common stock and $375,000 in preferred stock.

[23] The Hercules Tractor Company was incorporated on January 19, 1916, with capital of $300,000, being $100,000 in common stock (1,000 shares) and $200,000 preferred stock (200,000 shares).

In July of 1915 Hercules announced that a farm tractor would be manufactured by the company and that prototype machines were being produced.

Eugene Bradley [no relation to the principals of the Graham-Bradley tractor of 1938] and Ray Graham announced the development of a farm tractor, built in a shop at 1502 Washington Avenue and tested on Green River Road. They claimed the machine, the only one available which would cultivate and plow, replaced six horses. James Bradley held the patents on this device, but his name was withheld until actual production.

The tractor patents were secured by Hercules (eventually) and the tractor was tested at the Graham Farms, Washington, Indiana. The price "was expected to be around $600, which is well within the reach of most farmers." Hercules was prepared to produce 3,000 tractors in 1916, purchasing $25,000 in machinery to produce the engines, and planned a 150 foot by 100 foot addition to the existing engine plant. Plans included a free standing 150 foot by 500 foot building to be built south of the engine plant on Franklin Street. Total cost was estimated at $200,000 and would employ 250 men. The Bucyrus Steam Shovel Company (of Evansville) was to build the wheels, axles, and sprockets for the chain-driven tractor. Because of the war in Europe there was a large increase in the demand for American farm products and this, coupled with a general shortage of horses, made for brisk advanced sales of this tractor. L. L. Turney and Ray Graham had, by September, booked over 700 orders.

On September 25, 1916, Hercules announced tractor production was temporarily discontinued due to dissatisfaction expressed by farmers. Production was scheduled to resume after redesign was completed and the machine met farmers demands. On November 22, 1920, the Hercules Tractor Com-

pany was consolidated into the Hercules Corporation, and on January 6, 1921, the Hercules Tractor Company was dissolved. —Hercules Corporation files

[24] Over 45, according to C. H. Wendel in his *Encyclopedia of American Farm Tractors*.

[25] The history of Henry Ford and the Fordson tractor is a story in itself. Recommended reading would include *Ford and Fordson Tractors* by Michael Williams.

[26] With the sawtooth design, fully one half of the roof was composed of glass windows. This allowed a tremendous amount of natural sunlight into the work areas, proving to be energy efficient, and was preferred by the line workers over electric lighting.

[27] Production models featured a 133 inch wheelbase.

[28] *Automobile Industries* magazine reported in its March issue (As did the March 25th issue of *Motor Age*) that the new Graham Brothers truck utilized a Continental engine.

[29] The initial standard body styles included the express, the stake-platform, the double box, and the high rack/canopy.

[30] Those automobiles built during calendar 1914 were considered 1915 models.

[31] Estimates of the death toll for the short lived pandemic range from the most commonly given 22 million, to 40 million lives. The disease first began in the United States on August 28, l9l8 in Boston. A returning sailor was diagnosed that day. In a few weeks time over 15,000 lives were lost in Massachusetts alone. Over 24,000 service men died in crowded discharge camps following the war. Prompt medical attention was difficult because of the large number of medical personnel still serving in the armed forces. Precautions were almost immediately undertaken by civilian authorities, but were to no avail. Fortunately, the disease faded as quickly as it began, and for no apparent reason. Scientists still do not know exactly what prompted the killer strain of flu, and admit it could again strike at any time. There is no known "cure" for the flu.

[32] Much has been written concerning the exact cause of death for Horace and John Dodge. Most histories accept that Horace became ill with influenza, which was complicated by a number of debilitating factors, and then contracted pneumonia. His brother had been in attendance at bedside throughout the crises, and soon also became deathly ill. While Horace went on to recover, his dedicated brother died on January 14, l920, in an adjoining room. Only eleven months later, December 10, the grieving and weakened Horace also succumbed.

[33] Mr. Haynes was well known, and respected, throughout the automotive world. Prior to joining the Dodges in Detroit, Haynes was employed by Franklin as engineer and factory manager. Following his departure from the Dodge organization after its sale to W. C. Chrysler, Haynes became the president of Durant Motors, Incorporated. In 1929 *Automotive Industries* magazine called Frederick J. Haynes "an outstanding figure in the automobile industry."

[34] Over two hundred truck manufacturing firms failed to survive the severe recession of 1921.

[35] A total of 2644 units were actually delivered prior to Armistice.

[36] The major change during this production run was the addition of a panel side model.

[37] The day after John Dodge died, workers broke all production records as a tribute to their late leader.

[38] Begun in 1914, The Denby Motor Truck Company of Detroit built trucks in varying sizes during its sixteen-year existence. However, it was best known for its heavy-duty versions. With an eye toward increased production, Denby purchased an assembly plant at 475 Holbrook Avenue, Detroit on August 5, 1915. The facility was the original home of Briggs-Detroiter Company, manufacturer of the Detroiter motorcar. When Briggs-Detroiter failed in 1915, both Denby and Alfred Owen Dunk bid on the facility. Dunk intended to take over the failed Detroiter company and make the changes necessary to make it a going concern. Denby's bid of $63,500 was successful. Dunk subsequently put the Detroiter back into production in a plant on Stanley Avenue, Detroit.

[39] The tremendous increase of sales predicated an addition to the Meldrum plant later in the year (1922), giving it a total of 27,000 square feet. In 1923 that total footage was increased on site to 40,000.

[40] Designated "Model A."

[41] The Budd Company of Detroit, builders of Dodge bodies since almost the beginning of production, was now designing and manufacturing some of the truck beds for Graham. The beds were shipped "in white" from Detroit to Evansville.

[42] In a speech given in Evansville on April 26, 1926, following the absorption of Graham Brothers into the Dodge Brothers organization, President E. G. Wilmer said,

The merger will affect no material departures in the Graham Brothers production or distribution policy. Each industry, while under the control of one president, will retain its separate identity."

The structure was continued as it was successful.

[43] Original plans determined that Ray would manage the new Detroit plant, and Joseph would remain in Evansville, and Robert would handle sales. With a more than competent and loyal staff in Indiana, all three found themselves spending more and more time in Michigan.

[44] Shortly after Armistice, additional planes were purchased from Government surplus.

[45] Victor Baumgart also acted as airport manager and chief mechanic for Ray Graham.

[46] When the "new" Evansville Airport was dedicated in 1929 there was some support, led most notably by Richard Lythgoe, in naming the facility Graham Field. The city did not act on this suggestion.

[47] The bodies utilized at the Meldrum Avenue plant were shipped in from Evansville. The trucks assembled at the Detroit plant were to supply the east, north, and western parts of the United States. Those assembled in Evansville were intended for distribution in the south and southwest.

[48] The King Motor Car Company was the creation of automotive pioneer, Charles Brady King. King automobiles were produced in Detroit from 1911 to 1923, and in Buffalo, New York, in 1923 and 1924.

[49] A total of 10,743 trucks were produced in calendar 1924.

[50] In 1922 twenty-six standard body designs were available, including buses.

[51] The Evansville plant was not de-emphasized in any manner. In fact, the factory was added on to and employment by the Graham brothers was substantially increased. The brothers' commitment to Evansville was firm.

[52] A French delegation met with John Dodge about the project because of the inability of their nation to produce the intricate and delicate mechanisms in appreciable numbers. Built almost entirely by hand in France, their workers had incurred nagging assembly problems and far too few devices were being produced. The first two American companies approached to attempt production had failed miserably. Upon perusing the blueprints, John Dodge promised not only a building but production in a scant four months. True to his almost unbelievable promise, the structural steel building was finished by March of 1918, contained 129 newly designed machines to produce the recoil mechanisms (one designed by John Dodge himself), and immediately began shipping them to the Allied forces. By war's end in November, 8,000 men were employed at this ordnance plant. Production topped 30 mechanisms a day—more than six times the pre-Dodge production rate.

[53] License #1 was issued to the Graham Brothers for the Lockheed Internal Expanding Brake System.

[54] In 1922 sales in California alone accounted for 11% of total Graham Brothers truck production.

[55] Wheelbases now ranged from 118 inches to 158 inches, with over 15 standard model lines available.

[56] Stockton was situated on the tidewater of the San Joaquin River, the central point of the nation's fourth-largest producing agricultural county in the nation. In additional to this agricultural base, Stockton itself was home to nearly two hundred industrial plants, and the terminus of three major railroads.

[57] The Pacific Ocean is approximately 100 miles from Stockton, California.

[58] Stockton's previous association with the automobile industry was slight indeed. In April of 1899, *The Horseless Age*, (a trade publication), reported the Holt Brothers, manufacturers of agricultural machinery in that city, had produced a prototype of the Holt automobile, and that "they had engaged a prominent mechanic and inventor in their city to act as chief engineer." It is doubtful that any vehicles were produced beyond the prototype.

[59] The Kroyer Company was organized in 1917 when J. M. Kroyer and his associates sold the Samson Tractor Company to W. C. Durant and the General Motors Corporation. It was announced to the trade press in December of 1921 that manufacture of the Wizard 4 pull tractor would henceforth commence in Los Angeles, California. Kroyer was described as a $5,000,000 company in that announcement. The selling price of the property was approximately $90,000.

[60] The original plant, enlarged but fundamentally unchanged, is the present site of a cannery owned by Van Denburgh Foods.

[61] It was decided by the Grahams that the families of the approximately dozen employees to be sent to California be allowed to remain in Michigan during the holidays, allowing them to enjoy them with soon to be "distant" relatives. The courtesy and respect afforded Graham employees, tendered during the early glass and truck attachment years, was not lifted or forgotten when their production companies became the vanguard of the truck industry.

[62] Several thousand men applied for positions at the new factory, even prior to the arrival of the new plant manager. Notices were put in the local paper announcing nothing was to be done in regard to employment until the plant was properly prepared. However, the Grahams also announced that the new employees would indeed be Stockton citizens. Labor would not be imported from Evansville or Detroit, despite the fact that many had applied to be transferred to the Golden State.

[63] Over two hundred West Coast dealers were in attendance.

[64] The very first truck produced was purchased by Samuel Kahn. Mr. Kahn was the president of the Stockton Chamber of Commerce, and vice president and general manager of the Western States Gas and Electric Company.

[65] Following the dealers meeting, parade, and drive away, a golf tournament was enjoyed by the dealers and municipal dignitaries, with prizes provided by the Graham brothers.

[66] Trucks ranging from 1/2-ton to two-ton were produced in Stockton, with each utilizing the four-(initially) or six-cylinder (beginning in 1927) Dodge engine.

[67] Capacity would be increased to 60 trucks per day. On February 25, 1928, an additional 37 acres were purchased for future expansion. The Stockton plant was ultimately a victim of the Depression, producing its last Dodge truck in 1932. In 1933 the plant was vacant.

[68] Trucks built entirely in Canada, with no American attachments, included the Canadian (1911-1912), the Jennings (1911-1914), the Brantford (1911-1916), the Watson (1912), the Drednot (1913-1915), the Redcliff (1913-1914), the Symes (1914), the National (1915-1925), the Barton and Rumble (1917-1923), the Beaver (1918-1923), the Loughead (1919-1923), the Mapleleaf (1919-1922, this company based in Montreal, Quebec, should not be confused with the Maple Leaf built by General Motors, the US giant), the Ruggles (1921-1926), the Hayes (1928-1969, in 1969 this firm came under the control of Mack Truck, of the US), and the Boulton (1929).

Graham Brothers Tractors And Trucks

[69] The plant was shared with Dodge Brothers, in that they also produced Dodge automobiles at the site.

[70] In his classic book *Men, Machines, and Automobiles*, Theodore McManus indicated that the Graham Brothers truck firm has been "built up" to the point that it profited its owners $8,000,000 yearly.

[71] Horace Dodge, Jr. and John Duval.

[72] That figure was exceeded only by Ford, Chevrolet, and Buick.

[73] Mr. Wilmer became Chairman of the Board, and the functioning head of the corporation. Mr. Haynes was given the title of Chairman of the Executive Committee, an almost entirely titular position. Mr. Haynes was not fired.

[74] "Clarence Dillon actually had ideas of becoming a motor tycoon, and he was not without qualifications," according to historians Richard Langworth and Jan Norbye. "Born in Texas, he went to school in the East, graduating from Harvard in 1905. After holding management posts in iron, steel, and coal, he joined William A. Read & Co. in New York. After three years, in 1916, he was named its president. The firm became Dillon, Read, & Company in 1921, when it refinanced the Goodyear Tire and Rubber Company. Clearly, Dillon had a predilection for transportation. For example, his company handled all the bond issues for the Canadian National Railways, and he was personally involved with financing for Shell Union Oil Company. It became apparent that Dillon...had visions of a merger between Dodge, Packard, Hudson, and Briggs, feeling that such a group could rival General Motors, which was smaller than Ford Motor Company at the time." Langworth and Norbye also note that "Dillon had installed [Wilmer] as president of Goodyear four years earlier."

[75] Originally an independent custom body building firm, Fisher was purchased by General Motors (60% ownership in 1919 and remaining 40% in 1926) and eventually became the world's largest body builder. The company was one of the last major body builders to forgo wood frame construction.

[76] Ray Graham was reputed to be the largest single stockholder in Dodge Brothers in 1926.

[77] The career of Clarence Dillon proceeded with no undue restraints. The Wall Street investment firm continued to prosper. Dillon's son, Clarence Douglas Dillon, eventually headed the firm, and was named Ambassador to France in 1953. In 1961, President John F. Kennedy named the younger Dillon Secretary of the Treasury. He served until 1965.

[78] Clifford "Clen" Songer was an assembly line employee in Evansville who later became a test driver at the Evansville plant (His father, Burrell Songer, was employed at Graham Glass in that city). Family records show that in addition to test driving production trucks, he also was involved with experimental design testing. One design noted was this "hog nose" model. It was described as "...powered by a Continental engine...in which the front axle and wheels were directly under the driver, thus giving a shorter wheelbase. The engine and hood compartment stuck out front as a big hog snout. This design was so secret that Clen drove it...on only the remotest rural roads and isolated areas. For a load, the truck had a [temporary] dump bed loaded with sand." As with many other experimental models, this design never made it to production.

[79] Also introduced at the same time was a 29-passenger "street car style" bus. Powered by the "7-T" Continental six-cylinder engine, it was somewhat traditional in design with its only other distinguishing characteristic the 234-inch wheelbase it shared with the double-decker gas electric model.

[80] The engine was the Continental "17U."

[81] Beginning on March 22, 1927, this new "124" engine was used exclusively.

[82] A double belt molding was to be introduced in later models of the G-Boy.

[83] A one-piece windshield was introduced on the 1928 G-Boy.

[84] The fenders, hood, and cowl were black baked enamel while the body itself was lacquered in "Graham Brothers Blue."

[85] Realizing the wisdom of the Grahams' well-placed faith in Evansville, K. T. Keller, then head of the Chrysler Corporation, announced a half-million-dollar expansion to the Stringtown Road plant. Following the departure of the Grahams the plant was used by the Chrysler Corporation to produce Plymouth automobiles and Dodge trucks. Employment peaked at 650 during this period.
Directly after the attack by the Japanese on Pearl Harbor, the government effected contracts with the Chrysler Corporation to produce .45 caliber cartridges at the plant. The transition was dramatic, but the facility was able to contribute three billion .45 caliber cartridges, 500 million .30 caliber carbine cartridges, and 800,000 tank thread covers to the war effort. Over 4,000 Army trucks and 1,662 Sherman tanks were reconditioned at the plant as well. Just prior to the end of the war, a contract was signed which called for the manufacture of over 7 million incendiary aviation bombs.
Following the war, Plymouth automobiles continued to be produced in Evansville. Automobile production ceased when the Chrysler Corporation moved the plant to St. Louis in the 1950s. In the spring of 1997 it was announced automobiles would again be manufactured in the area when a new Toyota plant was planned for a site north of the city.

[86] Since March of 1926 Graham Brothers had been producing all Dodge Brothers commercial cars and had been badging them as such. To continue to build them on the automobile assembly lines was becoming increasingly burdensome. Graham produced over 24,000 commercial-sized cars during the calendar year.

[87] This engine was built by Continental to meet Dodge Brothers' requirements.

[88] The number of models, styles, and options available was truly impressive. According to a press release published by *Power Wagon* magazine in May of 1928 "...Graham Trucks are now available in 1,842 different types. This figure is reached by combining the standard equipped truck or motor coach body with the five capacities in which the trucks are built and varying the equipment, size of tires, type of wheels, special gear ratios, etc. The trucks are available in 1/2-ton, 3/4-ton, one-ton, 1 1/2-ton, and two-ton capacities."

[89] Chrysler had purchased the rights to the Dodge car, Graham truck, all the combined Dodge and Graham factories, the dealers organization, and all manufacturing materials on site. In direct contrast to the deal the Dodge widows had made only three years earlier, this was not a cash transaction. Chrysler transferred to Dillon approximately $170 million of Chrysler Corporation stock and assumed the existing Dodge debt, estimated at $55 million.

[90] Canadian advertising continued for some time to read "Graham Brothers (Canada), Ltd."

[91] The action was not unexpected, and can actually be considered belated, as the Grahams had been producing a most successful passenger car for a full year. The Chrysler Corporation did recognize the value of the Graham Brothers name and continued to use it on selected models for several years. Surviving examples include a Canadian-built 1935 Dodge fire truck and 1 1/2-ton truck.

Graham Brothers Tractors And Trucks

The first automobile produced by the Paige-Detroit Motor Car Company, serial number 1. Harry M. Jewett described the automobile as "junk...rotten..." (Courtesy of Henry Austin Clark, Jr.)

The Paige-Detroit Motor Car Company

CHAPTER FIVE

The Paige-Detroit Motor Car Company

Conversations in late 1902 between two engineers named E. O. Abbott and W. K. Ackerman laid the ground work. Together, in a converted street car barn on Amsterdam and Woodward Avenues in Detroit, they inaugurated a series of automobiles which proved to go far beyond their earnest discussions and expectations.

It was at that site Wilfred Leland assembled a group of engineers to develop what was hoped to be Detroit's first successful automobile. These men were involved in the initial development of the motor car to be named after the French nobleman and explorer Le Sieur Antoine de la Mothe Cadillac.

Cadillac engineers Abbott and Ackerman, however, had aspirations and ambitions of their own regarding the pioneer motor car field and left Leland's employ during that same year. While engaged at Cadillac, they concentrated their efforts on developing a one-cylinder engine which would eventually power the very first Cadillac automobile. Qualified and ambitious engineers, their free time was spent developing an entirely different type of automobile engine. These two men felt a properly developed two-stroke, three-cylinder engine would be much more powerful, efficient, and dependable than any other in use or development. The pair was confident such an engine would be seen by the scores of early automobile manufacturers as the best possible power source available and would soon become the standard of the fledgling industry. Full-time development of the engine commenced and within the year they had "perfected" their design, and entered into an agreement with the newly formed Reliance Automobile Manufacturing Company of Detroit. Organized in November of 1903, the somewhat undercapitalized company began producing a five-passenger, "canopy" touring car powered by Abbott and Ackermans' 15 horsepower engine mounted in an 86-inch wheelbase chassis. This side entrance tonneau featured shaft drive with a selective transmission and was offered at $1,250. It was, rather surprisingly, initially successful.[1]

By 1904 the undercapitalization of the firm became a severe problem and reorganization was in order. An associate and the largest stockholder from the beginning, J. M. Mulky became the new Reliance Automobile Manufacturing Company president.[2] In little time it was evident Mr. Mulky did not have the skills necessary to lift the company from its financial doldrums, and another businessman was called on to solidify its future. It was felt by the Board of Directors[3] that one Fred O. Paige was the answer to their problems. He became president of the firm in 1905.

Frederick Osgood Paige was a man of many interests. By the time he had come to the attention of the Reliance board of directors, he had made a name for himself in Detroit as a successful, if peripatetic, businessman.

Born in Cincinnati on September 25, 1863, to David Osgood and Mary (Wiggins) Paige,[4] young Frederick showed a bent toward business and promotion at an early age. His public school education in his home town was followed by graduation from business college there.

Determined his fortune was to be made in Detroit, Paige moved there in 1880 and quickly put his business school education to good use. For three years he was employed as a bookkeeper at a shoe and boot company. Although the job was what he was trained for and the pay was fair, the ambitious Paige was eager to better himself. His tenure as a bookkeeper was followed by a year of employment as a traveling salesman for the Detroit Printing and Engraving Company. In 1884, predicated by his success in the paper business, the 21-year-old businessman became a partner in the newly established Beecher and Paige Paper Company. Working with, and retaining, business partners became a real concern for Paige, however. A year later the firm was known as Paige and Strachan, only to be known three years later as the Paige and Chope Company. When Paige and Chope was incorporated in 1894, Frederick Paige was installed as president.

Eager for new business challenges, Paige entered the insurance industry that same year. Upon becoming the business manager for the Mutual Life Insurance Company of New York, Paige found he enjoyed and was adept at the intricacies of the industry. His monetary and professional success in this new field allowed him to acquire, only two years later, a partial interest in the Hartford Life Insurance Company (Conn.). In a short time, Paige was the district manager of the Michigan, Ohio, and Indiana regions.

Frederick Paige—through his marriage to Minnie Grant,[5] his business successes in several fields,[6] and his social standing[7]—became fairly well known in then-bustling Detroit. It was only natural a man of Paige's many and varied interests would take a keen interest in the automobile when it first appeared on Detroit's dusty streets. An early owner of a "horseless carriage,"[8] Paige's enthusiasm for the new vehicles was noted in one business publication when his only recreation was listed as "automobiling."

With the firm evidently on the right track under Paige, the corporation announced a new body style to the Reliance line, the "King of Belgium" tonneau. This new

Reliance was also a five-passenger vehicle, but the wheelbase had been stretched to 92-inches and the engine boosted to 18/22 horsepower. One reason sales had appreciably increased is the fact that this larger, more powerful automobile was still being offered at the same price as the first model, $1,250. On the heels of this newfound prosperity, the company was able to offer the Model C, Model D, and Model E in 1906. Priced at the same $1,250, the C and D were basically the same as the "King of Belgium" model offered a year earlier excepting a boosted horsepower rating on the three-cylinder engine. The final Reliance was the ill-fated Model E. This last offering rode on a 109-inch wheelbase, was powered by the same Abbott and Ackerman engine (now rated at 28 horsepower), and carried a hefty $2,500 price tag. Sales plummeted. It was evident Paige and the Reliance board of directors had not learned the lesson of consumer value very well when they offered the Model E at twice the price of the Model D. It was not twice the automobile.

As sales suffered, the company again appeared to be in dire straits. At that point emphasis was again shifted and, under the leadership of Fred Paige, the company began production of a commercial vehicle. Initial acceptance of this truck, based on the same chassis and engine as the Reliance automobile, was favorable and the board of directors elected to sell its automobile interests to a group of Detroit investors.[9] As of February 1907, the company concentrated on truck production only.

The local success of the Reliance truck was indeed limited, but the company was able to survive and catch the eye of one William Crapo Durant. As the founder of General Motors, Reliance was one of many companies he eyed for his fast-growing conglomerate. In 1909 the Reliance truck was absorbed into General Motors.[10]

Fred O. Paige, freed of obligations to any automobile company, now had the rights to a seemingly ideal automobile engine. With no shyness in regard to promotion, the former Reliance president made it known throughout Detroit he was eager to re-enter the automobile business. It wasn't long before Andrew Bachle, a mechanical engineer who had recently designed an entirely new automobile,[11] had the first of many conversations with Fred Paige. These two, like-minded men had the ambition and, they felt, the abilities necessary to build a successful automobile. Within the year a smooth-running, good-looking prototype had been assembled. All that was needed for prosperity in the field of automobile manufacture was backing for startup expenses. One of the numerous men they approached was Detroit businessman Edward Jewett.

Edward H. Jewett was able to proudly trace his ancestry back eight generations to Edwin Jewett, a prosperous cloth manufacturer in Yorkshire, England. The military career of Edwin Jewett's son, Joseph, brought him to the Colonies of North America. Joseph Jewett served with distinction for the British and, upon his return to England, influenced his son, Jeremiah, to follow in his footsteps. Serving the Crown during the Indian Wars of 1675, Jeremiah had the dubious distinction of being the first Jewett to be buried on American soil.[12]

The founding of Jewett City, Massachusetts, by Jeremiah's son, Eliezer,[13] was the proud achievement of the first Jewett born in America.[14] Success in their new country continued for the Jewett family, with Joseph Jewett, Eliezer's son, becoming a judge of note, and his son, Thomas Murdock Jewett, becoming a prominent Massachusetts politician in the mid-1800s. The calling of Arthur LeRoy Jewett, the

Fred, Edward, and Harry Jewett, upon matriculation at Notre Dame Preparatory School. (Courtesy of University of Notre Dame Archives)

The first University of Notre Dame football team, 1887. "Hal" Jewett is in the front row, far left. (Courtesy of University of Notre Dame Archives)

The Paige-Detroit Motor Car Company

son of Thomas, in the young and growing nation was that of manufacturer. When the first of Arthur Jewett's sons was born in New England, the Jewett name had long been respected on two continents.

Edward's parents, Arthur and Gertrude (Osborne)[15] Jewett, had begun their family with the birth of Fred Jewett in 1868 while living in Elmira, New York. Two years later another son, Harry Mulford Jewett, was born to the proud parents.[16] The family was complete when a third son, Edward Hunting Jewett, was born in 1874.

Blessed with loving and concerned parents, the boys enjoyed a typical and unremarkable rearing. At the age of 15, their middle son, Harry M. Jewett, suddenly distinguished himself by becoming an ex-student of his preparatory school. His penchant for athletics exceeded his desire for even the minimum effort required for academic satisfaction and he was summarily expelled. As Jewett's parents not only desired but insisted upon his continued education, arrangements were made for the young Jewett to matriculate at the preparatory school at Notre Dame in South Bend, Indiana. With a zeal for sports that consumed him for his entire life, Jewett found a ready and comfortable home on the athletic fields and in the gymnasiums of that institution. He soon became famous amongst his classmates

The University of Notre Dame recognizes "Hal" Jewett as one of the greatest athletes to attend that storied school. This photo was taken shortly after Jewett broke the world's record in the 100-yard dash.

as one with a tremendous amount of athletic prowess. Following him to that institution also was an almost total disregard for classroom studies. His successes on the playing fields were inversely proportional to his success with his studies.

Having been observed in a gymnastics class performing a difficult maneuver generally performed only by university athletes, a kindly and concerned teacher knowingly approached him. Following compliments for his energy and skill, the teacher inquired as to his standing in the classroom. After an embarrassing pause, Jewett replied, "At the bottom." Years later, Jewett recalled the teacher's reply,

> *Lad, you're blessed with wonderful vitality; you stand high in the regard of your classmates. And you're low in your classes simply because you never studied. You have found yourself in athletics. Why don't you find yourself in your studies? I am going to watch your work.*

Throughout his life Jewett never forgot the teacher's comments or concern. It was just the spark which was needed to give Jewett his direction and purpose in life, outside of athletics. From that point he found he did, in fact, have the ability to concentrate on both his studies and his athletic endeavors. Not only did he have the ability to satisfy the academic requirements, but also the ability to excel. By the end of the school year freshman Jewett was first in his class according to academic standing. But his fervor for athletics did not dim. As captain of the track and field team, he excelled. In that year, for the first and only time in Notre Dame history, the Preparatory Department track team defeated the University squad. As captain, Jewett won the 100-yard dash, the 220-yard dash, the 440-yard dash, the high jump, the broad jump, and the hop-step-and-jump.

But Harry M. Jewett's athletic involvement did not end at the preparatory

A small portion of H. M. Jewett's athletic awards and medals, as later displayed at the Detroit Athletic Club.

school. His entire collegiate career was decorated with athletic honors. On the University of Notre Dame football team, he was acknowledged as their fastest and most brilliant running back. He was presented a medal by his teammates for scoring the first touchdown in the school's history, tallied against the University of Michigan. It was a 110-yard run, the highlight of the season. On the baseball team he was the catcher for future major leaguer "Lefty" Inks, with broken bones in his right hand to show for it. "Hal" Jewett also stroked for the crew, and was a member of that national winner. Throughout, he excelled at track and was never far from the cinder oval, regardless of the season.

While at Notre Dame, Jewett not only won a letter in every branch of sport recognized at the University between 1886 and 1890, but was also the holder of the world's record in the 100-yard dash and A.A.U. national title for the 220-yard dash (21.20 seconds).

Blessed with athletic ability, Jewett never neglected his studies following his concerned teacher's intervention his freshman year. Upon graduation in 1890, he was presented with the medal (designating first in his class) for architectural drawing. Further distinguishing himself, graduation day saw him also carry off the medal for civil engineering, and that of the Science Department.[17]

As exemplary as these achievements were, the success of "Hal" Jewett were for the most part contained to the campus of the University of Notre Dame. During his senior year, however, Jewett was to be involved in a chain of events which would determine the course of his life.

Each June the Detroit Athletic Club was invited to Ann Arbor to meet the stars of the University of Michigan in a track meet. Although not associated with any university or college, the Detroit Athletic Club was an organization which fielded a strong team of amateur stars from the Detroit area. The University of Notre Dame track team was invited to this annual event in 1890. Well financed by the city's elite, the amateur athletes of the Detroit Athletic Club looked forward to trouncing the "college boys" each year.

When the Notre Dame team prepared for the first event, peals of laughter went up when a slender, well-muscled senior approached the starting line in an old pair of running shoes which were so ill-fitting they had to be tied around his ankles to remain in place. Further attention was drawn to Harry Jewett when he easily crossed the finish line ahead of all others. Mike Murphy, trainer for the Detroit Athletic Club,[18] immediately filed a protest, claiming Jewett must surely be a professional athlete. After documentation and further proof was furnished proving him to be a bona fide student, the next heat was run with Jewett again participating.

Lined up between Fred Bonine and John Owen (the first man to run the 100-yard dash in 9.8 seconds) in the second heat, Jewett placed a close second to Owen. He then added a first place finish in the high jump, then the broad jump, and finally in the hop-skip-and jump.[19] Before he had a chance to leave the field at the end of the competition, Jewett was approached by a delegation from the Detroit Athletic Club admonishing him to join their club following graduation. An application form was produced and he was encouraged to sign immediately. Promises of a job and a place on the team were offered without reservation.

Harry Jewett did not immediately sign the application, but he had made a formidable impression. These prominent young men, many of which were to go on to highly visible and powerful positions in business and politics, continued to be in touch with the senior after graduation.

Unsurprising to anyone who was familiar with his preparatory and college career, Jewett resolved to use his civil engineering degree to achieve like success in that field. Landing a job with the company that was doing the preliminary survey work for the Chicago Drainage Canal, Jewett started that career at the lowest level.

As a stake driver for the engineering firm he earned the princely sum of $50 a month. It was not what he expected following his high achievements and honors in civil engineering while at school, but he expected hard work would allow him to attain greater responsibilities. Little over a month after beginning work, his crew chief contracted a severe case of typhoid fever and was unable to carry on. By virtue of his degree, Jewett was put in charge of the survey team. Visions of quick promotions and a position more in tune with his training were hard to suppress. He imagined this to be the first fateful step in his climb to becoming a civil engineer of note and approached the job with ardor. But it was not to be. In just a few weeks those dreams were dashed when the same malady also put him flat on his back.

While convalescing, he was visited by members of the Detroit Athletic Club who were still trying to get him to their city and on their roster. Perhaps it was the offer of J. D. Hawkes, Chief Engineer of the Michigan Central Railway and ardent supporter of the club, which colored his decision to move to Michigan following his recovery.[20] The offer entailed a title—Assistant Engineer. His salary, again $50 a month, was de-emphasized during discussions but he was told advancement and increased salaries would follow hard work. He would also have the prestige of running for the Detroit Athletic Club.[21]

Employment during the following year provided a great deal of hard work, but little in the manner of advancement or increases in his pay packet. Youthful optimism gave way to the realization that winning honors in college did not necessarily pave the way to success and advancement in the real world of work.

During this period of self discovery, the railroad had been involved in a project concerning the construction of a drainage sewer from its stockyards to the River Rouge. The project was difficult from the start, and now quicksand had been encountered. The contract company given the project had failed. A brief order from his chief was placed in his box one morning. Years later Jewett recalled the memo:

You are appointed to put the drainage sewer through. Don't bother me with details. Put the sewer through.

Harry Jewett was thrilled to be given the opportunity to do some real engineering work, but at the same time he was filled with dread. Visiting the site, he discovered progress on the drainage sewer was at a virtual standstill. As fast as the sand was removed from the excavation, it flowed right back in. This was not the kind of problem which was presented in the textbooks, and one not covered by any college professor's lecture. Everyone, including Jewett, was perplexed.

While pondering the problem, Jewett observed a floating steam syphon pump at work on the River Rouge. The principle involved fascinated him and suggested an answer to his present predicament. Returning to the job site, he suspended all operations and contacted his supervisor. "Get me a steam syphon pump, a threshing machine engine, and some track." A confident Jewett predicted he would "finish the sewer."

The materials were rushed to the site, placed in the positions directed by the new project head, and progress commenced almost immediately. Within the next week it was evident the drainage sewer would be completed not only on time, but ahead of schedule. Even more amazing was the fact it was also completed under budget.

The Paige-Detroit Motor Car Company

When the project was completed, Jewett was called into his supervisor's office. He had been billed by his fellow engineers and employees as "the greatest engineer of the division" and "a construction genius", and one who would "rise high on the road." While accepting the compliments of all involved, not to mention the raise in salary to $145 a month, Jewett also accepted the fact there were others who could have and would have come to the same conclusion, and same end. He attributed this particular success, as he would others in his long life, as the "luck" of being in the right place at the right time. He contended it was a fluke that he was allowed to garner the solution, and not one of his equally talented co-workers. He was proud of his work and accomplishments, but he did not acknowledge himself to be a genius.

It was with this humble and honest evaluation of the situation, that when offered the position of Assistant Divisional Engineer, Jewett surprised everyone by resigning. In what was considered youthful boasting by Chief Engineer Hawkes, Jewett responded to the promotion by saying,

> *You as chief are getting $6,000 a year. I might never get that [at Michigan Central Railway]. But it's the limit. And if I felt that $6,000 a year was my limit, I would lose all my ambition. I believe I can earn more money than that. So I quit!*

Hawkes responded by saying, *More than $6,000 a year! At what?*

I don't know, but not at civil engineering! replied Jewett.

Hawkes was aghast at the pluck of his young charge, but valued his contributions and allowed that he would hold his job open for six months. *A railroad man never quits,* proclaimed Hawkes.

This is one who does. I'll never come back, was Jewett's response to the offer.

With no prospect of a job, and no idea of where to even begin to look, Jewett lost no time in making his way to the athletic field to work off some of his pent-up energy and frustration. It was there he ran into one of his friends from the Detroit Athletic Club, the Advertising Manager of the *Detroit News*. Within thirty minutes of this chance encounter, Harry M. Jewett was under contract to the newspaper to sell advertising space. Elated he was able to obtain a job in an entirely new business so quickly, Jewett again thought perhaps this was the fateful turn of events which would catapult him to his true lifelong calling. He was eager to become a newspaper man. However, it was evident all too soon the newspaper career of "Hal" Jewett, former college athletic star and former "genius" civil engineer, was not going to make him a wealthy or respected man either. It was only a matter of weeks before his newspaper "career" ended.

While working for the railroad in Michigan, Jewett had watched the long lines of coal cars roll into the industrial areas of the state. He had at that time found them fascinating and, now that he was unemployed, he resolved to contact an old Chicago friend, W. P. Rend. Based in New York City, Rend was a successful coal merchant. Shortly after Jewett contacted him in that city, Rend offered him a job as salesman in his company. Jewett's dismal failure in the newspaper business had given him some definite ideas and insight of what it took to be successful in the field of sales. While graciously accepting his offer of employment, Jewett insisted to Rend he learn the business first hand, by working in the mines. Taken aback, Rend found himself with his first college-educated coal miner on the payroll. At a salary of $75 a month, Jewett learned every practical aspect of his new industry. After eight months in the mines, he became the newest salesman of the W. P. Rend Coal Company. With a firm foundation of the basics, it was no time before he began experiencing success in sales. Recognition and income were starting to come to him, finally.

Unanticipated by any businessman, nor predicted by any economist, was the "Panic of 1894." America's thriving economy, especially the manufacturing industries, was practically paralyzed by this severe downturn. Throughout the nation business activity ground to a near halt. Reductions in manpower were forced in most industries, and the coal business was no exception. Rather than simply being laid off, with only the hope of being rehired with better times, Jewett approached Rend with a bold proposition:

> *I can't earn my salary now. And you can't well afford to keep me on the payroll. So I'll resign...let me take your coal from the Hocking Valley [in West Virginia] and Pittsburgh mines and sell it on commission...at ten cents a ton.*

With no better plan for keeping himself in business—and his friend employed—Rend accepted his offer. For two months Jewett contacted not only his regular customers but anyone and everyone who would conceivably need coal. Long days turned into long weeks, with little to show for his diligent, far-reaching, and exhausting efforts. During the next month his meager savings ran out (he had earned no commissions), and he relied on friends for his daily living expenses. Throughout this trying time, his efforts did nothing but intensify. Just at the point at which he felt he could not and should not continue, the tide turned. The economy began to come to life, and orders which he had been negotiating for months were realized in fact. Slowly at first, his volume of tonnage increased quickly to the point were he became the highest-grossing salesman for W. P. Rend Coal Company.

Having survived this challenge and by proving to his customers that "Hal" Jewett could and would produce for them, it was to this energetic salesman that industrial customers turned to during the Coal Strike of 1895. While local dealers were having no success bringing the much-needed fuel into Michigan during the strike, Jewett was able to supply their needs. This, however, required some outside help. The shipments needed to be paid for before leaving West Virginia, something even Rend was not able to do during the strike. Sensing a real opportunity, Jewett contacted a friend from his Detroit Athletic Club days. Jay W. Bigelow was the paying teller at a Detroit bank, and happily studied the proposition for his friend. With the admonition that the proposal was something the conservative banking practices of the day would surely not allow, Bigelow nonetheless introduced him to the president of the bank.

That same afternoon, no doubt aided by his newly developed skills as a salesman, Jewett left the bank with two drafts, totalling $10,000. One half was dated fifteen days, the other thirty days. The manufacturers desperately needing coal were contacted, and were told only cash transactions could be arranged. The manufacturers jumped at the chance. Within days long trains of industrial grade coal were making their way to Michigan. Jewett is credited with bringing the first West Virginia coal into the state. The notes were paid off on time, and no little profit was earned by the young Harry Jewett. These large customers stayed with Jewett following the coal strike and his prosperity continued.

Upon the suggestion of the notably impressed bank president, a partnership was formed in 1895 between Jewett and his financially skilled banker friend. The firm of Jewett and Bigelow[22] prospered from this early success and grew rapidly from retailer to wholesaler. With the addition of another substantial partner, the firm of Jewett, Bigelow & Brooks[23] became one of the largest coal operators in the nation.[24]

As the president of the thriving firm, Harry Jewett concentrated on the areas of mine acquisition, their development, and subsequent sale to large coal consumers. He enjoyed the work and was dedicated to its success. However, that dedication did not overshadow other facets of life. Like most of the nation, Jewett was outraged at the sinking of the battleship *Maine* in Cuba in 1898 and, upon the declaration of war in April, signed onto the Michigan Naval Reserve. Serving as a gunnery captain on the cruiser U.S.S. *Yosemite* during the Spanish American War, Jewett was at Manila Bay when Dewey defeated the Spanish fleet.[25] Just as his colonial great-great-great grandfather had done, Jewett served his country with honor.[26]

Returning to Michigan, Jewett also made the decision to end his bachelor days. On February 19, 1900, he made his long-time sweetheart his bride. The former Mary Visscher Wendell was the daughter of a prominent Detroit family, and their nuptials were quite a notable social event. The union produced a daughter, Eleanor,[27] and a son, Edward.[28] The marriage and family were looked upon as successful in every order.[29]

During the first decade of the century this letterhead was utilized by one of the nation's largest coal merchant.

This advertisement appeared in the Detroit Free Press, 1902.

For nearly a decade Jewett enjoyed the challenges of the coal business and prospered.[30] With the many business contacts made over the years he was able to invest in a number of successful firms outside of the coal industry, and became a wealthy man. Long gone were the days when $6,000 appeared to be the ceiling of his yearly earnings.

When Harry Jewett's brother, now a partner in the coal firm, approached him concerning his contact with Fred Paige, he was eager to hear more. Just as the long lines of coal cars had intrigued him while working for the railroad in Chicago, the current news reports of horseless carriages being manufactured in Detroit piqued his interest.[31] The infant motor car industry promised an interesting adjunct to common transportation of the day, and sharp businessmen could see profits being accrued from a successful manufacturing operation. This was a business which Jewett thought would perfectly complement his coal interests.

In the summer of 1909 arrangements were made for a meeting with Fred Paige and, shortly afterwards, a test drive of the Bachle-designed prototype was accomplished. The 25 horsepower, three-cylinder engine rode in a 90-inch wheelbase chassis, and a two-passenger roadster body was utilized. The prototype performed admirably during its test drive in and about the streets of Detroit, and was good looking. Jewett was favorably impressed. The slick presentation by Fred Paige of the automobile's superior characteristics was exactly what Jewett wanted to hear, and the thought of being a part of the excitement of automobile manufacture was almost irresistible. This appeared to the coal man to be not only a terrific car, but also a terrific opportunity.

Harry Jewett proceeded to organize a meeting of well-placed and financially capable friends[32] who might be interested in just such a venture. Upon only the word of the president of Jewett, Bigelow & Brooks, sufficient funds ($100,000)[33] were garnered at that first meeting to set up a corporation and lease a manufacturing facility. An old drug factory on a Detroit side street[34] served as the first assembly plant. It was small, housed neither an engineering[35] or manufacturing staff,[36] nor was there a sales department; but the young men were now in the automobile manufacturing business.[37]

Fred Paige had been elected to the young firm's presidency, by virtue of his presentation and reputation at Reliance. The directors of the firm, including Jewett, were all busy business men and had not invested their funds with the purpose of supervising or directing day-to-day operations. Paige was considered by all to be a "practical manufacturer." Such was their confidence that the name of the new corporation was to be the Paige-Detroit Motor Car Company.

When the production version of the prototype was announced, its good looks and construction brought immediate attention. The reputation of Harry Jewett and his associates was enough to convince prospective dealers a quality automobile was being produced.[38]

The 1910 Paige-Detroit[39] utilized the three-cylinder engine which had so impressed Jewett on the trial run, and was now rated at 25 horsepower. With a bore of 3 1/4 inches and a stroke of 4 inches, the two-cycle engine was valveless, the chambers were cast individually, and were suspended in the chassis at three points under the hood. The wheelbase of the single model, the roadster, was 90 inches, thread was the standard 56 inches, and the tires were 32 x 3. Atwater-Kent supplied the ignition, the cooling system was the industry standard thermo-syphon type, and a

The Paige-Detroit Motor Car Company

sliding, selective-type transmission was employed. The clutch was a leather-faced cone, the chassis was made of the best grade pressed nickeled steel, and the brakes were internal expanding and external contracting on the rear wheels. The Paige-Detroit carried two side oil lamps, one rear oil lamp, and top irons[40] as standard equipment. In addition to its good looks, the Paige-Detroit was—for all appearances—a well-built and well-equipped automobile.

National advertising extolled the fact it was the "highest grade small car in the world." In everything but overall size, the roadster was compared to the most expensive machines on the road. Its three-cylinder engine[41] was said to be " as smooth as any six being manufactured," while having no need for valves, cams, rollers, push rods, or rocker arms. Because of the engine's efficiency and the vehicle's light weight, the top speed was touted as an incredible fifty-five miles per hour.

Fred Paige, Harry Jewett, and the board of directors all felt confident in their product and their new corporation. Automobile men across the country were applying for dealerships in increasing numbers and the $800 vehicles were being sold at a healthy profit.[42] A very respectable 302[43] cars were built and sold in that inaugural season. Detroit's newest automobile concern appeared to be well on its way to acclaim in the fledgling automobile industry.

Jewett was still actively involved with the affairs of Jewett, Bigelow & Brooks and this entailed quite a lot of travel. As a hands-off investor, but yet a new "automobile man" eager for the excitement of this new business adventure, he made a point of stopping at distributors and dealers in his travels during the winter of 1909 and early spring of 1910.

With glowing reports from Fred Paige and from the company's bookkeeper, these visits were anticipated to be most pleasant. In his capacity of investor and company representative, Jewett thought he would be warmly greeted at each dealership and would endeavor to assist with any minor problems which may have come up. His eagerness was tempered, however, when each of his calls provided more than enough major problems to discuss. The routine calls developed a distinct and disturbing pattern.

Each stop provided Jewett a veritable classroom for automotive problems. Necessity insured he be an eager and studious student. It was quickly obvious to him there was much he did not know about automobiles when he had entered the industry only months before. Now, his eye was much more critical and of more a business and engineering bent than when he took his first ride in the three-cylinder prototype.

At the next regular board meeting, Jewett held his tongue while Fred Paige spoke eloquently about the Paige automobile and the success he was having in producing them, while the treasurer gave out glowing financial data, and when discussion was begun concerning the increasing of material purchases.

At that point the 36-year-old coal merchant and automobile investor stood to address the board. Solemnly he said:

You're broke right now and you don't even know it.

Jewett then related to the board his experiences in the field and the problems which were mounting each day. The directors of company were nonplussed. It was as much as a shock to them as it had been to Jewett on his stops.

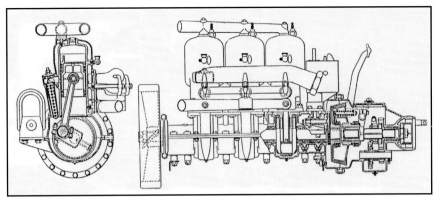

The Paige-Detroit three-cylinder engine, as designed by Ackermann and Abbott.

I can say we're broke because I have taken the trouble to find out from Paige dealers just what the public thinks of our car. It's rotten. A piece of junk. There isn't a director here who would be proud of the car. And I am going to prove it by showing you some of the gears that are going into the Paige car, Jewett explained.

On the meeting room table, Jewett spread out a number of gears which he had acquired from the factory prior to the meeting. Much more educated than he had been only months earlier, he asked,

Is there a single gear here that any one of you can be proud of? Measure them. Balance them. Look at the finish. I think the lot of them are terrible.

The directors objectively acknowledged the situation and a suggestion was made that the company be operated by an executive committee. This proposal was strongly contested by Fred Paige and a lively discussion ensued. With expressions of misgivings, the majority felt that Paige should be given a chance to rectify the situation and save the good name of the company. Even though it was their money which was being risked, they were not knowledgeable enough themselves to simply dismiss the only "experienced" automobile man they had known.

By July of 1910 the situation had not improved. Much to the board's chagrin it had deteriorated to the point that bankruptcy was a strong possibility. It was reported that Paige had "cracked under the strain."[44]

At the July meeting of the board, the investors elected a new president.[45] With his coal company well managed by his partners and brothers,[46] Harry Jewett was able to expend almost full time to the young company's survival.

With dispatch and no hesitation he proceeded to implement his recovery strategy. He had explained his four-point plan to the board and they had readily consented. First, he shut down production immediately. There was no need or reason to continue to send out inferior machines only to have them come back and further damage their reputation. Second, he called in the creditors and asked for extensions.

The Paige-Detroit Motor Car Company

*Side View Of Paige-Detroit Chassis
with 3-Cylinder, 2-Cycle Motor*

*The Paige-Detroit catalogue described this natty
roadster as "A Physician's Car $875 Fully equipped.
An ideal car for professional men. Entirely enclosed;
convenient to get in and out of. Very stylish."*

*Two views of the Plant of
the Paige-Detroit Motor Car Company*

The Paige-Detroit Motor Car Company

With Harry Jewett now involved in actual operations, it was not difficult to persuade these creditors to have a little more faith and patience. Next, the majority of the small engineering[47] and manufacturing staff was sacked and Detroit was combed for qualified and competent men.[48] From his successful coal operations, Jewett knew a solid organization was important to success. Having one man in control of all details, as Fred Paige had been, only invited disaster. And probably most importantly, he proceeded to phase out the three-cylinder engine in favor of the more reliable and powerful four-cylinder, four-stroke type.

Reports of those first few months of the new president's tenure indicate he worked "ruthlessly." Over $250,000 of inferior parts and stock were junked in addition to inadequate and sub-standard machinery. The stockholders—friends who had trusted him—were asked to come up with an additional $25,000 of capital. Authorized capital for the company was increased from $100,000 to $250,000. With those funds and an almost entirely new engineering staff and production force, Jewett started from scratch. Again.

The "new" Paige-Detroit for 1911 did not differ radically in appearance from the first automobiles produced in 1909-1910. But it was a much better automobile. The major difference was the use of a standard design four-cylinder, four-stroke engine in both of the two chassis now being offered.[49] Many of the improvements were not visible to the eye, but were evident in the machining, tolerances, and general construction principles involved in assembly. Other pronounced improvements involved the use of proven proprietary parts. For example, Bosch now provided the magneto, and the clutch was a multiple disc type (27 discs, alternating saw steel and phosphor bronze). Because of failures in gearing for the first production roadsters, advertising pointed out that for the new offerings the gears,

> *...are made from nickel alloy steel and properly heat treated. [The] Main shaft is mounted on imported annular ball bearings, and countershaft on nickel and steel rollers. [The] Universal joint is also carried inside of the transmission case and runs in an oil bath.*

These gears would not fail.

The basic 90-inch wheelbase roadster (now called the "Model E") was still available for $800,[50] and a fully equipped and canvas-enclosed Physician's Car (roadster body) was available on the same wheelbase for $875. Also riding on the same chassis was the Coupe. Described as a "Woman's Car"[51] for shopping, this rigid-topped and enclosed vehicle featured glass windows all around, full electrical equipment,[52] and a deluxe interior with "elegant" upholstery. Offered at $1,250 it was much more expensive than the basic roadster, but was much more impressive and substantial. This first enclosed car by the Paige-Detroit Motor Car Company was its styling and prestige leader, if not its sales leader.

Also available, on a 104-inch wheelbase, was a touring car ("Model B"). Designed as a "surrey" style touring, the automobile was a four-passenger car with removable rear seats. Described as both a family touring car and also a general utility car, it shared the same cast en bloc four cylinder engine which was used on the smaller chassis. With the rear seats removed, an additional 36 x 31 inch carrying capacity was available.

An aggressive advertising campaign, national in scope, brought the "new" Paige to the attention of the public. In November, a magazine titled *Paige-Detroiter* was created and sent regularly to dealers, salesmen, owners, and prospective owners. Automobile buyers heartily approved of the Paige-Detroit's improvements,[53] and the roadster became their most popular model. Sales increased dramatically, requiring increased production.

Within months, capacity was reached and demand outstripped production. By the end of the year Paige-Detroit was debt free, as each creditor and obligation had been paid in full. The Jewett-led automobile manufacturer had escaped bankruptcy, and now was producing quality vehicles which sold well. Production was more than tripled, with Paige-Detroit's 106 employees manufacturing 956 automobiles in 1911. This rapid and successful turnaround made the Paige-Detroit Motor Car Company a shining star in both the automotive and financial worlds.

Additional manufacturing space was acquired by leasing a building at Jefferson and McDougal Avenues, more machinery was purchased, and additional skilled labor was found. With the first signs of success the newly oriented engineering staff dedicated itself to a much enlarged and improved line. Optimism abounded at the Paige-Detroit Motor Car Company.

Enter the Lozier Motor Company. Production of the Lozier automobile began in 1905 in Plattsburgh, New York.[55] Based on the best—and most expensive—European automobile designs, the firm's initial note was in the racing field. The finely engineered chassis was known for its stamina and durability.[56] Success on the track quickly was followed by healthy sales of production cars. A reputation for producing luxury automobiles was established in short order. With a price tag near the $5,000 mark, it was a product that compared favorably with the luxury marques of Europe. Few American-made cars cost more at the time.

In 1910 a group of Detroit investors purchased $1 million in stock, took control of the company, and moved it to Detroit. Many of those investors were the same financial elite who had joined Harry Jewett in the Paige-Detroit enterprise. In fact, Harry Jewett was a major investor in Lozier, sat on its board of directors, and was joined by most of the Paige directors at the Lozier board meetings.[57]

The emphasis on the luxury market was continued with relish after the move. Advertising for Lozier cars was not only in mass market magazines nationally, but also in the publications meant for "high society" automobilists. Showing the vehicles in situations of wealth and social prominence, the full color advertisements were patrician by design. One tag line announced that Lozier sold "At a Higher Average Price Than Any Other Car In The World." Another boasted that "Price has always been the Last Consideration." The Lozier was portrayed as, and meant to be, an elite automobile for elite owners.

Ownership of Lozier stock, in addition to the actual vehicle, became very much a status symbol for wealthy investors in Detroit. To actually be on the board of directors was the pinnacle of social standing.

The success of the new Paige-Detroit offerings, coupled with the social and financial success of the Lozier enterprise, made Jewett's friends and fellow board members even wealthier, more prosperous, and prominent.[58]

Unfortunately, this increased wealth blinded them to the perceptions of the typical automobile buyer. The prestige associated with the production of an acknowledged luxury car was far greater than that associated with an entry-level, basic roadster. With the ability they possessed to purchase the latest and most expensive Packard,

The Paige-Detroit Motor Car Company

Pierce-Arrow, or Lozier, the wealthy board members mistakenly assumed all purchasers now wanted upscale and luxurious vehicles. The Lozier was targeted at only the cream of the very top level of the automobile market. This thinking was now starting to permeate the direction of the Paige-Detroit Motor Company.

When the 1912 Paige-Detroit lineup was announced ("Model 25"), it was impressive, and quite different from its most previous offering. Even though the chassis remained essentially the same,[60] there were major improvements. Touted in most advertising were the facts Paige was the first "popular price" motor car to include a self starter as regular equipment, to adopt a cork insert multiple disc clutch, and utilize the Delco system of ignition. The automobile's appearance, however, was what piqued the interest of the public.[61] The styling of the bodies was nothing less than the most modern, elegant, and sporty available. Even though the company found only limited success the previous year with its pricey and elegant Coupe, the company elected to cater to similar tastes and pocketbooks. The names of the new models set the tone for the company's new direction.

A major upgrade of the expensive, and slow-selling, coupe was made. The La Marquise was a four-passenger "Colonial Coupe" which sold for a pricey $1,600, twice the price of the basic roadster of the previous season. The Brunswick was the five-passenger touring car selling at $1,000, and the Pinehurst, a surrey-type touring car was available for $900. The roadster style was represented by the Brooklands ($975), and the Kenilworth ($975), a three-passenger sport design. The Beverly ($975) was a touring model carrying a torpedo body. The least expensive model available was the Rockland ($925), a runabout.[62]

With the introduction of this new and upscale line, a curious change was also made in corporate nomenclature. In addition to the elegant names assigned the new

models, the 143 employees of the Paige-Detroit Motor Car Company were now producing a vehicle called, simply, the Paige.

Although these were noteworthy, nicely appointed, and well-built automobiles,[63] sales began to immediately slump. The momentum gained only a year before was quickly slipping away, much to the chagrin of the directors and President Jewett. Although Paige-Detroit began exporting into Europe during 1912,[64] sales totals were disappointing. Whereas the moderately priced, well-built, basic roadster was embraced by the buying public the previous year, these higher-priced automobiles were being shunned by those same folks.

At the same time, Lozier was beginning to have financial and sales problems of its own. In June of 1911 well over $1 million was authorized for the development of a new six-cylinder engine and improved chassis. The new Lozier was introduced with a great deal of fanfare in the motoring press. However, reaction of the buying public to the new model was lukewarm at best. The rarified niche of the market so desired by the board and management was proving to be less than profitable to the company. When the downturn became drastic, management reluctantly turned to Wall Street financiers for assistance. With a considerable infusion of cash to assure continued operations, the financial deacons demanded two seats on the executive board. The reputation Harry Jewett had earned in the coal business, coupled with his impressive turnaround of the Paige-Detroit Motor Car Company only a year earlier, garnered for him Wall Street's nod for the presidency in August 1912.

His tenure was short lived, however, as reorganization was not the answer to the Lozier's problems. Even though additional capital was later raised,[65] the company was producing a series of vehicles which the market could not fully support. Jewett was president less than two years[66] before another re-organization saw his departure from the office. The company went bankrupt in September of 1914. New owners kept it alive until 1916, but no profits were made, and production ended in late 1916.

The lessons of the Lozier Motor Company were not lost on the management and directors of the Paige-Detroit Motor Car Company. Although Paige automobiles continued to be well built, carry elegant names, and be nicely appointed, the rapid escalation into the high-priced market was abruptly stopped. The aim of the company would henceforth be the upper middle class range, a price level where there were many more prospective buyers.

The Paige-Detroit Motor Car Company found success with its newfound restraint. Advertising for the next models introduced (1913) emphasized the touring cars,[67] moderately priced and aimed at the family man. The new Paige offerings were known as "Model 36" and were carried on a longer 116-inch wheelbase, had electric starting and lighting, and were touted as being "completely equipped." The Glenwood was the leader in this group, a five-passenger touring car selling for $1,275. The Brighton Raceabout and the three-passenger Westbrook roadster shared this same price. The top end of the offerings were the four-passenger coupe, the Montrose ($1,850), and the five-passenger sedan, the Maplehurst ($1,950). The public responded most favorably to the more moderately-priced offerings and the company again began to enjoy economic health.[68]

The Paige-Detroit Model 36 powerplant was radically different from the initial offering of the company in 1909.

The Paige-Detroit Motor Car Company

Paige "36" Closed Car —Model Montrose, $1850

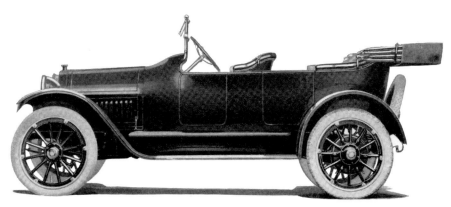

Paige "36" Model Glenwood
Five-Passenger Touring Car, $1275

By early 1913 the firm had begun to fully realize the success which accompanied courting the upper middle class market. Demand for the popular touring cars outstripped production, even at peak levels. Because of the value involved, and the ability to contain prices to a reasonable level, the enclosed top-end cars were able to be offered, even though they sold in far fewer numbers than the touring cars.[69] The company enjoyed sales totaling 4,631 motor cars.

It was soon obvious to the management a major expansion was sorely needed. The two buildings that housed the manufacturing plant had been simply outgrown. Predicated upon the overwhelming demand by the public, plans were put into effect to build an adequate factory to attempt to meet this demand.

Although it was acknowledged to be a transitional move, a large plant at 265 Twenty-First Street, Detroit[70] was leased. The strong demand for the new Paige offerings made the move necessary and did help alleviate the several months' backlog in orders. However, almost immediately after operations were established there it was evident this facility would be inadequate for the continued increase in demand for the new Paige models.

In May of 1913 the Paige-Detroit Motor Car Company announced its plans to erect a substantial and modernly equipped factory at 1203 McKinstry Street.[71] With over 12 acres of floor space under one roof, this plant was built with further increases in production in mind and proved to serve Paige-Detroit well. The entire Paige organization, both manufacturing and executive offices, was now located at one site.[72] The factory consisted of five units designed by the John Scott Company. Patterned in the shape of an "H" the two largest buildings were of four and three stories, two blocks in length.[73] The remaining buildings were one-story units. Construction was of fireproofed, reinforced concrete, and featured a modern sprinkling system. Considering the work force's preference to natural light, the wall surfaces of the new plant were almost entirely of glass.[74] Projected output from the new plant

was tabbed by Harry Jewett to be 15,000 motor cars for 1913, and nearly 25,000 for the following year.[75] A press release issued by the company noted that even with all of its facilities at full production,[76] production was lagging 22 weeks behind demand. The huge new plant, in addition to the three other facilities, were prominently featured in selected magazine advertising and sales brochures for 1914.[77]

The Paige-Detroit Motor Car Company, 1203 McKinstry Street, Detroit, Michigan.

The Paige-Detroit Motor Car Company

The 1914 Paige offerings were directed at the buyers who had made the most recent sales success possible and construction programs necessary. These models, the first to be produced in the McKinstry Street factory, were in the same class as the 1913 offerings, but there were major engineering and styling changes. Pre-eminent was the fact that these models not only had improved chassis design, but were also powered by a powerful six-cylinder engine.[78] Dubbed the "Model 46", these new models also carried bodies which featured a "New, Pure, Stream-line Body Design." The stream-lining of the cowl area into the body was an immediate hit at the important New York and Chicago Auto Shows that year,[79] and again the public responded with orders.[80]

The series continued to carry impressive names, solidifying the desire of the company to reach the upper middle-price niche. The export department also increased its efforts and a good number of Paige motor cars were going to Europe.[81]

The new Fairfield seven-passenger touring car, featuring the new six-cylinder engine and a 124-inch wheelbase, was offered at $1,395, as was the Meadowbrook roadster. The Hollywood, a five-passenger touring model with a 112-inch wheelbase was available for only $1,095. Even though the list price of these automobiles was beginning to creep higher, they were much improved automobiles. Not only did they feature longer wheelbases, complete electrical equipment, and powerful six-cylinder engines, special care was taken in designing, building, and finishing the "stream-lined" bodies. The advertising department pointed out that it took skilled Paige craftsmen a full 24 days to finish a body properly. A new radiator emblem, featuring a distinctive full-bodied font enclosed in a diamond shape, was featured for the first time.[82]

The "Model 25" continued to be offered, now at the reduced price of $975. It was touted as the only touring car with a full electric starting and lighting system available for under $1,000.

The automobile-buying public again responded, with a record 5,666 Paige automobiles finding owners in 1914. Nationally, the Paige-Detroit Motor Car Company was developing a reputation of producing well-built, well-appointed, stylish automobiles with reasonable prices.[83]

A breakdown of the over five thousand Paiges sold showed the majority of sales were in the open car genre. Production of closed cars continued, but the roadsters and touring cars were most popular with buyers.

There was a pronounced effort to produce an entire line of automobiles with sporting and fashionable bodies in 1915. Special attention was given to their fit and finish. European influences were made obvious with the introduction of a rounded, Bentley-like radiator shell. There was also a continued attempt to convince the public the closed models were of considerable value.

In 1915 two series were again offered, the "36" (now known as the Paige 4) and the Paige 6. First introduced at the Vanderbilt Hotel in New York City during the annual automobile show, the Glenwood touring ($1,075), the larger Fairfield touring car ($1,395), the Westbrook roadster (or Runabout-$1,075), and the Montrose coupe ($1,600) continued to be offered as the Model 36. The new "Model 46" was known as the Paige 6. Powered by a 29.4 horsepower (SAE) Continental engine (3 1/2 inch bore and 5 1/4 inch stroke) in a 124-inch wheelbase, the Fairfield seven-passenger touring car ($1,395) was offered on this chassis, as was the Meadowbrook runabout (also $1,395) and the Dartmore raceabout ($1,420). An interesting drive train feature offered in 1915 was the employment of a pressed silk intermediate helical timing gear. Positioned between two metal gears, it was designed to quiet even further the operation of that unit.

On May 17th the company announced its intent to double current production rates by erecting an addition to its McKinstry Street plant. An additional three-story

FOUR plants in Detroit quarters of a million squa space and 2,500 employes, led executive staff, make up the from which the inner Paige group is picked. This sele builders, in the plant units sively to that purpose, are ta and using all the knowledge experience to build still finer during Paige cars.

Every Paige car is given a the body is mounted, as a fina proper functioning of the units the chassis. This check is ma are thoroughly trained in the ing for small defects.

Paige Town Car Model Six "46" — Seven Passengers — $2250

Paige Coupe Model Six "46" — Three Passengers — $1700

The Paige-Detroit Motor Car Company

ree-
floor
eran
tion
ring
p of
xclu-
care
long
en-

efore
the
up
who
look-

ANOTHER Paige organization in Detroit, with a fifth plant of its own, attends to the service requirements of Paige and Jewett owners and stands back of the Paige and Jewett guarantees. Paige service is everywhere available through fifteen hundred service stations.

The Paige executive staff numbers twenty men who have been with the Company for more than ten years, and the same long tenure of service is typical of superintendent, foremen and inspectors; executives in secondary positions of responsibility. These men have grown with the automobile business and their practical knowledge of what is good practice is a strong factor in making the Paige the fine car that it is.

building, 60 feet by 500 feet, was to be completely outfitted with new machinery, with improved production methods put in place. One of the more newsworthy developments was the installation of a mechanical conveyor.[84] Although not the first automobile producer to do so, the use of "assembly line" techniques by Paige-Detroit marked its ascendancy to the status of major independent manufacturer.[85] When the addition was completed, the Paige-Detroit Motor Car Company had a total of over 600,000-square-feet of manufacturing floor in use. It was one of the largest automobile plants in the nation.[86]

Increased sales continued to greet Paige-Detroit board members at their regular meetings (7,749[87] automobiles during calendar 1915). By the end of 1915, Paige-Detroit occupied four large plants in Detroit, each operating at capacity. Paige-Detroit boasted that the new manufacturing facility on McKinstry Street was able to produce 150 Paige automobiles a day, making delays in delivery a thing of the past.[88] Management, dealers, and employees shared in this prosperity at the Paige-Detroit Motor Car Company. However, it was the 100% stock dividend paid to holders of common stock in 1915 that made it a highly sought-after commodity on Wall Street.[89] Association with Paige-Detroit was not only prestigious and socially acceptable, it was also highly profitable.[90]

It was obvious to management that their pricing restraint was paying off. Emphasis continued to be placed on producing beautiful bodies on well-engineered chassis.

With the introduction of the 1916 offerings, the four-cylinder engines were dropped from production. Hence, only six-cylinder power plants would be available in Paige automobiles.[91] Production was nearly doubled in 1916, with 12,456 Paige automobiles finding homes.[92]

Just as Jewett and his associates had been successful in the designing and production of a motor car of value, they had been successful in disseminating that fact to prospective buyers. "The Standard Of Value and Quality" was the catch phrase which had been used for several years on all print advertising. An active and enterprising advertising department had figured prominently in corporate disbursements. The Paige name had become well known, both nationally and internationally. Management had also been successful in establishing, and continually expanding, an aggressive and strong national sales network, with corresponding service available. A monthly magazine, The *Paige Radiator*, was a magazine mailed to all dealers, owners, and prospective buyers.

Paige's corporate attention was now also very much in tune with the female influence in motor car purchases. The upgrading to stylish and sporty bodies was not done entirely with the head of the house in mind. The elegant names, the plush and nicely appointed interiors, and elegant colors were admittedly done with the ladies' sensibilities considered. The introduction of a new slogan in 1916, "The Most Beautiful Car In America,"—although on the surface a neutral phrase—was

Paige Model "Stratford"
Six "51" — Seven Passenger
$1495

Paige Model "Brooklands"
Six "51" — Four Passenger
Convertible Roadster

Paige Model "Fairfield"
Six "46" — Seven Passenger
$1375

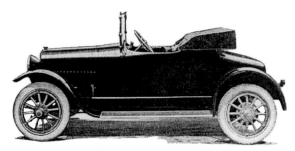

Paige Model "Dartmoor"
Six "39" — 2 or 3 Passenger
$1175

Paige Model "Linwood"
Six "39" — Five Passenger
$1175

Paige Convertible Winter Top
$185 Extra
Mounted on Five Passenger Body

one specifically used with women in mind. Although the thought of a "beautiful" car might be secondary to a male's judgment in the purchase of a motor car, it was a most important consideration for the fairer sex. Although Paige-Detroit did publish sales brochures specifically with the male in mind ("All That A Man Wants In a Motor Car"), this new tag line was used in all print advertising and was prominently featured. Numerous print ads did liken the refinements of the Paige interiors to those of the American woman's home. "Paige has long enjoyed the favor of dainty American womanhood," proclaimed one ad. Another observed, "The woman of refinement demands more than mere utility in her motor car." The magazine ad concluded, "Won't you make it a special point, please, to...inspect the exquisite new models? Or better still, merely call our dealer on the telephone and he will gladly arrange to give you, and **the other members of your family,** a most interesting demonstration."[93] (Emphasis noted by the author.)

The chic bodies, supplied in white by the Springfield Body Company,[94] were well received and highly regarded. 1916 was Paige's best year to date, with the company's nearly 900 employees producing 11,262 motor cars.[95] One financial tally by the press called attention to the fact that the company now had a monthly turnover equal to its capitalization. Authorized capitalization was increased to $1 million in May and $1.5 million in September. One thousand dollars invested in the Paige-Detroit Motor Car Company in 1913 was worth $36,998 in 1916. The company's reputation as a successful manufacturing enterprise was firmly entrenched in the mind of the public.

It should also be noted that Paige automobiles were often raced during the second decade of the century,[96] but seldom by the factory. A multitude of racing and hill climbing wins were made known, but nearly always these entries were privately sponsored. One such privately entered racer of note was the winner of the 273-mile road race between Douglas and Phoenix, Arizona,[97] in 1916. A Paige, driven by a salesman from the Phoenix dealership, finished ahead of a pack which included a Stutz, Cadillac, Hudson, National, Franklin, Pierce-Arrow, and Stearns-Knight. The salesman's name was E. L. Cord.[98]

The Paige-Detroit Motor Car Company

The Paige Seven Passenger Phaeton

The 1916 season saw the introduction of the "Model 38." Although the Model 46 was still offered on its unchanged 123-inch wheelbase chassis,[99] this offering was for corresponding Paige models on a smaller 117-inch wheelbase. The asking price for this Model 38 (Fleetwood Six)[100] was accordingly less,[101] and the "companion" models sold well.

Cognizant of the fact that offering two series each season was profitable for them, Paige offered not only two series for the 1917 season, but three. In addition to the previously introduced Six-39 and Six-46 models, a "Six-51" chassis was offered.

Each of the touring models in each series featured a double cowl,[102] square-edged, nickel-plated trim on the headlights, and a distinctive V-type windshield which complimented the V-shaped radiator. A seven-passenger touring car, the Stratford ($1,495) was available, as was the four-passenger Brooklands roadster ($1,695), and the seven-passenger town car ($2,750). The cars featured a larger engine, and most unattractive prices. The "Six-51" model was dropped from production within the year. Predictably, Paige returned to the successful corporate policy which had served them so well.

As the trend toward practical, reasonably priced enclosed bodies was becoming evident in the automotive industry, Paige was also noticing the slight shift from overwhelming sales of touring models. Although the majority of sales continued to be for the well-received touring cars, manufacturing technology was now allowing greater economies in closed car production. The ability to style these enclosed cars in more streamline designs made them more appealing to the public.

Paige was a leader in this development, most notably for its "convertible" sedan and coupe introduced on the Paige 6 chassis.[103] The C. R. Wilson Body Company, manufacturer of the 1917 Paige bodies, worked together with Paige to pro-

duce this advanced and unique body style.[104] The models were convertible in that when the side posts were removed, the side windows could be lowered into the body.[105] The body was then converted into a "fixed top open car." To further distinguish the 1917 offerings, two-tone paint jobs were available on selected models. The buying public responded by purchasing 14,952 of the stylish cars.[106]

While bodies were receiving the most obvious improvements by designers, engineering was not de-emphasized in any manner. Continual improvements were made to the engine and drive train. The clutch (now a multiple disc with cork inserts: there were 14 discs, with 36 corks in each of the seven driving discs) was redesigned to make it smoother. A device for electrically pre-heating gasoline prior to its introduction into the cylinder was introduced, as was the use of a Model 10-D Continental engine for the larger series models (Rutenber supplied the engines for the smaller series). An "automatic valve polishing device" was now also incorporated into that engine. To insure owner security, a locking transmission was incorporated in all models. A Stewart Power Tire Pump was an ancillary feature (an air pump which was permanently attached and available under the rear floor boards) used as a sales aid while discussing tire longevity.

It had been quite a turnaround for a company that less than a decade before had been on the verge of bankruptcy. But Harry M. Jewett was a dedicated man, and his board of directors had stood solidly behind him. His dedication and drive did not end in the board room, his office, or the factory floor, however. His love of sport continued to grow, even as his ability to compete on the cinder oval faded. From Maplehurst, his estate at 625 Lakeshore Drive in Grosse Pointe Shores, Jewett was able to enjoy his love of boating. *Nandoma*, his 66 1/2-foot yacht, was anchored directly across from his home and the six-member crew often was called on for business and pleasure excursions into Lake St. Clair.[107] The winter season found Jewett enjoying his passion for ice boating near his home.

In a monograph penned years later, Jewett explained "Being a lover of gun and rod and, in fact, all forms of sport,"[108] he avidly continued those sporting interests. He continued to run and swim, although not competitively. He maintained a stable of thoroughbred horses, and regularly rode his favorite Algonquin mare in local contests. His true love, however, one which would remain strong for the rest of his life, was that of hunting and fishing.

Harry M. Jewett, the president of the Paige-Detroit Motor Car Company, 1917.

It became obvious to him through his years of game hunting and fishing that natural resources, especially those of the Midwest, were being depleted at an alarming rate. His love of nature would not allow him to idly stand by while this trend continued. A regular visitor to the woods surrounding his large and impressive Grosse Pointe Shores home, he enjoyed a kennel of 23 Llwellin Setter hunting dogs.[109] But Jewett did not simply use the woods for his personal pleasure; he also felt a need to preserve its natural treasures. Harry M. Jewett was to become one of Michigan's pioneer conservationists.

After a study of hunting techniques and hunting dogs, Jewett had imported the Llwellin setters from Britain. The breed was developed by R. L. Purcell Llwellin, a conservationist and hunter from Shrewsbury, England. Through both correspondence and personal visits, Llwellin had convinced Jewett that the sorry state America found itself in concerning natural game was due to its inability to control hunting and natural habitat. The two agreed that,

> ...the propagation and liberation of game animals and destruction of vermin by co-operative efforts of farmers, sport clubs, and state conservation departments would accomplish the restoration of fish and game.

While it was to be a humble beginning, these founding plans of conservation were implemented in the comparatively thickly populated areas around Grosse Point Shores. In the mid-teens, even the woods around that urban area lacked even a meager quail or pheasant presence. On the spacious grounds of his home, Jewett began a program to re-populate the native birds. Eggs and birds were obtained from the State of Michigan and they were raised in buildings specially built for the purpose. Within a few years, Jewett's program of "raise and release" made the sighting of both quail and pheasant a common sight. According to the same monograph,

> By (my) propagation and liberation from eggs and birds..., today we have two large golf clubs and all the adjoining country is well supplied [with quail and pheasant], the people feeding them in their gardens to the great delight of all.

Hunting and fishing in the lower peninsula of Michigan was a preferred pastime of Harry M. Jewett, and he was often accompanied by fellow automobile manufacturers and friends. The first of many trips to the Rose City, Michigan, area was made in 1916, and soon the area became a favorite of his.

The 1917 Paige models sold well, even after the winds of war began to blow in Europe. Many citizens and business leaders earlier felt the war in Europe was just that, and would stay that way. America's entrance into that "foreign entanglement" was hotly debated and strongly opposed. Many believed the United States would never be directly involved. America's entry into the war in April of 1917 initially did not affect the automobile industry, at least not immediately. Jewett's company recorded a 64.9% increase in sales for the first six months of 1917 over the same period during the record-breaking 1916 season.[110]

Just as most all other automotive firms did, Paige-Detroit introduced new models for 1918 and operated at full capacity. Again there would be two series, and they would be completely restyled and engineered. A multitude of engineering improvements were incorporated, including a completely new manifold design. A unique mechanical feature was the use of a built-in keyed Yale lock on the transmission. The "6-55" was the larger of the two series, based on a 127-inch wheelbase and powered by the familiar six-cylinder Continental engine. The larger series was the prestige line for the year. The Essex seven-passenger touring car was the least expensive of the line, selling for $1,775. The enclosed sedan and coupe shared the $2,850 price, and the elegant town car and limousine shared the $3,230 level.[111]

Again Paige management learned that the more reasonably priced smaller series sold in greater quantities. The "6-40" also was powered by the six-cylinder Continental engine, but the chassis was the smaller 117-inch wheelbase. The prices were much more reasonable, and much more in line with what had propelled the success of the past few seasons. The price for each of the three body styles offered on the "6-40" chassis was $1,330. A five-passenger touring car was called the Linwood, the roadster was rated for two or three passengers, and the Glendale was a "cloverleaf" or "chummy" roadster. The "winter top" sedan was $1,950.

In truth, the nation began its quest for war readiness only after formal declaration, and it was some time before there was any indication from Washington what the course of manufacturers and heavy industry would be. If nothing else, this indecision on the government's part propelled the public into Paige showrooms in even greater numbers than before. Of course, no one really knew how long a world war would last, or when and how automobile production would be affected. Buyers prepared for the unknown by purchasing Paige automobiles in record numbers.[112] Paige-Detroit not only pleased the new owners of these quality automobiles, they continued to please the owners of the company's stock—dividends paid on common stock in 1918 totaled 130%.

As the government became more organized in its war effort, American industry became involved in supplying that effort. There was no real need for passenger cars in the fighting across the Atlantic, so there was no immediate demands placed upon the automobile manufacturers. There was, however, a very definite and urgent need for trucks—especially those of larger capacity. The Ordnance Department of the United State Army made plans to have the trucking industry contribute to this increasing need.

The Jeffery Quad, a four-wheel, two-ton truck produced by Nash of Kenosha, Wisconsin, was ideally suited for the needs of the Army. However, even at full capacity the Nash Motors Company was not able to supply all the trucks the government requested. During the second week of February 1918, it was announced the Paige-Detroit Motor Car Company would be building the Nash Quad under license and under Nash patents. Erection of a building specifically for the assembly of the trucks[113] was begun at the McKinstry Street site and the required machinery was installed as the building was finished. Paige-Detroit was contracted to build 2,000 Nash Quads by the end of April 1918.[114] Production continued until Armistice.

Paige-Detroit was eager to get involved with truck manufacture for several reasons. Of course, patriotism was the official rationale. But Paige had been trying to enter the burgeoning truck industry for some time. Jewett and most automobile industry leaders were able to see that the war would eventually impact their ability to produce and sell motor cars. Truck manufacturing appeared to be a reasonable parallel product. In 1917 the firm announced to the press it "had developed a two-ton truck. Immediate steps are being taken to place the truck in production." Evidently the truck had not been totally developed as the press release also noted; "it will be some time before the truck is placed on the market."[115]

With a desire to shorten the development time for this Paige truck, Jewett and his board attempted to acquire an established motor truck manufacturer, the Signal Truck Company of Detroit.[116] In March of 1918 an offer was tendered to purchase the company's plant and assets. The next month the offer was officially spurned by the stockholders of the Signal Truck Company.[117] Undaunted, development of the Paige-Detroit Motor Car Company truck continued in-house.[118]

As the war progressed it was clear all parts of American industry would be contributing to the effort. The federal government requested and ordered changes in motor car manufacturers' operations, gradually but steadily. The first step mandated was the freezing of production levels for passenger cars, requiring all surplus materials to be used for the war effort.[119]

By the end of September 1918, the majority of work being done at the Paige-Detroit plant was war work, even though the assembly line did continue to produce passenger cars for the public.[120]

During the almost nineteen months of World War I, print advertising for Paige consisted almost entirely of non-illustrated text. Paige proudly proclaimed they were helping the war effort in every manner possible. Indeed, many employees left their jobs in Detroit for the jobs "over there." There were also considerable[121] defense contracts awarded to Paige to aid the needs of the government in pursuit of victory. One of the government's contracts called for Paige-Detroit to provide depth charges for the United States Navy.

It wasn't until October of 1918 that the federal government requested Paige produce only one quarter of the automobiles it had the year before. As this was an industrywide request, Paige willingly complied. A series of advertisements stressing the importance of supporting "our boys" in the fighting had run during the year, and the contributions of the Paige-Detroit Motor Car Company were noted. Considering the active patriotism the president of the company had personally shown during the Spanish-American War, it was not hard to imagine the company would comply fully and assist the effort. The automobile manufacturer's stated purpose read:

> To meet every need, to comply with every request of our Government, to contribute our utmost to Win the War is the one task and ambition of the Paige-Detroit Motor Car Company.

In November of 1918 the company announced the government had requested an even greater volume of war work from the factory. Per its request, the company would cease production of Paige automobiles until the end of the war.[122] Again the stated purpose and intent of the company was widely published:

> We have no alternative and we seek none. Instant and cheerful compliance is the obvious duty of us all. We shall put our organization, our factories, and every dollar of our large resources, every ounce of our energy on one-hundred per cent War Basis. We shall give our hands, our heads, our hearts to the Service of the Colors—until the War has been won.

The resolve so stated was never tested in any meaningful manner. Armistice was November 11, 1918. The transition to full and total production of war materiels had not been actually effected when the proud intent to supply the war effort became a moot point.

Subsequently, text-only print ads extolled the virtues of the returning veterans and the appreciation of those who welcomed them home. "We Shall Remember These Men" was the heading of one typical ad. The future was considered bright due to the sacrifices of those involved: "Now for the Peace and the Work, Responsibilities and Rewards of Peace."

Everything related to the war was looked upon as a character-building and strengthening factor. According to the company,

> It was the great privilege of Paige to stand shoulder to shoulder with scores of other great American Companies and fight, not in the trench and turret, but beside lathe and drill press.
> Our service with the Colors has brought us recompense, which lies, not only in the consciousness of having given our best to Uncle Sam and Victory, but actually, in the invaluable experience we have secured in meeting and solving the unprecedented problems which War forced upon the resourceful men, the strong men, the indomitable men of American Industry.
> We have built new factories, added vastly to our equipment, expanded our facilities tremendously. We were given the War and War Work new Visions of the need for motor cars and motor trucks. And now that Peace has come and the Markets of the World are re-opened to us—we are prepared.

With those comments of preparedness in mind, it is interesting to note the 1919 Paige, announced in January of that year, models were basically the same as those of the previous war year.[123] The prestige line, the Six-55, was continued with the same war time prices. The more popular, and less expensive, Six-40 offerings featured increased prices. The Linwood and the two- (and three-) passenger roadsters were now $1,555, and the cabriolet was $1,885. The war tax enacted by the government was partially responsible for these increases, but the popularity of those Six-40 models was primary. That popularity allowed Paige-Detroit to spent over $400,000 during the summer to purchase new equipment and enact improvement in production; a 25% increase in total production was announced as its goal.[124]

Paige was proud to tally 15,766 sales for the year; again, a new production record. Sales would have been even more impressive if labor troubles at several parts suppliers had not hindered production.[125]

The Paige-Detroit Motor Car Company

The development of a truck prototype, aided by the successful completion of the Nash Quad contract, came to fruition with the announcement of a two-ton Paige truck prior to the war's end. In April of 1918 the company announced,

Having studied the motor hauling situation and making an exhaustive investigation of the problems involved, [Paige] will market a complete line of Paige trucks, ranging from 1 to 5 ton capacities. A separate truck department is being organized and a complete truck factory equipped, comprising several buildings in addition to those already...at Paige.[126] The new truck plant will be entirely distinct from the passenger factory, but the product will bear the Paige name and will be exclusively and completely a Paige product.

The truck's availability was due to the fact that "the demands of war work have been met to an extent which permits the production of machines for peaceful purposes." The formal introduction of the truck came during the first week of November 1918. Known simply as 'Model 4," the two-ton chassis had a wheelbase of 150 inches and was fitted with solid rubber tires.[127] A four-cylinder 27-horsepower[128] Continental engine[129] with worm drive powered the $2,950 commercial hauler.[130] One feature of the truck touted by Paige was the massive drop-forged radius rods. Available from the factory first only as a chassis, a completely enclosed cab was later available as an option. One other item of note was the fact that the chassis was not fitted with a electrical starting or lighting system.[131]

Later truck advertising explained the truck as a positive by-product of the war:

The War has been a sort of gigantic demonstration of the value and wide range of usefulness of trucks. Never again can there be any doubt of the overwhelming superiority of the truck in almost every field of transportation.

The Paige trucks were available from the already existing Paige automobile dealers throughout the nation. There was not a great deal of advertising done, print or otherwise, because it was felt the quality and reputation of Paige automobiles would easily be transferred to the truck field.

The November announcement pointed out only a limited number of trucks would be distributed while the war in Europe still raged, but "as soon as war conditions make it possible, production of the trucks will be increased and other models will be added."[132]

Even with lukewarm reception by the motoring press,[133] sales for the two-ton Paige truck the first year were as expected: 100% of those produced. However, because of material limitations, that meant less than 400 trucks were sold

throughout the nation. The next year, as an adjunct to the passenger car models Six-42 and Six-55, an expanded heavy truck line was offered. The Model 4 was continued unchanged except for the change of name to Model 50-18. The larger Model 51-18 shared much of the initial model's design but featured a 40 horsepower Continental engine,[134] 160-inch wheelbase, 3 1/2-ton capacity, and heavier-duty chassis equipment.[135] The first six months of 1919 saw a total of 164 chassis produced and sold.

Nineteen-twenty saw the designation the Model 50-18 increased to a 2 1/2-ton chassis, the Model 51-18 continued as the 3 1/3-ton chassis, and the introduction of the Model 52-19 as a 1 1/2-ton offering.[136] A year later the three models remained the same in tonnage, but the 2 1/2-ton chassis was known as the Model 54-20. Nomenclature then continued unchanged into 1923.

The expedited development of a heavy truck prototype during the latter half of 1918 was at least partially in response to the perceived needs of the government and a hope of continued production. When the war abruptly ended and all war contracts were cancelled, Paige rethought its entry into the already crowded truck field.

Production[137] was to continue until the spring of 1923,[138] but truck production was limited by poor sales each year. A lack of advertising and strong competition from well-established truck manufacturers were the main reasons for the sales failure of "The Most Serviceable Motor Truck In America."[139]

The Paige Six-55 models for the 1920 model year were basically the same automobiles as the year before (127-inch wheelbase). Prices ranged from $2,060 for the seven passenger touring car to the elegant town car and limousine for $3,330.[140] The Glenbrook phaeton and roadster were the price leaders of the Six-42 offerings, carrying a price of only $1,670. The sedan sold for $2,395, and the coupe $100 less.

2 1/2 ton Paige Truck showing stake body.

The Paige-Detroit Motor Car Company

Garnering much more interest in the motoring press—and by the public at the New York Auto Show in January—was the first showing of a new, smaller Paige. This vehicle was distinguished by not only its entirely new chassis and mechanics but, more importantly, by the fact that it was the first time an engine made entirely in the Paige shops powered a Paige motor car. Riding in a 119-inch wheelbase chassis, the new Paige was using a propeller shaft in a single unit, rather than the divided yoke shaft used on past models and on the larger Six-55. The new six-cylinder engine displaced 231 cubic inches (3 1/8 x 5), and was of the L-head design. First-rate proprietary components were used throughout, such as Borg and Beck clutches, Detroit axles, Kelsey wheels, Jacox radiators, National Can radiators, Gray and Davis starters and lighting, and Atwater-Kent ignition. This new light-weight six was an exciting first for the company and they stressed it in much of their national advertising.

Paige was proud of the fact production totals had increased every year since the company's founding. However, the war year of 1918 broke that record. The indecision of both the government and the industry as a whole during the war had given the business a pause. Nineteen-nineteen again saw an increase in total production at the Paige-Detroit Motor Car Company. The year 1920 provided a slight increase in production (16,090), but an increase nonetheless. Although dividends on common stock paid a respectable 33% for the year, it was not in line with the huge dividends of past years. Undaunted—with their customary success undoubtedly to continue—management began planning future developments in earnest.

Although 1920 had been another year of record production for Paige-Detroit, and for the automobile industry as a whole, the much expected post-war prosperity did not materialize. The war tax was continued even after the conflict's end, and combined with other economic transitions following the world war, a deep recession afflicted the country. Automobile sales, including those at Paige-Detroit, began to fall dramatically. Since Harry M. Jewett had been able to continue his policy of no corporate indebtedness since the second year of his tenure,[141] the recession was able to be endured.

In fact, the two series offered in 1921 included the familiar 6-42 lineup,[142] and the all new 6-66. The new series had been in planning since the latter stages of the war, and Paige-Detroit had definite plans for its market niche.

The "Six-Sixty Six"[143] sedan was the new seven-passenger closed car, and it was complemented with a five-passenger coupe. The seven-passenger touring car was dubbed the 6-66 Lakewood, and the close-coupled four-passenger model was named the Larchmont II. These were large cars, carrying a powerful six-cylinder engine (3 3/4 inch bore, 5 inch stroke, rated at 70 horsepower)[144] in a 131-inch wheelbase chassis. Although these cars were impressive in themselves, it was the two-passenger speedster which was to become the most famous Paige model of all.

It was obvious this new Paige line was aimed at the buyer who wanted not only a well-appointed and well-built automobile but also a sporty, fast model. The introduction of the Paige speedster in June 1921 was done with a great deal of forethought. When the finishing touches were put on the prototype body, it was agreed the final product was equal to or better looking than any production sports car, American or European. To make sure the public understood the brute force that lay

January of 1920 saw the introduction of the first motor produced in-house by the Paige-Detroit Motor Car Company. Displacing 231 cubic inches, the powerplant was of the L-head design.

beneath the sport car's hood, the company strayed a bit from its decade-long policy of no corporate sponsorship of racing or hill climbs. The services of the famous driver Ralph Mulford were acquired and he proceeded to show the public what a powerful speedster he was given to drive. The car, completely stock, sans fenders,[145] was driven well over 100 mph in a number of demonstrations. On May 18, 1921, the prototype was campaigned at the Uniontown Speedway in Uniontown, Pennsylvania. The Mulford effort resulted in World's Stock Chassis records in nine categories and eight distances.[146] At Daytona, Florida, the class B speed record was attained in the prototype. In commemoration of that event, the production model was named after the site. The "Paige Daytona" was also sponsored by the factory in a series of races at Pike's Peak,[147] showing well and providing a great deal in the way of advertising photos and copy.

Print advertising pointed out the records which Mulford tallied, and showroom sales brochures assured prospective owners they could expect over 80 mph in the completely stock version. Realizing the buying public "wanted it all," brochures also pointed out,

> *...at no sacrifice to [body] lines a large carrying space has been provided under the rear deck...and [features] an auxiliary seat on the right hand running board. Close-fitting top and side curtains and ample carrying space make it a practical car for all season service without detracting from its fleetness.*

These disclaimers were, for the most part, ignored by buyers as it was obvious this was a fast, stylish, and powerful sports car; nothing more, nothing less.

The Paige-Detroit Motor Car Company

THE 6-66 DAYTONA
(Two Passenger Speedster)

MODELLED after the car in which Mulford set new records at Daytona and Uniontown, the Daytona Speedster epitomizes the qualities of unusual speed and flexibility inherent in the Paige 6-66 chassis.

Better than 80 miles an hour has been obtained with this car. At sixty it still has the smoothness you expected and found at thirty-five.

At no sacrifice to lines a large carrying space has been provided under the rear deck of this model and an auxiliary seat for the right hand running board.

Close fitting top and side curtains and ample carrying space make it a practical car for all season service without detracting from its fleetness.

A well upholstered auxiliary seat pulls out over the right running board of the Daytona and a special footrest is provided.

Advertising highlighted the Daytona, although the remaining 6-66 and 6-42 models were well represented. Unfortunately, the fact the Daytona became the best known American sports car since the Stutz Bearcat did not take away from the fact America was still in a deep recession. For only the second time in company history, sales did not exceed that of the prior year. Only 8,698 Paige automobiles were produced in 1921, slightly over half of production during the previous season. The product was just as well built, easily as stylish as previously, and now a particular model had become universally known. But it was not enough to keep production totals from tumbling.

Realizing both the market and the industry were changing in fundamental ways, Harry Jewett and his management[148] decided to act. That decision to confront the situation resulted in a change in corporate thinking which was to quickly lead to unprecedented sales success. The next big step in the direction of the company was not to simply announce the next season's styling and engineering advances. Soon to follow was a much more important announcement.

With a decade of production and sales experience behind them, the board of the Paige-Detroit Motor Car Company had become comfortable with the market niche it established.[149] The upper middle price range had been profitable for them, and had allowed them to increase production almost yearly. During the war it had become obvious to all astute businessmen the automobile industry was changing radically. General Motors, and especially Ford, had shown mass production was going to be a stiff challenge for all smaller volume makes, regardless of their quality or value. To prosper, or even survive, these smaller producers would need to expand beyond their customary markets.

The first to attempt this type of expansion was the Hudson Motor Car Company. It was the intent of company head Roy Chapin to market a completely separate make of automobile; not to compete with its current product, but to complement it. In the years since its founding in 1909, Hudson had slowly left the low price field and had become more upscale. Chapin wanted to regain the foothold Hudson once had in the low price field. Plans were begun during World War I to design this new automobile, and in 1919 the Essex was introduced to the market. A separate company, Essex Motors, was set up to produce the lesser-priced car. In truth, the newest entry in the low-priced market was entirely a Hudson product, built in Hudson factories and designed by Hudson engineers. Chapin's decision was an auspicious one, in that the Essex met with immediate success, and in most years its production and sales exceeded the parent company.[150]

The automotive industry and financial world looked upon the Hudson's move with a great deal of interest. The desire of Harry M. Jewett and his board of directors to regain their former prosperity led them to seriously study the implications of a similar move. The constraints of being a limited volume producer of upper middle class automobiles were becoming oppressive. It was exceedingly difficult for Paige-Detroit to compete with large volume producers. The time honored method of careful and skillful manufacture was fast giving way to the high speed modern assembly line.[151]

Andrew Bachle, now vice president in charge of the engineering department, enlarged his staff and began working in earnest directly after the war in the designing of a "companion car" for Paige. Subsequently, the McKinstry Street facilities

Harry Mulford Jewett, 1924, Detroit, Michigan.

themselves were completely redesigned for the production of two lines of automobiles. On November 17, 1921, Harry Jewett made the formal announcement to the motoring press.

The new six-cylinder Paige product would be a "light" six, to sell in the medium price class field. In deference to the man who had brought the Paige-Detroit Motor Car Company from near bankruptcy over a decade earlier to a much respected manufacturer in the upper middle class range, the new make was to be named "Jewett." The president of Detroit's newest company—Jewett Motors, Incorporated—proudly announced at the first showing at the Hotel Commodore in New York City,[152]

> *In designing the new car we had the experience of all the other makers in the popular priced field before us, and were able to profit thereby. Careful study and thorough tests of existing sixes and fours in the low priced field convinced us that the six was the most efficient and satisfactory, and in the long run the most economical automobile. We are also able to design a real modern car with many marked improvements.*
>
> *The absence of vibrations in a six means longer life and lower upkeep costs for the entire car. It also means greater driving comfort. The great advantage of the six under normal driving conditions is obvious. It runs smoother, picks up faster, and is in every way more desirable from the owner's standpoint.*
>
> *Coming into the market at this time, with no handicaps, we are able to secure our materials at a price to enable us to offer values never before possible.*
>
> *The Jewett Six will be low in cost and in operating cost with a vibrationless six cylinder motor and sound construction. It will show low costs of upkeep and long life. In beauty, and comfort and performance, we feel that the new car will be a real and pleasant surprise.*

Jewett Motors, Incorporated, was to be a wholly owned subsidiary of the Paige-Detroit Motor Car Company. Jewett declared the new make would be made in the Paige factories in Detroit, but by an entirely separate work force and an entirely separate management team.[153]

The Jewett would be carried on a 112-inch wheelbase and powered by a beefy 50-horsepower Continental engine (3 1/4 inch bore, 5 inch stroke). Although the car was touted as a completely new product, the engine had been in the Paige line up for some time. First produced in 1917, the motor originally powered the Paige 6-42. Following an updating, the Continental-based engine was used in the Paige 44.[154] The Jewett was completely new in appearance however, and its sharp and up-to-date styling was refreshing. The J. C. Widman Company was engaged to provide bodies for the new motor car.[155] Although the new Jewetts maintained Paige quality, it was a smaller car than the usual Paige fare, and much more affordable. The 1922 Jewett line up, available in March of that year, consisted of only a touring ($1,065) and a sedan ($1,395). Working out engineering and production problems delayed actual production until March.[156]

The Paige-Detroit Motor Car Company

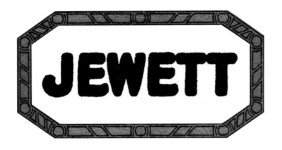

When the Jewett was made available to Paige dealers for showroom display, the reaction was nothing less than overwhelming. By the end of July nearly 10,000 Jewetts had found owners, and by the end of the year that total numbered over 20,000.[157] Just as it had done for Hudson, the "companion car" had more than complemented the existing line. Once again, Paige-Detroit stockholders were treated to triple digit dividends for the year (100%).

Upon the first signs of success the engineering department was put to the task of enlarging the line. The 1923 Jewett line up proffered not only the sedan ($1,465) and touring car ($995), but also a roadster ($995) and four-passenger coupe ($1,445). Now known as the Jewett Six, the sales success continued into the new season. Note was made of successes in hill climbing events across the country and much was made of the power of the Jewett engine and components. The company was proud to advertise that since its introduction in March of 1922, the total number of Jewett Sixes sold by the end of July 1923 was 46,780.[158]

The company was more than pleased with the results of the companion car concept. More Jewetts had been sold since their introduction in 1922 than cumulative Paige sales since 1919.[159] Clearly the public was eager to get the well known Paige quality at a Buick or Hupmobile price. Advertising clearly pointed out that the Jewett Six was a product of the Paige-Detroit Motor Car Company.

Early in 1923, the Paige-Detroit board of directors[160] realized another bold decision needed to be made. While acknowledging the poor sales of Paige automobiles, they could not help but be elated and encouraged with the sales totals for the new Jewett light six. Even with additional manpower at the big McKinstry Street plant, production could not keep pace with orders.[161]

In contrast to the phenomenal success of the new Jewett, Paige motor car sales were simply dismal. During 1922 Jewett production took over the entire capacity of the McKinstry Street plant. Actual assembly and production of Paige motor cars were transferred to the recently acquired plant of the former Hinckley Motors Corporation.[162] This gave Paige-Detroit three plants in the city, the remaining site an exclusive engine plant.

Flush with cash and a belief the Jewett would continue to exceed production capacity, a 45-acre parcel of land just over the Detroit city limits was procured and the services of architect Albert Kahn,[163] famous for his successful industrial designs, were obtained. Plans were immediately put in effect to erect a million-square-foot, state-of-the-art manufacturing facility. The factory which Kahn designed for the Dearborn site was one which would become a jewel in Michigan's motor car industry. Construction of the massive plant on West Warren Avenue began on June 4, 1923, and featured a distinctive sawtooth roof design.[164] All operations would be on one floor, a somewhat radical concept in factory design. Completion of the plant proper was projected for November 1, with full production to be commenced at the year's end. The double assembly line plant would contain only the most modern, accurate, and sophisticated production machinery available.[165] Three miles of automatic conveyors assisted the labor force in building the new car. The construction, inspection, testing, and shipping[166] of the Jewett was done under one roof. Capacity was designed to be approximately 500 cars a day. Included in the building proper were "physical and chemical" laboratories which rivaled those at private and institutional sites. The plant was referred to as the Jewett Assembly plant of Paige-Detroit Motor Car Company.[167]

An extensive reorganization of manufacturing methods at Paige-Detroit resulted in the decision to erect the new facility. The intent was to have Paige production transferred back to the original plant on McKinstry Street,[168] allowing each make to be produced in its own factory.

Reorganization, remodeling, and construction proved to be somewhat disruptive and expensive in the short run: dividends paid out in 1923 totaled a modest—for Paige-Detroit at least—50%.

The 1924 Jewetts, the first series to be produced in the West Warren Avenue plant, included the now familiar standard touring car, roadster, sedan and coupe,[169] plus deluxe versions of each.[170] A new offering at $1325 was the Brougham. This five-passenger car was highlighted as an ideal family vehicle, and its closed nature was emphasized. Construction features were also a favorite topic for the advertising department. Great lengths were taken to insure the public realized the Jewett was

How New Plant Looked Three Weeks Ago

The company that erected the framework of the new Jewett Assembly Plant is so proud of the work they did on the building that they want to use a picture of it on their next year's calender. The problem arose to get a photograph that would give some idea of the plant's immense size. The chief of erection solved it by slinging a platform from the end of one of the big locomotive cranes that helped build the plant and having himself lifted on it with a camera as high as the crane would carry him. This picture was the result. It was taken nearly three weeks ago. Today, the building is almost roofed over, a large portion of the side walls are up, the entire site has been graded and the workmen have begun laying the floors.

*The **Paige Radiator** proudly featured this illustration and caption in its August 6, 1923 number.*

One of the most distinctive features of the new Paige-Detroit factory on West Warren Avenue was its nearly all glass "sawtooth" design. This photo illustrates the northeast corner of "The Most Modern Plant In The Automobile Industry" shortly after its erection. The roof design allowed the maximum amount of natural light into work areas. Line employees much preferred natural light over artificial lighting. (Courtesy of Albert Kahn Associates, Detroit, MI)

The Paige-Detroit Motor Car Company

not simply another "light" six.[171] The weight of the vehicles was accentuated (2,805 pounds for the Brougham), and the "new" Duco finish (three separate dippings in enamel and then baked) prominently featured.[172] Advertising proudly featured the new manufacturing facilities. Sales continued to be impressive for the new offering,[173] both domestically and abroad. Sales in Britain were so impressive a subsidiary was established, Paige-Jewett Cars, Ltd. in London.[174]

The two makes were now mentioned in the same breath by the public. The company logo changed in print advertising, now equally featuring both the Jewett and Paige emblems on a shaded circle.

In 1925 the standard and deluxe versions of the Jewett touring, sedan, and brougham were retained.[175] The addition of a business coupe and a coach expanded the successful line even more.

Even with the runaway success of the Jewett, the company's namesake automobiles were given a great deal of attention by Harry Jewett and his men.[176]

The 1922 season saw two series Paige automobiles being offered, a continuation of the 119-inch wheelbase Model 6-44 and the much publicized 131-inch wheel base Model 6-66.[177] The Daytona was the talk of all knowledgeable sports car enthusiasts, and was well received nationally. In addition to the Daytona speedster, the 6-66 for 1922 included the seven-passenger touring car, five-passenger coupe, seven-passenger sedan, and limousine.[178]

Unfortunately, the effects of the recession had not receded to the point where higher-priced automobiles, especially Paige, were selling well. Even though the Jewett was to eventually exceed all optimistic expectations, the initial start-up was delayed, and the first few months were at less than capacity.[179] The end result was that while Jewett production—and sales—were eventually gotten into high volume production, only 9,323 Paige automobiles were shipped from the McKinstry Street and Hinckley plants in 1922.

As the post war recession continued, more than a few undercapitalized and ill-managed automobile companies failed. Paige-Detroit was strong in both areas, and was able to carry on. Strong management, a quality product, and a faith in the future of the upper middle price niche brought them through other hard times, and this attitude led to an optimism at the Paige-Detroit Motor Car Company, regardless of the dismal sales for the 1922 edition of the Paige.

This optimism, coupled with past successes, allowed the Jewett brothers to invest in industries unrelated to automobile production.

In 1906 Dr. Lee de Forest, a radio transmission pioneer, invented the three-element vacuum tube at his laboratory in New York City.[180] By the next year he was able to broadcast music to the small number of equipped listeners in the nation's largest city. The utilization of his tube made commercial radio transmission a reality to a gradually expanding audience. By the end of World War I, the availability of commercial radio broadcasts had become more common throughout the urban areas of the East Coast. Capitalizing upon his patents and expertise, the scientist established the DeForest Radio, Telephone, and Telegraph Company in Jersey City, New Jersey, following the war. In March of 1922, the rapidly growing company moved into the former Campbell Soup Company building on Franklin Street at Central Avenue in that city.[181] Although the company was continually waging wars in the courts concerning patents, royalties, and manufacturing rights,[182] it was immediately successful in the marketplace.[183]

Jewett Six De Luxe Roadster

That success was noted by Edward Jewett. Convinced of the medium's commercial future, he purchased the company. The firm was moved in its entirety to Pontiac, Michigan, and it was renamed the Jewett Radio and Phonograph Company. Detroit's existing radio station, WCX, was only two years old in 1924 but had experienced tremendous success; the station had recently moved its studios into the prestigious and plush Book-Cadillac Hotel. In December of that year, Edward Jewett[184] approached E. D. Stair,[185] the station's owner, and proposed his newly formed radio station WJR (representing **W**e're **J**ewett **R**adio), and WCX join forces in the Detroit market.

The first joint broadcast from the shared studios was on August 16, 1925. A live show, featuring the Jean Goldkette Dance Orchestra, played from the Blue Room of the host hotel. In September of that same year local celebrity Leo Fitzpatrick presented the first of his regular Sunday night programs titled, "The Jewett Jesters."[186]

Although the station appeared to be successful to the public, it had become obvious Edwin Jewett was much more at home in an automobile manufacturing plant than in a radio studio management role or radio manufacturing career. In short order a "huge" deficit had been accumulated and there were grumblings about poor reception. The reports of poor reception made sales of advertising more and more difficult, and the financial situation worsened. At the same time the parent company, Jewett Radio, was experiencing a sharp dip in sales of radios themselves. Both companies were near insolvency when the assets of both companies were ordered liquidated in March of 1926.

Leo Fitzpatrick was named administrator of the two firms, and he quickly worked to save the companies. To save the station itself he quickly installed taller and better towers to improve reception, and began an association which would then insure the success of the fledgling station. When approached, the clergymen of Detroit's largest congregations realized the power of radio and began to regularly purchase blocks of radio time at full commercial rates. Detroit's most famous radio preacher, Father Charles Coughlin, was to later become a national figure and political commentator.[187]

With the Jewett brothers now out of the WJR picture, Fitzpatrick ended the association of the radio station with the radio manufacturer and retailer.[188] In a short time the radio manufacturer was out of business, while WJR went on to prosper.[189]

While the Jewett brothers continued to invest in other companies, it was to be Edward's last hands-on investment while he and his brothers continued in the automobile business.

Harry Jewett also continued to invest in companies quite distinct from the automobile industry, but his true—non-automotive—love was that of outdoorsman and sport.

His hunting and fishing visits to all parts of the lower peninsula of Michigan during the decade had given him an added incentive to promote his conservation ideas on a larger scale. Although he made regular trips to many areas, the Rose City area soon became his favorite following his initial 1916 trip. With sales of Jewett automobiles at their frenzied height, with a fortune accumulated from both the coal and automobile industries, he was now able to live his dream of conservation. As he recalled several years afterwards,

> *Enthused with the idea, I spent a year prospecting every corner of lower Michigan and selected what I believe to be an ideal location.*

Over a period of several years Jewett was able to gain possession of a large tract of near-wilderness land and in 1925 commenced to pursue his conservation goals. He said,

> *It [his acquired property] comprises over 4,500 acres with eight lakes and two trout streams, splendidly watered all over, with ideal game cover...It is located 200 miles north of Detroit, near Rose City and Lupton, Michigan, on the highest ridge in the lower peninsula, with a cold, vigorous winter climate with plenty of snow and produces hardy stock.*

At the lower end of the Rifle River and the lakes, Jewett located a large game farm. Just as he had in the Grosse Pointe Shores area, he obtained eggs from the State of Michigan and began large scale propagation efforts. A number of large hatching sheds were erected and a multitude of open and covered pens were established in the English manner. The propagation of pheasants and ruffled grouse were of special attention to Jewett.

He also intensified his campaign of limited time seasons for hunting, "one buck" laws for deer, and reasonable limits for fowl. The eradication of vermin—a favorite subject and theory with his mentor R. L. Purcell Llewellin—was vigorously promoted among the local farmers and fellow hunters.[190]

A deal with the federal government was struck in which large quantities of trout were raised for release. Half were used to stock the two trout streams and the Rifle River, the balance was given back to the government for release in streams off the Jewett property. The same type of arrangement was made with the Michigan state government regarding the purchase of mature bass from Lake Huron. Their young

were seined out of his 30-acre lake at the proper age and half released to the government's restocking program, half to his waters.

The propagation programs were wildly successful, and Harry Jewett was justifiably proud. To encourage the idea of game and fish restoration he continued his activism in game law revision and encouraged his neighbors in his conservation efforts. Each September he brought in renowned conservation speakers to speak at a barbecue given for Rose City area farmers and land owners. Moving pictures were shown under large tents and displays and exhibits explained exactly what was being done. In 1927, "the entire countryside" was invited and over 700 enjoyed the Jewett

Harry M. Jewett, 1924.

hospitality, a lecture by the famous Canadian goose conservationist Jack Miner, and a Harvest Dance which followed the complimentary barbecue.

By 1928, the Jewett holdings had grown to 7,360 acres.[191] Three years later the restocking program had progressed to the degree that 160,000 fingerling speckled trout were raised and released. A year later the total was 180,000. With its success came more involvement by fellow conservationists.[192] The University of Michigan-Fish Research Department became involved, as did the state and federal game and fish commissions. In a short three years since its inception, over 15,000 Ring-necked and Mongolian pheasants were released in addition to a like number of Hungarian partridge. Later, Chinese Ring-necked pheasants were introduced, as were prairie chickens and quail. A working farm was included in the system, featuring purebred Guernsey stock, Belgian horses, and polo ponies. Riding trails were cut through the area. A staff of 30 men maintained the private reserve.

When it was established that the restocking and propagation policies were successful and the reserve was doing just what Harry Jewett had envisioned, he indulged himself a bit. He made trips to the site as often as his business schedule would allow, and enjoyed bringing friends to hunt and fish. But it was a rustic sportsman's environment, not really suitable to all—including his wife and children.

Construction began on a log lodge, built on a peninsula in the midst of the four main lakes. The high ridge afforded a magnificent view of the entire reserve. In that he had the finest private game reserve in the nation, Jewett resolved to have the

The Paige-Detroit Motor Car Company

finest log architecture available. Finnish "axmen" were brought in from the logging camps in the upper peninsula of Michigan to fell and trim the logs for the project and numerous tradesmen from Detroit were brought in. Because of the rural nature of the setting, water was pumped from the lake for concrete and other construction work. Other logistic problems due to the remote location were encountered and overcome. The large, two-story structure featured all the modern conveniences, including steam heat, electric lights, a private bath in each of the multiple bedrooms, a large living room featuring a huge fireplace, and an abundant dining area. An observation cubicle was erected to enhance the spectacular view. It was reported that the lodge cost Jewett over $100,000.

The lodge, as was the entire reserve from that point, was named "Grousehaven" in honor of his initial, and favorite, conservation project. It was reported in the local press that Harry Jewett had invested over a quarter of a million dollars in "Grousehaven." The reserve was truly a fitting retreat and future retirement home for the successful businessman and sportsman. It was the crowning achievement for his conservation efforts.

When the business concerns in Detroit came to command most all of his attention, his visits to Grousehaven became less and less frequent. In 1928 the lodge and grounds were opened to the first time to sportsmen not personally acquainted with Harry Jewett and his family. Brochures were printed explaining the purpose and manner of "Grousehaven Shooting Preserve" and the (English or Scottish) manner of hunting. A decidedly upscale get away for well-to-do sportsmen from the city, the shooting preserve enjoyed success almost immediately as a for-profit entity.[193] The shooting preserve prospered until Jewett's death.

As with most all successful businessmen, Jewett and his brother were not single minded. The challenge of multiple tasks and goals propelled them to greater achievements. However, the production of Paige and Jewett automobiles was foremost of their responsibilities.

For the first time since the early days of the company, only one series of Paige automobiles was offered for the 1923 season. The 6-70 was the only series offered, if only for reasons of economy during an enduring economic downturn. The 6-70 was basically the continuation of the well publicized 6-66.[194] The engine was virtually unchanged,[195] and the wheelbase remained at 131-inches. The Daytona speedster was the loss leader of the line, joined by a seven-passenger touring car ($2,195), a four-passenger sport touring car ($2,245), coupe ($3,100), sedan ($3,155), and limousine ($3,350). These high prices kept away most prospective buyers. A total of 4,047 Paiges were shipped from the Hinckley plant site during the 1923 season. Without the phenomenal success of the modestly priced Jewett, the Paige-Detroit Motor Car Company would have had to deal with a great deal of red ink in its books.

More manpower and equipment was going over to Jewett production at this time. By July of 1923, nearly 50,000 examples of the new make were shipped and sold. Fewer of the higher-priced Paige automobiles were sold.

The Paige line for 1924 was introduced in January and was a continuation of the same cars from the previous season. The Model 6-70 was again the only series offered and, excepting a boosted horsepower rating from 70 to 75[196] and the use of a flat radiator, was almost identical to the 1923 model.[197] The only noteworthy change overall was the use of four-wheel brakes on all models.[198] The nation was well on its way to economic recovery, but the market for upper middle class automobiles continued to waiver. Paige production for the year was increased to 5,913, but remained disappointing in every aspect.

A real concern to Paige management was this rapidly evaporating demand for their well-built, nicely appointed, and sophisticated automobiles. The fears and apprehensions which prompted the creation of the Jewett in 1921 were well founded and continued. The future course of the parent company was a real concern.

Grousehaven, near Rose City, Michigan

Persevering, the company presented a single series of Paige models in 1925. Presented to the public in July of 1924, the "new" 6-70 was a warmed-over version of previous seasons, with only a slight change in styling and appointments.[199] The aging 70 horsepower engine was without appreciable change or improvement.[200] The line had been pared to five offerings,[201] the four- and seven-passenger touring cars, the brougham, the sedan and the limousine.[202] New and exciting developments were not occurring in the Paige line-up, and its styling was aging rapidly. Although the Daytona was now internationally famous, it was no longer offered. Poor sales of the limited production speedster prompted its dismissal. Buyers responded with a total of 39,479 vehicles purchased, again concentrated mostly on the Jewett line.

Elegant advertising continued to expound the quality and social correctness in owning a Paige automobile, but the offerings for 1925 were little different from those of several prior seasons. It was a buyer's market and Paige was not responding. Management did understand the situation, as is evident from the text of a sales catalog from that year:

The perfected performance of Paige cars is not achieved through radical change in design; rather it is the logical result of continuous progress. With the high reputation these cars have won,

it would be both wasteful and hazardous to experiment at your expense with something new and untried. The Paige motor, which out-performs more expensive multi-cylinder engines, is now more notable than ever for its smoothness, its quietness and its swift surge of power. It is better balanced, better cooled, better lubricated.

In the midst of the "Roaring 20s", the public did not buy the company line.

By necessity, Paige-Detroit was now putting even more effort into its profitable Jewett line. Although the bore and stroke of the Jewett engine remained the same, it was reworked by Paige engineers to increase its output. New axles were utilized and numerous small improvements were made to the chassis. Although the advertising and press reported "new" Jewett bodies for 1925, it, too, was in reality a warming over of existing designs.

The Paige offerings for 1925 now included balloon tires, and a $70 increase in list prices. Lockheed hydraulic brakes were offered for an additional $45.[203]

Regardless of the dwindling sales of automobiles from the parent company, Harry M. Jewett remained optimistic about future sales. At the annual meeting of Paige and Jewett Dealers on January 10, 1925,[204] Jewett declared,

General business conditions hold out promises for the greatest year in Paige history.

The projections of Jewett sales for 1925 made this comment reasonable and eminently believable.

His business attitude was further reflected when he announced:

Development of a satisfied patronage which will feel it has been given its money's worth and treated honestly and fairly is one of the first ideals for which the automobile dealer should strive.

Harry M. Jewett was not going to panic and enact any rash or radical policies. As he had done years earlier, the company would be made successful by offering a quality product at fair prices; a product of which the public would approve.

One step made by the Paige-Detroit management in 1925 was the introduction of an entirely new model in the Paige lineup. A DeLuxe Brougham was added to the Paige line,[205] in the hope it would mimic the success of the Jewett Brougham.

But it was the continued high volume sales of the Jewett which now drove the company. In response to dealer and customer demands, a bargain-priced Jewett roadster was now added to the line on April 1. For only $1,630, the new open car would feature five balloon tires, have a complete complement of equipment and have four-wheel brakes and steel wheels as an option.

The success of the Paige-Detroit Motor Car Company's Jewett line had become a common topic in both automotive and financial circles. A financial report made public at the end of April showed the

Although the 1921 Paige Daytona speedster defined the season for the Paige-Detroit Motor Car Company, this Standard Brougham, Model 70, is what the buying public perceived as the signature Paige offering during 1924. Priced at a reasonable $2,195, the formal and dignified brougham sold fairly well. (Courtesy of Karl Zahm)

The Paige-Detroit Motor Car Company

The Albert Kahn-designed administration building of Paige-Detroit fronted Warren Avenue. Its design and construction were considered the finest in the industry. (Courtesy of Albert Kahn Associates, Detroit, MI)

parent company had never been in better financial shape. Current assets were tallied at \$8,959,289 with liabilities of only \$2,867,462.[206] Shortly afterwards application was made to issue over a half-million new shares of common stock. The company's reputation for reimbursing its stockholders well insured the immediate sale of shares.[207]

With the Jewett models fueling the success of the company, Paige-Detroit now found itself at the center of numerous Wall Street rumors. Although merger rumors were ubiquitous in the automotive and financial worlds, those concerning Paige were now being written up regularly in the motoring press. Those most commonly circulated involved the merger of Pierce-Arrow, Paige-Detroit, and Hupp. This backroom talk was summarily dismissed by all principals, but rumors continued to swirl. In June, production records for Paige-Detroit were publicized, and the records set fueled even more speculation.[208]

Increased production prompted the reduction of the recently introduced Jewett roadster's price to \$1,500, and the popular DeLuxe sedan was reduced to \$1,680. Other results from the success of the fast-selling Jewett line include the confirmation of rumors that Paige-Detroit was going to introduce an additional line of automobiles to complement the Paige and Jewett offerings. Harry Jewett and other executives were tight lipped about details, but did allow,

> *...considerable attention was being given to development of an automobile to fit into the unoccupied place in the price scale below the present Jewett.*

They did also confirm that several experimental and prototypes had been road tested for several months, but no further details would be published until the "appropriate" time.

In September of 1925 the company declared another dividend, this time 35 cents on common stock, giving a single share a \$1.40 annual basis. Of course, available shares were hurriedly acquired by eager investors.[209]

With more than adequate cash on hand, management publicly announced its decision to reinvest it in the company. Major additions were made to the Warren Avenue plant. Over 500,000 square feet of manufacturing area was added to the existing plant, in addition to the erection of a classically elegant administration building. Again the services of Albert Kahn were requested, and the result was a beautiful two-story, white stone administration building which was designed to front the factory buildings on West Warren Avenue. The Paige-Detroit Motor Car Company now truly had a state-of-the-art manufacturing facility.

The plant was reconfigured to produce both the Paige and the Jewett under one roof. The McKinstry Street plant was not abandoned, but was used for the busy factory service and export departments.

With both Paige and Jewett automobiles now being produced at the West Warren Avenue plant, manufacturing and purchasing economies were able to be effected.

The first week of July 1925 saw the introduction of the Paige lineup for 1926. Indicative of the lessened clout in the market, only four body styles were available. The seven-passenger landau sedan carried a list of \$2,395, making it the least expensive Paige sedan ever mounted on their traditional 131-inch chassis. Phaetons were available in either a four- or seven-passenger configuration, as was a seven-passenger sedan.[210] Hydraulic four-wheel brakes were now standard as was an enameled trunk. The most distinguishing feature of the new sedan was the D-shaped rear windows at the rear. Sales were expectedly spurred, while Jewett sales continued to be profitable. By mid-July of 1925 Harry M. Jewett was able to announce,

> *We have on hand today $4,770,000 in cash. There is no abatement in orders for cars. We have all the business we can handle at present, and indications are that this condition will continue throughout the summer.*

That month also saw the announcement of a new Jewett. Not at all new in an objective sense, this new line of Jewett[211] was mounted on a longer (115-inch) wheelbase, featured "more attractive color combinations," the adoption of a coincidental lock on the steering gear,[212] and an air cleaner on the engine.[213] Every opportunity to expand into the lower priced market without a major retooling was considered a valid business move. The "new" Jewett was announced at the same time price reductions from $15 to $120 on the existing Jewetts took effect.[214]

Production was such that Murray, the Detroit body shell builder who had been providing shells for both Paige and Jewett, was now engaged for Jewett production only. Mullins,[215] a Salem, Ohio, body firm, contributed to the manufacture of ancillary sheet metal parts for Paige and Jewett bodies. Jewett sales success continued with this new series.

In 1925 Paige-Detroit achieved a standing of 14th[216] place in a listing of American automobile manufacturers.[217] Regarding this noteworthy accomplishment, Harry Jewett was quoted as saying,

> *Paige Jewett has the men, the money, and the machinery to build good automobiles and to keep on building them.*

It was only natural this sustained volume success prompted continuing takeover rumors. In October the press reported "a large producer of fours" had acquired the Paige-Detroit Motor Car Company. It was common knowledge the large producer of fours referred to was the Dodge Brothers firm. The deal was said to be announced on November 1, 1925.

Of course, such a deal would make sense to a company in Dodge's position. As a volume producer of four-cylinder automobiles, the addition of a prestigious, well-built, and fast-selling six-cylinder line would be distinctly advantageous to them. The rumors were no doubt based on recent Dodge history which saw this manner of acquisition allowing them to enter the heavy truck field in 1921.

When F. J. Haynes, president of Dodge, returned from a European business trip in early November, he categorically denied the rumor. On November 10, Harry M. Jewett "flatly denied" that any such deal was in the works. Jewett's announcement included the statement,

> *The Paige-Detroit Company, not only has not changed hands, but there has been and will be no negotiation. The company has*

been operating most successfully under the present management for many years and is planning to push its present advantage in the six cylinder field by aggressive policies of manufacturing and merchandising.

The announcement was followed by news that the West Warren Avenue plant would undergo even further remodeling and expansion. A materials storage building, 530 by 70 feet, was being built, in addition to a nickel plating building, a building for riveting frames, and additions to the power house and a new large boiler system. Four large compressors would be housed in a new building. A motor conveyor was installed in the existing plant, capable of handling over 300 motors every eight-hour shift. The motor paint oven was substantially enlarged, as was the chassis assembly conveyor. Over $300,000 was invested in the improvements. These preparations initiated additional rumors that Paige-Detroit shortly did confirm.

On December 3, 1925, Harry M. Jewett announced to the trade press that a third line of automobiles was indeed going to be offered by the Paige-Detroit Motor Car Company. This Paige product was to be priced even lower than the current Jewett and would provide a "new day" for the buying public. Dubbed the "New-Day Jewett," the company was entering the low-priced field.

Prompted by the discouraging sales of Paige automobiles, even with their reduced list prices, management decided that this market would allow them to continue their lower-priced success.

To reach that market, the list prices on the New-Day Jewett models began at less than $1,000. The all-steel bodies by Murray were mounted on the shortest chassis ever utilized by Paige-Detroit (109-inch wheel base) and carried a 40 horsepower L-head Continental engine[218] (2 3/4 inch bore and 4 3/4 inch stroke).[219]

Considered a 1926 model, the New-Day Jewett was simply a smaller, less powerful version of the standard Jewett line. In that the Jewett was advertised as the "Thrifty Six by Paige," the New Day Jewett prices were really eye openers for new car buyers. The standard sedan was available for an amazingly low $995, and the same sedan with deluxe equipment was only $1,095. A deluxe touring model was later added to the line for the same price as the deluxe sedan.

Sales continued at their torrid pace with the addition of this new offering, and the Warren Avenue site was again failing to meet demand.

This continued success in the lower-priced field prompted the Paige-Detroit board of directors to have the namesake line of automobiles follow the lead. On March 31, a 1925 special Paige Model 6-70, was introduced. Priced at a reasonable $1,295, this Paige Brougham was designed to be midway between the New Day Jewett and the standard Paige offerings. Based on a 115-inch wheelbase, the new Paige was said to be the lowest-priced Paige ever offered. However, expected sales failed to materialize.

Introduced in January, the "new" 1926 Paige offerings were in showrooms nationwide.[220] The new Paige 6-72 used the same 72 horsepower engine as the previously announced Paige,[221] but rode in a longer 125-inch wheelbase chassis. Abandoning the longer chassis which had been used for years by the marque, the company explained that this shorter configuration was designed to "make it easier to park, to be more economical, and to be better suited to present driving conditions."

The Paige-Detroit Motor Car Company

The New-Day Jewett DeLuxe Sedan

Descendant of a long line of distinguished fine cars, famous for their mastery of road and hill, the New-Day Jewett is the first automobile ever to be engineered from initial conception to finished production as an answer to present day conditions.

In a single stride, it sweeps past the inefficiencies and limitations that the motor car has shown in crowded highways and close-packed city streets.

With its innumerable new-day features and improvements—with its dashing performance, its mastery of traffic, its beauty, roominess, comfort, substantial quality—with all that you could or would expect in a true new-day automobile—this Jewett DeLuxe Sedan is still by a very wide margin the lowest priced Jewett closed car ever built.

The Paige-Detroit Motor Car Company

PAIGE & JEWETT SIXES

New-Day Cars for New-Day Needs

enced. It was becoming evident to the board their policy of lower-priced automobiles of true value, coupled with an absence of corporate indebtedness and conservative management, was going to bring them back to the success they had become accustomed. However, that optimistic outlook and seemingly confirmed tack was to be suddenly and dramatically dismissed.

Since the beginning of his tenure at Paige-Detroit, Harry Jewett had insisted upon using the very best proprietary parts available. To do so made it possible to obtain state-of-the art components for his product, while not having to invest in-house development and production. It was an ideal situation for many smaller independent manufacturers, although the larger mass production companies derided the end product as simply "assembled cars."[223] The inherent danger of relying upon these procured units was the manufacturer's dependence upon their availability.

Of course, competing in a capitalist economic system insures the product will be of the highest quality, and competitively priced. However, by 1926 the automotive industry had matured to the point where there were a somewhat limited amount of suppliers available for any given part.

Over the years Paige-Detroit had obtained their bodies "in white,"[224] that is unfinished, from a number of body and sheet metal suppliers.

A real effort was made to have the new models appeal to buyers who were looking for the best value. The body was not extensively reworked,[222] but a "modish" belt molding was introduced, a much more plush interior was standard, a heater was included, and sharp disc wheels set off the new look. When a buyer considered that for only a few hundred dollars more than the smallest Paige offered, the 6-72 five-passenger Deluxe sedan was indeed a real value for $1,670. A standard version was available for only $1,495. Later in the year a seven-passenger sedan was added to the line ($1,995), as was a seven-passenger touring car, seven-passenger limousine, cabriolet, and four-passenger phaeton.

This move by the company seemed to be exactly what was needed, as a considerable increase was experienced with Paige sales. The board of directors was pleased when sales took off, with a total of 15,870 Paige automobiles finding new owners. Employment totaled 2,300, a highwater mark for the company.

Jewett and New Day Jewett sales continued to amaze the industry and now more healthy sales were being experienced with the venerable Paige lineup. The first six months of 1926 were the best two quarters the company had ever experi-

Murray, Robbins, Griswold and Central Manufacturing[225] had produced shells for the company in the past. The Murray Body Corporation had been supplying much of Paige-Detroit's sheet metal needs ever since the body maker was established in 1924.

The famous "Flying J" atop the radiator of a New Day Jewett

Paige-Detroit Motor Car Co., Detroit, U. S. A.

The Paige-Detroit Motor Car Company

For many years the city of Detroit had Paige-Detroit manufactured vehicles in its livery. This photo shows
a 1925 Jewett brougham in the service of the Detroit Police Department. (Courtesy of John A. Conde)

When Jewett sales skyrocketed, bodies and other components were simply ordered in larger quantities. The motorcar industry's suppliers were usually able to handle such fluxes and, generally, both companies would profit.

Oddly, there was occasionally too much success for these automotive industry suppliers. Unfortunately, this proved to be true for the Murray Body Corporation— much to the detriment of the Paige-Detroit Motor Car Company.

Murray was established on November 15, 1924, as the result of the combining of the assets and facilities of the Towson Body Company[226] (formerly the Anderson Electric Car Company), the C. R. Wilson Company, and the J. C. Widman & Company—supplier of Jewett bodies.

Almost immediately after its creation, the Murray firm was supplying bodies to Marmon, Hupp, Lincoln, Packard, Jordon, Reo, and a host of others. The company, headed by Allen Sheldon Murray, immediately embarked on a program of expansion and acquisition. In July of 1925, the firm contracted to produce Hupp bodies for a period of five years. Included in the agreement was the purchase by Murray of the Hupp body plant in Racine, Wisconsin. This $1 million investment was followed the next year by the purchase of the Marmon body plant in Indianapolis for $200,000.

This obvious outward success was tempered, however, by the inability of the company to completely surmount the transitional woes that were presented daily to the amalgamation. Although there were almost daily increases in production and many deadlines were successfully met, there were also the inevitable delays and problems. The demands of the Jewett assembly line were one of the problems at Murray, and the needs of the Paige-Detroit Motor Car Company were not being fulfilled. The popular Jewetts were selling at a pace which Murray was not able to sustain. The Warren Avenue plant was experiencing slowdowns for the first time since the introduction of the Jewett.

It was obvious to all involved the new Murray Body Corporation had grown too large, too fast. By supplying their other contracted customers at any expense, they had gotten themselves into a problem not only with the Paige concern but also with other customers and suppliers. There was a dearth of working capital for a large corporation with major obligations. Not all of those obligations were being met.

In December of 1925, the company—and their customers—agreed the firm should enter a "friendly" receivership. *Automobile Topics* magazine described it as a financial reorganization, reporting,

> *In light of all the facts brought out at the meeting[227] it [receivership] was deemed the best move for the interests of the company, especially as it would insure no let up in production which would prove a detriment to some of their customers.*

To insure the industry and public knew that Murray was not in any threat of insolvency, the receiver[228] issued a statement insuring them of continued production,

> *There [will be] no interruption in the working program of the corporation and [this] receivership is not the result of excessive liabilities but due to the lack of working capital.*

A mortgage bond was issued to assure the company's $3,750,000 debt, and holders of bank indebtedness were issued stock and cash in return for their cooperation.[229]

Subsequent reports indicated this plan was more than successful. In early 1926 negotiations began which resulted in a $15 million contract with the Marmon Motor Car Company.[230] A similar multi-million dollar contract was agreed to shortly afterward with the Hupp Motor Car Company.[231]

In July of 1926 Vice-President Widman was able to report to the press that from January 1 through June 30, Murray had been able to produce over 66,000 units, profiting a little over $930,000. The company had done so well, once it had overcome the hurdle of inadequate working capital, that there was talk during the summer concerning the ending of receivership and sale of the company.

Meetings were held in July and August concerning this sale with all creditors and customers. Most all agreed with the terms, but there was a problem with Paige-Detroit. Deliveries had been excellent during the first half of the year, but now that the two large contracts had been secured by Murray, they had become a forgotten customer. In addition, each body was now costing them considerably more than prior to the receivership. Sales for Jewetts had boomed during the first six months, but because of a lack of body shells hardly any Jewetts or Paiges had been shipped since the end of June. Of course, the larger customers were happy with the new arrangements (they could easily spread the increased price over a large number of units) and projected sale of the company—especially since their supply of bodies was to be uninterrupted.

Paige-Detroit was not in that situation. The first six months of 1926 was the best half year in the company's history and this surge in sales was expected to continue. The garnering of Murray's big contracts spelled disaster for Paige-Detroit. Body shells into the Warren Avenue plant slowed to a veritable trickle. The company was able to sell all the Jewetts it could produce, but was unable to do so at capacity due to deficiency of outside supply.

The response of Paige-Detroit was twofold. They tried to persuade Murray, soon to be renamed the Murray Corporation of America,[232] to supply bodies to the desperate motor car manufacturer. They were less than totally successful, although progressively more bodies were delivered to them in July and August. Harry M. Jewett and Paige-Detroit then entered a claim into federal court in the amount of $294,794 against Murray.

Paige's balloon had burst just as it was enthusiastically inflated with high hopes and brimming order books. Instead of increased production, year-end totals showed almost 2,000 fewer units being produced than the year before.[233] For only the second time since the war the Paige-Detroit Motor Car Company produced fewer cars than the previous year.

Even more shocking was the fact that Paige-Detroit had produced precious little profit during one of the automobile industry's more profitable years.

The annual report to the stockholders of the Paige-Detroit Motor Car Company had Harry Jewett explain the "extraordinary situation"—and financial stumbling block—in this manner,

The losses referred to [in the September 30, 1926 report to stockholders] had to do almost entirely with the fact that our body

THE FAMOUS JEWETT SIX MOTOR—PAIGE BUILT

The Heart of Jewett's Spirited Performance
Perfected Through Two Billion Miles—Seven Years' Service

HERE'S the motor that has made Jewett Six winner in a hundred hill-climbing contests. The motor that accelerates Jewett from 5 to 25 miles an hour in 7 seconds, in high gear. The motor that pulls Jewett ahead first when the traffic whistle blows. It is the BIGGEST motor ever put into a car in the $1000 class—and the best proved! The Jewett buyer is not experimenting.

When Paige engineers first created this Jewett Six motor in 1917, it was for the Paige 42—a $1900 car. It was greatly improved and continued in the Paige 44, with ever-increasing success. In 1922 this Paige-built motor with many betterments became the heart of the Jewett Six. More than a billion miles of service in 110,000 cars have proved Jewett's motor! Constant refinements have kept it the leading motor in its field.

1 *Big cylinders, big power.* Extra cylinder size gives Jewett amazing power—actually 50 horsepower. Each cylinder is 3¼-inch bore, 5-inch stroke—giving the motor 249 cubic inch piston displacement. Piston displacement determines power. Don't be misled by claimed "horsepower." Figure piston displacement this way (for example using Jewett bore and stroke):

Bore	Bore	Constant	Stroke	No. of cylin.	
3.25 in. ×	3.25 in. ×	3.14 ×	5 in.	6	= 249 cu. in.
		4			

Prove to yourself Jewett's extra power by figuring this for any $1000 car.

2 *High pressure oiling.* Jewett Six motor is oiled like the big Paige and other top quality cars. Jewett's oiling system isn't just a "splash" system or a "pressure" system to main bearings. It's a HIGH PRESSURE, hollow crankshaft system that forces 2 gallons of oil per minute through main bearings—AND CONNECTING ROD BEARINGS—and sprays the entire internal mechanism. Metal never rubs metal—always a thin film of oil between. When you drive for miles at high speed or at slow speed on bad hills or through soft going, there is always enough oil forced under 20 to 40 pounds pressure, to lubricate all working parts thoroughly. Hence Jewett's long motor life—smooth, quiet, "peppy" performance. Overhauling need is long postponed. No better oiling anywhere than in Jewett's time-tested motor!

3 *Extra large wrist pins.* Wrist pins are hidden, but vital to a motor's success. The power blow at each explosion is transmitted through the wrist pin in each piston. Jewett's pins are large—much larger than the pins used in other cars in its class. A Jewett wrist pin is the size of a quarter, others the size of a dime. Extra strength of Jewett's wrist pins contributes to Jewett's long motor life and continued sweet-running harmony and silence.

4 *Oil bathed valve-gear.* The oil sprayed by the high pressure system reaches the camshaft and pushrods of Jewett's valve assembly. They are bathed in oil. Small wonder at quiet operation! Valves are 1 9/16 inches in diameter. Valve springs are made of expensive electric furnace vanadium steel. The entire valve assembly is utterly accessible. Adjustments are easily made, so there need never be noise through wear. Truly, a marvel of mechanical ingenuity.

5 *83-pound crankshaft.* That's a heavy shaft—much heavier than is used in comparable cars. Jewett engineering standards require a crankshaft material that rests to an elastic limit of 70,000 pounds per square inch. It's an immense shaft to handle Jewett's immense power. In precision of manufacture, in composition of metal, in care in inspections, in balance—Jewett's crankshaft compares point by point with those in far more costly cars.

6 *Easy acting clutch.* With the new Paige-type clutch, however fast you lift your foot you can neither stall the motor nor jerk the car. The reason? A light-weight driven clutch member, weighing less than 3½ pounds, has one-third the usual weight, and with one-third the momentum, quickly adjusts itself to speed changes. Jewett's clutch positively amazes those who are accustomed to pause to avoid clash or "missing." Having six springs instead of one, it engages smoothly and releases under the gentlest foot pressure.

Now you understand why this veteran Jewett Six motor performs so well and stays so good! Among all $1000 cars—yes, including cars up to $1500—Jewett welcomes expert comparisons as to power, performance, ruggedness and HISTORY! Your demonstration in a Jewett Six will open your eyes to the advantages of buying this proven motor—will show you, when you sit at the wheel and drive—why Jewett Six tops the $1000 field. (609)

Touring $1065
Brougham $1325
Sedan $1495

Special Roadster $1195
Special Touring $1220
Special Sedan $1695
Prices at Detroit. Tax extra.

JEWETT SIX
—PAIGE BUILT—

Callout labels (on diagram):
- ④ Oil bathed valve-gear
- ⑤ 83-pound crankshaft
- ⑥ Easy acting clutch
- ③ Extra large wrist pins
- ① Big cylinders, big power
- ② High pressure oiling

source, a combination of units, with whom we had been doing business on a satisfactory basis for a great many years, unexpectedly went into the hands of a receiver. The receiver extracted an increased price per body, which took away more than half of our normal profit. Arrangements were made for a supply of bodies from another source, but inasmuch as a period of four to five months is required to get tooled up for new body production, we necessarily had to continue for a time to take bodies from our then existing source at the increased prices. These direct losses were substantial, without taking into account the intangible loss involved in the unavoidable interruption of our production resulting from the necessary change in our principal body source of supply...Notwithstanding this, the financial condition of your company has been well maintained...Net earnings, after provisions for depreciation and all other charges, and after elimination of inter-company profits, amounted to $500,206.

The Paige-Detroit Motor Car Company was putting its best face on a bad situation.

Although the management at Paige-Detroit had as its foremost concern the securing of an ancillary body supplier, advance planning continued for the company.

In August the trade press reported Jewett would cease to exist as a separate make of automobile in January of 1927. The New Day Jewett would become the Paige Model 6-45 with virtually no chassis or styling changes.[234] The company quietly allowed the model to fade away, and it was neither featured nor noted in the 1927 prestige showroom catalog.

September saw the introduction of two "new" six-cylinder models by the Paige-Detroit Motor Car Company. Although the company had proclaimed its models "The Most Beautiful Car In America" for years, some allowed that these motor cars did indeed fit that description.

The two series for the 1927 season included the 6-65 and 6-75. The prestige showroom catalog delineated the quality construction and sophisticated refinements which had been traditional on Paige automobiles since almost the beginning. However, it was the new body work which was emphasized. The new bodies, finally again being supplied in reasonable quantities by Murray, were said to,

...endow each Paige body with a new symmetry and refreshing grace—an atmosphere of regal luxury. Paige continues as the style leader among fine cars as well as master of the highway.

Advertising hyperbole, of course, but the newly designed bodies were good looking and distinctively different from the tired designs of the past few seasons. A double bead body belt was incorporated into the refreshing design, and was especially distinctive on the two-tone models.

Even though the new-looking Paiges were attractive, their mechanics were little changed. The smaller, 115-inch wheelbase Model 6-65 was mechanically identical to the discontinued 6-72.[235] The only open car available on the 6-65 chassis was the

four-passenger roadster ($1,540). This model featured a rumble seat and detachable rear curtain and windshield wings. The closed cars featured a one-piece roof with an integral sun visor. The two-door, five-passenger brougham ($1,395) carried landau bars, and was so named. Rounding out the junior Paige lineup was the standard five-passenger, four-door sedan ($1,540). Each of the closed cars featured walnut[236] instrument boards and trim panels.[237]

The 6-75 was the larger, 125-inch wheelbase Paige offering. It, too, carried the same basic motor as the discontinued 6-72.[238] However, the Paige engineering department had bored out the powerplant by 1/8-inch, marginally boosting its horsepower. Except for the longer wheelbase, longer springs, and larger tires, the automobile shared all chassis specifications with the smaller 6-65. The standard five-passenger, four-door sedan ($1,695) was available to prospective customers, in addition to the seven-passenger sedan ($1,995). For those buyers of means, the seven-passenger sedan could be ordered as a "Suburban Limousine" ($2,245) complete with sliding glass partition and leather upholstery for the front seat. These bigger sedans carried aluminum trunk bars for touring convenience. All models featured a coincidental lock. The four-passenger coupe ($1,995) featured a sporty belt line treatment, as did the cabriolet roadster. The closed cars also featured an extension of the roof line which formed the windshield visor. The only true open car shown in the showroom catalog was the seven-passenger phaeton ($1,655), but a four-passenger cabriolet roadster was available for $1,995.

Even though the chassis' featured attractive new bodies, the buying public was able to perceive these "new" six-cylinder Paige offerings for what they really were: mechanically, the same cars offered for the past several years. The automobile industry, and especially motor car engineering, was progressing rapidly—but Paige-Detroit was not offering anything new nor improved to their loyal customers, excepting a pleasant new body styling. As might have been expected, sales for the remainder of the calendar year were, quite simply, dismal.

These disappointing motor cars would be the last introduced by Harry Mulford Jewett, president of the Paige-Detroit Motor Car Company.

When Harry M. Jewett entered the automobile industry in 1909, he was a successful and wealthy 39-year-old coal magnate. After taking the reins of the Paige-Detroit Motor Car Company in 1910, he dedicated himself to the success of that enterprise for nearly two decades. He gained not only the respect of his fellow manufacturers, stockholders, and the automobile-buying public, but also amassed another fortune from its profitable operation. The road to success was one strewn with considerable obstacles, but Harry Jewett was equal to the task.

Approaching his 56th birthday, Jewett began to consider his retirement years. Flush with the announcement his company had posted a record profit of over a half million dollars during the first six months of 1926,[239] Jewett began to contemplate the wisdom of turning over the presidency to a trusted corporate officer. For well over a decade he had been faithfully served by a hardworking and intelligent management team. He felt comfortable handing over the day-to-day operation of the firm to them, and allowed that he would indeed enjoy spending more time with his family[240] and pursuing his many other interests.

As it had done in the past, the company would surely overcome the nagging body supply problem, and go on to be profitable.[241] After all, he had begun planning

Paige Four-Passenger Sports Roadster - Model 6-65

Paige Seven-Passenger Sedan - Model 6-75

some time ago for an entirely new Paige which would undoubtedly be accepted by the public to the same extent the Jewett was in 1922. Jewett's policy of no corporate debt had served the company well, his company was housed in one of the finest state-of-the-art manufacturing facilities in Michigan, and Paige-Jewett had earned a well-respected name in the industry. The crowning achievement of his automotive career, his motor car company, was a valuable commodity.

During the last quarter of 1925, Dodge Brothers, Incorporated, made a corporate decision which would prove to be far-reaching. Its association with the Graham Brothers truck firm had been exceedingly successful, and enhanced its market position considerably. Cognizant of its value, Dodge Brothers purchased a minority stake[242] in the firm, netting the Graham brothers in excess of $3 million.[243] When the Graham brothers resigned their positions at Dodge only a few months later,[244] they sold the remaining stock to Dodge Brothers, Inc., for a reported $13 million. The three Graham brothers were well capitalized.

The motoring press reported the brothers had "retired," having deserved a well-earned rest.[245] Nothing could have been further from the truth.

The Graham brothers team had been successful in the bottle industry, the truck industry, and the automobile industry. They believed these successes could be repeated, especially with the familial trio in total control of whatever industry they might decide to enter.

Having left the Dodge management team, the Grahams became even more involved in the business world. As it had been in the past, business decisions were to be made by the brothers as a team, not as individuals.

Although the Grahams had exerted a great deal of effort in making the truck manufacturing enterprise successful, they continued to be very much involved in the glass and bottle industry.[246] When they sold their bottle interests to Owens Bottle in 1916, John D. Biggers took day-to-day control of the four Graham plants. The Grahams still held positions in their former company and were duly impressed with Biggers' abilities, so much that when they assumed positions of authority at Dodge Brothers they quickly acquired the services of Mr. Biggers at that firm. In late 1926 Biggers was named managing director of Dodge Brothers Britain Limited, of London, England. Following the example set by the Graham brothers, he would now be well versed in dual industries.

The Paige-Detroit Motor Car Company

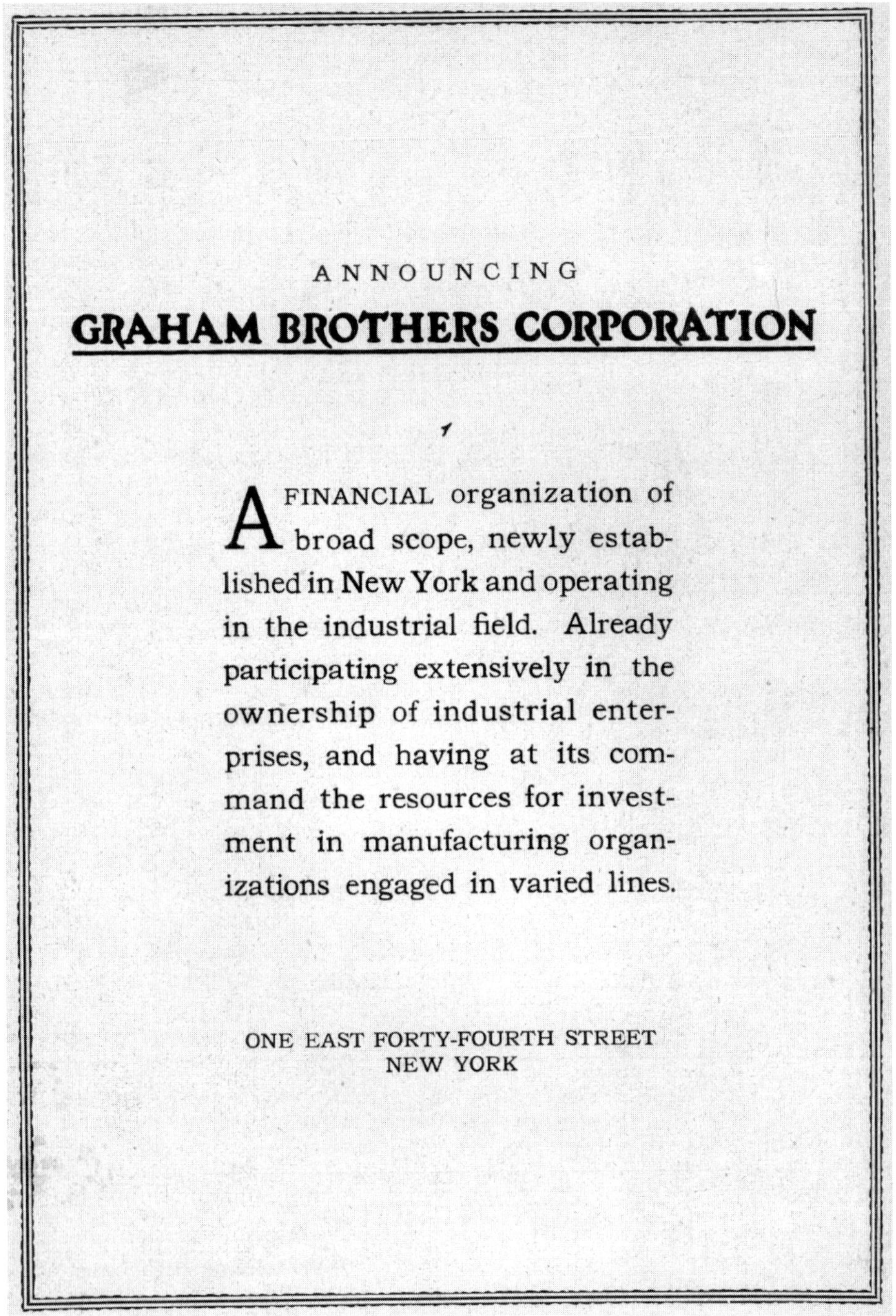

ANNOUNCING

GRAHAM BROTHERS CORPORATION

*

A FINANCIAL organization of broad scope, newly established in New York and operating in the industrial field. Already participating extensively in the ownership of industrial enterprises, and having at its command the resources for investment in manufacturing organizations engaged in varied lines.

ONE EAST FORTY-FOURTH STREET
NEW YORK

With the capital realized from their withdrawal from Dodge, the Grahams formed a holding company. Graham Brothers Corporation was announced in April of 1927 and was officially described as,

A financial organization of broad scope, newly established in New York and operating in the industrial field. Already participating extensively in the ownership of industrial enterprises, and having at its command the resources for investment in manufacturing organizations engaged in varied lines.[247]

One of the first endeavors of the new corporation was to begin negotiations with representatives of the estate of the late Edward Drummond Libbey to obtain his considerable holdings in the Libbey-Owens Sheet Glass Company. The end result of the negotiations was the creation of the Libbey-Owens Securities Corporation, whose sole purpose was to obtain those holdings.[248] Ray Graham was elected president of the corporation.

This new corporation made a bid of nearly eleven $11 million to the executors of Libbey's estate,[249] and it was eventually accepted.[250] Management of the company was not affected, but the new investors were given places on the board of directors. Joseph Graham was elected directly to that post, but the next year John Biggers was elected to represent the Graham interests.[251]

At the same time the re-entry into the glass industry was taking place for the Graham Brothers, inquiries were quietly being made in the automotive industry as well. Representatives of the Graham brothers had canvassed the motor car industry to learn what firms might be available. According to accounts published later, inquiries and investigation of the Paige-Detroit Motor Car Company were made beginning in September of 1926.

The Graham brothers liked what they saw and what was reported to them. In addition to the very much respected Paige name, the firm had no indebtedness, had a nearly new and thoroughly modern manufacturing facility, and was possibly available. Surreptitious meetings were held and, within two months, the first signs of change at Paige-Detroit were evident.

Innocent at first blush, the announcement of the stepping down of Harry M. Jewett from the presidency of the Paige-Detroit Motor Car Company was not entirely unexpected. Jewett had reached an acceptable age for such a move, and he was to become the chairman of the board.[252] W. A. Wheeler, first vice-president of the firm since 1924, would take over the presidency during the first week of 1927. To the public, it would be a normal business strategy at the respected firm. The immediate goal of the new president would be getting the company back into regular production, and profitability. The vehicle which would duly impress the automobile-buying public had been planned while Harry M. Jewett was still president. Its introduction by the new president of the Paige-Detroit Motor Car Company would be the start of a new era.

[1] This first model is considered a 1904 model, even though later factory advertising claimed 1903 to be the first year of Reliance production. The rationale for this deceptive sales ploy was the desire of the Reliance to be acknowledged as the first side tonneau model to be introduced in the United States. The fact the Peerless and Orlo for 1904 both offered this feature necessitated the false advertising. Freedom in advertising appeared to be a strong trait at the company. According to the Standard Catalog of American Cars, 1805-1942: "Overkill in sloganeering seemed to a Reliance penchant. If one motto was good, a half dozen might be even better. The brochure for 1905 had a different one on virtually every page—"The Car Too Good For The Price," "The Light-Heavyweight Touring Car," and "Reliance-All Made Under One Roof."

[2] Mr. Mulkey was prominent in the salt and portland cement industry.

[3] The board of directors was made up of financially able men. In addition to Mulkey, the directors included Hugh O'Connor, president of the Michigan Wire Cloth Company, and George Wetherbee, a woodenware manufacturer.

[4] Most references indicate David O. Paige was born in 1833 in New Hampshire, although one federal census report gives his place of birth as New York. At the age of 27 he was a clerk in Cincinnati, and a year later he listed his occupation as salesman. About 1867 Paige moved to Detroit and became the superintendent of the Detroit Safe Company. There is some confusion as to the veracity of records found in Detroit that fellow New Hampshire native Mary Wiggins was indeed the mother of Frederick and his sister Glenna (b. January 1862). Census records show that in 1880 Abby Paige is the wife of David O. Paige (m. 1879), the household recorded to be at 70 Canfield Avenue in Detroit. In 1900 the household is listed as 24 Canfield Avenue and David's wife is listed as Maud (m. 1895).

[5] The Paiges were married in Detroit in 1890. The marriage produced four children: Frederick O., Junior (born April 1891), Mildred born April 1893, Clarence G. born March 1895, and John S. born September 1897. Minnie was born in Michigan in April 1869 and died in a sanitarium in Los Angeles on June 19, 1959.

[6] Paige directed his varied business interests from an office at #406 Penobscott Building. His home address was 1115 Woodward Avenue.

[7] Prestigious clubs that included Paige on their membership roles included the Detroit Club, the Detroit Country Club, the Detroit Automobile Club (serving as president), the Harbor Beach Resort Association, the Ohio Society, and New England Society.

[8] The make is lost to history.

[9] The Crescent Motor Car Company was organized in May of 1907 to continue production of the Reliance touring car and the former Marvel roadster. Capital stock totaled $75,000. Experiencing no more success than the original Reliance, the company was taken over by the Constantine Motor Company in September of 1908. Plans included using the former Hawley Motor Car factory as the main manufacturing site. Amid confusion by management and investors from the start, the company produced nothing more than prototype models for anticipated production. The company ceased to exist within a year.

[10] The Reliance truck evolved into the GMC Division of General Motors. The General Motors Truck Company was created in 1911 from the consolidation of the Reliance enterprise and the Rapid Motor Vehicle Company, which was founded in 1904 in Detroit. In 1943 the GMC Truck and Coach Division was formed when the Yellow Truck and Coach Manufacturing Company and the Yellow Cab Manufacturing Company were merged with the General Motors Truck Company.

[11] According to an unpublished, typewritten account of the early years of the Paige-Detroit Motor Car Company,
"Mr. Bachle became interested in the automobile industry when one of the first automobiles built, which was being driven by a newspaper man from New York to Chicago, refused to labor further than Adrian, Michigan. In this little town there was a stationary engine manufacturing plant of which Mr. Bachle was the chief engineer. He undertook to put the "horseless carriage" in running order. His success in this aroused his interest in the "new contraptions," and seeing the future of such a motor conveyance, he interested the principals of his company in the building of motor cars. He began at once to design such a car for the Church Manufacturing Company, this car being placed on the market about 1900. Mr. Bachle was thus one of the very first designers of motor cars."

[12] In Ipswich, Massachusetts.

[13] The probate and estate papers of Jewett show his first name spelled as Eliezer. This is the accepted spelling, and the manner in which it appears on his grave marker (December 7, 1817), although other references note it to be Eleazor and Eleazer.

[14] Jewett was born in Norwich, Connecticut. According to the estate records of Jewett in the State Library in Hartford, Connecticut, Jewett "began with only a small farm and a mill seat on the Pachaug River, also called Jewettville, or Jewett Farms. He had the first grist mill and sold portions of land to induce others to settle near him. According to Dr. Emmons, 'Eliezer Jewett has the most uncommon kind of sense—and this made him a prominent man. For a man who left so little in material wealth [$206.72] his persevering interest and influence made a lasting impression on the community.'" The community officially took the name Jewett City in 1895.

[15] One reference gives Gertrude's maiden name as Mulford.

[16] August 14, 1870

[17] Jewett's eldest brother, Fred, left the university in 1889 without earning a degree. His younger brother, Edward, graduated in 1894 with a B.S. degree. On June 5, 1900, he married Emma F. Farwell.

[18] Murphy was formerly the trainer at Yale. An expert in his field, he was an integral part of a winning team. When Murphy left the Detroit Athletic Club for the University of Pennsylvania, the fortunes of the Detroit Athletic Club's track team began to wane. Success followed Murphy to Pennsylvania also, as it did when he was official trainer for the victorious American teams in both the 1908 and 1912 Olympics. (He was an assistant trainer with the Olympic team in Paris in 1900.)
As with Harry Jewett, Murphy's ties with the Detroit Athletic Club were lifelong. Back at the University of Pennsylvania in 1913, his ill health did not allow him to get to the school's track and stadium without a great deal of discomfort. A group of Detroit Athletic Club alumni, headed by Harry Jewett and others who remembered his valuable contributions to past glories, presented him with a new Paige automobile to ease the burden.

[19] One indication of the degree of "Hal" Jewett's athletic fame can be found in the April 11, 1896, edition of the *Notre Dame Scholastic*, official publication of the University. Quoting that edition,

An apparently unsophisticated chap introduced himself at the Olympic Club in San Francisco the other day as Detroit's retired crack sprinter, Harry Jewett. They did not do a thing but gave him the run of the club, feed (sic) him a few French dinners, and tender

him all kinds of hospitalities. The sublime joke of it all was discovered when a friend of Harry's came in and asked for his ex-chum's address. A description was given and the chap was discovered to be an impostor. The real Harry Jewett is still in Detroit. The other fellow is—heaven only knows where.

That same issue also notes the athletic prowess of his brother, Edward Jewett,

Harry Jewett, the noted sprinter, has a brother who recently ran his first quarter in fifty-one seconds and beat him [Harry] in the 100 by two yards.

[20] John C. Lodge, future mayor of Detroit, also claimed to have personally encouraged the Notre Dame star to join the Detroit Athletic Club.

[21] Jewett's association with the Detroit Athletic Club continued for the rest of his life. His loyalty to the organization did not end with his athletic pursuits (In addition to winning the amateur world's record in 1892 for the 220-yard dash—the first man to break the 22-second barrier—under the Detroit Athletic Club banner, he also became the American amateur champion in that same year for the 100-yard dash.) When the Detroit Athletic Club was reorganized in 1913 (supplanting the original charter of 1888), Jewett became a charter member, serving as a director from 1914-1927. He served as president of the organization in 1924.

As the club prospered, it became an important social and business fraternity for the wealthy and powerful of Detroit, especially for those associated with the motor car industry. Other Detroit Athletic Club presidents with automobile industry ties included Hugh Chalmers, Henry B. Joy, William E. Metzger, Walter O. Briggs, A. T. Waterfall, B. Everett, Charles Fisher, Edward Fisher, K. T. Keller, William Knudson, and Carl Breer.

[22] Initial office space was located at No. 27 Whitney Opera House Block, Detroit.

[23] Walter Brooks was a native of Detroit, born on September 18, 1870. A graduate of Harvard (B.A. 1894) and Olivet College (B.S. 1895), Brooks was associated with the Michigan Drug Company prior to his partnership with Harry M. Jewett. Other coal industry connections included the J.B.B. Colleries Company, Twin Branch Mining Company, and the Maher Coal and Coke Company. Like Jewett, Brooks was a Republican. He resided at 255 Burns Avenue.

[24] Edward Jewett became a partner in the firm shortly after its incorporation as Jewett, Bigelow & Brooks.

[25] The chief machinist of the U.S.S. *Yosemite* during the Spanish-American War was Charles Brady King. King is acknowledged to have driven the first gasoline-powered automobile on the streets of Detroit on March 6, 1896. King later manufactured automobiles in both Detroit and Buffalo, New York. Although there is speculation that the two men came to know each other during their tenure on the battleship (or knew each other previously, as they were both members of the Detroit Athletic Club), there is no documentation that any association or contact was made. Jewett's brother Edward also served aboard the U.S.S. *Yosemite* during the war.

The U.S.S. *Yosemite* played an important part in the brief three-month war. The battleship that the Jewetts and King served on was credited with driving the "Antonio Lopez" to destruction, effectively shortening the war.

[26] Throughout his long business career, Harry Jewett remained active in veterans organizations and "planning for national preparedness."

[27] Eleanor Jewett was born on June 12, 1902. She later married Christian Henry Buhl, son of Willis Buhl, an original investor in the Paige-Detroit Motor Car Company. Her husband's grandfather was a former mayor of Detroit and the family owned much of the land on which present day downtown Detroit is located. Mrs. Buhl had a very active social life and was also involved in humanitarian causes. She died in 1987.

[28] Edward was born on May 29, 1909.

[29] Mary Vischer Wendell Jewett died on November 16, 1955, at the Henry Ford Hospital in Detroit.

[30] Jewett was also president of the J.B.B. Coal Company of Twin Branch, West Virginia. His brother, Edward, was a vice-president of Jewett, Bigelow & Brooks and was a director on the board of J.B.B. Coal Company.

[31] A letter written by Harry M. Jewett on May 24, 1915, indicates that he was an early automobilist. Although the purchase date is not noted, Jewett wrote to the editor of the magazine, *The Automobile*,

...I gave Mr. Henry Ford his first order for an automobile. He picked out number seven, as being a good one and it certainly proved so.

This statement would appear to indicate that Jewett owned the seventh Model A produced by the Ford Motor Car Company in 1903. This purchase of a 1903 Ford Model A is further corroborated by an account by Theodore F. Mac Manus and Norman Beasley in their landmark work *Men, Money, and Motors*. This volume, printed in 1929, relates that James Couzens became sales manager for Henry Ford during the initial days of the Ford Motor Company. According to Mac Manus and Beasley,

A.Y. Malcomson, one of the two largest stockholders in the company and Couzens' former employer, sold a car at at discount. He sold it to Harry M. Jewett...and Couzens protested so vigorously that the other stockholders voted to compel Malcomson to pay the difference.

[32] Jewett's friends who became stockholders and directors were among the city's financial elite. Theodore D. Buhl was a multi-millionaire whose family controlled Buhl Stamping Company and Buhl Malleable Company, two major metal fabrication firms in Detroit, in addition to being president of the Buhl and Sons Company hardware store. He was also on the board of Old Detroit National Bank; Parke, Davis & Company; Detroit Copper and Brass Rolling Mills; and National Can Company. E. D. Stair, publisher of the *Detroit Journal* and the *Detroit Free Press*, was on the board, along with Charles B. Warren, a socially and professionally eminent lawyer who had organized the Michigan Sugar Company (in conjunction with the Havemeyer Sugar Trust) and was later ambassador to Mexico and Japan. Gilbert W. Lee operated a wholesale grocery in five midwestern states and acted as vice-president. William Cady was both an attorney (Charles B. Warren's law partner) and an investor, with large investments in railroad, manufacturing, and paper concerns. Charles Hodges was the president of the Detroit Lubricator Company (automobile carburetors) and the American Radiator Company. Sherman Depew had inherited a fortune and through shrewd investments had increased it considerably. Alex McPherson had been president of the Detroit National Bank for nearly two decades. Just as it had done for his brother, Edward Jewett had profited mightily from the coal industry and was also able to invest in the firm.

[33] One source indicates this amount was $75,000, but this is not substantiated. Only $23,575 was paid in cash.

[34] The leased building was located at the corner of Leib and Larned Streets.

[35] The engineering staff at that time consisted of Andrew Bachle, designer of the prototype.

[36] By mid-1910, 150 men were employed at the McKinstry Street plant.

[37] One description of that first factory indicated ten men were employed initially and the factory was "about four times the size of an ordinary private office."

[38] This automobile should not be confused with the Paige automobile produced in Batavia, New York, in 1900. According to the Standard Catalog of American Cars, 1805-1942,

The Paige-Detroit Motor Car Company

"Edison W. Paige was a paperhanger from Batavia and the builder of the first automobile in town. It was completed and had its maiden run to Rochester on August 9, 1900. 'That was really something,' he recalled to a Batavia reporter decades later. 'All the people of Batavia lined the streets to see me take off about 10 o'clock in the morning. It was a gray runabout with white stripes, an elevated rear section and the front seat rounded toward the dash...a one cylinder buggy without top or fenders. It made the trip to Rochester at the rate of 22 miles per hour.' The car had been built in the kitchen of his home. Paige later sold it for $355 to Fred Remsen, the ticket agent at the New York Central railway station in Pembroke. He never built another car."

Also, the October 16, 1901, number of *The Horseless Age*, in its column entitled "Minor Mention" tells us that, "F. E. Paige has just completed an automobile for Hooker & Brown, Batavia, New York, proprietors of the Enterprise." This effort was likewise not associated with Fred Paige of the Paige-Detroit Motor Company.

[39] Although the first Paige automobiles were produced and delivered in 1909, the company considered them—both in advertising and technical papers—as 1910 models. The initial model never carried a name in any national advertising, but in later factory listings the 1910-1911 three-cylinder models were dubbed "Challenge," the four-cylinder models the "Challenger." The three-cylinder models of that year were also given the "Model A" designation while the four-cylinder version was designated the "Model B."

[40] The actual top was an extra cost item.

[41] The utilization of a two-cycle, three-cylinder power plant was not considered unusual in the early years of the fledgling automobile industry. Other manufacturers to use this type of engine included the producers of the Elmore, Atlas, and Hatfield (cars and trucks). Truck manufacturers to use this principle included Chase and Brockway.

[42] The Paige-Detroit Motor Car Company first showed its offerings at the New York Auto Show during the first week of January 1910. Its display at the show featured the three-cylinder chassis and a single runabout. It was the only two-cycle, three-cylinder motor car shown.

[43] This figure was provided by a later magazine advertisement which featured the signature of Harry M. Jewett. Another source, *Moody's Manual of Investments*, gave the figure as 267. Both documents were created well over a decade after actual production.

[44] The report that Paige had "cracked under the strain" is only found in one reference and cannot be corroborated. An indication that he quickly resumed his business career can be inferred from the fact that by 1912 he had moved to Philadelphia and was the vice president and treasurer of an unnamed firm, probably insurance related. There is evidence that Paige prospered in his post Paige-Detroit career in that he was later listed as a former vice president and treasurer of the Menhaden Fishing Company, in addition to being vice president of the Bird Archer Company. By 1920 he and his family were living in New York City, were he was the president of the Paige and Jones Chemical Company. His success in these new fields of business endeavor are reinforced by his membership in the prestigious Sound Beach Golf and Country Club and the Belle Haven Beach Club (Greenwich, Connecticut).

[45] It is interesting to note Harry Jewett was not a majority stockholder. Fred Paige held the most stock with 200 shares, Andrew Bachle tallied 100, and Gilbert Lee had 75, as did Willis Buhl. Sherman Depew held 80 shares and E. P. Stair owned 70. Those owning 50 shares of Paige-Detroit stock were Charles Hodges, Alexander McPherson, Charles Warren, Edward Jewett, and Harry M. Jewett. Twenty shares were owned by William Cady, and 15 shares each were held by David Clay and Fred Aiken.

At that same meeting, Willis Buhl was elected vice president; William Cady, secretary; and Gilbert Lee, treasurer.

[46] Jewett's eldest brother, Fred, was also now a member of the coal firm.

[47] Andrew Bachle was retained as chief engineer.

[48] James F. Bourquin was made general manager. Bourquin was a former superintendent at the Chalmers Motor Car Company and was a qualified and competent automobile man.

[49] Even though the three-cylinder engine had been abandoned for all practical purposes, it was still available from the factory upon request. A sales booklet explaining the 1911 model year offerings notes that "...we shall continue to make Paige-Detroit two-cycle motors and furnish this type of power plant to any of our cars. We firmly believe in the efficiency and future of this type of motor, but we have been forced by the larger demand for the four-cycle type to make this our leader. Many manufacturers of four-cycle motors are now experimenting with the two-cycle and we thoroughly believe that it will be eventually used in many cars." Contradictory as this may sound, the booklet went on to explain, "Owing to the slight attention which has been given by automobile engineers, in general, to this type, it has not reached the degree of efficiency that the four-cycle has, except in the Paige-Detroit."

[50] The top was still an option.

[51] It, too, was described as a "Physician's Car" in factory literature.

[52] *The Horseless Age* described the use of electric head and side lamps as "scintillating."

[53] *Cycle and Automobile Trade Journal* gave the 1911 Paige a complete writeup in its September 1910 number. At the conclusion of its recitation of mechanical features, the article ended with paragraphs titled "On the Road." The reviewer, identified only as S. L. G., said,

"Recently the writer was permitted to ascertain at first hand what the Paige-Detroit can accomplish when on the road under trying conditions. With W. C. Kron (sic), of the Detroit Motor Sales Company, local distributor of the Paige-Detroit, at the wheel, the car was headed out into the country for Clarkston, thirty-eight miles away as the objective point. As it was not a case of establishing a speed record, for the trip was purely for pleasure, the distance was negotiated in two hours and five minutes. From Detroit to Pontiac, twenty-six miles, the road was in fair condition, although a portion of the way considerable sand was encountered, and there were several good hills to negotiate. From Pontiac on there was little but sand and hills, the road being of a nature calculated to test the most thorough manner the staying qualities of a car. Indeed, if one was to judge by the number of machines that were having trouble of one sort or another along the way, the course was living up to its fondest hopes. Only twice on the way was it found advisable to shift from high speed, this being in negotiating two particularly bad hills. Absolutely no trouble was experienced, and the car seemed at all times to have plenty of power in reserve, although heavier machines came to grief. The next day the return trip was made in a little more leisurely manner, and with equally satisfactory results. No exact record of the fuel consumed was kept, but a little less than five gallons was required for the round trip, including a limited use of the car while at Clarkston."

[54] By the end of 1910 Harry M. Jewett owned 100 shares, and by the end of 1913 he held 150 shares.

[55] The Lozier was first exhibited at the fifth annual auto show at Madison Square Garden in January of 1905. Development of the vehicle had begun in 1904.

[56] According to the Standard Catalog of American Cars 1805-1942: "The Lozier prowess in racing was not because it was the biggest and fastest; it was neither of those, but there was no car anywhere that had its stamina and durability. If anything ever broke on a Lozier, it was a major news story."

[57] Lee, Warren, Paige, Hodges, Stair, Willis, Buhl, Depew, and the Jewetts sat on both boards.

[58] Having established himself financially, Jewett became involved in the upper levels of Detroit society. In addition to organizations for which his profession demanded his membership (the Automobile Board of Trade, Detroit Board of Commerce, and the Appalachian Engineers' Society), he also maintained membership in the Detroit Country Club, the Detroit Athletic Club, The Grosse Pointe Riding and Hunt Club, the Yondotega Club, the Turtle Lake Club, and the New York Yacht Club. He was also a Mason and a registered Republican. He made his home in upscale Grosse Pointe Shores, Michigan, and had offices in the prestigious Penobscot Building and at the Paige-Detroit plant.

[59] The concept of "conspicuous production" is extremely well detailed and explained in a volume of the same name by Donald Finlay Davis (Temple University Press, Philadelphia, 1988). It is recommended reading.

[60] Only the four-cylinder engines were offered. Paige-Detroit was never again to offer a three-cylinder power plant. However, automobile design seems to have gone full cycle.

Saab used a three-cylinder engine from 1956 through 1967. Their model 93 GT roadster was capable of over 100 mph, and was the winner in the R.A.C. rallies in 1960, 1961, and 1962, and the Monte Carlo rallies in 1962 and 1963.

In 1991 an illustrated 111-page book titled, *Two Stroke Engine Design and Development*, was published for automotive engineers. The book dealt with fuels, flow, fuel injection, and related topics. The book's thesis could be summed up, and was advertised as, "Possibly the engine of the future for the auto industry."

The Geo Metro, a product of the Chevrolet Division of General Motors from the 1990-1997 model years, featured a three-cylinder engine on some models. A single overhead cam engine, this three-in-line design displaced one liter (61 cubic inches). It featured a bore and stroke of 2.91 inches by 3.03 inches and was rated at 49 horsepower at 4,700 XFi. The motor had a compression ratio of 9.5:1 and utilized electronic fuel injection.

Prior to its use in the Geo Metro, Chevrolet used the same engine in the Chevrolet Sprint beginning in 1985.

[61] The line was first shown at the annual New York Auto Show. From January 1-17, 1912, the Paige models could be seen at the Grand Central Palace. During the Chicago show later in the month, the cars were introduced at the Hotel La Salle.

[62] One example of the parallel corporate direction was model nomenclature. Sophisticated names used by Lozier included: Briarcliff, Lakewood, Riverside, Meadowbrook, Montclair, Fairmont, and Touraine.

[63] These 1911/12 models were considered "Model 25" and all rode on a 104-inch wheelbase. Improvements included a self starter as standard equipment, as was a cork insert, multiple disc clutch. All models carried Delco ignition equipment.

[64] The first Paige shipped abroad was a touring car sold in Antwerp, Belgium.

[65] Two million dollars in March of 1913.

[66] The reorganization which saw Harry M. Jewett vacate the presidency was in May of 1913.

[67] Emphasis in most advertising was directed at these fast-selling touring cars. In 1917, one magazine ad delineated the prices of each of the open cars available and then added, "A complete line of closed cars is also available."

[68] The "Model 25" body styles continued to be available, at $50 off the 1912 prices.

[69] The industry did not see a nationwide trend to closed cars until the new decade. The ratio of closed to open cars produced by the Paige-Detroit Motor Car Company is telling, and indicative of the entire industry. In calendar 1922, with a work force of 2,101, Paige-Detroit manufactured 21,916 open cars and 7,826 closed cars. The next year, 26,302 open cars were produced by Paige's 2,429 employees as compared to 16,565 closed cars. The actual turning point came in 1924 for Paige when 1,984 men produced 22,305 closed cars and only 12,356 open cars. Calendar 1925 saw that ratio expanded even more when 2,332 Paige employees produced 33,478 closed automobiles to only 5,024 open styles. During 1926 a reduced work force (1,711 men) produced 35,812 closed cars to 1,248 open cars.

[70] Advertising over the next few years gave the address as: 224-258 21st Street, 225-235 21st Street, 21st and Baker Streets, 303 21st Street, 262 21st Street, 220-260 21st Street, and 240-250 21st Street.

[71] The building was erected on McKinstry Street, between West Fort Street and the tracks of the Wabash and Pere Marquette railroads. This was near the Detroit River, within a block of the huge Timken factory, and close to one of the Studebaker assembly plants.

[72] Although a great many more parts were able to be manufactured in the new plant, the engines and transmissions were made elsewhere "under the plant's supervision." Paige would not produce its own engine until 1920.

[73] The land purchased for the plant was 900 feet long by 170 feet wide. The main building was 406 feet long and 60 feet wide, four stories in height, giving a total working area of 2.5 acres under one roof. The storage and stock building was of three stories, 94 feet by 94 feet, and had its own power plant. The executive offices were on the second floor of the main building, and were made up of 16 departments.

[74] The front of the factory, facing the west, utilized ribbed glass to lessen the sun's glare. The east side of the plant featured plain glass panes.

[75] The new plant was not totally functional and at capacity until February of 1914. *The Automobile* commented that "not a single car was held up in production by the change." Increased production was immediate. January, February, March, and April of 1913 showed totals of 124, 213, 354, and 504 motor cars being produced in the old factories. Corresponding totals for 1914 in the new factory totaled 329, 459, 807, and 1,223, respectively. This represented an increase of over 136%.

[76] Total employment numbered 513.

[77] Later in the year a service department was established at Lafayette Boulevard and Twelfth Street.

[78] Although Paige-Detroit was not a pioneer in the six-cylinder field, it was an early entry. The other builders of six-cylinder automobiles in 1914 were prestigious makes: Pierce-Arrow, Packard, Marmon, Buick, Reo, Studebaker, Hudson, and Franklin.

[79] The Paige-Detroit Motor Car Company displays at these shows featured five automobiles. Touring cars and runabouts were featured, but the stand did include a coupe, and a specially prepared speedster. The traditional Paige color was dark blue with black chassis; the streamlined speedster body was done in a light green and was accentuated by a highly V'ed radiator.

[80] In addition to the automobiles on display at the Paige-Detroit stand, there was a novelty which would become a Paige-Detroit tradition over the years. A completed chassis was split lengthwise from bumper to bumper. Exposed by this center cut, the internal workings of the engine, transmission, differential, and all other parts could clearly be seen. Electric motors moved the pistons and other mechanical parts to illustrate their operation. This split chassis concept was used for more than a decade by Paige-Detroit at the shows.

[81] Paige automobiles were regularly shown at the European shows, and there is some evidence they were also raced and entered in reliability tours.

The Paige-Detroit Motor Car Company

[82] The basic design would serve the company until its final automobiles came off the assembly line in 1927. Although the design was used first in 1914, it was not registered with the United States Patent Office until October of 1918.

[83] In May of 1914 the company was able to proudly announce that "Paige-Detroit Motor Car Company has a small capitalization. It does not have to earn dividends on watered-down stock. It has no indebtedness, hence no interest charges to pay. Demand has always been in excess of production. When you buy a Paige you buy only the car."

[84] There were actually four conveyors, or assembly lines, installed. The first was a frame line, 735 feet long with a load capacity of 75 tons. At 18 inches per minute, its capacity was 150 completed cars in a 10-hour shift. A return truck conveyor was 760 feet long and was moved at 20 feet per minute. The oven conveyor was actually three units, each with a length of 134 feet, a width of 18 feet, and height of 6 feet. The oven reached a temperature of 180 degrees Fahrenheit by means of steam. The oven conveyors had a speed of 24 inches per minute. The double body conveyors were 350 feet in length and were rated at 10 feet per minute.

[85] The July 20, 1916, issue of *The Automobile* magazine commented on the body drop technique of Paige-Detroit, "Paige might be mentioned as a good example of the method where the wheels are applied half [of the] way [through] the assembly journey and carry the car on to the end. An electric hoist picks the chassis, sans wheels, from the truck, lowers it to a wheel-attaching platform, and after these are in place, drops it through a chute to the floor below where the vehicle begins the last part of its journey on its own tires."

[86] The most progressive manufacturing methods were utilized. The third floor of the main building at the plant was used for the painting and assembling of frames and wheels. The frames were riveted there, and placed on a cable conveyor which carried them to a huge tank where they were cleaned with gasoline and given one coat of paint. The conveyor brought them to the heating ovens for 110 minutes. A second coat was applied and they proceeded to the next set of ovens. Each frame received three coats of paint, at which point the fully assembled wheels were attached to the frame. A chute at the end of the building was used to lift the frames to the floor above where the various components were added. The fourth floor conveyor was a double track system, one for each series of Paige automobiles. The tracks ran through the center of the building, with stock booths arranged on the walls so workmen were within a few steps of their work. The winter tops, special paint, and equipment departments were on second floor, while the entire first floor was devoted to machine work, block testing, and the adjustment of engines. The

engine block testing room was 125 feet long, and the blocks were suspended on an overhead cable on which they entered and exited. About 150 engines were tested each day.

[87] Another source lists 7,743 as the total.

[88] This figure was increased in later advertising to 175 completed cars in each work day. A working day was considered ten hours at this time.

[89] Total sales for 1915 were tallied at $7,471,033.37, allowing a net income available for dividends of $609,775.87. Authorized capitalization was increased to a half million dollars. The stock was listed on Wall Street, but no shares were ever offered for sale. The 18 shareholders were not interested in selling a stock as productive as Paige-Detroit.

[90] The monthly dividend to Paige-Detroit stockholders for July totaled 10%. Because of the fact that dividends had grown exceeding large by the company's prosperity, it was decided at the August 3, 1915, meeting to increase the capitalization from $250,000 to $1 million. In 1915, 18 stockholders owned the company in its entirety. The majority stockholders, owning between 100 and 150 shares each included H. M. Jewett, Charles B. Warren, Gilbert W. Lee, William B. Cady, Willis E. Buhl, Charles H. Hodges, and M. Augusta Hartnell. Those possessing from 15 to 85 shares included E. H. Jewett, Emma F. Jewett, and F. L. Jewett, Andrew Bachle, F. M. Aiken, David D. Cady, E. D. Stair, Grace E. Stair, Sherman I. Depew, Hazel Pingree Depew, and James F. Bourquin. That meeting also saw the authorization of the distribution of $250,000 par value of the new stock pro rata among the company's stockholders in the form of a 100% stock dividend, and transferred $250,000 from the surplus amount to capital stock.

[91] The small six was supplied by Rutenber and the large six was supplied by Continental.

[92] Private owners were not the only purchasers of the fast-selling Paige automobiles. In December of 1915, the Detroit Fire Department purchased a touring car, followed by a sedan in April of 1916. The Detroit Fire Department also purchased a Paige roadster in December of 1917, and in October of that year, a sedan. The tradition of fire department purchases continued following the creation of Graham-Paige Motors Corporation, with a sedan added to the department's livery in February of 1929 and a Special Coupe in 1931.

[93] In a sales brochure written to tout its "enclosed" models for winter driving, the company again emphasized the female buyer's viewpoint. In addressing the limousine and town car models, the text read: "To the American woman especially, with her love of comfort and demand for every available con-

venience, Paige enclosed models will make a compelling appeal. The interior of the Limousine and Town Car possess those various little feminine trinkets so indispensable to the heart of the woman of to-day. There are panel mirrors so ingeniously hung that Milady may see herself almost full length; there are toilet requisites, note books for social or business memoranda. There are charming silk curtains for the rear and side windows; there are large dome lights and rear quarter lights to permit reading or visiting during the drive. There is an automatic step light to guard against the possibility of mis-step on the darkest nights."

[94] The Springfield Body Company of Springfield, Massachusetts, was a successful body supplier to not only Paige but also Abbott-Detroit, Cadillac, Cole, Davis, Haynes, Interstate, Marmon, Mitchell, Oldsmobile, Overland, H.A.L., Reo, Sterns, Studebaker, Velie, Wescott, and Winton. Hinsdale Smith was the company's president and chief designer. On August 26, 1916, the company reported the previous 12 months had seen an increase in orders of over 1,000%. The plant was later taken over as the custom body firm which supplied the Rolls-Royce Company of America.

[95] Total sales for the first ten months of the year were $9,899,790.48, with a net income available for dividends of $964,442.21.

[96] Dealers and distributors also entered endurance contests. On September 6, 1916, a Paige-Detroit roadster began a transcontinental run from New York City to San Francisco, via the Lincoln Highway. Four drivers were to navigate the roadster, with Joseph Nickrent and Robert Evans beginning the contest. The contest was sanctioned by the Automobile Club of America.

Although not directly involved, the company did not discourage stunts either. That same year a Paige Six-46 was driven to an altitude of 9,500 feet on the face of Mount Hood in Oregon. Driven on latticed boards over the snow, sometimes at grades approaching 40%, the attempt to go even higher was ended only because of a sudden blizzard at that height. Magazines covered the feat and Paige-Detroit later issued a sales brochure touting the qualities of such a car.

[97] The route of the race, beginning in Douglas and ending in Phoenix, included Bisbee, Tombstone, and Tucson. It was not a direct route.

[98] Cord had done other racing, and his stint as a salesman at the Phoenix dealership (Smith Brothers) was one of many automobile-related jobs prior to his finding success at Moon Motor Car Company dealership in Chicago. The total elapsed

time for the race was eight hours and 12 minutes according to *The Arizona Republican* (newspaper). The Paige was "absolutely a stock model, with special gears, privately entered by its owner." According to the newspaper, "The finish line was in front of the Phoenix Fair Grounds and, when the Paige arrived, its driver was so caked with alkali that Helen [his wife], who was in the stands, did not recognize her husband and panicked. Leaving little Charlie [their son] in friends' care she rushed to the Paige. She was almost delirious with joy to discover that the spectre at the wheel, and the overall winner, was her man."

[99] The seven-passenger sedan was offered at $1,900, the three-passenger cabriolet sold for $1,600, the seven-passenger town car was available for $2,250, the seven-passenger Fairfield touring car carried an asking price of only $1,295, and the basic three-passenger coupe was available for $1,700. The automobiles were basically unchanged from the previous year's design.

[100] The Fleetwood Six-38 replaced the slow-selling Hollywood.

[101] The list price was $1,050.

[102] *Automobile Trade Journal* commented, "The cowl of the Paige Larchmont model contains three large compartments and a light located in the center. ...the light is operated by push buttons located on the right side of the lamp on the metal plate, and the three compartments are fitted with locks." The illustration showed that in reality they were actually what we would today call "glove boxes."

[103] Although Paige was a leader in this type body style, there were other marques which introduced their own version of the "convertible" during the model year. Those manufacturers included Hudson (on the Super Six Touring Sedan), the Maxwell (on the Sedan), Chandler (on the Springfield Sedan), Chalmers (on the Six-39 Touring Sedan), Cole-Springfield (on the Toursedan), Willys-Knight (on the Touring Sedan), Cadillac (on the Open Sedan), Studebaker (on the Convertible Sedan), Inter-State (on the Touring Sedan), Westcott (on the Springfield Touring Sedan), and Haynes (on the Light Six Touring).

[104] In 1917 Wilson was the second largest body supplier in the nation. Employing 1800 men, the Detroit company had a capacity of 500 bodies a day. The firm's major customers included Ford, Hupp, Liberty, Oakland, Premier, and, of course, Paige-Detroit.

[105] A modern description of this type body would be "hardtop."

[106] Sales were not confined to the United States. For example, the Paige-Detroit dealer in Tokyo, Japan, was Fujiwara Shokai. He also sold Packard and Chevrolet.

[107] The *Nandoma*, formerly known as the *Friendship*, was a wooden hulled ketch designed by Harry L. Friend. Built by W. I. Adams & Sons of East Boothbay, Maine, it was launched in 1910. The brigantine had a four-stroke eight-cylinder (6 1/2 x 8) Sterling engine installed in 1913. Jewett was a member of both the Detroit Yacht Club and the Grosse Pointe Yacht Club. During the 1920s the *Nandoma* was replaced by a yacht approximately 25 feet longer, the *Tramp*.

[108] Taken from "The Idea Behind Grousehaven," published in 1928.

[109] An early riser, Jewett enjoyed training his hunting pups prior to breakfast.

[110] Six dealers increased their sales by over 200%. Nearly all 1,500 dealers recorded increases in total sales.

[111] In the 6-55 series, the sedan was priced at $2,850, as was the coupe. The limousine and town car were both priced at $3,230, and the 6-39 sedan was $1,925. The Brooklands model was priced $20 more than the Essex, which was a $1,775 vehicle. The Linwood and the Dartmoor were both priced at $1,330, as was the Glendale. The "39" winter top, an emphasized accessory, was $198.50 installed at the factory, or $230 shipped separately.

[112] Sales abroad had been steadily increasing, and in 1918 Paige-Detroit published a sales brochure with French text.

[113] A later report indicated two buildings had been erected for truck manufacture.

[114] National and Premier, both of Indianapolis, and Hudson of Detroit were also licensed to produce the Nash Quad for the government. Hudson was also requested to produce 2,000 trucks by the end of April, 1918. Nash freely contributed all the necessary blueprints and patent rights.

[115] A building formerly occupied by the Williams Pickle factory was leased for development and eventual production.

[116] According to the Standard Catalog of Light Duty Trucks,

Starting with a 1 1/2 ton truck, this firm made its 3/4 ton light-duty available in 1914 at $1,350 for the chassis. Four one tons, the D, DL, F, and FL were marketed in 1915 at between $1,400 and $1,700. The FS-F, of 1917, was a $1,700 one ton with a choice of a 10

or 12 foot chassis. Also available concurrently, was the FL one ton, having a 14 foot chassis and $1,775 price tag. A one ton "F" returned to the line in 1920. It had a 4 1/8 x 5 1/4 inch Continental four cylinder engine that produced 27.23 horsepower and scaled in at 4,500 pounds. Also available was the lighter (3,575 pound Model NF, which used the same engine. Both were carried over into 1921. The following season, the NF got a new 22.50 horsepower engine of 3 1/2 x 5 inch bore and stroke, which remained available in 1923.

[117] C. P. King and W. K. Hoagland, voting trustees of the Paige-Detroit Motor Car Company, offered a cash buyout to stockholders of Signal. A price of $106 and accrued dividends was tendered to the owners of preferred stock, with the value of common stock to be determined at the time of the sale.

Signal Motor Truck Company was evidently having financial problems at the time. The press reported that following the rejection of the Paige-Detroit Motor Car Company offer,

"The Signal stockholders agreed to decrease the par value of their stock from $10 to $5 and each stockholder will be entitled to one share so reduced in par value for each share now held by such stockholders. A local stock broker will supply the credit for the funds required to carry on the business for which Signal will give him long time notes."

In 1924 the Signal Motor Truck Company ceased to exist.

[118] Development of the truck continued and it was ready for manufacture well before actual production began. During the war the federal government ruled that a moratorium be observed concerning the start-up of any new projects in the automotive and truck manufacturing industries.

Just as Paige-Detroit had done, other automobile manufacturers (Oakland, Willys-Overland, Olds, Briscoe, and Columbia) sought to supplement dwindling passenger car production by manufacturing trucks. They, too, simply froze their truck manufacturing plans until the government approved resumption of production.

[119] The War Industries Board was put in charge of the transition of the automobile industry to war mobilization. It wasn't until late 1918 until restrictions of any type were put on automobile manufacturers. It was determined in late 1918 that production should be one half of what it was in the corresponding month of 1917. The board's mandate was achieved in that passenger car production for 1918 totaled only 925,388 as compared to the 1917 total of 1,740,972. Most historians maintain this decrease in production was due as much to material and labor shortages as to formal government intervention.

[120] The federal government continued to allow automobile firms to assemble existing stock, with the understanding that assembly would cease when that stock was exhausted.

[121] On the 28th of September 1918 *Motor Age* noted that "The Paige-Detroit Company is fast approaching the 100% war business. In a few weeks all the resources of the company will be devoted exclusively to Government service. When the company has used its present supply of materials it will make no more passenger cars."

[122] Production would cease when automotive materials on hand were exhausted. Of course, production totals for 1918 were substantially less, amounting to 8,898 vehicles for the year.

[123] It is interesting to note that in addition to the traditional, and famous, Paige split chassis (from an Essex 55 model) being shown at the show, was a Paige-Detroit touring car with headlight lenses which were V-shaped with one side of the "V" being frosted so

...direct light was thrown to the right and a diffused light to the left, thus removing the glare from approaching drivers but giving a brilliant light at the side of the roadway, where it is needed.

Another improvement concerned the rear window treatment. The traditional five small windows of isinglass were replaced with beveled plate glass in metal frames.

[124] Capacity prior to the improvement was 125 cars and 50 trucks daily. Expected capacity was to be 175 cars and 75 trucks daily. Because of a shortage of materials, truck production dipped to three to ten trucks per day.

[125] Because of that lack of materials, only 60 to 75 cars per day were produced (capacity was approximately 125 automobiles).

[126] A note in the "Factory News and Capital Increases" section of the *Automobile Trade Journal* of June 1918 noted that,

...two new units, which will provide space for the new truck department which the company has established, and will increase by one-half the space of the executive building.

[127] The wheels were wooden, with square hickory spokes.

[128] S. A. E. rating.

[129] Bore and stroke were 4 1/8 x 5 1/4 inches.

[130] Carburetion was by Stromberg, ignition was provided by Bosch, a Pierce governor was used, and Timken manufactured the rear axle (worm type) and the bearings throughout. The chassis weighed 5,200 pounds.

[131] Later, "dash lights" were available as an option. Mounted on the cowl, these lights were used in the manner of head lamps.

[132] The announcement also noted,

At present the Paige plant is devoted almost entirely to Government work, and few passenger cars are coming through.

The delay in production since the introduction in spring was attributed to the fact that,

The company has been building Government trucks for more than a year, which has delayed its entry into the market.

A study of serial numbers given to the 1918 chassis indicate that no more than 400 units could have been produced (10000 to 10400).

[133] One truck industry journal said of the Paige chassis, [that] "in every respect, it conforms to standard practice."

[134] The SAE rating for the engine was 32.4. Bore was 4 1/2 and stroke was 5 1/2. The Continental engine was the E-7.

[135] Bore and stoke for the four-cylinder engine was 4 1/2 by 5 1/2 inches. The smaller 2-ton chassis had engine dimensions of 4 1/8 by 5 1/4 inches. The larger chassis weighed 7,000 pounds.

[136] The call of the open road and the desire to modify stock vehicles was strong even in 1920. *Motor Life* magazine showed a photo of a 1920 Paige truck which had been modified by a Mr. G. L. Price of Knoxville, Tennessee. Built in the manner of a touring bus, Mr. Price anticipated modern motor homes by constructing a steel-bodied vehicle which featured eight Pullman-like chairs (converting into upper and lower berths at night), a kitchenette, dining compartment, running water, shower bath, and electric lights. The magazine described the vehicle as a "portable palace."

[137] Actual construction of the Paige trucks was at the Paige-Detroit engine plant, not the McKinstry Street site.

[138] The author and most historians believe that production ended during calendar 1922. Only 137 trucks were manufactured during that year. There is no proof any trucks were actually assembled after the latter part of 1922.

[139] This logo, or phrase, was used on all Paige truck advertising but it was never explained or expanded upon in the text of that advertising. Except for the rationale for increased use of trucks on America's highways and the specifications of the models produced, no special "serviceability" of Paige trucks was pointed out. From extant data, it appears the trucks were conventional in every manner, and no extraordinary engineering or designs were used.

[140] The Larchmont touring sold for $2,165, the four-passenger coupe was $2,950, as was the seven-passenger sedan.

[141] Advertising continued to point out this fact. There was no corporate debt, except for "current billings."

[142] The 6-42 series carried their models on a 119-inch wheelbase. The Glenbrook touring, two-passenger Lenox roadster, sedan and coupe were continued almost unchanged, with held over prices. The only new model offered was the four-passenger Ardmore "sport" touring car. On both series Remy electrical equipment was now standard.

[143] Advertising nomenclature used both "Six-Sixty Six" and "6-66."

[144] A Continental Model 8A was used, displacing 331 cubic inches.

[145] It is believed by most historians that the Daytona which broke the existing world's records had a specially prepared engine, and the production Daytona had a detuned, production engine. All information from the factory indicates the chassis was a stock chassis (thus the stock chassis world's records) and the prototype was simply stripped of fenders and unneeded equipment. It was claimed that the production Daytona model would exceed 80 miles per hour "fully equipped."

[146] The categories, time, and speeds were as follows:

5 miles	3:15	91.8 mph
10 miles	6:31	91.9 mph
15 miles	9:45	92.1 mph
20 miles	13:01	92.1 mph
25 miles	16:37	90.1 mph
50 miles	33:16	90.1 mph
75 miles	50:00	89.9 mph
100 miles	66:53	89.7 mph
One hour		89.0 mph

[147] The factory encouraged dealers and owners to engage in hill climbs and contests nationwide. The Pike's Peak exhibition was a climb over nine miles of track used by the Pike's

Peak Cog Railroad. It was noted that "four of the miles have a grade of 25% and more than three miles have a grade of better than 20%. The half mile at the summit varies from 25% to 28%." The Paige used by Mulford was the Lakewood model. No other automobile had ever made this climb, and it was believed to be the longest, steepest, highest climb ever made by an automobile. Other hill climbing exhibitions included Corey Hill in Boston, Scarboro Hill in Toronto, Ensign Peak in Salt Lake City, Pacific Avenue Hill in San Francisco, South Monroe Hill in Spokane, Miller Avenue Hill in Brooklyn, Lookout Mountain and Ruby Hill near Denver, Camp Baldy at Pomona, California, the Pali Road near Honolulu, and the Continental Divide at Raton Pass, New Mexico. Following the 102.8 miles per hour record at Daytona, the factory issued a challenge to any stock car at any price to compete. The demonstrations were to include hill climbs (in high gear), slow hill climb (in high gear), acceleration, five to 50 miles (high gear), and speed on a straight away.

[148] Frederick Jewett became vice president in 1921.

[149] The company's success had allowed them to accumulate assets totalling $9,224,354.

[150] The trend toward companion cars was not to end with Hudson and Paige-Detroit. In 1925 Nash introduced the Ajax, in 1926 Oakland brought out the Pontiac, in 1927 Overland began production of the Whippet. That same year saw Reo introduce the Wolverine, Cadillac brought out the LaSalle, and Studebaker produced the Erskine for the first time. Later Marmon was to experiment with an eight-cylinder car in the $1,000 range called the Roosevelt. In 1930 Buick followed suit and introduced the Marquette. All of these automobiles were attempts to succeed in a less-expensive market niche.

The only attempt at a parent company attempting to introduce a more expensive "companion car" was that of Oldsmobile's introduction of the Viking. The make lasted only two model years (1929-30).

The last attempt of a companion make in the early thirties was that of Nash's introduction of the LaFayette. Some historians consider the LaFayette simply an additional Nash model; others considered it a companion car.

[151] Paige-Detroit's imminent entry into mass production was indeed radically different from previous policy. In a magazine ad for the Brunswick model in 1912, the company stated:

We take time to build the Paige right. There is a rule against rushing work in the Paige plant. It is a fixed established rule, and every Paige workman obeys it. He wouldn't take the risk of breaking it. This Paige factory rule means a whole lot to you if you are buying

an automobile. We will build only 3,500 Paige cars this year. We could turn out three times that number if we were willing to rush things—if we were willing to build them haphazardly. We take the time to build Paige cars right.

[152] This was done during the annual New York Auto Show.

[153] The Jewett Motor Carriage Company of Jewett, Ohio, (1922-27) was not associated with Harry Jewett's automobile firm in any manner.

[154] Advertising claimed that the power plant was a proven success in that it had been utilized in 110,000 Paige automobiles since 1917 and had provided over 2 billion miles of customer satisfaction.

[155] Initially, Widman was contracted to only supply the open car bodies. Widman also listed as its customers Chalmers, Franklin, and Earl.

[156] Only 186 Jewett automobiles were produced in March of 1922.

[157] Production for both the Paige and Jewett amounted to 29,892.

[158] Production for calendar 1923, according to Jerry Heasley's "Production Figure Book For U.S. Cars" was 25,900. Nineteen-twenty four production totals showed an increase of 1,762 over that 1921 total.

[159] Production for both nameplates totaled 43,556 for calendar 1923.

[160] The management and board of directors remained exceptionally consistent throughout the life of the company. Of course, the Jewett brothers themselves continued in positions of authority, and Andrew Bachle continued to be vice-president of engineering. The death of Willis E. Buhl created the only vacancy on the board. It was quickly filled in 1916 by Jerome H. Remick, a music publisher and president of the Detroit Creamery Company.

Edward H. Jewett continued on the board and his brother, Frederick L. Jewett, was first vice-president.

Many employees had been with the company for nearly its entire tenure. Those in management included Bachle, Henry Krohn (vice-president of the sales division since 1910), Thomas Bradley (vice-president in charge of purchasing since 1910), W. A. Wheeler (vice-president in charge of production since 1914), George Peterson, G. Clark Mather (both engineers were coworkers of Bachle for a decade prior to the formation of Paige), B. C. Young (assistant treasurer since

1911), John Germonprez (production engineer since 1913), T. E. Quinlan (factory auditor since 1912), Fred B. Rosenau (superintendent of final testing since 1910), C. F. Huntoon (superintendent of the tool department since 1911), J. H. Connors (superintendent of stock and receiving since 1913), J. W. Mitchell (superintendent of Plant 2, an employee since 1911), F. W. Jenning (director of services since 1911), F. W. Bowen (manager of the technical division since 1913), and William Degalan (assistant service manager since 1911).

[161] In May of 1923 press releases were given all the motoring journals reporting the notice of discontinuation of the Paige truck. The official reason given was the rapidly increasing demand for Paige and Jewett automobiles. Harry Jewett was quoted as saying,

This will enable the company to devote all its facilities to passenger car production. Despite extensive additions to factory floor space in the past year, it was found impossible to satisfy the demands of the Paige-Jewett dealers, although the Paige plant has been working to capacity all winter. The present move is expected to offer material relief. The company's service department will continue to service all Paige trucks as in the past.

Automotive Industries magazine noted,

When the passenger car business became brisk again in 1920 there was a let-up in truck activities and since that time not many Paige trucks have been produced, the company centering its activities on passenger car production.

Motor Age magazine reported,

Truck construction was formerly carried on in a part of the engine plant now devoted exclusively to building Jewett motors. The truck material was sold to individual buyers.

[162] Or Hinkley, as both spellings have been used. The Hinckley Motors Corporation built engines for the federal government during World War I. Begun in 1914, the corporation was founded by Carl C. Hinckley, former chief engineer for Chandler and Oldsmobile. Although automobile production was contemplated, according to the Standard Catalog of American Cars, no vehicles were produced. Following the sale of the factory to Paige-Detroit, the enterprise was dissolved and Hinckley joined the Buda (motor) Company.

[163] Kahn first came to the forefront of plant design in the automotive industry when he designed Packard Building Number 10 in Detroit. Although he had built several conventional buildings prior to this time for Packard, this 1905 construction was one of the first to use reinforced concrete.

In 1906 he constructed a large plant for the George N. Pierce Company in Buffalo. The Ford Highland Park facility followed in 1909. Hundreds of factories designed by Kahn followed, including the River Rouge plant for Ford, the Hamtramck plant for Dodge, Hudson's main assembly plant, Buick, and the GM (Durant) Building on Grand Boulevard in Detroit. He also designed homes for several automobile magnates, including Horace Dodge.

[164] The sawtooth design was intended to increase the availability of natural light. This natural light was much favored by the labor force in that it was a great deal less stressful on the eyes than the artificial lighting of the day.

[165] The new factory boasted of having the only overhead frame painting and drying ovens in the industry. This allowed the floor space below to be utilized for other manufacturing purposes.

[166] The loading docks were reported to be able to accommodate 100 freight cars at a time.

[167] The factory referred to this plant in internal publications as Plant 2. The McKinstry Street site was known as Plant 1.

[168] The Hinckley site was used for a time and then sold.

[169] The touring car continued to be offered for $1,065, the sedan was now $1,495, and the coupe $1,250.

[170] The DeLuxe touring car was $1,220 and DeLuxe sedan listed at $1,695. The "Special" roadster was $1,175.
The equipment supplied with the DeLuxe models included: spare tire and cover, front and rear bumpers, rear view mirror, combination stop and tail light, automatic windshield wiper, and heater in all enclosed models.

[171] The racing abilities of the Jewett motorcar were emphasized when the famous Cannonball Baker drove a stock Jewett to second place in the Thanksgiving Day "Hill and Dale" race at Ascot Park in 1924. The 250-mile race was over a five-mile course.

[172] Paige-Detroit had always been proud of its bodies and especially the first class paint jobs they acquired in the factory. Starting in 1918 all Paige automobiles were sprayed with a coating of paraffin before leaving the factory to protect that paint job during shipping. The policy and process continue to this day for some manufacturers.
In 1916 Paige-Detroit became one of the first manufacturers to include a can of "body polish" with the tools and equipment which accompanied each automobile shipped.

[173] Production was overwhelmingly concentrated on the Jewett, with total sales slipping for the two makes to 34,091.

[174] This was not the only wholly owned subsidiary of the Paige-Detroit Motor Car Company. In addition to Jewett Motors, Incorporated, the company had established Paige Sales and Service Company, Detroit; Paige-Detroit Company of New England, Boston; Paige Ohio Company, Cleveland; Paige Company of Northern California, San Francisco; Paige Company of Southern California, Los Angeles; Paige-Jewett Company of Washington, Seattle; Paige-Jewett Company of Texas, Dallas; and Paige Motor Car Company of Oklahoma, Oklahoma City.

[175] The "Special" touring was $1,375. Special versions of the sedan ($1,770), Brougham ($1,550) were also available. The standard version of the touring and roadster were $1,135, the standard version sedan was $1,570, and the standard brougham was $1,410. The three-passenger business coupe was now $1,335.

[176] W. A. Wheeler, a longtime executive, became vice-president in 1925.

[177] This 1922 offering was the first Paige to have a cross bar at the front of the frame horns. Those units produced in the latter half of the year used Timken bearings.

[178] The prices for the 6-44 were basically unchanged. The sedan sold for $2,570, the roadster $1,625, the coupe $2,450, the touring car (seven-passenger) was $1,635, and the Ardmore $1,925. Wheelbase for the 6-44 continued to be 119 inches.

[179] Both makes of motor cars were being built in the McKinstry Street plant at that time.

[180] Many historians consider de Forest the "Father of the Radio."

[181] The plant, encompassing an entire city block, had been used by the Franco-American Food Company since 1897.

[182] These disputes were generally with either Crosley Radio or RCA, and de Forest usually won the legal battles.

[183] In 1929 Dr. de Forest moved his research facilities back to Jersey City, New Jersey. On April 7, 1930, the first broadcast of a television program with simultaneous sound and picture was achieved in that city. Working with the engineers at radio stations WHOM in Jersey City and WRNY of New York, de Forest helped develop the 139-meter wave length transmission of experimental television station W2XER of

Jenkins Radiovisor Company, Jersey City. The event was a tremendously welcomed event with addresses by politicians, entertainment, and a statement by Dr. de Forest, radio pioneer and scientist. About 50 television receivers were placed in schools, clubs, and newspaper offices in the city. At the Lincoln Lodge, a public gathering place and casino, over 200 policemen were dispatched to control the crowd of approximately 20,000 people who had massed to watch the single television screen.

[184] Harry M. Jewett was an investor and silent partner.

[185] Mr. Stair was also the owner of the Detroit Free Press newspaper.

[186] According to an official history of the station: "Apparently, what the program lacked in originality of title, it made up in content, for it became [another] radio success. One of the favorites on the program was a young blind singer, Harold Kean, who was billed as "The Sunshine Boy."

[187] Father Coughlin's first broadcast was on the third Sunday of October, 1926. Controversial even in his hometown, Coughlin garnered huge audiences with his high blown oratory, his anti-New Deal attitude, and anti-Roosevelt rhetoric. The Catholic Church forbade him from further broadcasts in 1946.

[188] Occupied by a succession of businesses since Jewett Radio failed, the manufacturing plant still stands in Pontiac. Although it is in a state of disrepair, the large, dark brick chimney in the rear of the plant features the name Jewett, vertically, in white bricks.

[189] WJR is today one of ABC's flagship stations. A division of Capital Cities/ABC, Inc., it has a format of news/talk/sports and can be found at AM 760.

[190] Jewett's description of vermin included, great horned owls; house cats; stray dogs; crows, goshawks; sharp shinned, cooper, red shoulder hawks; weasels; skunks; mink; gophers; ground squirrels, blue jay; grackle, and wolf. His actions against these animals was the result of their destruction of those game birds which he raised. The exception, of course, is the wolf which he blamed—in conjunction with an unlimited bag and unspecified length season—for the sharp decline in the deer population. It is interesting to note that wolves are at present an endangered and protected species per the federal government.

[191] A brochure for the reserve noted that two of Michigan's finest trout streams, the Au Sable River and its tributaries, along with 10 contained lakes which formed headwaters of

the Rifle River, were at the reserve. The Houghton, Gamble, Fontinalis, and Brown were trout creeks noted for their excellence. The four main lakes-Devoe, North, Loon, and Spring—"are in a nest and abound with brown trout, bass, pike, and perch, with four additional lakes with bass, blue gills, sun fish, calico bass, crappie and rock bass." The remaining lakes were Grebe, Lodge, Scaup, Pintail Pond, Mallard Pond, South Pond, and Devil's Wash Basin, Grousehaven Lake, and Jewett Lake. Jewett Lake is a 12.9-acre lake with a depth of 17 feet.

[192] In 1928 Jewett was able to convince Frederick M. Alger of Detroit to purchase 8,000 acres adjoining Grousehaven. Encouraged by Jewett's success as a private game farm and reserve, Alger vowed to dedicate it to the same purpose.

[193] When Harry Jewett died suddenly in 1933, his heirs lost nearly all their interest in "Grousehaven." Twelve years later it was sold by the Jewett heirs to the State of Michigan Department of Conservation for the give-away price of $75,000. The Department of Conservation used the area as a field laboratory for fish and game research. In 1963 the lands were deeded to the Michigan Parks Division. The lodge was torn down in 1967. The only thing to remain today from the time of "Grousehaven" is the concrete slab which was the foundation for the huge fireplace. At present the reserve, renamed the Rifle River Recreation Area, is comprised of 4,329 acres and ten lakes. There are two modern campgrounds located on Grousehaven Lake which contain over 80 sites, in addition to 101 rustic camping sites. There is also a swimming beach, playground, and boat launch. Hunting and fishing (no boats with motors are allowed on any lake) are popular activities and there are snowmobile trails throughout the wooded areas. Fourteen miles of pathways meander throughout the area for hiking, biking, cross country skiing, and snowshoeing.
When Jewett's widow died on November 16, 1955, it was reported that part of the reserve had been donated to the City of Rose City, and that the family had erected several of the cabins as a contribution. Her obituary also noted,
"In 1948 the Chamber of Commerce [Rose City] planned a monument to Mr. Jewett. They placed a large natural rock at the park entrance and had a bronze plaque made, honoring him, but to date the memorial is incomplete."

[194] The most notable changes were the first time use of automatically adjusted chain drive timing gears and the locating of the spare tire recessed into the running board in back of each front fender. Gauges on the dash were now under a glass oval and the tops of open cars were lined. The brake drums were increased from 14 inches to 15 1/2 inches. During May of 1923, the closed cars featured a double belt line molding.

[195] Continental provided the engine, Model 9A.

[196] A Continental powerplant, Model Special 9A was used.

[197] The only other styling change was the abandonment of the triangular aluminum windshield support previously used. An iron frame was now standard. A four door-brougham was introduced in May, replacing the two-door brougham previously offered.

[198] Most historians acknowledge that Packard, in 1923, was the first volume manufacturer to use four-wheel brakes on production cars. Duesenberg did earlier use four wheel-brakes on its "Model A," but production was limited to very small numbers. Later in 1923 Rickenbacker, Buick, Oakland, and Cadillac used the four-wheel system. When Paige introduced them to their 1924 models they were also in use on Marmon, Chalmers, Elgin, and Locomobile.

[199] An example of the motoring press' reaction to the new Paige models was that of *Automotive Industries*. The trade journal simply dismissed the new Paige models by reporting "the Paige is changed but little."

[200] The engine—Continental Model 10A—featured an L head design, with pressure pump fed lubrication, and four-bearing crankshaft. Remy components were again used for starting and lighting, and Atwater-Kent provided the ignition. Timken axles were used, with Hotchkiss drive. Four wheel Lockheed hydraulic brakes were optional. To allow for the use of balloon tires, a new steering gear was employed. An electric clock on the dash was standard.

[201] The five-passenger Brougham was priced at $2,395, both the seven-passenger and four-passenger phaeton were priced at $2,165, the deluxe sedan was $2,770. The Suburban (limousine) was priced at $2,965. The only difference between the deluxe sedan and the limousine was the sliding glass partition and speaking tube featured on the latter. After July 8, 1925, there was no extra charge for the Lockheed hydraulic braking system. The Brougham was the lowest-priced Paige ever to be offered on the 131-inch wheel base.

[202] Both phaetons were priced at $2,165, the brougham was $2,395, and the limousine was $2,965.

[203] Later in the year they became standard equipment.

[204] During the New York Auto Show. The banquet was held and remarks made at the Blackstone Hotel.

[205] On March 4th a standard brougham was made available for $2,195, which was $30 more than the Paige touring car.

[206] Harry M. Jewett noted in June that "the company has $2,515,000 cash on hand, with no current liabilities except current bills."

[207] On April 1 a 2 1/2% stock dividend was paid to holders of common stock and in July a 10% dividend followed.

[208] According to factory officials, dealers "clamoring for immediate delivery" prompted the increased production. On May 31, 1925, the largest single day production of Paige and Jewett cars was achieved, with 403 automobiles being shipped. This record exceeded the recently set records of 330 on March 7 and 330 on March 14. During the month of May, production totaled 5,841, or 169 more than the existing monthly record (set in March of 1924).

[209] Net pre-tax profit for the six months which ended June 30 were $2,208,094. This was an increase of over $350,000 over the same period in 1924. Total cash assets now amounted to $16,574,087, over $5 million of which was cash. Over 24,000 automobiles were produced during the first six months of 1925.

[210] Both phaetons were priced at $2,165, while the seven-passenger sedan was $2,840.

[211] Factory technical papers referred to this as the Second Series Jewett for 1925. Those produced in the first half of the calendar year were referred to as First Series.

[212] A Hershey coincidental lock.

[213] Ireland and Methews produced the air cleaner.

[214] The deluxe roadster was $1,500, deluxe touring was $1,320, standard coach was $1,245, deluxe coach was $1,400, and deluxe sedan was $1,680. This represented a reduction to five body styles from the previous eight. These remaining models were equipped with Lockheed hydraulic brakes which increased the list price by $40. The sedan and roadster were painted in two tone, while the other body styles were monochromatic except for trim.

[215] It is important to note that Mullins did not supply complete bodies, only selected components. In 1925 Mullins provided body parts for not only Paige and Jewett, but also Chrysler, Cleveland, Cunningham, Franklin, Hupmobile, Jordan, Lincoln, Locomobile, Marmon, Maxwell, Nash, Packard, Peerless, Pierce-Arrow, Reo, Rickenbacker, Stearns-Knight, Wills Sainte Clair, and Willys-Knight.

[216] One reference indicates tenth place.

[217] This plateau was reached with sales totals of 39,479.

The *Paige-Detroit* Motor Car Company

[218] Model 9U.

[219] The piston displacement of the Continental engine was 169 cubic inches, and it developed 40 brake horsepower at 2400 rpms. Maximum torque was tested at 115 pounds at 800 rpm.

[220] The Model 6-70 was discontinued when the Model 6-72 was introduced in January of 1926.

[221] A Paige-produced engine, it displaced 248.9 cubic inches, and had a bore of 3.25 inches and stroke of 5 inches.

[222] One national automotive reporting service described the new automobiles as "...no radical departure from standard practice as designs closely combine those of [the] larger Paige and Jewett.

[223] This derision, regardless of how commonly accepted, ignored the fact that no automobile has ever been produced which had all its components produced in-house. Even the corporate giants used a percentage (although admittedly smaller) of proprietary parts in their automobiles.

[224] Following the stamping of sheet metal body parts or bodies, the metal was prepared for painting. The metal was etched with an acid either by dipping or spraying. The acid cleaned the metal surfaces of all acids, residues, and other foreign compounds. The acid was strong enough to actually eat away at the metal a bit, allowing primer and paint to adhere more completely. Following the acid "bath", the bodies were given a neutralizing bath allowing the bodies to be shipped and/or be painted. This neutralizing bath was achieved by submersion into a compound which resulted in an off white color given to the surfaces.

[225] Central Manufacturing was located in Connorsville, Indiana, and was later acquired by E. L. Cord for Auburn, Cord, and Duesenberg production.

[226] Towson customers included Velie, Davis, and Packard.

[227] A meeting between the creditors and customers of Murray was held with the corporation's officers the first week of December 1925.

[228] The Guardian Trust Company was designated the receiver by the court. Guardian's Chairman of the Board, W. R. Wilson, was the former president of the Maxwell Motors Corporation.

[229] Twenty five per cent of the amount was paid off in cash, with the remainder to be common stock (at $45 a share).

[230] The contract was inked on July 17, and guaranteed Murray would supply Marmon with all its body needs for the next two seasons. It was estimated this would total approximately 75 shells a day. A separate contract, approved by the court also, was the purchase of the Marmon body plant for $200,000.

[231] The Hupp contract, dated August 12, 1926, involved supplying all its body requirements for the next four years.

[232] Receivership ended on November 24, 1926, when the company was sold and renamed.

[233] Total for 1926 was 37,474.

[234] The five-passenger sedan was $1,295, the five-passenger brougham was $100 less, and the five-passenger touring car was listed for $1,150. The asking price for the four-passenger cabriolet roadster was $1,360, and the two-passenger coupe was $1,165.

[235] Bore of 3 1/4 inches, stroke of 5 inches.

[236] The wooden portions of the appointments were walnut stained, not actual walnut.

[237] Although the sales literature shows only disc wheels in its illustrations, they were an extra cost option. Standard wheels were of wood, artillery type. All spares were rear mounted, and all wheels were of the demountable type.

[238] The power plant was considered a 68 horsepower unit at 3,000 rpm. This was five more horsepower than its predecessor.

[239] $505,369.

[240] Perhaps the illness of his brother, Frederick L. Jewett, weighed upon his decision. A business partner nearly from the start, Frederick had been a business associate of his brother beginning in the coal business and later as first vice-president and respected member of the Paige-Detroit management team. Serious illness afflicted him during 1924, and he retired two years later. His death in June of 1928 at New London, Connecticut, affected Harry M. Jewett deeply.

[241] Total production for calendar 1926 was 15,870 vehicles, nearly all produced during the first six months of the year. The loss, the first ever for the company, totaled $185,789.

[242] Dodge acquired 49% of the existing stock, and obtained options on the remaining stock held by the three Graham brothers.

[243] A like figure was realized from options given on the remaining stock held by the Graham brothers.

[244] In April of 1926.

[245] In April of 1926 a reporter at Evansville, Indiana, asked Joseph Graham what the plans were for the three Graham brothers. In an attempt to deter any speculation concerning their business future, he commented that they "would make no definite plans for the immediate future until they had secured a lengthy rest." The "lengthy rest" ploy worked well, as speculation in print subsided for quite some time. This time was used to survey the automobile, and other industries, for investment vehicles. Their involvement in the Libbey holding in the glass industry and the investigation of the motor car industry made these months some of the most intensive in their careers. Incidentally, Joseph Graham was in Evansville to preside over a directors meeting of the Hercules Corporation, of which he was president.

[246] See Chapter Four, endnote #22.

[247] The corporation was based at One East Forty-Fourth Street, New York, New York. *Motor Age* described the corporation as "an investment company similar in set up and purpose to Fischer and Company."

[248] Incorporators were listed as the Graham Brothers Corporation, and the Mutuelle Solvay Bank of Brussels, Belgium, and the investment firms of Lehman Brothers and also Marshall, Field, Glore, Ward and Company.

[249] C. J. Wilcox, James Blair, and C. A. Schmettau.

[250] The holdings consisted of 858 shares of Toledo Glass Company common stock (valued at $9,000 per share), 11,506 shares of Libbey-Owens Sheet Glass Company common stock, and 9,712 shares of preferred stock.

[251] Biggers was later to head Graham-Paige International Corporation and to sit on the Graham-Paige Board of Directors.

[252] Prior to the meeting of the board of directors of the Paige-Detroit Motor Car Company during the first week of 1927, there was no chairman of the board. Harry M. Jewett controlled the company in its totality as president. The directors established that post during that meeting, expressly for the purpose of Jewett's transfer of the presidency to Wheeler.

The Paige Model 8-85 four passenger coupe. (Courtesy of Karl Zahm)

Transition – 1927

Since its inception in 1901, the New York Auto Show had become the most well attended annual event in the motor car industry and the traditional arena for manufacturers to introduce new models. Just as had been done in years past, the new Paige-Detroit offerings were stylishly and proudly shown.[1] However, it was obvious to longtime members of the automobile industry—and the interested public—that the Paige presentations were quite different from those of the past. Not only were the presentations made by the new Paige-Detroit Motor Car Company president, W. A. Wheeler,[2] they included a major departure from past corporate policy: Paige-Detroit would be showing an eight-cylinder motor car.

Dubbed the "Straightaway Eight," this new model is what Harry M. Jewett anticipated would bring the company back to unabashed sales success. Planning for this impressive new vehicle began in mid-1926 when Jewett was still at the helm.

Entry into the eight-cylinder market was achieved by using a 80 horsepower Lycoming (4H) engine displacing 298.6 cubic inches,[3] carried in a 131 1/2-inch wheelbase chassis. The engine was of the "eight in line" L-head type, and featured alloy pistons and Invar struts.[4] This powerful motor was mounted at four points in the chassis by means of rubber cushions, insuring smoothness. A Lanchester vibration dampener insured the same end in the engine itself.

Linked to this impressive power plant was a four-speed transmission specially designed for Paige by the Warner Gear Company.[5] For the first time, Paige-Detroit would be utilizing a four-speed transmission[6] in its motor cars. This "Hy-Flex" transmission was a double drive unit,

> *...by which it is possible to reduce materially the engine speed and fuel consumption, and obtain smoother operation by using the fourth speed for fast driving or along straight level roads.*

Earlier four-speed transmissions were classed as the "over-speed"[7] type. This new four-speed transmission was described in a sales brochure as an under-speed unit, and its advantage explained as having fourth, or direct drive, being a "stepped-up" drive. Internal gears were used, rather than spur gears, reducing friction and noise. According to that catalog,

> *Third speed was through two sets of internal gears built directly into the transmission. This, in effect, gave the drive an additional high speed with a gear ratio suited for hill climbing and fast get away. The most important of the several advantages that result is that you get the*

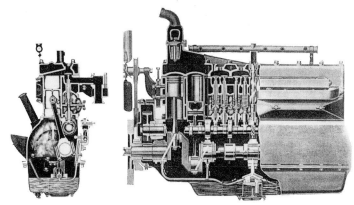

This cutaway drawing illustrates the 80 horsepower, "Eight-In-Line", engine Paige first used in its 1927 models. The powerplant displaced 298.6 cubic inches and was dubbed the Model 4H by Lycoming, the engine's manufacturer.

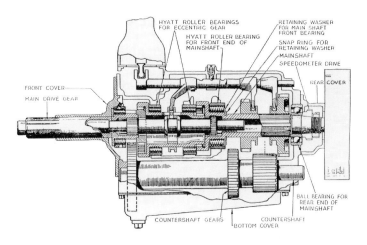

The Warner Hy-Flex four speed transmission (Model T5) was a double drive, under-speed unit.

The Model 6-75 touring car was available for $2295 following the purchase of the firm by the Grahams. The Model 6-75 was the largest of the six cylinder models offered.

same smoothness at high speeds as at normal driving speeds. No wracking from an over-worked engine—no whipping in the propeller shaft—no over-heating—no axle noise.

The "Straightaway Eight" was geared at a 3.69 to 1 ratio, allowing 70 miles per hour in fourth gear.[8] Powerful Lockheed external contracting brakes were used on the "Straightaway Eight," also known as the Model 8-85.

Another feature of the novel chassis design was reported by *Motor Age* in its national show issue. It commented on,

...the unusual feature of the chassis [in] mounting the battery between the engine and the frame on the right side where it is readily accessible.

Placing the battery under the hood was a Paige first, and a feature which was to be copied by virtually all of the automobile industry in only a few years time.

The six body styles presented at the show were virtually the same as those worn on the six-cylinder models appearing first in September. Open cars included the seven-passenger touring car ($2,295) and the cabriolet roadster ($2,655). The five-passenger sedan was the least expensive closed model at $2,355, with the seven-passenger sedan listing at $300 higher. A four-passenger coupe was available for the same price as the cabriolet roadster and a seven-passenger limousine occupied the high end at $2,795.

The reception of this new in-line eight was expected by the Paige chairman and board of directors to be momentous and as encouraging as the Jewett introduction proved to be in 1921. To increase the emphasis on this new flagship model, prices of the slow-selling 6-65 and 6-75 were cut at the time of show.

When the reaction of the press and public became clear, the management of Paige-Detroit Motor Car Company could only be disappointed. The Straightaway Eight was fairly well received on the show floor and was written up in the press in a somewhat positive way, but it was nowhere near what they had expected. The six-cylinder models had been dismissed by the buying public as old cars with pleasant new bodies. When the eight was introduced, the powerplant and transmission did pique the interest of knowledgeable consumers, but it was a buyer's market and there were many fine automobiles in Paige's price range. Too, the bodies that the eight-cylinder motor cars carried were identical to the recently discounted sixes.[9]

It was not an appealing situation. Paige-Detroit and its new president were beginning 1927 in a decidedly weak manner.[10]

Compounding the lukewarm reception the eight was receiving in showrooms around the country were the problems the Warren Avenue production staff was having. The transition to the production of the new eight encountered more than usual technical and production bugs at the plant. Body procurement continued to be a lingering and bothersome problem. Far less than capacity volume was being shipped to distributors from Warren Avenue, and there was an ominous lack of sales for available units. Paige's problems were becoming rather well known, even to those not attuned to the daily activities of the automotive industry.

Interestingly, it was longtime sales manager Henry Krohn—not President Wheeler—who wrote the lead article in the January number of the *Paige Radiator*. In that article he wrote of the company's competition at the New York show and how well Paige compared to competing makes. He allowed, indirectly, that the less than revolutionary changes in Paige bodies was not a major concern in that there were few radical body developments in the industry and,

...the show would be one of...colors—that appointments, fittings, appearance and colors of the bodies would hold precedence over chassis features...In this regard Paige stood up 1000% with the competition.

This five passenger Paige sedan was photographed on the west side of the Warren Avenue plant during the late spring of 1927. (Courtesy of Karl Zahm)

And this was indeed true. New colors now adorned the 1927 Paige models and magazine advertising noted the "20 separate body styles and color combinations," as did other print advertising. The ads and brochures also proclaimed,

There's an air of custom built exclusiveness about this Paige. Its lines suggest speed and outdoor sports — and moonlight drives when Romance rides with two. The smartly shaped, bright finished fabric top and blue and walnut interior give it an atmosphere that is truly Parisian.

The addition of stylish tubular Balcrank bumpers on the cabriolet roadster and coupe was termed "swanky" by Krohn.

Full color ads in the *Ladies Home Journal* appealed to the female members of the family, explaining "Paige cars mirror her individuality as her gown does—or her hat!" Comparing her attire accessories to her automobile, the text actually stated, "Men are so impossible...Will they never know that beauty is only beauty, but that style...ah, Madame...that is different."

However, Paige's style was not different. It was much like that of the past, recent and otherwise.

Krohn then, almost as an afterthought, continued in the *Paige Radiator* article to extol the Straightaway Eight's engine and chassis features and the "most interesting mechanical feature announced..at the show, that of the Paige Hi-Flex" four-speed transmission.

The introduction of the company's first eight plus the introduction of one of the first four speed transmissions in the industry would seemingly be the central point of any text directed to the public or dealers. It was not. The Paige-Detroit Motor Car Company was obviously unfocused, and unsure of the tack it should take in merchandising. When the sales manager concentrated on the color combinations available, rather than the introduction of a radically new powerplant (for Paige) and a progressive, technically advanced transmission, customers and dealers alike wondered aloud what condition the company and its leadership might be in. The truth was that since Paige could not produce motor cars at anywhere peak production—and those they did produce were not the best available for the price—it made advertising verbiage of any sort mute. The Paige-Detroit Motor Car Company was in dire straits.[11]

The continuing slowdown in sales was filling the Paige financial journals with more and more red ink. It appeared that Paige's situation was untenable. Dependence upon an outside supplier was critically harming the respected manufacturer, and the motor car which was to be their savior was being unenthusiastically received. Paige-Detroit common stock was now selling for an all time low of 7 7/8, compared to 20 during April of 1926. Less than a year after Jewett's boast of his company having over $4 1/2 million in cash in their coffers, the amount now totaled less than $300,000.[12]

Shortly after the introduction of the new eight, rumors began to circulate freely in the Motor City concerning the future of Paige. Many of these rumors were based on pure speculation, fed by the abysmal sales reports filed by the firm and the timely stepping down of its longtime president. Flaming those rumors was the fact it was exceedingly difficult to keep absolute secrets in an industry as localized as that of automobile manufacture.

In March and April of 1927 it became more commonly known that the chairman of the board of Paige-Detroit had been involved in secret discussions with Joseph, Ray, and Robert Graham.

For those who did not actually know what was being said behind those closed doors, the speculation concerning outright sale of Paige-Detroit to the Grahams made a great deal of sense. The physical plant Paige had recently erected, its venerated name and goodwill, its established dealer network, and its now apparent availability, made it a most logical target of the Grahams—or any other manufacturer seeking to expand its lineup.

Even as Paige-Detroit was daily adding red ink to its books, the all but confirmed rumors of negotiations with the Graham brothers began to push Paige-Detroit stock higher and higher. The word on the street was that the only thing remaining to consummate the sale was the actual announcement. Between New Year's and the formal announcement during the first week of May 1927, Paige-Detroit Motor Car Company stock more than doubled in value.[13] Such was the faith Wall Street and individual investors put in the reputation of the Graham brothers, and their ability to make the crippled company prosper.

A letter to registered Paige-Detroit stockholders dated May 7, 1927, from Sherwin A. Hill, secretary of the company, indicated control and management of the company would be transferred to the brothers, subject to the ratification of the stockholders.[14] Considering the financial condition of the company, that ratification was a foregone conclusion.

The Graham brothers were to purchase the stock held by the Jewett brothers,[15] giving them controlling interest.[16] When the Grahams announced the purchase of the Jewett interests in the company they also made it clear that they would begin steps to make the firm profitable[17] post haste.

Even though the Paige-Detroit plant on Warren Avenue was one of the most up-to-date in the motor car industry, the Grahams announced an initial investment of over $4 million would be made in the company, and a promised additional $4 million would be made available for expansion and improvement as it became necessary. The legal document which allowed the passage of ownership to the Grahams also authorized an increase of 500,000 shares of common stock (to 1 1/2 million) and the issuance of $4 million worth of 7% cumulative, voting, convertible second preferred stock. Press releases concerning that increase of common stock did not indicate whether the stock would be available to the public.

The skilled labor force was to remain intact, but changes almost immediately began in regard to management of the company. Graham men began moving into offices directly after the announcement, and began their work of converting the floundering company into a viable, profitable enterprise. Former president W. A. Wheeler was retained, no doubt to ease the transition.[18]

Letters were sent out to dealers explaining to them the existing line of cars would be continued and there would no radical changes in the company's dealings with them.

Lest any investor or dealer be misled by the Graham brothers' intentions, a press release revealed the goal of the trio when Joseph Graham said,

> *In taking control of the Paige organization we realize that the Paige factories in Detroit with over a million square feet of floor space are the most modern and efficient in the industry. My brothers and I are in the automobile industry to stay.*

It became obvious at once the Grahams had not "taken a rest" but had been hard at work since their leave taking at Dodge Brothers. Prior to the approval of the purchase of Paige-Detroit, the brothers had personally purchased the Wayne Body Company[19] in nearby Wayne, Michigan. The 200,000-square-foot factory[20] was exactly what the company needed to solve its immediate body supply needs. On June 29, the Paige-Detroit Motor Car Company purchased the plant from the brothers, for exactly the same price the Grahams had paid for it. The perplexing situation of body supply had been successfully addressed.

In fact, it had been addressed both short and long term. Confident of the fact they would bring Paige-Detroit to a level of a volume producer, the brothers harkened back to their Indiana ties. A $500,000 contract was awarded in July to the M. J. Hoffmann Company of Evansville for the erection of a 600 foot by 80 foot concrete and steel building, with a 200 foot by 80 foot warehouse, and a 92 foot by 80 foot garage to be located on Graham-owned property in that city. It was promptly evident the new management of the Paige-Detroit Motor Car Company had their adopted hometown in mind when planning the future of the new enterprise.

With the Graham brothers in place, work at the management level proceeded at a frenzied pace. Details of plant production procedures were analyzed and modified, new schedules and methods instituted, and structural changes were made at the plant.

As this work became more visible, the brothers themselves were more and more in the public eye. Suppliers were contacted, industry organizations were joined, and contacts were again made with influential members of the press and government. Advertisements for the Egyptian Lacquer Manufacturing Company now featured a 1927 Paige Cabriolet Roadster in its trade advertising, and a similar ad for the Hyatt Roller Bearing Company featured an eight-cylinder coupe. In September an illustrated article appeared in the news section of *Automotive Industries*, "How Flywheel Housings Are Finished At The Paige Plant." Some of the Graham clout was beginning to be seen. Later in the year Robert Graham was elected to a directorship of the National Automobile Chamber of Commerce.

The July 16 issue of the *Saturday Evening Post* carried an impressive two-page ad headed simply: "A Message from the three Graham Brothers." Carrying no graphics, the text-only ad succinctly noted the brothers' industrial past, present, and plans for the future.

> *More than a year ago we sold our entire holdings in Dodge Brothers, Inc., (manufacturers of motor cars) and Graham Brothers, Inc. (manufactures of motor trucks) and severed our active and financial connections with both organizations.*
>
> *On June 10th we acquired control of the Paige-Detroit Motor Car Company, assumed full responsibility for management and invested over four million dollars in the company, thus providing substantial working capital.*
>
> *The Paige-Detroit plant is modern, well located, well equipped and with the addition of the Wayne Body Plant which we have just purchased provides manufacturing facilities of a high order.*
>
> *Twelve months investigation among users of Paige cars gave us satisfactory reports as to the worthiness of this product. Our policy will be to continue the production of Paige six and eight cylinder models in their several price fields. The public expects motor car executives to keep abreast of the times and make their product constantly better. We shall earnestly strive to do so.*
>
> *We shall endeavor to protect the merchandising organization now existing and progressively advance its interest, keeping in mind that the owner of Paige cars is best served through dealers who have the fundamental three C's—Character, Capability, and Capital. By our business conduct we shall strive to make the Paige dealership a profitable enterprise for a substantial business man in every community.*
>
> *During the twenty-five years of industrial accomplishment we found that to Sell well was to Serve well. We shall continue upon the simple belief that the foundation under a greater Paige-Detroit Motor Car Company should not consist of brick and mortar but of the confidence of the American public in our integrity and ability as manufacturers.*
>
> *We pledge ourselves to build that solid foundation for the future, step by step—stone by stone.*

The statement was signed by the three brothers. It was a statement which they would live by for the rest of their careers.

Ever so slightly, sales of Paige automobiles increased.[21] The public was well aware of the brothers' reputation for solid business practice and value for dollars

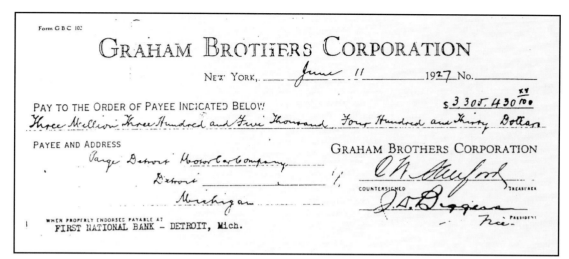

John D. Biggers, Vice-President of the Graham Brothers Corporation, signed the $3,305,430,000 check transfering control of the Paige-Detroit Motor Car Company to the three Graham brothers. (Courtesy of David Graham)

spent. Too, the division of Dodge Brothers, Inc., which continued to carry their name was experiencing unparalleled success. During June it was announced more Graham Brothers trucks had been shipped by Dodge than any other week in the division's history.[22] The public was indeed aware of the Graham name.

To further accentuate the vitality of the corporation and its intent to be an enthusiastic player in the automobile marketplace, August saw the introduction of the "1928" Paiges.

A new showroom sales brochure followed the introduction of these new Paiges during the first week of the month.[23] In addition to illustrations of the existing 6-65, 6-75, and 8-85 models,[24] the brochure delineated an additional model to the lineup. The 6-40 was available only in the touring car body style, and was identical to the 6-45 except in use of a smaller engine.[25] The next month two additional body styles were introduced on the 6-45 chassis. Advertised as the first six-cylinder Paige in the history of the company to sell "for less than $1,000,"[26] the new brougham and sedan were known as the "6-45A."

Considerable effort was made by the new engineering staff at Paige to improve the existing chassis and powerplants as much as possible. Gas mileage and output was increased by a redesign of the intake and exhaust manifold on the 6-75. Cast in one piece, the manifold had all sharp intake curves eliminated,[27] and was given a porcelain finish. The exhaust manifold gradually increased in diameter and split at the ends to provide for expansion. An oil filter and the Lanchester vibration dampener were now also standard.

Four point engine supports were common to all the sixes, with the 6-65 and 6-75 utilizing rubber insulated mountings.[28] The 6-45 did not go without improvement either, as the compression ratio was increased by decreasing the combustion chamber by 1/32 of an inch. An air cleaner was now being fitted to all the models. The manner of radiator attachment was also changed. Previously, the radiator cores were bolted directly to the front frame member. Beginning with the 1928 models they were hung in the radiator shells (shrouds) and the shells were bolted to the frame member.

The engine compartment's appearance was greatly enhanced by the use of nickel plating on radiator hose clamps, spark plug wire conduit (to protect against shorting), spark and throttle rods, and various other fittings. All gasoline, oil, and hydraulic brake lines visible under the hood were finished in a dull nickel finish.

As much as possible was done about body design short of a complete restyling. The overall height of the motor cars was reduced by using smaller 20-inch wheels[29] and 30 x 5.25 balloon tires. The rear of the cars were rounded off at the top, shortened, and the use of an abbreviated visor contributed to the appearance of a lower body. Window reveals were painted in contrasting colors and completely new color schemes were made available. Much was made of an "advanced new process"[30] of painting the motor cars. The interiors were not neglected, with a new style oval instrument panel being used in addition to built-in arm rests.[31] One of the more noticeable external changes was the use of "conical headlamps" with matching cowl lamps.

Although it made up a minuscule part of the automobile, perhaps one of the most telling parts of the 1928 Paige motor cars was the new radiator emblem. The familiar white diamond framing the Paige name had been used for the most part unchanged since 1914. That basic design was continued for the 1928 Paige motor car, but beneath the Paige logo the phrase "Graham Built" was proudly placed.[32]

At the time the 1928 Paiges were unveiled, the company also announced the reduction of prices on ten of the new models. The reductions ranged from $100 to $160 on the selected models.[33]

In addition to improvements to the automobiles themselves, the Grahams had been hard at work to improve their sales and distribution network. Issues of *The Paige Radiator* were widely distributed to dealers and prospective customers, and featured much more in the way of illustrations and testimonials. Monthly sales contests were held for salesmen, with cash awards ranging from $10 to $100.[34] Robert Graham penned articles such as "The Four Steps of A Sale" and "Building Confidence Through Advertising." As vice-president in charge of sales he also began a campaign to visit all the major distributors in the nation. After having visited the central and far western districts, Robert Graham addressed the Paige dealers in the Cincinnati territory. He was quoted in the national and local press saying:

> [We] have the utmost confidence in the immediate future of the automobile industry.

On August 1, they announced the opening of five factory branches in as many states. A formal release informed the motoring press,

> ...the company has adopted a policy of establishing a network of factory branches throughout the country to make possible a more direct contact with the dealers in all trade territories, as well as with the public.

Later that month the Graham brothers also announced "plans are being formulated for an aggressive pursuit of foreign business." Incorporation papers were filed in New York state to establish the Paige-Detroit Motors International Corporation for the expressed purpose of handing all export business. The company was a wholly owned subsidiary of the Paige-Detroit Motor Car Company, and no stock was offered to the public. Robert Graham was the president of the new corporation, and John Biggers (also an officer of the Graham Brothers Corporation) was named vice-president. Walter Morrison, the former export manager under the tenure of Harry M. Jewett, was retained as secretary and treasurer.[35]

Advertising of the Paige line continued on a national level. *The Saturday Evening Post*, soon to be a favorite advertising medium for the Grahams, featured a two-page advertisement which showed and discussed the facilities on Warren Avenue and in Wayne, Michigan. The eight-cylinder power plant was highlighted in other ads, garnering a headline that read, "The Eight That Commands Respect." Later in the fall, the brothers placed an ad in the *Post* and *Liberty* which was titled simply "Paige Progress."

With laconic prose the Grahams set forth what they had done since taking over the Paige organization, and why the public should consider Paige automobiles. The all-text ad read:

> *Within sixty days after acquiring control of Paige, we announced substantial improvements on all Paige sixes and eights, and lower prices on ten of the twenty models.*
>
> *Thirty days later two new models, a sedan and brougham, were added to the Paige line at still lower prices, making a Paige available for the first time for less than a thousand dollars.*
>
> *The recently acquired body plant at Wayne has been equipped with machinery and tools of the latest type. Construction has been completed on two additional factory units at Detroit, contributing manufacturing facilities of a still higher order.*
>
> *Thus stone by stone we are laying the foundation of a great Paige organization, holding fast to the belief that this foundation must rest upon the confidence of the public in our integrity and ability as manufacturers.*
>
> *The Paige line includes twenty body types on four chassis in sixes and eights, at prices ranging from $995 to $2695. f.o.b. Detroit.*
>
> *We invite your inspection.*

Again the advertisement was signed by the brothers.[36]

By September it was evident to all observers the Paige-Detroit Motor Car Company was being revitalized, reorganized, redirected, and put hard to work. The trio of brothers had definite ideas of how the company was going to be perceived by the automobile-buying public. Those plans were proceeding according to schedule, and were being implemented by an enthusiastic Graham-trained staff.

Unfortunately, September was also a time of great sorrow for the Graham family. On September 7, 1927, Ziba F. Graham—father and business associate of Jo-

Ziba F. Graham, always a dignified and proper man, enjoyed getting away from the demands of business by spending time at the Graham Family Compound at Conway, Michigan. Fishing was a pastime enjoyed by all the Grahams, especially Robert. (Courtesy of Robert C. Graham, Jr.)

Again, the reputation of the business abilities of the Grahams allowed all the available stock to be purchased in short order.[42]

The "stone by stone" philosophy was being implemented with all due dispatch. In November it was announced the C. H. Jennings Dodge agency in New York City—one of the most well known and respected automobile agencies in the metropolitan area—had severed its 13-year association with Dodge Brothers, and would henceforth be associated with the Graham brothers venture.[43] Highly publicized in both Gotham newspapers and the national press, it was one of many high profile dealerships to sign on with the Grahams. Jennings visited the Paige plants and was quoted as saying,

> *The Graham brothers' name today stands for good workmanship and honest salesmanship wherever it is known, here and abroad. Last week Joe Graham and I walked through the new Paige plants at Detroit and Wayne, which the Grahams now control and operate. I was deeply impressed with the manufacturing plans and fair dealer policies they are developing.*

Joseph Graham told him,

> *We can build fine cars here. And economically, too. The capital investment is moderate, profit requirements reasonable, production and prices have no financial overload to carry.*

seph, Robert, and Ray Graham—succumbed to heart disease while at his retirement home in Conway, Michigan. The body of the 75-year-old patriarch was taken back to Washington, Indiana, for a funeral mass said at St. Simon Catholic Church.[37] Burial was in the family plot in St. John's Catholic Cemetery.[38] As a fitting mark of esteem for the Graham family, Ziba's death was not only written of and eulogized in Indiana papers, but also in the national motoring press. It was a sincerely grief-filled and distressful time for three sons who had so recently taken on major responsibilities.[39]

The end of September also saw the Paige-Detroit Motor Car Company make available 300,000 new shares of common stock at ten dollars a share.[40] According to the announcement,

> *The authorized common shares would be increased from 1,500,000 to 2,000,000, with 300,000 to be issued. There would be no underwriting; the Graham brothers would take over any of the new stock not subscribed. The proceeds are to provide funds to meet increased business and for enlargement of facilities.*[41]

Robert's abilities as a salesman were becoming more and more evident as hundreds of automotive businessmen, all deemed to possess the three fundamental C's (Character, Capability, and Capital), also signed on with Paige.

The immediate future was looking better all the time. The Grahams reported in the first week of December that production during November was the best of any November in the company's history. Sales had increased by 18% over the previous month.

During the fall of 1927 the manufacture of Paige automobiles continued, but not at the frenzied pace some expected. Inventory was being moved and enough cars were being produced to meet the demand. However, much more effort was being placed in the design, engineering, and production methods for the firm's next offering.

Chapter Six
End Notes

[1] The new six-cylinder offerings had been available at Paige dealers since September of 1926. This was the first national showing of the entire Paige lineup.

[2] The board of directors at the beginning of 1927 included E. D. Stair, E. H. Jewett, H. M. Jewett, Gilbert W. Lee, Charles R. Warren, Jerome H. Remick, Sherwin A. Hill, and W. A. Wheeler.

[3] The bore of the Lycoming-produced motor was 3 1/4 inches and the stroke was 4 1/2 inches.

[4] The six-cylinder models, the 6-65 and 6-75 also used alloy pistons and Invar struts.

[5] It is interesting to note that the Graham Brothers truck division of Dodge Bros., Inc., announced on September 24, 1927, that their new series of 162-inch wheelbase, six-cylinder trucks also featured a four-speed transmission.

[6] Warner dubbed the transmission as Model T5.

[7] The sales brochure which extolled the new four-speed transmission reported that the "old-style" four-speed transmissions (with the over-speed concept and spur gears) had never caught on with American drivers, but were "widely used in Europe."

[8] That same brochure detailed the "high speed" expectations a new owner might expect: "5 to 25 miles per hour in only 5.6 seconds—and up to 40 miles per hour in five seconds more!"

[9] Harry Jewett noted to stockholders,

By utilizing existing dies and tools, it has been possible to get the new Eight into early production with a negligible increase in investment, and substantial increase in our sales and profit possibilities.

[10] Perhaps anticipating continued problems with production, advertising in early 1927 still touted the 1926 models. During January the company's advertising in the *Saturday*

Evening Post—the nation's largest circulation magazine of the day—was headlined, "Paige-Jewett Forecasts the New Year's Fashion." The advertising went on to say,

...*The Most Beautiful Cars in America now possess in addition to Paige Beauty—a smartness and exclusiveness that stamp them style leaders in the coming season.*

This was published during the month the Jewett nameplate was dropped, the 1927 six-cylinder models had been in showrooms for several months, and an eight-cylinder offering would be introduced at the January shows. This advertising was an indication of the tenor of the company.

Another indication of the poor leadership and product planning was the fact that during the 1925 model year Apperson featured a "Straightaway Eight." This Apperson automobile featured a 60 horsepower engine, 120-inch wheel base, and ranged in price from $2,550 for the five-passenger sport phaeton to $2,850 for the five-passenger sedan. The last Apperson was built in 1926.

[11] Full page ads in *Motor Age* during February appealed to readers to invest in a Paige-Detroit franchise. They were the first of such ads in the company's history.

[12] The cash balance was $287,679.40.

[13] The low for the stock prior to May 1927 was 7 7/8. By the time the actual purchase was announced on May 4 it had risen to 14.

[14] That stockholders meeting was to be held at the Warren Avenue offices at 10:00 a.m. on Friday, May 25, 1927. The board of directors meeting which recommended this special meeting was held on Tuesday, May 3.

[15] Harry M. Jewett, Edward H. Jewett, and Frederick L. Jewett. The Jewett brothers immediately resigned their positions in the company and, according to *Motor Age*, "retired."

[16] One account gives the purchase price of the Jewett brothers' shares at $11 per share, or approximately $840,000.

[17] Interestingly, the initial press reports indicated Joseph B. Graham would assume the presidency of the Paige-Detroit Motor Car Company and Robert C. Graham would become the new vice-president in charge of sales, but it was "unknown" if Ray A. Graham would be involved with the new venture.

[18] Although Wheeler was retained, there was a gradual and steady leave-taking by other high level Paige executives.

The transfer was not nearly as dramatic as the much written about Chrysler takeover at Dodge, but it was done with dispatch. The Graham men definitely took charge immediately.

That is not to say that the upper level Paige-Detroit executives were abandoned by the automotive industry. For example, Henry Krohn was general sales manager of Paige-Detroit for 18 years and became a vice-president in 1926. Upon his departure from Paige-Detroit Krohn became the director of Senior Six Sales at Dodge Brothers, Inc. In May of 1930 Krohn was associated with the Federal Motor Truck Company as a top executive.

[19] The Wayne Body company occupied the facilities of the former Harroun Motor Car Company. Ray Harroun is remembered primarily as the winner of the first Indianapolis 500 mile race. Harroun Motors Corporation was incorporated for a reported $10 million on September 14, 1917. According to the Standard Catalog of American Car 1805-1942,

Construction of a factory...with a 24,000-unit-per-year capacity was immediately begun. In the meantime, Harroun went into production at the Wayne plant of the Prouty and Glass Carriage Company. Approximately 500 cars were produced prior to April of 1918 when the company received a large government contract for the manufacture of munitions. A half million dollars in new machinery was installed by Harroun to produce them, and after the Armistice the company had more than a little difficulty settling with the government on its war claims. This delayed the return to full-time automobile production and represented the death knell for Harroun Motors Corporation. ...Harroun Motors Corporation found itself in receiver's hands in June of 1922. Its factory was purchased by Gotfredson Truck Corporation.

The Gotfredson Truck Corporation later used the site as the home of one of its divisions, the American Auto Trimming Company. One of the notable employees of Gotfredson was Gordon Buehrig, who left in 1927 for employment provided by E. L. Cord.

[20] The plant was appraised at $1,250,000. Immediately after its purchase a 40,000-square-foot addition was begun. It was announced that full capacity production for Paige automobiles would be achieved by early fall.

[21] Production in June of 1927 was 1,552 cars. The May total was 1,507. During the halcyon days of June 1926, 2,748 Paige and Jewett Motor Cars were produced.

[22] The week ending June 18 saw 1,415 vehicles delivered to domestic and Canadian distributors and dealers. On Au-

gust 20 the Dodge division announced a new two-ton truck with a six-cylinder engine. The Graham Brothers truck division now made models ranging from the 3/4-ton to 2-ton. The new 2-ton offering featured the same power plant as the Dodge Senior automobiles.

[23] There is some difference of opinion amongst historians whether these August 1927 offerings are indeed 1928 Paige automobiles, or whether they should be simply considered revised 1927 models. The author believes them to be a distinct model year. Contemporary motoring journals also considered them likewise: *Automobile Topics*' August 6, 1927, number included an article entitled, "1928 Paige Line Bear Graham Brothers Stamp."

[24] The models illustrated included the 6-45 brougham, sedan, cabriolet, and coupe. The 6-40 phaeton was shown, as was the 6-65 roadster and the 7-75 touring car, five-passenger sedan, and coupe. The 8-85 models shown were the five-passenger and seven-passenger sedans, coupe, and cabriolet.

[25] The Continental "9U" was the same engine that had been used in the New-Day Jewett. The 109-inch wheelbase was also identical to that previous model.

[26] The published price was $995. Although the model was considered part of the "twenty charming body types" available, the five-passenger "6-45A" brougham and sedan were first introduced and available on September 10.

[27] The exhaust manifold increased in diameter from the rear to the front, as the exhaust was attached to the front of the motor. This front exhaust design had been used on other previous models as well. The company stated,

...this gradual increase in diameter... materially improve[s] engine performance—by preventing the building up of the back-pressure near the front cylinder exhaust ports.

[28] The front supports were rubber mounted, while the rear supports were of the trunion type carried in brackets. This design allowed for the motor to be removed without disturbing the rubber mounting itself.

[29] Steel, or disc, wheels were available as optional equipment, at no extra charge, excepting the 8-85 models. Disc wheels were not available for the "Straightaway Eight."

[30] The new process was never named or explained in any 1928 Paige advertising or technical releases. The *Paige Radiator* did mention "The new colors are applied by an ad-

vanced process which adds to the appearance of the cars and to the durability of their finish. The high lustre of the new finish is the result of the painstaking care with which it is applied, and the additional work in the preparation, application and finishing of its many coats. Each coat is thoroughly baked to remove any moisture that might detract from the durability of the finish. "

[31] Mohair was used in the closed six-cylinder models and broadcloth in the eights.

[32] The phrase replaced "Reg. U. S. Pat. Off."

[33] The 6-45 cabriolet roadster was reduced $100 (from its original $1,295) as was the 6-65 roadster (from $1,495), the 6-75 cabriolet roadster (from $1,995), the 6-75 four-passenger coupe (from $1,995), the 8-85 phaeton (from $2,295), and the 8-85 five-passenger sedan (from $2,395). The 8-85 seven-passenger sedan was reduced $130 (from the original $2,655), the 8-85 cabriolet roadster and coupe were both reduced $160 (from the original $2,655), and the 8-85 limousine was reduced $130 from the original $2,795. The remaining models were continued at their original prices.

[34] The September 20 number listed how the 550 cash prizes would be distributed.

[35] The officers of the corporation and Robert Graham's brothers made up the board of directors. The offices of the new corporation were located at 1 East Forty-fourth Street, New York City. Biggers and Morrison maintained their offices at that address.

[36] An article in the *Paige Radiator* explained the advertising policy of the company,

For some time the advertisement of Paige motor cars, appearing in newspapers and national magazines, have differed considerably from the general run of automobile advertising. This difference has been carefully planned.

The severe simplicity that marks Paige advertisements today, the entire absence of illustrations or decorations, the generous margins of white space, the restrained and dignified wording of the messages and the reproduction in practically every advertisement of the signatures of Joseph B. Graham, Robert C. Graham, and Ray A. Graham—all these contributed to the general effect desired. This is the building up of widespread confidence in Paige and the quality and value of Paige cars.

[37] Ziba Graham's death was unexpected and sudden, probably from a heart attack suffered during the night. Family members accompanying the body back from Conway on two special cars of the B & O Railroad included his widow, Mrs. and Mrs. Joseph Graham (and their children, Eleanor, Virginia, Joe, Charles, and Betty), Mr. and Mrs. Robert Graham (and their children, Robert, Ziba, and Tom), and the son of Ray Graham, John Phillip Graham. Mr. and Mrs. Ray Graham, and the remainder of their children, were touring Europe at the time of Ziba's death. Coincidentally they were scheduled to set sail for the United States the very morning of Ziba's death. It is interesting to note that Ray Graham and his family were not able to arrive in Washington until the week following the funeral mass. However, he and his family were able to pay their final respects in that following the visitation at the home of Robert Graham and the funeral mass at church, Ziba Graham was not buried. Actual burial was delayed until their return and subsequent viewing of the family patriarch.

[38] Ziba Graham's wife, Margaret Agnes Cabel, was also buried in the family plot when she died on September 20, 1944.

[39] At the time Ziba's death, his wife, sons Joseph and Robert, and other family members were present. Ray Graham was in Europe setting up branches for the Paige Motors International Corporation.

[40] On a pro rata basis to present shareholders.

[41] A stockholders meeting was called for October 14 to vote on the stock offering.

[42] The faith investors put into the reputation of the Graham brothers is even more impressive when one considers the financial situation at that time. In order to get the firm's finances in order, $1,056,510 of charge offs in the second quarter were recorded. That meant for the first nine months of 1927 a loss of $1,796,104 was recorded by the company. This compared with a profit of $755,452 for the same period in 1926. At the end of the first six months of 1927, Paige had reported a loss of $1,426,463; shrewd investors were able to see early that improvement was already being made directly after the Grahams took over.

[43] Jennings had the Dodge metropolitan district which included Manhattan, Bronx, and Westchester County. With his alignment with Paige, he would control the entire city, in addition to Long Island, most of the rest of the state, Connecticut, and New Jersey. His New York City showroom was located at Broadway and 56th Street. Jennings also operated several ancillary showrooms and service stations.

Transition – 1927

Le Baron custom Phaeton on Graham-Paige 629 Chassis.

The Graham-Paige Motors Corporation – 1928

The Graham-Paige Motors Corporation
1928

Upon purchase of the Paige-Detroit Motor Car Company, the Grahams' publicly pledged to continue production of Paige automobiles and to make the company a more profitable enterprise. Production did continue, and a respectable—considering the condition of the company and the transition to an almost entirely new management team—21,881 Paige motor cars were produced and sold in 1927. However, much more than continued production was being planned by the brothers. It was the desire of the Graham brothers to introduce a new line of automobiles which would bear their name.[1] Even before the ink was dry on the contract, work involving the design of this new series of automobiles was well under way.

Initially, one may have thought it unusual a business and personal relationship developed between the Graham brothers and one Lorado Taft in 1927. Natives of the Midwest, the brothers had been successful for decades in several highly competitive industrial and business enterprises. Lorado Taft was also of Midwestern heritage[2] but his successes had been in the world of fine art, particularly that of sculpture.

Taft was a graduate of the University of Illinois[3] and subsequently studied at the prestigious Ecole des Beaux-Arts in Paris. Returning to Illinois, Taft became a well known lecturer,[4] author,[5] and teacher.[6] His lasting fame was achieved, however, as a highly successful sculptor of larger-than-life portraits,[7] massive fountains[8] and other monumental public works.[9] Regarded as the *major-domo* of this type of art,[10] he was well known nationally, and especially in

Lorado Taft, sculptural romanticist.

the Midwest. His artistic opinions were well chronicled in the press and his residence at the Art Institute of Chicago was a point of civic pride. History associates Taft with impressive allegorical works of art using gracefully composed figures to represent the theme of the piece. His work is typified by sculptural romanticism, shown through naturalism and "the expressive potential of the human form." By 1927, Taft was one of the most influential sculptors in America.[11]

To designate this new series of automobiles, the Grahams commissioned Lorado Taft to design an emblem to symbolize the re-entry of Joseph, Ray, and Robert Graham into the automobile industry.[12]

Detroit had been abuzz with rumors of what the Grahams had in mind for the Paige-Detroit Motor Car Company. Full well realizing the inability to keep complete secrecy in the Motor City, the brothers nevertheless remained mum concerning any future planning details, while enthusiastically calling attention to their improved sales network, plant enhancements, and emendations to those Paige models in production.[13]

Not unexpectedly, a full page teaser advertisement appeared in the December 31, 1927, number of the *Saturday Evening Post*. Featured was an engraving of a sculptor at work on what appeared to be a medieval shield. The lower portion of the emblem was obviously incomplete, but the helmeted profiles of three knights in mail were clearly visible in the upper half. The caption was purposely vague:

> *VERY SOON—An advertisement of more than ordinary interest to the public and the automobile trade will appear in this and other publications.*

The following Saturday a two-page ad appeared in the *Post* and a number of other periodicals. The left hand page featured the now completed emblem. The sculptor had obviously finished his work, and the lower half of the shield had the name "Graham-Paige" engraved in a very singular and distinctive font. A quote by the famous Lorado Taft was discreetly placed near the shield:

> *My studio has designed this symbol of the integrity and unity of purpose back of the Graham-Paige.*

The facing page had text which read:

> *An INVITATION from the three Graham brothers—The public and the automobile trade are cordially invited to the first showing of passenger cars bearing our name.*

The ad was signed by the three brothers, in the familiar manner. In smaller-scale type, the showing of the inaugural models at the Grand Central Palace in New York during the second week of the year was noted.[14] The frenzied effort exerted by the brothers and their associates since Spring had reached a climax with this simple announcement.

To all who attended the New York Automobile Show,[15] it was obvious the new Graham-Paige automobile[16] was distinctively different from its predecessor. The motor cars the Grahams invited the public to see were almost entirely new in design and appearance.

Already, the Grahams had contacted LeBaron Studios to contract for an altogether new body style design for their proposed new automobile.

In the spring of 1920 Thomas L. Hibbard and Raymond H. Dietrich founded LeBaron, Carrossiers. The firm created numerous classic designs during the next decade and was highly respected in the automobile industry. In 1926, then under the direction of Ralph Roberts, the body builder was purchased by the Briggs Corporation, with LeBaron Studios becoming its custom design division.

It was in the New York[17] atelier of LeBaron, Inc., that the preliminary design for the new Graham-produced automobile was completed. A product of the combined efforts of R. L. Stickney and Hugo Pfau, the new Graham-Paige was neither radically different from accepted designs, nor "reminiscent of any competitors offering."[18]

Deemed "a complete modernization of design features," the overall design was set off by a most distinctive radiator shell, or shroud. Obviously influenced by the then current Hispano-Suiza, the radiator shell was slightly V'ed and had a gently curved leading edge with rounded corners. Quite different from any other manufacturer's offering, it did set the new Graham-Paige apart from the rest of the pack. The radiator shell also carried a highly polished brass emblem of Taft's recently introduced design.

Four six-cylinder models were to be introduced, in addition to one straight eight.

All of the Graham offerings featured powerplants of the L-head type design, used Nelson-Bohnalite aluminum pistons, Invar struts, forced pressure lubrication to all camshaft bearings, full length cylinder water jackets, air cleaner, and mechanical fuel pump. Chassis commonality included four-point engine support, Lockhead hydraulic brakes, Timken bearings, North East ignition and lighting, semi-floating axles, and two plate clutches.

The Graham-Paige Model 610 five-passenger sedan sold for $875.

List price in early 1928 for this Graham-Paige Model 614 five-passenger sedan was $1,295.

The Graham-Paige Model 619 four-passenger coupe, powered by the identical 97 horsepower engine that drove the Model 629, was available for $1,575.

Stately with its disc wheel equipage, the Graham-Paige Model 629 seven-passenger sedan was offered at $2,110.

The Graham-Paige Model 629 coupe featured a rumble seat and sporty lines.

The Graham-Paige Motors Corporation – 1928

The smallest model, the Model 610, rode in a 110 1/2-inch wheelbase chassis, and used a standard three-speed transmission. The 52 brake horsepower six-cylinder motor featured a bore of 2 7/8 inches and a stroke of 4 1/2 inches, displacing a respectable 175 cubic inches. A sales brochure handed out at the New York and Chicago shows (and later supplied to all distributors and dealers) proudly pointed out that the "motor is of our own design...and built in Graham-Paige plants."[19] That same brochure said, "The bodies are built in our own modern plant in Wayne, Michigan." The five-passenger sedan sold for a most reasonable $875[20] while the two-passenger coupe—available on May 31—was only $860.[21]

Announced, but not shown, at the New York and Chicago shows was the Model 614. (Model designations were the convenient combining of the number of cylinders and the last two digits of the wheelbase.) This series carried a larger 71 brake horsepower engine displacing 207-cubic inches. With a bore and stroke of 3 1/8 by 4 1/2 inches, it was a slightly more powerful power plant on a longer wheelbase. When available later in the spring,[22] the five-passenger sedan sold for $1,295, while the four-passenger coupe was offered for $1,275.

The Model 619 and Model 629 shared the powerful 97 brake horsepower,[23] 288 cubic inch powerplant, while utilizing a 119-inch and 129-inch wheelbase chassis, respectively.[24] The Model 619 five-passenger sedan was only $1,595,[25] while the four-passenger coupe $1,575.[26]

On the Model 629 chassis, a five-passenger sedan was proffered at $1,895,[27] while the seven-passenger model was $2,110. An elegant-looking town sedan was also available, at $2,085.[28]

To assure the first showing of the Graham-Paige automobile would be as impressive as possible, special custom bodied models were shown along with the standard production models. In addition to creating the production models, LeBaron was commissioned to create custom, one-off designs specifically for the New York Auto Show. The six-cylinder, 129-inch wheelbase chassis was used as the platform for these truly custom creations. Sophisticated in every sense, a dual cowl phaeton, roadster, an elegant town car, cabriolet, and sport sedan were featured at the Graham-Paige stand. Distinctive belt moldings, appealing color combinations, and luxurious interiors distinguished these custom jobs from the standard factory offerings. Show-goers were duly impressed.

Although not shown at the New York show, the new straight eight was emphasized at each opportunity. Positioned on a 135-inch wheelbase chassis, the Stickney and Pfau design was portrayed at its best on the Model 835. Massive and impressive, the straight eight was powered by the 85 horsepower, 299 cubic inch Lycoming engine that had formerly been used on the Paige Straightaway Eight. When the existing supply of engines had been exhausted, an even more powerful 120-horsepower, 322-cubic inch Continental-based engine[29] was used. Few manufacturers boasted of a larger power plant.[30] It was an automobile of which the Graham brothers could be unabashedly proud.

The initial offering of body styles on the straight eight was to be similar to the Model 629 body styles and, like the Model 614, prices were announced when the cars were available in April. (The five-passenger sedan was $2,285,[31] the seven-passenger sedan was $2,410, the town sedan was offered at $2,385, the rumble seat cabriolet was $2,485, as was the coupe with rumble seat.)[32]

Le Baron Custom Town Car

Le Baron Custom Roadster

Le Baron Custom Convertible Cabriolet

The Le Baron custom-built show cars used to introduce the Graham-Paige lineup at the New York Show in 1928 were one-off, and distinctly different from production models. All three models were built on a Graham-Paige 629 Chassis.

Noted in most advertisements was the availability of custom-built bodies by LeBaron on the Model 835 chassis, in addition to the factory-bodied styles. Available first on May 23, a town car and phaeton were available through all dealers. The five-passenger dual cowl sport phaeton was available for $3,755 and the four-passenger town car was listed at a pricey $4,285.[33] Swank and distinguished in every way, the largest Graham-Paiges were a symbol of the effort the Grahams had exerted to bring a well-built and popular automobile to the American public.

With the impressive chassis Graham-Paige was providing on its top end model,[34] it was hoped other custom body builders would use it as a foundation for equally impressive automobiles.[35]

The chassis were well-engineered and distinctly different from the former Paige offerings. Seven bearing crankshafts were featured on the six-cylinder models, while the straight eight had but five. The larger sixes and the eight also featured Lanchester vibration dampers. However, one of the most enthusiastically touted features of the new chassis was the continuation of the Warner Hi-Flex four-speed transmission (on all models excepting the 610.) In addition to noting its features in the flood of advertising which followed the national introduction of the Graham-Paige automobiles, a special brochure titled "Four Speeds Forward-Standard Shift" was given to all prospective buyers.[36]

Four days after the opening of the New York show, the Graham-Paige Motors Corporation held its first sales convention. Over 1,100 dealers (many of which had signed on simply upon the strength of the Graham brothers' reputation) and 200 invited guests were present at the prestigious Roosevelt Hotel in New York City. Complimenting the medieval theme as created by Lorado Taft, Ray Graham had commissioned Norman Bel Geddes, noted Broadway set designer, to transform the large ballroom into a knightly banquet hall. The walls were entirely covered with painted canvas, depicting medieval scenes. A half circle canopied stage was erected at one end of the room for the evening's speakers, guests, and orchestra. Forty Graham-Paige pendants hung from the balcony. Two hundred and fifty candles, each over two feet high, provided the only illumination for the "baronial hall."

The proceedings were presided over by Vice-President Robert Graham, whose remarks followed a sumptuous meal. Each of the three Graham brothers made short speeches, expressing their appreciation and extolling the virtues of their new product. Each model was detailed and highlighted on a huge motion picture screen on the dais. Special guests offering their remarks were heavyweight boxing champion Gene Tunney and Notre Dame football coach, Knute Rockne.

Displaying the modesty and solid Midwestern work ethic all three brothers shared, Ray A. Graham—when introduced to the assembled dealers and distributors and greeted with "tumultuous" applause—said,

> Thank you. I appreciate the welcome, but applause has always meant just one thing to me and that is 'Young man, you've got a good job—see that you don't lose it.'

At the end of the evening an enormous Graham-Paige banner was unfurled from the valance.

As general sales manager, Robert Graham was also the firm's representative at the West Coast dealer's convention held the following week in San Francisco. The same warm welcome and approval of the new Graham-Paige models was expressed likewise in the Golden Bear State.

Upon arriving in Chicago on February 2 from California, Robert Graham was proud to report that 79 orders had been placed during the one-week show in California. Prior to addressing the Midwestern sales organization during the annual car show in Chicago,[37] he was to learn that the recently named local distributor (Byrd-Sykes)[38] had sold 87 Graham-Paige automobiles in the first few days of the Chicago show. Concerning the successful debut of their namesake automobile and the state of the automobile industry, Robert Graham was quoted as saying,

> In June we started with 600 retailers and in December this figure had climbed to 1,780. There still is a big task ahead but this growth certainly indicates that there will be steady progress. The industry has grown by leaps and bounds. Where production formerly was uppermost in the manufacturer's mind he now is bending every effort to enlarge his outlets by helping the dealer. Production is past the point where the country will absorb automobiles as fast as the factories can make them. Watch your retail salesmen. Compensate them well in proportion to their loyalty and productive effort.

As they had done in New York, each of the brothers addressed the Chicago luncheon, but it was Robert who presided. In addition to acknowledging the enthusiastic approval of the show floor crowds and the encouraging early sales, he spoke about the principles which formed the basis for the Graham-Paige Motors Corporation.

He went on to explain that "integrity and unity of purpose" were the foundation of the brothers' beliefs. As later printed in a brochure, he explained,

> Integrity of product. That means honest manufacturing and substantial value to those who purchase from us.
>
> Integrity of policy. A full recognition of our obligations both to those who work with us and those with whom we deal.
>
> Unity in thought and operation between ourselves and through-out our entire organization so that, from veteran executive to youngest mechanic, every man's daily work is a true expression of the company's policies and represents the best he has to give.
>
> During twenty-five years of industrial accomplishment we have believed in these principles and ideals. They shall continue to guide us and all who are associated with us. You will find them reflected in the Graham-Paige car and in your dealings with the Graham-Paige organization.

Special guests that evening were Lorado Taft and Knute Rockne. Following their introductions, Joseph Graham detailed to the dealers the Model 835 and its anticipated date of availability.

Production of Graham-Paige bodies was accomplished in plants at Evansville, Indiana and Wayne, Michigan. This photo illustrates one corner of the huge plant in Wayne. Purchased in June of 1927, the facility was ideally suited for the Grahams' needs and was only a few miles from the Warren Avenue plant. The plant was operated at full capacity during 1928 and most of 1929.

While acknowledging gratefully the initial success of their new automobiles, the Grahams took no time to savor that early success. The complete transformation of the Warren Avenue plant to the Graham manner of manufacturing continued[39] with all due speed. An enthusiastic nationwide advertising campaign was employed to bring the news of the new motor car to the public. Fulfillment of the brothers' longer term plans were also being developed.

Shortly after its purchase in June of 1927, the Wayne, Michigan, body plant began to produce bodies for the Graham-produced Paige automobiles. To insure they would never face the problems in body procurement Harry Jewett experienced, the Grahams formed another subsidiary—Motor Bodies, Incorporated—to furnish bodies in the much larger quantities for which they anticipated a need.

It was no surprise to friends of Joe, Ray, and Robert Graham that when the wholly owned subsidiary (capitalized at $100,000) was incorporated, the legal papers were filed at the capitol in Indiana. The brothers very much had their "adopted" home town of Evansville, Indiana, in mind when they bought the Paige-Detroit Motor Car Company.[40]

It was announced on February 19, 1928, that Motor Bodies, Incorporated, had purchased the former Johann Manufacturing Company plant in Evansville. Located at Morgan and Read Streets, the building formerly housed the Karges Wagon Works.[41] In early 1926, while still with Dodge, the Grahams contracted with Johann Manufacturing[42] to manufacture special truck, bus, and commercial bodies for Graham Brothers (then a division of Dodge Brothers, Inc.). W. H. McNeely, chief engineer at Graham-Paige Motors Corporation, was named president of the new firm, while Joseph B. and Robert C. Graham were on the board of directors.[43] Remodeling of

the plant for production of Graham-Paige bodies was begun immediately, and it was anticipated 150 men would be employed in building of roadster and touring bodies.[44] Production in Evansville was intended to supplement production of the Wayne body plant.[45] Evansville papers were enthusiastic in welcoming back their successful "sons."

Because of the unprecedented initial success of the Graham-Paige automobiles, the Wayne and Evansville body plants concentrated on producing bodies for the Model 610. The Model 619 and the Model 629 were, by necessity, contracted out to the Briggs Manufacturing Company of Detroit.

February was also the month the Graham-Paige Motors Corporation severed all formal ties with the former Paige-Detroit Motor Car Company. At the end of the month $2,662,408 was written off due to the old materials and equipment made obsolete by the transition. When that figure was appended into the actual loss for the year, a deficit of $4,643,351 was entered into the books.

The transition of Graham-hired men taking their place in the executive office building of Warren Avenue continued apace. F. R. Valpey, a longtime Graham associate,[46] was named general sales manager[47] and W. R. Heilman, another employee of long tenure, was tabbed as his assistant.[48] Many former colleagues from Dodge and Graham Brothers trucks came to positions of authority at Graham-Paige as the orderly transition continued.

Much to the surprise of the casual industry observer, Graham-Paige sales began to skyrocket. With nearly 1,800 dealers in place, coupled with the Graham's reputation for value in their products, sales were much more than brisk, and the factory was hard pressed to keep up with the flood of orders.

The Graham-Paige Motors Corporation – 1928

Progressive Assembly Lines
Graham-Paige Body Plant, Wayne, Michigan.

Progressive Assembly Lines
Graham-Paige Main Plant, Detroit, Michigan.

The engineers and management had done wonders on Warren Avenue, but more production was called for. Over 3,000 employees were in place at the Warren Avenue plant,[49] which was almost 500 more than were employed by the Paige Motor Car Company at its peak. The Wayne body plant employed 1,086 men and was beginning to set production records almost daily.[50] At least 300 bodies were shipped from nearby Wayne to Warren Avenue each day.[51]

Construction people were ever present at the Warren Avenue site. Erection of a new engine assembly building was begun, just as a large concrete test track was completed behind the main manufacturing building on Lonyo Road. Located inside that oval was the new (480 foot by 100 foot) final car testing building.[52] Plans and initial foundation work were also put into place for a large engineering building to front Warren Avenue.

A great deal of effort was expended by the Graham brothers to make known their business policies and philosophies to the public. Robert Graham adopted the phrase "To sell well is to serve well," as a guiding principle for the sales department. Those words were reinforced often, just as they had been in the glass and truck enterprises. The integrity and prosperity of their sales agents were also of much concern. When the torrent of initial advertising was released during the spring, the brothers invited those who exhibited the "three C's"—Character, Capability, and Capital—to become agents and distributors.

Established in spring also was the "Graham-Paige Legion." Press releases explained the Legion was,

> *...an honorary organization of employees, male or female, of the Graham-Paige Motors Corporation. Its purposes are to promote the principles of Integrity, Honor, and Loyalty.*[53]

The medieval theme was continued in all aspects of the organization. It was explained that the knights in the Graham-Paige emblem recalled,

> *...the heroic element that is in every good man.*[54] *It goes back to the olden days when knights were pledged to uphold the right. It harkens back to an ancient system, which is not dead, but which lives today in all vigor and vitality of its ancient glory—the system of chivalry...These mail clad men are no more. But today, in the great battle of modern business, young knights still go forth, hold aloft the flag of uprightness, and fighting courageously for the cause of honesty and loyalty. Their weapons are different; but their hearts still beat high, and their lives still are marked with the great virtues of ancient knighthood.*

Upon election to the Legion, the members were asked to sign a pledge card, and accept a gold lapel pin.[55] This pin showed the three helmeted figures of the Graham-Paige emblem. Communication from the Grahams noted,

> *Members of the Legion should be worthy members. The little gold button should remind them that they are modern knights,*

The Graham-Paige Motors Corporation – 1928

fighting an even greater battle than was the clash of arms in ancient days. They are fighting the battle of clean living and honest business. They have pledged themselves to be true to themselves, true to their fellow men, and true to the nobler impulses of their own hearts.

Through the Graham-Paige Legion, we shall develop and foster the fundamental virtues on which our organization should rest. We set ourselves a standard when we strive to be that which we know we should be; in the end the persistent practice of good behavior against natural impulses affects character for the better.

The Graham-Paige Legion figured prominently in all dealings the Graham brothers had with their organization. Each dealers meeting was considered a gathering of the Legion, and was treated as such.

Just as they had done when they needed an appropriate emblem for their organization, when the Grahams felt a need for an appropriate and characteristic theme song for the Legion they engaged one of the best artists in the field. Arthur Pryor, well known for his arrangements when he was with the John Philip Sousa band (and subsequently his own band), presented the brothers the *Graham-Paige Legion March* in May of 1928.[56] As one of America's foremost composers and musicians, Pryor was a proper choice for the Grahams. A phonograph recording[57] of the theme, with words by Earl C. Donegan,[58] was made available and was played at all gatherings of the Legion.

Later, the company proudly announced,

> *Wherever this spirited marching song has been played or sung, it has met with immediate favor, not only from members of the Graham-Paige*

Arthur Pryor, formerly of the John Philip Sousa Band, was commissioned by the Graham brothers in 1928 to pen the Graham-Paige Legion March. (Courtesy of Frederick Williams)

The Spirit of the Legion was engraved by well known artist Roy F. Heinrich. Tyrone Power, Sr., modeled for the image of the medieval knight. Power donned the same garb for his appearance at the elaborate 1929 dealers convention stage show.

Legion but from the general public. It has been played by many well-known bands and orchestras, has been broadcast many times, and as a recording is in the homes of Graham-Paige men in all parts of the world.

In the same sense, an artist of high regard developed the image used for all Legion matters. "The Spi___ __he Legion" was the title of an engraving by Roy F. Heinrich.[59] That image showed a medieval knight in full battle regalia, clutching a Graham-Paige shield and massive lance. This image was used, as was the

The Graham-Paige Model 835 coupe with rumble seat was available for $2,485.

At $2,385, the elegant Graham-Paige Model 835 town sedan was intended for an upper level niche of the buying public.

With classic open car lines, this 1928 Model 835 phaeton by Le Baron is perfectly at home in this toney neighborhood. Pauline Fredericks, Hollywood starlet, is shown with the top-of-the-line Graham-Paige. Although not a factory option, the dual running board spotlights were not an uncommon accessory on these models. (Courtesy of Karl Zahm)

Legion March, in connection with all Legion dealings. The picture was hung in all the offices of the Graham-Paige Motors Corporation, in addition to being conspicuous in all Graham-Paige salesrooms. According to the company the image was,

...a constant reminder that permanent success is achieved only by a strict adherence to those chivalric principles of character, honesty, loyalty, integrity, and unity of purpose.

The second week of March saw the availability and formal introduction of the Model 614. The motoring press was quick to point out that the 614 was the lowest-priced car on the market with a four-speed internal gear transmission. According to *Automotive Industries* magazine, the powerplant of the already introduced 610 was based on the 614 engine design. A considerable number of engine parts were interchangeable but, because of the 1/4 inch larger bore, the 614 developed 35% more power than the 610. Of note also was the submerged master cylinder, which was designed to keep the system automatically filled for the Lockheed hydraulic brakes.

By the end of March the Model 835 had been put into regular production. Five body styles were available: the five-passenger sedan was $2,285, and the seven-passenger version was $125 more, the five-passenger town sedan was $2,385 and the rumble seat cabriolet was $100 more. The four-passenger coupe was also priced at $2,485. Six wire wheels were optional for $75.

A total of 200 automobiles were built by the Grahams by January 20; by the end of March 13,339 Graham-Paige motor cars had been shipped to dealers nationwide. From 300 to 350 automobiles a day were being produced in May. First quarter totals showed a gain of 7,279 motor cars produced over the same period in 1927, an increase of 121%.

Obviously, the automobile-buying public was impressed with the Graham brothers' product, found value in their philosophy, and motor cars it produced.

It was then no surprise when the Grahams held true to another of their promises. Upon their purchase of the Paige-Detroit Motor Car Company they promised an additional $4 million[60] in facilities in equipment "when they became necessary." On May 2 of 1928 the firm announced the board of directors had approved plans for additional facilities in Detroit. Those additional facilities would be put in place immediately and increase current production by a third.

Later in that same week the Model 629 had additional body styles added to those already available.[61] A four-passenger (two in the rumble seat) cabriolet would now be available, as would a four-passenger (same seating arrangement) coupe. Both side mounted models[62] were priced at $2,185. The availability of these two body styles on the Model 835 chassis was announced at the same time. The Model 835 coupe was priced at $2,485, identical to that of the cabriolet.[63]

It was with much pride that the Graham-Paige Motors Corporation[64] announced on May 2 production for 1928 surpassed the total for the entire calendar year of 1927 (21,881). Shipments during the week of April 23-29 totaled more than 10% of the entire 1927 production.[65] On June 1, the 30,000th Graham-Paige was shipped from Warren Avenue.[66]

****

Robert Graham continued to crisscross the country visiting auto shows and dealers, exhorting salesmen to full effort in presenting the new automobiles to prospective buyers. "First Anniversary Week" was promoted for June 10-17, and special showroom decorations were provided to each dealer.

Joseph Graham spent the majority of his time in Detroit, continuing the supervision of the spectacular rise in production, distribution, and plant enlargement.

Ray Graham found himself spending more time in New York City, the financial center of the nation, positioning the Graham-controlled firm as a major independent in the automobile industry.

While at a sales convention in Buffalo,[67] New York, Robert Graham shared the dais with John D. Biggers, newly appointed vice-president of Graham-Paige International Corporation, New York. Even before the spectacular success of the new Graham firm, associates and former employees from the glass and truck businesses, in addition to those at Dodge Brothers, were migrating to Detroit to assist the brothers in their efforts. The courtesy, respect, and fairness shown employees—from Loogootee to Evansville to Detroit—had not been forgotten.

When queried about the omnipresent rumors of mergers in the automobile industry, Robert Graham allowed that they were of little interest to the brothers.

The Grahams are in control of the Graham-Paige factory and we mean to stay that way. I believe that the independent company has a place in the industry, and an important place.

He also pointed out the company's desire to have the sales organization keep pace with the production increases to serve the consumer as best as possible.

Even the brothers' expectations for their new firm had been exceeded during the first half of the year. Net income for the first half of the year had been $1,878,502 after all charges. Most of those earnings came in the second quarter[68] when production got up to speed. A healthy $1.44 dividend was paid on each share of common stock, as compared to 15 cents paid to Paige-Detroit Motor Car Company stockholders for the second quarter of 1927.

Then disaster struck.

An investigation later revealed it was probably a short circuit in the electric system at Motor Bodies, Incorporated, which started a fire late Friday night, July 20. When the electrical spark ignited a paint storage area, a spectacular blaze followed which resulted in $80,000[69] in damages to the structure.[70] Forty-five completed bodies, ready for Saturday shipment from Evansville to Detroit, were destroyed in the blaze, in addition to a number of unfinished bodies.[71] Cleanup started on Saturday, and plant manager William Allen optimistically predicted operations would resume in three weeks.[72]

It was a devastating blow, not so much for the financial and structural loss, but for the shutdown of the much needed body production. The inevitable slow down of Model 610 assembly on Warren Avenue predicated an even longer wait on existing orders.

Stockholders of Graham-Paige Motors Corporation were beneficiaries of $1.44 dividend for the second quarter of 1928. The Paige-Detroit Motor Car Company paid a 15-cent dividend for the same quarter in 1927. (Courtesy of Ken Dunsire)

The Graham-Paige Motors Corporation – 1928

Ironically, another recently formed subsidiary—Graham-Paige Body Corporation—announced earlier in the month it had secured 40 acres of land on East Columbia Street[73] in Evansville for the construction of an entirely new factory dedicated to the manufacture of Graham-Paige automobile bodies. It was common knowledge the bankers[74] of Evansville, mindful of the tremendous impact the Grahams had on the economic prosperity of their city in the past, had cooperated with the Grahams to bring this plant to their city.

It was the intent of the Graham brothers to erect a substantial factory in Evansville to supplement body production at Wayne. Because of the tremendous need for body components to keep up with demand, the "rush" construction job was given to the Hoffmann Construction Company of Evansville. The $1 million building was to be 480 feet by 570 feet. There was 700 feet of frontage on East Columbia Street, and the factory would be served by three railroads. As with the Warren Street plant in Detroit, the building would be of the sawtooth design, with the roof and one half of the walls made entirely of glass panes. The one-story building would be two blocks long and one and one half blocks wide.[75] When completed, the building contained over 800,000 bricks and 14,000 tons of structural steel. The power plant portion of the building would feature the tallest structure in the city of Evansville, a 225-foot-tall chimney.[76] The railroads built spurs into the building, so railroad cars could enter in one end and leave at the other end.

It was also announced that the plant would eventually employ more than 1500 men,[77] with a capacity of 350 bodies a day when fully operational.[78] All body styles would be manufactured there.[79] Two-thirds of the Graham-Paige body production was to come from the Wayne plant, with the remaining third to be shipped from Evansville.

In addition to the utilization of natural daylight on the production lines, the plant also featured another "employee friendly" concept: the interior walls were painted a soft white with green trim. A rest area for women and girls was incorporated as was an infirmary with rooms for both men and women (with a matron). An on-site registered nurse was also provided.

Plant manager A. Stone announced,

> *The welfare of employees, and consid-*
> *eration for their health and comfort has been*
> *an important factor in the planning and*
> *equipment of our entire plant.*

Aesthetics were also considered, as the buildings were set back from the street, with a pleasant lawn and shrub arrangement.[80] The building was meant to be an architectural showcase, and a credit to the city of Evansville.

Manufacture of Graham-Paige bodies was expected to begin on January 7, 1929.

Throughout the spring and summer, Robert Graham continued to travel the United States building on the base of the sales network and expanding into new territories.[81]

Nineteen twenty-three was the year in which the Paige-Detroit Motor Car Company reached its production zenith. On July 18, 1928, Graham-Paige announced it had manufactured 43,556 automobiles, exceeding the 1923 production record of Paige-Detroit and doubling the 1927 mark. Plans were put in effect immediately to enlarge the main manufacturing plant[82] to keep up with continuing increases in demand, with a corresponding increase in production facilities in Wayne. Over $700,000 was designated for immediate improvements. That same announcement stated the former Paige-Detroit factory at Fort and McKinstry Streets had been purchased[83] for the purpose of setting up a service and export shipping department, freeing up more floor space for manufacturing on Warren Avenue.[84]

Sales records continued to be set into August, a most unusual achievement. The automotive industry was used to a falling off of orders and general business during the hot summer months, a traditional seasonal trend. On August 11, the factory reported its most productive week ever with 220 cars being shipped. On August 18, the 50,000th Graham-Paige was produced.

On August 8, 1928, this eight-cylinder coupe became the 50,000th Graham-Paige automobile produced at the Warren Avenue plant. (Courtesy of David Graham)

Ray Graham's love of guns and shooting never waned. This tidy club house headquartered the Graham-Paige Motors Corporation Gun Club on the grounds of the Wayne body plant.

Not all effort was put into production, however. To penetrate even deeper into the market, the designers and engineers continued to increase the number of body styles available on the original chassis. During August the Model 835 was being shipped in the five-passenger coupe form (at $2,385) as was the Model 629 in the same body style (at $2,085). A two-door "sport" phaeton, designed and built by Griswold[85] for Graham-Paige, was now being made available on the Model 614 and 619, at $1,435 and $1,745, respectively.[86] This two-door phaeton was of "new" design and was intended for

> *...those who desire a car having space for four passengers in any weather, instead of a rumble seat arrangement.*[87]

The seven-passenger phaeton was now also available on the straight eight for $2,410 and the Model 629 for $2,110.

These new models were likewise enthusiastically greeted, and Graham-Paige set another record on August 14 when it produced 516 automobiles during a regular nine-hour working day. Even higher production levels were expected as September saw the completion of the superstructure of the Evansville plant.

During the first week of September the Graham-Paige Motors Corporation—barely nine months old—announced total assets of $29,578,770.[88]

The company continued to be innovative in both production and sales. A meeting of sales managers and distributors at the plant in Detroit during September included tours to the much enlarged and improved plants in Wayne and on Warren Avenue. However, rather than have the assembled group addressed by the brothers and department heads, each district manager and field representative was scheduled to have one hour of personal conference with the Grahams and factory department heads. The Graham tradition of serving both their customers and their employees with a personal touch had continued in all their business pursuits, beginning in Loogootee many years prior.[89]

In a further attempt to control and increase production, the Graham brothers acquired acreage and property in Perry, Florida. Perry was the center of a thriving hardwood timber industry in that state. Erection of a new sawmill began on September 10 in Perry, under the direction of manager Charles Hastings. As a division of Graham-Paige Body Corporation, the mill would ship dimension-cut hardwoods (maple, magnolia, and ash) directly to the three Graham-Paige body plants.[90] It was explained that this Florida operation would be an asset to Graham-Paige because it would no longer be dependent upon outside suppliers and,

> *...the new mill will effect savings in transportation costs, these operations (milling to dimension-cut pieces) will eliminate 20% of the weight.*

The Graham-Paige Lumber Mill at Perry, Florida, was an extensive operation, served by its own railroad spur.

The Graham-Paige Motors Corporation – 1928

Known locally as "Graham Timberlands", the Florida acreage bought by the Grahams to supply their hardwood needs involved not only a dimension sawmill, but also a complete system of train tracks, locomotives and other special equipment. (Courtesy of John Conde)

பொது சம்மதம் சம்பாதித்
துக்கொண்டிருக்கிரது.

இந்த கிரகம் பேஜ்மோட்டார்
வண்டிகளுக்கு ஜனங்கள் அதி
கசந்தோஷத்துடன் ஏற்றுக்
கொண்டதற்கு திரட்டாந்தமா
கஜுலைவரிமாதத்தில் ஆரம்பித்
ததிலிருந்து இந்த மந்தமா
தங்களிலும் இந்த கம்பெனியா
ருக்கு பதினெட்டுவெரு22ங்க
ளில் எந்தமாதத்திலும் கிடை
யாததவ்வளவு வேலை கிடைத்
திருக்கிரது.

அனேக விதமான பாடிகள்
6, 8, சிலிண்டருடைய
இந்து வித்தியாசமான
சாசிஸ் மேல் எரிற்கும்.
எ14 மாடல் படம் காட்டியி
ருக்கிரது. 5பேர் ஓட்கா
ரும் செடான் கார்.
4ஸ்பிட் டிரான்ஸ்மி22ன்
மொத்தவடி உல.

Joseph B. Graham
Robert C. Graham
Ray A Graham

GRAHAM-PAIGE

Graham-Paige Motors Corporation was truly an international entity. A series of advertisements featuring the Model 614 were issued early in 1914 by Robert C. Graham and his Sales Department staff. This newspaper ad, written in the Tamil language, was intended for prospective customers in southern India and Ceylon. (Courtesy of Robert C. Graham, Sr.)

The new mill was projected to cost $150,000 when completed, have 50,000 square feet of floor space, and have nine dry kilns of 20 feet by 150 feet. Daily production capacity would be 60,000 board feet a day.

On September 28, 1928, Robert and Bertha Graham[91] set sail on the ocean liner *Ile de France* to attend the London and Paris auto shows and "to make a study of conditions and potential sales possibilities."

Since the introduction of the Graham-Paige, the European motoring press, especially the British, had been enthusiastic in their reviews. Even though the vast majority of English automobiles at that time were of four speed configuration,[92] the press was extremely favorable about the Graham-Paige version. Considered a "twin-top gear box," it was mentioned in nearly every write-up. The staff writer at the *Sunday Times* said "Driving the Graham-Paige is really fascinating...Graham-Paige has earned my highest respect." The prestigious automobile journal, *Motor*, said "the car is an exceptionally attractive proposition, being possessed of a fine performance and providing the comfort of many vehicles costing nearly double." The *Sheffield Independent* found the Graham-Paige "an altogether remarkable car, with road performance of unusually appealing qualities." *Auto* said "Graham-Paige is sure to command a deal of attention from a motorist who wants speed and accommodation..." The *Bradford Times* remarked that "One of the leading American cars making a great name for itself in this country is the Graham-Paige, a fact which, considering the many remarkable features of the engine lay-out, is hardly surprising." *The Daily Telegraph* said, [The Graham-Paige is]" One of the few American cars that appear to have been designed to give pleasure to the driver handling it." Mr. E. M. Wright, writing in the *Graphic*, said, "The Graham-Paige is not a sports car; it has the feather bed comfort of the best type of touring car combined with super performance." There were so many complimentary comments from England the factory issued a 20-page booklet titled "Expert Testimony" which detailed the comments. This was especially satisfying in that the English press was predisposed to portray American products as inferior to their domestic products.

Robert Graham's trip in September, coupled with the groundwork John D. Biggers did prior to the trip, resulted in almost immediate results. It was reported that Robert Graham met with, and was host to, dealers representing 80 countries.[93]

One major stop during his time in Germany was at Johannisthal, an industrial suburb of Berlin.[94] Issued during the first week of October, a press release explained the creation of Graham-Paige Automobil G.m.b.H., a corporation organized to operate an assembly plant and to act as Graham-Paige distributor for the entire country. An existing plant of 57,000 square feet was acquired, and long time Paige distributor Baron Edgar von Spiegel[95] was named general manager.[96]

Meanwhile, domestic production at the end of October was reported to be 274% greater than in October of 1927. The automobile industry was well aware of the presence of the Graham-Paige Motors Corporation.

But sales were not the entire emphasis in the rebuilding of the company. Just as Robert Graham and his sales staff kept in close and constant contact with the ever-growing dealer network, the service department was dedicated to building an equal degree of camaraderie and vitality in that facet of the business. Before the end of the year, the Technical Services Division of Graham-Paige established a school[97] at the Fort and McKinstry Street site for mechanics. Salesmen had been urged to greater success by a succession of contests and bonuses ever since the takeover by the Grahams. That tack was similarly employed by the corporation in regard to the service department. Beginning with the production of Graham-Paige automobiles in January, the service department kept in close contact with the mechanics and technicians in the field by means of Confidential Service Bulletins. These technical bulletins were directed at proper service, improved operation, and detail changes in production. A multitude of helps were given in regard to the details of the Graham-Paige automobiles, how they were built, and proper service. In September a contest designed to reward aggressiveness and initiative in the service field was begun. Twenty district supervisors shared $2,300 in prize money, the top prize being $500. The winners were awarded prizes on Christmas Eve. The Grahams really did appreciate and understand their employees.

During November an announcement was made which seemed to logically follow the course the company was taking. Corporations were set up as subsidiaries in major urban areas, essentially making those dealerships direct branches of the factory. These were the higher-volume dealerships, those which had substantial buildings, service areas, and staff. As with all other facets of the business, the Graham brothers attempted to control as much of the corporation's direction as possible. Beginning with the Graham-Paige New York City Corporation, the factory acquired and controlled 21 subsidiary branches[98] by year's end.

The Grahams' attempt to produce a quality product at reasonable price had allowed the effort of the past 18 months to succeed beyond anyone's expectation. A supreme effort in all areas of manufacture, sales, and financing made that effort a truly satisfying one, with end results which all of the nation and the automobile industry readily acknowledged.

Mindful of the importance the new Graham-Paige body plant was to the economic health of their city, the leaders and city fathers of Evansville decided to honor the Grahams with an officially designated "Graham Brothers Day" in November. Coordinated by the Evansville Chamber of Commerce, a day-long series of events was planned to commemorate the brothers' faith in the city and to coincide with the opening of the new plant. Beginning with a breakfast honoring the brothers at the McCurdy Hotel,[99] followed by a noon luncheon at the Vendome Hotel sponsored by the local Rotary Club, the city was virtually shut down by noon for the celebration, highlighted by an afternoon parade.[100] The school board excused all pupils at city schools at that time so they could attend the big event; both businesses[101] and factories throughout the city also closed at noon to give their employees an opportunity to participate. The *Evansville Courier-Journal* estimated over 100,000 people viewed the 2:00 p.m. parade[102] on that clear, yet gelid,[103] day.[104] With nearly 100 floats,[105] 15 bands, and a caravan of Graham-Paige automobiles, the three-mile-long parade was the largest civic event ever held in city's history.[107] Completed only days before the celebration, the new Graham-Paige Body Corporation plant was open to the public for tours beginning at 9:30 a.m. A huge number of people were ushered through the plant that day, accompanied by the strains of the live band in attendance.

As the city's largest employer, the Grahams were held in high regard. One local publication said,

Like generals returning from conquests, like kings going to coronation, the three important figures in the motor world will find an entire city massed to show them its gratitude.

Robert C. Graham, Joseph B. Graham. Lieutenant Governor Harold Van Orman of Indiana and Ray A. Graham as they appeared during the Graham Day celebration in Evansville, Indiana on November 20, 1928. (Courtesy of David Graham)

The Graham Day Parade in Evansville focused on Joseph, Robert and Ray Graham. Over 100,000 people attended the parade to honor the three brothers, here shown sharing the back seat of their parade car, a custom-bodied Model 835 phaeton.

Following the parade there was a 4:00 p.m. reception held at the Evansville Soldiers and Sailors Memorial Coliseum feting the brothers.[108] The entire affair was broadcast on WGBF radio for those who could not attend. The entire balcony of the Coliseum was filled with Evansville grade school children who sang "America" to begin the festivities. A twenty-four piece band played the Graham-Paige Legion March prior to the short addresses by the Graham brothers. Everyone was then invited to close the evening with a dance held in the Coliseum.[109]

The return of the Graham brothers to Indiana was dear to them for reasons quite distinct from the parade and factory opening. From their childhood in Washington, each of the brothers had dutifully followed the teachings of the Roman Catholic Church and had been known to all as fervent Catholics. A special Mass was held at their home parish in Washington the day before the Graham Day parade, one which they would remember with reverence for the rest of their lives. The Mass held at San Simeon Catholic Church that day honored the brothers for "notable deeds, outstanding services rendered to the welfare of society, and to the Church and its welfare." Bestowed by the Vatican's Papal Court upon deserving laymen, the honorary title of "Knights of St. Gregory the Great" was given each brother. This distinction was one of the highest honors a layman could garner from the Vatican. It was the first time in Church history that three persons from the same family had been honored with Knighting. The Grahams were humbled with the honor[110] and became even more dedicated in their resolve to operate successful businesses by treating their employees with respect and fairness.[111]

Satisfying as it might have been for the brothers, they did not have the luxury of staying long in Evansville and absorbing the accolades and appreciation. There was much work to be done before year's end, and they approached it with relish.

Since their purchase of the Paige-Detroit Motor Car Company, the three brothers had more than doubled the capacity of the manufacturing plants. Square footage increased from 950,000 to over 2 million square feet.[112] Improvements had been made in every area of manufacturing and, by year's end, production had more than trebled.[113]

However, the erection of the new engineering building was considered by many their most visible symbol of their dedication to the automobile industry and their place in it.

The new engineering building was a 300 foot by 60 foot structure and faced Warren Avenue, as did the Jewett-erected administration building. Built in a complimentary style and connected by an enclosed bridge, the cost of the two-story white reinforced concrete building was said to be over $200,000.[114]

Nonetheless, the expenditures for the machinery, equipment, and laboratories contained by the structure far exceeded those figures. To say the building contained one of the most advanced and professional automotive research laboratories in the world would not be an understatement.

The first floor of the imposing building was dedicated to a chassis and engine experimental laboratory. The second floor contained the experimental body room, machine shop, drafting room, and offices for the entire engineering staff.

In addition to the laboratory equipment usually associated with an automobile engineering department, the Grahams had installed four features which made it stand out among its peers.

A "cold room" was built (38' x 16') into the first floor lab in which an entire automobile could be tested. Equipment had been installed which allowed the Graham-Paige engineers to study the company's products at a temperature as low as -47 (°F). It was said the refrigeration equipment installed was of capacity equal to an ice plant producing 60-tons of ice every 24 hours. A powerful industrial fan was positioned at

This illustration of the Warren Avenue plant shows the newly erected Engineering Building. The Albert Kahn-designed Administration Building (in the foreground to the left) was connected to the Engineering Building by means of an enclosed above-the-street walkway.

Graham-Paige issued literature proclaiming: " In the new engineering building at Detroit there is provided every facility for the scientific study of motors and the rigid testing of every phase of motor performance.

The Graham-Paige Motors Corporation – 1928

the end of the room to produce a "wind" in front of the car equivalent to a speed of 35 miles per hour. These conditions of arctic cold were used to test the operation of engines, starters, carburetors, and oil pumps, in addition to observing the effect of cold on paint, top material, rubber parts and other materials.[115]

A corresponding "heat room" was installed on the opposite end of the building. Temperatures approaching 140 (°F). were attainable in this specially insulated room designed to examine cooling systems, carburetion systems, manifolds, gasoline pumps, gasoline gauges, thermostats, and automatic radiator shutters.

In addition, "silent rooms" were positioned on the first floor. A full chassis dynamometer was installed so the staff could bring in an entire automobile to monitor noise under operating conditions. Three other smaller silent rooms were established with power shafts driving individual components. A special water brake dynamometer was used for long continued tests. The testing of axles, transmissions, valve assemblies, and other chassis units were carried on in adjacent rooms.

Another corner of the first floor accommodated the chassis and body road shock testing equipment. With an eye toward safety, tests were conducted with the front and rear wheels placed on steel rollers, the car anchored firmly against displacement. The rollers were then either driven by the car's own engine or electric motors. These rollers were designed not to be smooth, but had wooden blocks of differing sizes attached to simulate hitting a road bump or pot hole. A test of 160 actual miles (per the speedometer reading) was said to subject the car to approximately 4,000 miles of road use. The apparatus used was designed to specifically test springs, shackles, and shock absorbers.

Perhaps the crowning feature of the new laboratory was the use of a stroboscope, used in the study of high-speed motions. The Graham-Paige stroboscope, of French design and construction, was one of only five in the entire nation.[116] Utilizing a cluster of 1,000 candlepower neon tubes, the stroboscope could illuminate and light an entire engine or chassis at speed. The lights were timed so it would flash in synchronism with the rate of motion of any given part. This allowed the engineers to study—as if it were standing still—any component of a chassis or engine while in motion. The use of smaller stroboscopes for the inspection of smaller units was not unheard of in the automotive industry, but Graham-Paige's installation of a unit capable to studying an entire car or chassis or car was an industry first. The close proximity of the new concrete test track on Lonyo Road made "real life" testing more than convenient.

In preparation for the introduction of the 1929 Graham-Paige models and the sales convention to be held in conjunction with the annual New York Auto Show, the Graham brothers again were innovative. The December 1 number of *Automotive Industries* magazine best described that effort:

Graham-Paige has gone and done it again. After staging something really new in the way of dealer meetings during automobile show time last January, the Graham brothers are stepping into the merchandising limelight again by being the first automobile company—in fact the first industrial organization—to utilize the "talkies" for sales purposes. They have just completed a talking film some 30 minutes in length which can be projected by

means of portable equipment carried in three relatively small trunks. The film records talks by each of the three Grahams as well as other interesting material shown to the accompaniment of an extremely impressive musical score.

...the faithfulness with which it records the personalities as well as the words of the three men who head the organization is so marked as to be quite impressive. The film begins with the same sort of symbolic picture as was used...last year, emphasizing the qualities of courage, loyalty, and service upon which the Graham-Paige Legion is founded. Then comes a talk by Joseph B. in which he describes briefly the technical development in the company during the last 12 months and invites the dealers—for whom the film is designed—to come to a special gathering in Detroit shortly after the first of the year to see what is to be at the New York Show. Joseph is followed by Ray A. who re-emphasizes and revivifies the principles upon which the Legion is based and then discusses the future of Graham-Paige business, while Robert B. is the final speaker. He tells of the success the organization has been having abroad and also emphasizes his hope to meet each dealer personally at the January meeting.

The plan is to show the film in as many centers as possible between now and January 1, primarily with the idea of building up to the special sales convention and also with the thought of bringing to as many dealers as possible a clearer feeling and contact with the men who are heading the organization whose product they are selling in the field. The equipment being used is one of the first portable sound projection machines ever produced. Only two or three such machines exist today.

While the movietone is an entirely new stunt so far as use by business organizations is concerned, the importance of this particular film, as we see it, lies not primarily in its obviously practical and utilitarian relation to the working out of a carefully laid sales plan. The film is designed exclusively for use among dealers and in no sense as a means of reaching owner prospects.

The goal of the brothers to become an important independent producer of motor cars was taken very seriously.

As 1928 drew to a close the brothers were able to reflect upon the growth of their new endeavor during its first year. Over $5,800,000 was expended during the year to more than double the manufacturing area (to 2,017,430 square feet). Employment was increased from 1,800 to 6,100 men and women, and the number of dealers increased from 781 to 2,270.[117] By producing 72,965 motor cars they had become the 12th largest producer of automobiles in the United States, producing a profit of $1,055,678[118] on $61,464,397 of total sales.[119]

But there was little time for reflection in the lives of these busy businessmen. This record-breaking year was simply to be the foundation for an even greater year of accomplishment.

The Graham-Paige Motors Corporation – 1928

[1] There had been other automobile firms bearing the Graham name which had no association with Joseph, Ray, and Robert Graham:

Graham [steam car] (1899-1900), a product of the Graham Equipment Company of Boston, Massachusetts.

Graham (1903-1904), a product of the Graham Automobile and Launch Company of Chicago, Illinois.

Graham-Fox (1901-1904), a product of the Graham Fox Company, New York, New York, and Middleton, Connecticut. In 1904 Graham Fox merged with the Eisenhuth Horseless Vehicle Company.

Graham Motorette (1902-1904), a product of the Sefrin Motor Carriage Company of Brooklyn, New York.

[2] Taft was born in Elmwood, Illinois, in 1860.

[3] Both a B.A. and M. A.

[4] Taft joined the faculty of the Art Institute of Chicago in 1886, remaining on staff during his highly successful career as a commissioned artist.

[5] Taft authored the first comprehensive treatment of American sculpture in his 1903 volume entitled "The History of American Sculpture." In 1921 he published "Modern Tendencies in Sculpture." He was also a regular contributor throughout his career to art magazines and newspapers.

Hamlin Garland, a well known and respected American author, was Taft's son-in-law.

[6] Following his election to the National Academy of Design in 1911, Taft participated enthusiastically in the planning of public education in art. He also served from 1914-17 as the director of the American Federation of the Arts.

[7] Examples include "Marquis de Lafayette," 1896, at Lafayette, Indiana; "Schuyler Colfax," 1887, at Indianapolis; "Philo Carpenter," 1888, at Chicago; and "Ulysses S. Grant," 1899, at Leavenworth, Kansas.

[8] Taft's most well known and acclaimed work is the famous "Spirit of the Great Lakes." Dedicated in 1913 the huge fountain was located on the grounds of the Art Institute of Chicago and brought Taft lasting fame and respect. Renderings of the fountain were shown in some of the early 1928 magazine advertising for Graham-Paige. Other well known fountains include the Columbus Memorial Fountain (1912) in Washington D.C.; the Thatcher Memorial Fountain (1917) in Denver, Colorado; and the Fountain of Time (1920) in Chicago.

[9] With the support of Chicago attorney Wallace Heckman, Taft established an artists colony in 1898 near Oregon, Illinois, on the Rock River. At least partially to escape the heat of the city during summer months, the establishment of "Eagle's Nest" by Taft soon made it a very stylish and socially acceptable place for artists to be seen during the summer. A huge and impressive memorial to native Americans titled "Blackhawk" was erected on the bluffs overlooking the Rock River in 1912. Other examples include the "Peace Pylon" and "Prosperity Pylon" (1899) in Chicago, and the "Randolph County Soldiers and Sailors Monument" (1890) at Winchester, Indiana; "Midway Bridges" in Chicago; and "Solitude of the Soul" (1900) at the Art Institute of Chicago. One of Taft's better known works is "Eternal Silence," a memorial at Graceland Cemetery (Chicago) for the Dexter Graves family plot.

[10] Taft's name was linked to Augustus Saint-Gaudens, Daniel Chester French, Frederick MacMonnies, Bela Lyon Pratt, and Cyrus Dallin as one of the most influential sculptors of the age.

[11] Taft's former home and studio, Midway Studios, is located on the campus of the University of Chicago and is preserved as a national monument.

[12] The Grahams were, of course, not the only brother team to be in the automobile and transportation industry. Other familial management included these brother-headed organizations:

Fischer Body (Fred J., Charles T., Lawrence P., William, A. Edward F., Alfred J., and Howard A.); Studebaker (Henry, Clement, John M., Peter E., and Jacob F.); Kissel (George A., O.P., A.P., and W. L.); Duesenberg (Fred and August); Marmon (Walter C. and Howard C.); Firestone (Leonard, Harvey, Jr., Raymond, and Russell); Dodge (John and Horace); Widman [J. C. Widmann and Company] (J. C., Frank E., Charles H., David, George, and Arthur); Stranaham [Champion Spark Plug] (Frank A. and Robert A.); White [White Motor Company] (Windsor T., Rollin H., and Walter C.); Jeffery (Charles and Harold); Gardner (Russell E., Jr., and Fred W.); Fageol [Fageol Motors and later Twin Coach Corp.] (W. B. and F. R.); Davidson [Harley-Davidson] (William, Arthur, Jr. and Walter); Mack (J.M. and J.C.); Remy [Delco-Remy] (Frank and B. Perry); Owen [Owen-Magnetic] (Ralph R. and Ray M.); Becker [Elmore automobiles] (James H. and Burton A.); Davis [Davis Motor Car Co.] (George W. and Walter C.); Watson [Watson Stabilators] (John W., and Richard A.); Timken [Timken Roller Bearings] (H.H. and W.R.); Lipe [Brown, Lipe Gear Co] (Charles E. and William C.); Apperson [Haynes-Apperson] (Elmer and Edgar); Duryea (Charles E. and J. Franklin); Stanley [Locomobile and Stanley Steamer] (F.E. and F.O.); Packard (J. W. and W. D.); Clark (Louis S., John S., and James K.). Nor were the brother teams limited to domestic marques. These brother-managed companies operated in Europe: Stoewer (Emil and Bernhard), [Stoewer automobiles], Germany; Reichstein (Carl, Adolph, and Hermann), [Reichstein automobiles] Germany; Opel (Carl, Wilheim, Heinrich, and Fritz), Germany; Michelin (Edouard and Andre), France; Goudard (Maurice and Felix), [Solex Carbs] France; Farman (Henry, Maurice, and Dick), Farman auto, France; Renault (Louis, Marcel, and Fernand), France; DeJong (Sylvain, Jacques, and Henri), [Minerva automobiles] Belgium.

[13] Complete and absolute secrecy regarding the new corporation was not of the highest concern to the brothers. In fact, while encouraging the retail salesmen involved in the sell-off of the remaining Paige automobiles, Robert Graham developed a plan to give them even more incentive to produce sales. Contests and bonuses had been issued to successful salesmen throughout the fall of 1927. Just prior to Christmas 1927 a brochure was issued to all retail salesmen indicating the Graham-Paige Motors Corporation had instituted a new policy of benefits. In addition to the regular commission earned, those salesmen selling reasonable numbers of automobiles would be eligible for life insurance policies in amounts from $1,000 to $5,000. Entitled "A Gift of Life Insurance to Graham-Paige Salesmen," the inside cover of the brochure carried a letter from Robert Graham explaining the purpose of the benefit, and how they felt a benefit to the salesman's entire family was most appropriate. (The policy was at no cost to the salesman and no medical exam was required.) In addition to the references throughout to "Graham-Paige salesmen," the December 25, 1927, brochure carried a large representation of Lorado Taft's recent creation on the cover. By March, a half million dollars worth of insurance was placed on Graham-Paige salesmen.

[14] The Graham-Paige offerings were assigned space A-5. The new automobiles could also be seen in the main lobbies of the Roosevelt and Pennsylvania hotels.

[15] Sponsored by the National Automobile Chamber of Commerce, the annual show was held January 7-14 in 1929.

[16] A special meeting of the stockholders of the Paige-Detroit Motor Car Company was called for January 5, 1928, to act specifically on the name change. *Automobile Industries* noted the name change would "identify the company and its product more fully with the three Graham brothers who are now in control."

[17] Pfau reports that after the original design was determined, the scale drawings were sent to the Detroit studio where they were adapted to the various chassis to be offered.

[18] In his book, *The Custom Body Era*, designer Hugo Pfau offered the following comments on the Graham-Paige design and its introduction at New York,

> *At that time, space in the New York Automobile Show was assigned by the National Automobile Chamber of Commerce, on the basis of dollar volume of each member firm's sales during the preceding year. By pure chance, Graham-Paige and Hupmobile were assigned space on opposite sides of the same aisle.*
>
> *When I visited the show, I could not help smiling at the comments of people who stood between the Hupp and Graham exhibits and made remarks about how everybody in Detroit was copying everybody else. I was one of the few people there who knew that the Hupmobile, with a Murray Body, had been styled by Amos Northup and his staff in Detroit, while Stickney and I worked out the Graham-Paige in New York. Neither of us had any idea what the others were doing.*
>
> *Of course, a considerable amount of copying did go on, but many similar designs came from different people simply because design is essentially a process of evolution. One idea suggests another, and it is not unnatural for more than one designer to get the same inspiration at the same time.*

[19] It is important to note that when Graham-Paige said that it built its own power plants, that is exactly what it did. According to Scott McKibben, Graham-Paige engineer from 1928-1932, "engine blocks were supplied by Ferro, and periodically, others. The block was delivered bare, and Graham-Paige then assembled the powerplant to their specifications." This was true in each case, except for those cases in the text where it is indicated that Continental supplied the engine blocks. Even in those cases, it was only a base engine block which was purchased.

[20] Canadian sales literature indicates the price at Windsor was $1,165, Canadian.

[21] Five wire wheels were $35 extra, and front and rear bumpers were $15 extra.

[22] Brochures handed out at the show indicated that formal introduction would take place at "important shows" on February 15 and production would begin about February 25.

[23] This engine was larger and more powerful than the eight-cylinder motors of Auburn (88 hp), LaSalle (80 hp), Cadillac (90 hp), and Cunningham (95 hp). These motor cars are classified as true classics by the Classic Car Club of America.

[24] Standard production bodies for the Model 619 and Model 629 were produced by Briggs. The Evansville and Wayne plants were employed full time in trying to meet Model 610 production needs. Custom and special bodies were being procured from LeBaron Detroit Company.

[25] Five wire wheels were $60 extra, while front and rear bumpers were standard equipment.

[26] The prices at Windsor were $2,265 and $2,235 Canadian, respectively.

[27] Front and rear bumpers were standard equipment, while five wire wheels were $75 extra.

[28] A chassis sans body was available for "custom mounting" in each of the six-cylinder series, as was later true for the eight-cylinder chassis. The Model 610 chassis was available for $695, the Model 619 for $1,230, and the Model 629 was $1,375.

[29] The Continental motor used was the Model 14K. This powerplant, built by Continental to Graham-Paige specifications, was derived from the Continental 12K. The 12K was stock engine, built "for the trade."

[30] Only America's biggest and best motorcars exceeded the power and size of the Model 835 chassis: Cunningham's Model V7 (441.7 ci), Cadillac's Series 341 (341 ci), Lincoln (384 ci), Locomobile's Model 90 (371.5 ci) and Model 48 (524 ci), Marmon's Model E-75 (339.7 ci), McFarlan's TV6 (572.5 ci), Packard's 4-43 (384.8 ci), Pierce Arrow's Model 36 (414.7 ci), Rolls-Royce of America's Phantom 1 (468.0 ci), Stearns-Knight's Model J-885 and Model H 885 (385 ci), Studebaker's Commander (354 ci) and President Six (354 ci),

and the Willis 9 of Maywood, Illinois (432.5 ci—only two prototypes of this nine-cylinder motor car were built).

By comparison, the Duesenberg for 1928 utilized an engine which displaced only 259 cubic inches.

[31] Advertised prices in Australia were 395£ for the Model 610 sedan, 525£ for the Model 614 sedan, 635£ for the Model 619, 750£ for the 629 sedan, and 895£ for the 835 sedan.

[32] Front and rear bumpers were standard, disc or wood wheels were no charge options, but six wire wheels were a $75 option. All variations included four 31 x 6.20 tires.

[33] Neither the roadster nor the convertible coupe, as shown on the Model 629 chassis, was available on the straight eight-platform.

[34] The custom built town car and phaeton were also available on the Model 629 chassis. The phaeton was $3,485 while the town car garnered $4,015.

[35] In Australia, Richard Motor Body Builders, Ltd., of Adelaide, S.A., built special bodies for that continent's trade on the Model 614 chassis. Coupes and phaetons of their own design were distributed by Maughan Thiem Motor Company, the sole Graham-Paige distributor at that time.
A year later, the Melbourne Motor Body Works of West Melbourne built five-passenger phaetons (tourers) and two-passenger coupes on the Model 612 chassis. They were distributed by Walter Whitborn, Pty., Ltd., of that city.

[36] The emphasis on the four-speed transmission was continued into 1929 when the brochure was issued in several variations under the title "Four Speed Advantages".

[37] The sales convention was held at the prestigious Blackstone Hotel in downtown Chicago.

[38] Byrd-Sikes had also been a leading Paige distributor for many years.

[39] The start-up, although impressive in its speed, was gradual. By January 20, the 200th Graham-Paige automobile was produced.

[40] In addition to the three brothers, the board of directors included E. D. Stair, Gilbert W. Lee, Sherwin A. Hill, W.A. Wheeler, J. D. Biggers, W. H. Neely, and F.R. Valpey.

[41] Kargas Wagon Works was concerned with much more than wagon production. They also were involved with furniture production and architectural endeavors.

143

[42] When Johann took over the former Kargas Wagon Works for the purpose of building Graham truck and bus bodies, the plant was considerably remodeled and up-to-date machinery was installed.

[43] William Allen was named vice-president and general manager and R. C. Hicks was secretary-treasurer. Named superintendent of body painting and trimming was Charles Gamber, E. A. Campbell was superintendent of body samples, and Donald Whister was metal work superintendent.

[44] Actual manufacturer of Graham-Paige bodies commenced on March 1, 1928, with a work force of 100 men.

[45] The first bodies were produced in Wayne on February 6, and daily production was approximately 150 bodies. It was anticipated that 200 bodies would be produced daily within a month.

[46] Valpey began his career in the automotive field in 1914 when he joined the Willys-Overland Company. He remained there until 1917 as factory representative of the New York district, when he joined the Franklin Company in New York, also as a distributor. He was first associated with the Grahams when he became a Graham Brothers Truck distributor in the early 1920s. From November of 1924 until April of 1926, Valpey was director of districts and then sales manager for Graham Brothers Trucks. Until 1917 he was assistant general manger for Dodge Brothers, Inc. When the Grahams purchased Paige, Valpey became executive assistant to Robert C. Graham until his appointment as general sales manager.

[47] Valpey took the place of longtime Paige sales manager, Henry Krohn, who resigned on March 1. Krohn had been with Jewett almost from the beginning, and was considered a valued executive for Jewett.

[48] Heilman began his career in the automotive industry with Peerless in 1909. He was then associated with the Vulcan factories in Evansville, Indiana, in their sales department until 1921. Heilman then became a district representative for Graham Brothers trucks on the coast, and then became an assistant of Robert C. Graham. In 1926 he became southern division sales manager for Dodge Brothers, Inc., and became director of commercial car and truck sales in that same year.

Heilman took the place of G. B. Gaunt, a Paige employee for 12 years. Before taking the position with Paige in Detroit, Gaunt was a distributor for Paige (and Pierce Arrow) in Dallas and was also associated with the Knight Tire and Rubber Company.

[49] 3,030.

[50] During the start-up months of the Graham-Paige Motors Corporation, the standard workday was ten hours. This was later reduced to nine hours when a consistent production was achieved.

[51] For example, the March 7, 1928, total from Wayne was 311 bodies.

[52] Over one acre of floor space was under its roof. This building would later contain the Graham-Bradley tractor assembly plant.

[53] The Grahams defined the terms in this manner: Integrity is the fundamental virtue of good life. In its most appropriate meaning it stands for uprightness in all dealings. It goes to the very heart and does not confine itself to external actions, which may be nothing but hypocrisy. Honor we take as honesty in dealing with fellow men. Honor in this sense is the natural result of integrity. Loyalty, or unity of purpose, is the virtue that cements men together in a common cause.

[54] With a perspective which was not common in that day and age, the Grahams included in their announcement, "Since women as well as men possess these virtues, we greatly encourage women to join the Legion. They have the same right as men to become members, providing they fulfill all the requirements. Hence, everything here said regarding men is to be likewise understood regarding women." Those requirements included being proposed for the Legion by his or her boss, association with Graham-Paige (or Paige-Detroit) for at least 12 months, and exhibiting the virtues of Integrity, Honor, and Loyalty.

[55] When the brothers had their formal portraits taken in 1928, each of their lapels showed the Legion lapel pin. An article in the New York Sun noted that the Taft design "showed the helmeted heads of three knights, visors raised to show stern and serious classic faces above shoulders covered with chain mail. Done in clear cut relief on art metal, three faces bear a family resemblance and appear to be those of three men of somewhat different ages."

[56] In addition to being assistant conductor for the Sousa band for 12 years, Pryor also gained a reputation for his memorable solos and for arranging the ragtime music used by Sousa. Pryor is also known for his composition "The Whistler and His Dog" (1905), in addition to the fact that his band—70 members strong—premiered George Gershwin's song "Swanee" at New York City's Capitol Theatre in 1919 for the Demitasse Revue.

According to The Big Band Years by Bruce Crowther and Mike Penfold, "Arthur Pryor, a trombone player of phenomenal ability...[whose] popularity led to his becoming a band leader in his own right. Phil Wilson, trombone star with Woody Herman in the 1960s, still considers Pryor's technique and mastery of his instrument to be second to none. 'You listen to those old records and you can hear between the scratches that Arthur Pryor can still hold his head high with the wizards of today.'"

In 1997 a compact disc was released by Crystal Records, Camas, Washington, entitled Arthur Pryor/Trombone Soloist of the Sousa Band. The CD is part of its Historical Series (CD451) and features 26 of Pryor's recordings. The recordings date from 1901 to 1911. The liner notes state, "Arthur Pryor is the most acclaimed trombonist of all time."

[57] Available on the Victor Records label (Camden, New Jersey), the recording could be ordered from the factory for 60 cents. The piece was performed by the Victor Orchestra.

[58] It is interesting to note that the lyrics were written by Donegan, a New York writer, prior to the composition of the music. When Donegan turned over the lyrics to Pryor "...within 24 hours he [Pryor] returned with the 'Legion March' substantially as it stands today."

The lyrics are of but two stanzas:

Commerce does not kill the manly spirit—
Does not turn all aims toward gain;
Sell and serve can be the watchword
Of the Legion we maintain.

Comrades in effort, with one purpose,
Value—service-is our gauge,
Working always for the Legion
And the good name Graham-Paige.

[59] A native of Indiana, Heinrich was raised in the East and studied art in Connecticut. Establishing a commercial art studio in Detroit in 1910, Heinrich was engaged by Graham-Paige to make a series of drawings for the initial public relations campaign. Examples of these drawings can be found in the initial 1928 prestige catalog. Entitled "Beauty," "Smoothness," and "Swiftness," these drawings were also used in magazine advertising and prestige showroom brochures. Heinrich was invited by the Grahams to attend the 1928 New York Automobile Show and a meeting of the executives and dealers. The room in which the meeting was held was done in the previously described medieval theme. The presentation by Ray Graham at that meeting impressed him and appealed to his idealistic viewpoint of art and, now, his idealistic view of business. According to the company, Heinrich "returned to his studio, and of his own

The Graham-Paige Motors Corporation – 1928

volition began to draw a picture that should represent—as he saw it—"The Spirit of the Graham-Paige Legion." Posing for the portrait was well known actor Tyrone Power, Sr. In 1929 Heinrich illustrated two booklets for Graham-Paige. Titled "*Motor Cars for Farmers*" and "*Motor Cars for Railroad Men*," they bore the distinctive Heinrich style.

[60] In addition to the $4 million needed to acquire the firm.

[61] A bulletin from the factory indicated the Model 629 coupe would be shipped beginning about June 1. Its price was $2,185 f.o.b. The coupe and cabriolet featured six-wheel equipment, with wood or steel (disc) wheels standard. Wire wheels were a $75 option.

[62] Either wood or disc wheels were initially available, and both bumpers were standard.

[63] Communication from the factory on June 23, 1928, indicated the entire production of Model 835 cabriolets for the year had been ordered and dealers should not place any further orders for the body style. The Model 629 cabriolets were similarly sold out. Continued demand for the popular cabriolets and subsequent dealer pressure forced the factory to put the body style back into production in July. Popularity of the Model 629 and Model 835 coupes had outstripped production, and dealers were advised to not order these body styles until after August 1. Sales and orders of the Model 610 coupe far exceeded each dealer's allotment, and dealers were admonished to not order more Model 610 coupes than they could realistically deliver.

[64] It is interesting to note it was in June of 1928 the Graham Brothers division of Dodge Brothers, Incorporated, widely publicized their conversion to all six-cylinder engines. This advertising and publicity no doubt helped, at least in a tertiary sense, the public's recognition of the brothers' new motor car offering.

[65] Even though the production records of Graham-Paige exceeded all domestic producers by a large margin, nearly all manufacturers prospered during 1928. This was due at least partially to the repeal of the war tax enacted ten years earlier, and the booming "Roaring 20s" economy. Nearly all manufacturers reduced prices slightly, enhancing sales.

[66] By comparison:

	1927	1928	% increase
January	1374 automobiles	1497	8.9%
February	2102 automobiles	4019	91.2%
March	2477 automobiles	7616	207.4%
April	2830 automobiles	8275	192.4%

[67] The gathering was on June 23 at the Statler Hotel with over 150 dealers from Buffalo and western New York in attendance.

[68] Second quarter net income totaled $1,620,719.

[69] Originally reported to be a $65,000 loss, the total was later increased to this figure. The loss was only partially covered by insurance.

[70] Perry Neal discovered the blaze, and night watchman A. C. Grayson sounded the alarm "almost simultaneously." Two firemen were overcome fighting the fire.

[71] Two rail box cars filled with completed bodies were pulled to safety by an alert train crew who happened to be near the plant.

[72] Actual production would not resume until August 16, 1928.

[73] The plot of land purchased extended from East Columbia to Crown Avenue to the C.& E.I. railroad line.

[74] The formal announcement was made at the Evansville Clearing House Association at the Mercantile Bank on July 18, 1928.

[75] In addition to the plant building there was to be an employment office, two clock houses, and three watchmen's houses.

[76] The chimney had a diameter of 18 feet.

[77] In addition to 100 women. It was explained that it was best to give the vast majority of employment to men, as they would then be able to support their entire families. Forty-four high-powered sewing machines were installed for interior fabric work. Almost the entire 100 women worked in the sewing department as it was found men "could not do satisfactory work" in that department.

[78] The payroll was expected to be near $3 million a year.

[79] Initially, two- and four-door sedans, touring cars, and roadsters were to be produced in Evansville. The first body produced was a four-door sedan.

[80] With the introduction of nearly 1200 new employees (expected) the Grahams also considered their adopted hometown's well-being in a social sense. The influx of new residents would no doubt make drastic changes around the

plant. Graham-Paige officials requested an appearance at the Evansville city council at which they appealed for "discretion in building permits" near the new plant. It was the stated position of the officials that "bootlegging joints" be strongly discouraged from the area to "keep it clean and healthy."

[81] The week of July 21 was spent with the managers of the 12 factory branches of Graham-Paige Motors Corporation. Along with assistant Valpey, Robert Graham conferred with the managers at Detroit and tours of the main plant on Warren Avenue and the Wayne body division were conducted. On Monday of that week, following the tours, a competition was held among the executives and managers at the Graham-Paige Gun Club grounds in Wayne. Ray Graham's love of guns and shooting had never left him. Following the Detroit portion of the conference, the men left for Mackinac Island for the rest of the week. Discussions of the plans and policies of the factory, future sales strategy, and each factory branches' role were concluded there on Saturday.

[82] A total of 126,800 feet of additional floor space was being constructed.

[83] Prior to this time the facilities at that site had been leased from the Jewett/Buhl interests.

[84] A subsequent press release revealed the original plans for the Evansville plant had been enlarged and the amount of additional floor space would increase building costs by over $100,000.

[85] The Griswold Body Company was a rather small scale body producer in the motor city. According to historian Karl Zahm, "The company was established in July 1909 in Detroit and was situated on Commonwealth Avenue. The original factory was a wooden structure which measured 90 feet by 110 feet. An addition of approximately 42 feet by 85 feet was added in January 1910. H. F. Marsh was president; M. Griswold, vice-president; A.F. Marsh, treasurer; Louis Smith, secretary and general manager; and Elmer Day, superintendent. A fire of unknown origin destroyed most of the oldest portion of the plant in 1911. Reconstruction began, almost before the fires were contained, upon a larger all-brick facility, half again as large as the former plant. A large 3-story addition valued at $12,300 was completed in the summer of 1915 enabling the concern to increase production."

A specialty firm, Griswold had produced commercial bodies over the years, in addition to a myriad of smaller automobile manufacturers, including Partin-Palmer, King, and Columbia. In 1928 (at the end of the fiscal year) Griswold reported that the firm was in good financial shape, having over

$500,000 of sales during the year to Chrysler, Jordan, Graham-Paige and others. The concern also produced roadster bodies for Willys-Knight, a major client. It was also during this period that Griswold produced the famed cabin speedster for E. L. Cord at Auburn.

A year later Griswold would produce a unique automobile for Graham-Paige with which they anticipated future sales. Deemed a "semi-convertible," this convertible victoria featured stationary side window frames contained in a fabric body. Still later another version was produced on a Model 615 chassis, but no contract was garnered from Graham-Paige.

The Griswold Body Company should not be confused with the Griswold Motor Company. J.P. La Vigne formed the Griswold Motor Company in May of 1907. Located at 520 Lincoln Avenue, Detroit, the company was capitalized at $200,000. The Griswold Motor Company shared a building with the C. M. Bloomstrom Manufacturing Company, manufacturers of the "Bloomstrom 30." The Griswold Motor Company was out of business by the end of 1907. The Griswold automobile made in Quincy, Massachusetts (1905-06) and the Griswold automobile of Troy, New York, (1906) were likewise unrelated business ventures.

[86] In mid-August, production of the sport phaetons was up to speed, and the factory announced price reductions. The Model 614 was available, with painted wooden wheels, for $1,295. It was also available with natural wood wheels for ten dollars more, with five steel (disc) wheels for $1,310, six steel wheels for $1,355, and six wire wheels for $1,380. The Model 629 had a base price of $1,595 with painted wheels, $1,605 for natural wood wheels, $1,615 for five steel wheels, $1,655 for five wire wheels, $1,655 for six steel wheels, $1,745 for six wire wheels, and $1,705 for six natural wood wheels.

[87] The announcement went on to explain that the doors were of unusual width, one on each side, serving as the entrance to both the front and rear seats. The front seat is divided and either half may be folded forward, giving easy access to the rear passenger compartment.

[88] The period reported on was to June 30, 1928. This amount included the sale of $3 million 6% sinking fund gold debentures. Common stock and surplus totaled $12,612,768; current assets of $17,277,665; and current liabilities of $7,864,573. Current assets included cash of $6,305,677; dealers' accounts of $3,128,423; open accounts of subsidiary companies, $1,860,331; accounts receivable of $205,742; and inventory valued at $5,777,749.

[89] The Graham brothers not only accepted suggestions and criticism, they encouraged it. To insure there was good communication between Warren Avenue and the field, a letter was posted to all distributors and dealers. That letter, authored by Service Manager W. L. Kessinger, recounted a conversation he had with Joseph Graham addressing his concern. The president of Graham-Paige Motors Company said, "I wish our Distributors and Dealers didn't feel that it was necessary to begin or close with an apology, when they write us letters of valuable suggestions and constructive criticisms. I'd like for you to write...making it clear that we need and value these criticisms, that no apologies are necessary, and that one is going to be catalogued as a chronic kicker because he has given us his honest constructive opinion."

[90] The company was proud to point out the operation was done entirely by Graham employees on Graham-owned land. "Graham-Paige timber experts fell [the trees] and...are taken to the mill and rough cut." The timber was then stacked on open air racks for 90 days of seasoning. The kiln dried aspect of seasoning was for a period of eight days to four weeks, depending on the size and moisture content of the lumber. Heartwood, finely grained and strong, was utilized for the sills, pillar posts, and body top side rails. Soft wood was used "only where the factor of strength does not enter into its use."

[91] Their sons, Ziba and Charles, also made the trip.

[92] *Autocar* magazine listed the 248 makes produced in Europe and totaled 163 of those which utilized a four-speed internal gear transmission.

[93] Print advertising abroad not only featured the familiar languages of Europe, but also Tamil (southern India and Sri Lanka), Cusarati (Ethiopia and Somalia), Chinese, and Bengali (eastern India).

[94] Johannisthal is 18 miles from the capital of Germany.

[95] The Baron was the first Paige distributor in Germany, being appointed by Harry M. Jewett on October 16, 1924.

[96] The announcement noted that "S.M. Berg and Hans Wollner, experienced engineers and layout men, have been sent to Berlin by Detroit to make a thorough survey of the manufacturing, assembling, and export possibilities of the Johannisthal plant. The buildings will be laid out to assemble Graham-Paige chassis on the American system of continuous production and to receive bodies built in Germany under Graham-Paige supervision. It is expected that the manufacturing and assembly plants will be completed shortly, and that volume production will be attained by the early spring of 1929."

[97] The school established at the McKinstry Street plant (Plant No. 3) consisted of class rooms with component parts available for study, in addition to complete chassis of each of the company's offerings. The classes were of two weeks duration, and were held during the fall, winter, and spring months. In addition to instruction regarding the repair and maintenance of Graham-Paige automobiles, the classes also addressed proper stock keeping methods, shop management, and proper dealer/factory relations in regard to stocking and returns. Class size was limited to 50 men. For those mechanics who could not attend the factory school, a series of filmstrips was produced for viewing at the district level. The author owns a set of these filmstrips (including the projector) which were produced for Graham-Paige by Wilding Picture Productions, 1538 Mullet Street, Detroit, Michigan.

[98] Wholly owned subsidiaries included Graham-Paige Company of New England, Graham-Paige Company of Texas, Graham-Paige Company of El Paso, Graham-Paige of Indiana, Inc., Graham-Paige Company of Southern California, Graham-Paige Company of Nashville, Graham-Paige Company of Nebraska, Graham-Paige International Corporation, Graham-Paige Motors, Inc. (Canada), Graham-Paige Automobil G.m.b.H, S. A. Graham-Paige (Belgium) and the Graham-Paige Body Corporation (both Evansville and Perry). Those which were controlled but not wholly owned were: Graham-Paige of North Carolina, Graham-Paige of Cincinnati, Inc., Graham-Paige of Michigan, Graham-Paige Company of Evansville, Inc., Graham-Paige of Louisville, Graham-Paige of Louisville, Graham-Paige of New York City Corporation, and Graham-Paige of Northern California. This was also true of the subsidiaries established later: Graham-Paige Motors, LTD, London; Graham-Paige of Minnesota; and Graham-Paige of Washington, D. C..

[99] Joseph and Robert flew into Washington for the festivities, while Ray Graham drove from the Graham Farms in Washington.

[100] The Grahams rode in a Model 835 phaeton. Riding a horse directly in front of the touring car was "Miss Evansville" for 1928. The reigning Miss Evansville was eight-year-

old Evanline Ingleheart, daughter of Mr. and Mrs. Austin Ingleheart (200 Sunset Avenue).

In 1984 the Graham Owners Club, International, held its annual meet in Washington, Indiana. Dubbed "The Graham Homecoming," the gathering paralleled the original parade in that it, too, was officially designated "Graham-Paige Day" in Washington, was highlighted by a long parade including numerous Graham-built vehicles, and a band (the Washington High School Band) played the Graham-Paige Legion March as it progressed through the streets of Washington. Mrs. Evanline Hamilton, "Miss Evansville 1928," was a guest of honor at the 1984 gathering.

[101] Many businesses took out ads in a special section of the day's Courier-Journal. Typical of the messages included in the ads was that of Bittermann Brothers. Along with photos of the Grahams, the text read (in part): "Welcome Joe-Bob-Ray/We wish to commend you on your faith in Evansville. You have played a big part in the industrial life of our city, and we trust that Evansville will continue to merit your confidence and good will."

Most downtown merchants displayed photos of Graham-Paige automobiles and many displayed automotive parts. The Andres Company window displayed an entire motor painted in black enamel.

[102] The parade started on Riverside Avenue, and was headed by a lone horseman in medieval costume. He was followed by two heralds with trumpets, and three knights in helmets. More than 200 Graham-Paige motor cars caravaned from Loogootee and Washington, Indiana, to participate in the parade. They were accompanied to Evansville by an escort of state police motorcycles. A 35-piece band met the caravan at the Evansville city limits and led the group into the parade proper.

[103] Every surviving attendee of the parade interviewed by the author first commented on how cold it was that day, prior to relating other details of the parade.

[104] The only civic celebration to rival that of Graham Day was the parade held in 1937 to celebrate the manufacture of the 1,000,000th Electrolux refrigerator by the Servel Corporation. On that day an estimated 50,000 people viewed the parade and then proceeded to Bosse Field for speeches. It is interesting to note that it was Joseph Graham who convinced Servel, a subsidiary of Hercules, to locate in Evansville.

[105] Many businesses and civic groups entered floats in the parade. Typical of those was the *Evansville Press* (newspa-

per) float. A seven-ton truck carried a plaster cast of the new Graham plant, 16 feet high, 7 feet wide, and 30 feet long. It was distinctively painted in green and white, mimicking the interior of the new factory.

The employees of Graham Glass were also included in the festivities, and marched in the parade. Examples of their "handy work" (glass canes, door stops in the shape of turtles and other animals, and abstract shapes) were given away to spectators.

[106] One reference indicates that the Graham brothers, in appreciation to the gesture extended by the city, donated an eight-cylinder sedan to the Evansville Police Department. The archives of the Evansville Police Department indicate this was not the case.

[107] The interest Ray Graham had in aviation was not forgotten on Graham Day. The media wrote of the arrival of a "Mystery Plane" which would arrive the day before the parade. The "huge bi-motored amphibious ship" was to arrive at the local airport the afternoon prior to the Graham Day celebration. Sponsored by real estate dealer John W. Castle, the plane was piloted by H. G. McCaroll and its designer, Lt. George R. Pond. Built in secrecy, the trip to Evansville was its maiden flight. According to its designer and builder, the plane would embark on a world flight in an attempt to break existing records. Following its display at the airfield the plane was brought to the Ohio River for exhibition.

[108] Master of ceremonies was former Evansville postmaster, John J. Nolan, friend of the Graham family. Evansville Mayor Herbert Males gave the welcoming speech.

[109] No admission was charged for the dance.

[110] The Order of St. Gregory the Great was to commemorate the life of Pope Gregory XVI. The order was established in 1831 and had six ranks or titles. The highest honor was The Supreme Order of Christ, followed by the Order of Pius IX, the Order of St. Gregory the Great, the Order of St. Sylvester, The Order of the Golden Militia (or Golden Spur), and the Order of the Holy Sepulcher.

[111] That respect was indicated by the comments of John Thurman, president of the Central Labor Union, upon the celebration of Graham Day. Interviewed by a local reporter, Thurman said, "I am personally heartily in favor of this civic achievement. It is a big help to the city. The labor movement in Evansville is in favor of any large concern locating here.

The location of the Graham Brothers here will be of distinct benefit to the labor movement in Evansville."

[112] From 950,554 to 2,017,430 square feet. The Warren Avenue plant had been increased from 359,460 square feet to 1,063,644; the Fort and McKinstry Street site was 262,000 square feet; the Evansville body plant was 273,600 square feet; the Wayne body plant was increased to 228,370 square feet (from 203,810); the Perry dimension lumber plant was 50,000 square feet; and the assembly plant at Johannisthal, Germany was 57,000 square feet.

[113] From 21,881 in 1927 to 72,956 automobiles in calendar 1928.

[114] Prior to the erection of the new engineering building the engineering department was in that part of the plant which was directly behind the executive parking garage.

[115] The "cold room" at Cadillac or Auto-lite (in Toledo) was used prior to the erection of the Graham-Paige Engineering Building. In addition to the obvious disadvantages of using a competing automaker's facility or one in another state was the fact that neither was large enough to contain an entire automobile.

[116] One similar stroboscope was located in the laboratories of the General Electric Company. Another was in use by the Navy Department.

[117] The overseas dealer network increased from 51 to 307.

[118] A gross profit of $6,156,016 was recorded on the total sales of $61,464,397. However, the net profit after all charges but before depreciation was $2,014,068. Factoring in depreciation reduced that figure to $1,440,087, and a loss from subsidiaries in the amount of $384,408 further reduced it to $1,055,678.

[119] Joseph Graham noted in his annual report to stockholders that the financial picture would have been even more markedly positive had not "production for the last quarter [been] curtailed and profits adversely affected by extensive re-arrangements necessary for manufacturing expansion and by unavoidable delays in production of the new models." Because of the fact they were introducing a completely new automobile these numbers were also affected by the "substantial deductions for experimental and development expenses and the customary operating and depreciating reserves."

The Graham-Paige Motors Corporation – 1928

Following the formal presentation of the Graham-Paige Model 837 to Pope Pius XII in the Court of San Domaso, His Holiness inspected the engine compartment and other mechanical features of the gift. (Courtesy of Musei Vatican/Archivic Fotografico)

As Another Year Begins – 1929

As Another Year Begins
1929

When the Grahams returned to Detroit from the civic paean in Evansville, they returned to a company where both management and labor were working at a fevered pitch. Production of the nation's most popular new make of motor cars continued on Warren Avenue at record levels. The engineering staff had the task of both outfitting and operating the most advanced research laboratory in the industry, in addition to finalizing the design of the new models to be introduced at the beginning of the new year. And the office and sales staff had thrown itself into the details of what was hoped to be the most impressive dealer convention ever.

Even though the public realized that new models of Graham-Paige motor cars would be introduced in January of 1929, sales for the brothers' initial offering continued unabated. Although production had risen to nearly three times what it had been in 1927, the four Graham-Paige factories struggled to keep up with demand. The labor force strained even more during the last quarter of the year when the transition to the new models was being effected.

It was at the most elaborate and majestic dealer's gathering (please refer to the preface for details) in Detroit's history that the new 1929 Graham-Paige models (second series)[1] would be formally introduced.[2] Similar gatherings were held in New York, Chicago, and other major American cities.

The success of the introductory models of the Graham-Paige Motors Corporation had not precluded the engineering department's quest to improve the Graham brothers' product. Clearly evident to the public and industry watchers were the many changes and improvements made to the chassis, power plants, and bodies of the new 1929 offerings.

The most evident and pleasing changes in body design included the use of one-piece crown fenders, chromium plating on all exterior bright work,[3] the upward curving hood molding serving as a visor support, a more concise arrangement of finer hood louvers, and the repeat of the distinctive radiator shell's shape in the front of the roof and visor. Perhaps the most visible change was the employment of a Graham-Paige radiator emblem which now featured a bright red cloisonne background. As on all models, the taillight housing was now in the shape of the familiar Graham-Paige shield and featured the helmeted profiles and the marque's name in its distinctive font.

Formally introduced by the Graham brothers at the Detroit show was the new Model 612, an evolution of the Model 610. The wheel base for the smallest Graham-Paige had increased by an inch and a half, giving the motor car its new designation. By boring out the Continental-based motor by 1/8th inch,[4] the brake horse-power for the (now rubber-supported) power plant was increased to 62. The power plant was further distinguished[5] by the arrangement of the positive drive water pump and the entirely new exhaust manifold. The water pump was designed so it was driven by the timing chain, rather than the fan. Thus the engine was being cooled whenever it was running, in addition to being further cooled by the water jackets extending the full length of the cylinders. Contrary to traditional practice, the exhaust manifold was designed to carry the engine's exhaust forward, to the front of the engine. It was then directed back along the side of the frame and motor, and under the body of the automobile. At no point was the exhaust pipe any closer than ten inches to the floor boards. With this innovative design, no excessive heat was transmitted to the passengers during the summer months, and the entire side of the engine was now open for maintenance and repair. The electrical system[6] was now a Delco-Remy product,[7] and both a Lanchester dampener and Johnson carburetor were standard. Also, standard equipment on all models were internal expanding hydraulic brakes. The frame itself was beefed up with the institution of two cross channel members at the rear, replacing the single wide plate used previously.

The Graham-Paige Model 612, an evolution of the Model 610 offered in 1928, was available for a modest $995 in the sedan configuration.

The roadster offered on the Model 615 chassis was priced identical to the sedan, coupe, and phaeton—$1,195.

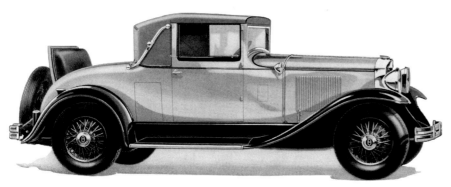

Powered by a 97 horsepower engine, the Model 621 cabriolet was an attractive open car priced at $1,810.

The Model 612 was the line's least expensive offering, and thus the standard three-speed transmission was retained. In contrast to the previous January, nearly every body style was available to dealers and distributors almost immediately. Of course, the most popular version of the Model 612 proved to be the two-door coach, offered at a reasonable $885.[8] The four-door sedan was also a great value with its $995 price tag. A coupe was available, with and without a rumble seat, for $955; the five-passenger phaeton and roadster shared the $970 price.[9] The most expensive body style for the Model 612 was the cabriolet, priced at $1,025.

Just as the 610 evolved into a larger and improved automobile, the Model 614 was markedly improved and also carried a new designation. By virtue of its lengthened wheelbase (to 115 inches), the motor car was now known as the Model 615. The engine was made more powerful—to 76 horsepower—by boring it out an additional 1/8th inch.[10] This larger car carried Lovejoy shock absorbers and the famous four-speed transmission. All other chassis improvements evident on the Model 612 were similarly made on the Model 615, and the same body styles were made available. The Model 615 was adorned with the familiar radiator badge, backgrounded with a rich blue cloisonne. The two-door coach was the least expensive body style at $1,155, while the four-door sedan was $1,195. Sharing the $1,195 price with the

fast-selling sedan[11] was the coupe (available with and without a rumble seat), the roadster, and the phaeton.[12] Again the cabriolet was the most expensive offering of the model designation, at $1,295.

The Model 621 was created by the addition of two inches to the wheelbase of the former Model 619. While it carried all the chassis improvements and visible body changes exhibited on all motor cars in the series, this bigger six-cylinder model offered additional refinements and features. Again, by boring out the engine (to 3 1/2 x 5 inches), a more powerful (97 horsepower) car was created. In additional to more power and speed, the cooling system also featured thermostatically operated radiator shutters. The chassis featured Bijur chassis lubrication,[13] Houdaille two-way hydraulic shock absorbers, and an AC fuel pump. Considerably more of an automobile than the two smaller sixes, the price of the big six reflected that fact. The four-door sedan[14] and coupe were both offered at $1,595, the roadster was $1,795, the cabriolet was $1,810, and the classy swept panel dual cowl phaeton was $1,865.

The 1929 second series lineup was the first proffered by the Graham brothers that featured two eight cylinder motor cars.

The Model 827 was created by powering a 127-inch wheelbase chassis with the Continental based 120 horsepower powerplant from the previous season.[15] Carrying all the more refined attributes of the biggest six-cylinder offering, the eight was available in similar body styles. The standard four-door sedan was the least expensive at $1,925, while the four-passenger coupe and roadster were available for $2,125. The cabriolet was offered at $2,145 and the five-passenger phaeton was the most expensive at $2,195. A two-piece oval cloisonne emblem featuring the company's shield logo was used on all of the eight-cylinder offerings.

The largest automobiles ever created by the Graham-Paige Motors Corporation were also the most impressive and imposing. Riding on a wheelbase of 137 inches, the Model 837 was the natural improvement upon the Model 835 of the previous season. All the mechanical and body improvements available on the smaller 1929 second series eight-cylinder model were also featured on this flagship model. As the most stately and majestic model in the line, only the most elegant and stylish body styles would be available from the Warren Avenue plant. Standard factory bodies

The Model 827 five-passenger phaeton was the most expensive body style of the 127-inch chassis offering, retailing at $2,195.

As Another Year Begins – 1929

The dignified and impressive Model 837 town car was a five-passenger motor car and sold for $2,355. Only the seven-passenger sedan was more expensive on the 137-inch wheelbase chassis.

included a refined seven-passenger phaeton at $2,195; while a swank five-passenger town sedan, five-passenger coupe, and five-passenger sedan were $2,355. The seven-passenger sedan was available for $2,425.

These large eight-cylinder automobiles would have been an impressive offering from almost any automobile manufacturer in 1929, but the Grahams enhanced that impression by again making true custom bodies available. The New York show featured a custom-bodied dual cowl sport phaeton on the 137-inch chassis, again created by Le Baron and again, truly impressive. The phaeton, built specifically for the annual automobile show and subsequently displayed at a number of dealerships around the country, was later used as the personal car of Joseph Graham.[16] The dignified motor was deemed so striking that it was the object of a feature article in the October number of swanky *Country Life* magazine.

Featured in showroom catalogs and other print advertising was an illustration of the Le Baron seven-passenger limousine-sedan with disappearing division glass. The imposing automobile was available for a reasonable $3,865. The Le Baron town car carried a price of $4,180, while the limousine commanded $4,430. It was the Grahams' fervent hope that their impressive chassis and powerful powerplant would entice other custom body builders to use the Model 837 as a platform.

With an impressive array of motor cars to present to the public, the advertising and sales department was able to present a formidable advertising campaign to the nation. The traditional print media was liberally used, featuring brochures, catalogs, magazine and newspapers, in addition to more use of the motion picture medium[17] and radio.[18] "As Another Year Begins", "Abreast of the Times", and "The Thrill of Two High Speeds" were common titles for the advertising thrust. Just as they had done for the inaugural models, the Graham brothers were low key in their advertising, politely inviting the public to view and drive their offerings. A typical showroom catalog[19] was prefaced by this simple statement:

We present a new line of Graham-Paige sixes and eights, with refinements and improvements which represent our earnest en-

deavor to keep abreast of the times, and to make our product constantly better. We believe you will appreciate the added beauty, increased size, improved performance, and substantial value of these motor cars. You are invited to enjoy a demonstration.

At the bottom of the page were the three familiar signatures.

Pausing only shortly to enjoy the kudos and enthusiasm generated by the introduction of the new 1929 (second series) models, the brothers continued to improve and enlarge their company.[20] Production at the new body plant in Evansville began on January 14,[21] and more urban dealerships and distributors were purchased and made factory-owned subsidiaries.[22] Robert Graham proudly announced on May 30 that 254 new dealers were signed on in the United States during the past 32 days, bringing the domestic total to over 2,500. Those dealerships employed over 8,000 salesmen. Foreign distributors were also added at a record pace, as were dealers.[23] The factory service school was operated at full attendance and the financial officers of the company provided a revised accounting and reporting system to better help individual dealers. Retail salesmen were urged on to greater totals by the continuation of cash bonuses and increased life insurance. The underlying rationale for developing a strong and well-served dealer network was capsulated by the phrase present in all trade advertising: "Twenty-five years of successful manufacturing experience has taught us that the prosperity of the dealer comes first."

The omnipresent talk of mergers in the automobile industry again began to center on the Graham-Paige Motors Corporation. Those rumors predicated a formal statement by Joseph B. Graham on January 21, 1929. Titled simply, "A Statement," it read:

We are not interested, directly or indirectly, in consolidation or merger with any other motor car manufacturer; nor are we interested in the purchase of stock in any other motor car company. We are definitely pledged to the upbuilding of Graham-Paige and Graham-Paige only.

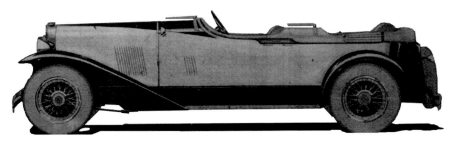

The original Le Baron sketch for the one-off show car created for the 1929 New York Auto Show. The handdrawn legend reads "Especially designed for the Misses Eliner and Virginia Graham." The phaeton was later the personal car of their father, Joseph Graham.

FOUR WORLD'S RECORDS IN CLASS B!

Mr. D. M. K. Marendaz driving the record-breaking Graham-Paige.

GRAHAM - PAIGE uses Wakefield CASTROL and averages over 86 m.p.h. for 24 Hours!

At Montlhery on the 24th December, Mr. D. M. K. Marendaz driving a Graham-Paige broke the following World's International Class B Records.

2000 Kilos. at 87.25 m.p.h.   2000 Miles at 86.69 m.p.h.
3000 Kilos. at 86.47 m.p.h.   24 Hours at 86.36 m.p.h.

(Subject to confirmation)

Wakefield CASTROL lubricated the record-breaking engine, proving once again its outstanding suitability for the Graham-Paige—that is why Messrs. Graham-Paige Motors Ltd., use and recommend CASTROL exclusively.

13 RECORDS IN 1929 BY GRAHAM - PAIGE USING CASTROL!

C. C. WAKEFIELD & CO. LTD.
All - British Firm
Wakefield House, Cheapside,
LONDON, E.C.2.

o26   KINDLY MENTION "THE MOTOR" WHEN CORRESPONDING WITH ADVERTISERS.

This advertisement appeared in the January 7, 1930, number of The Motor, the British automobile magazine. This advertisement is of note because it illustrates the second body used on Marendaz's Model 835. Stiff competition predicated that he forgo the heavier, factory-issued sedan body.

As Another Year Begins – 1929

Unhampered by the previous year's startup concerns, Graham-Paige was able to get into peak production in short order.[24] On March 20 the production at the plants exceeded the number of cars manufactured and shipped during all of calendar 1927 (21,850).[25]

March 1929 saw the publication of a rumor which had been spread in industry circles since late in 1928. A trade journal, *Automotive Industries*, reported in its March 18th issue that they "understand on good authority that a Graham-Paige truck will be introduced in about 18 months." This short paragraph was to raise eyebrows in many executive offices around the industry. It was a well known fact when the Grahams left Dodge, part of the agreement was the Graham brothers were restricted from producing trucks for a period of five years. Although rumors continued to swirl throughout Detroit, little more made it to print until later in the year.[26] It is interesting to note that during the first week of January, Dodge Brothers—no doubt predicated upon the success generated by a Graham-manufactured automobile—dropped the Graham Brothers name from its truck line. From that point on Dodge Brothers produced only Dodge Brothers trucks, and no free advertising of the Graham name was given from the corporate giant.

April brought manufacturing totals which exceeded all predictions. A 72% increase over the same month of the previous year was notched (11,550 cars shipped, including exports totaling 1,465.)[27] When the financial statement for the first four months of 1929 were released by the thriving company, it was reported a profit of $931,532 was realized for that period.[28]

During its regular monthly meeting, the board of directors voted to increase the amount of non par common stock from 2 million to 2 1/2 million shares. The additional capital was to be used once again to increase production to meet the unrelenting demand. The company reported in early June that 99% of the stock had been purchased by eager investors, raising $7,093,950 in working capital.[29]

As each succeeding month's totals were reported to the press, a new record was being set at the Graham-Paige Motors Corporation.[30] The 50,000th Graham-Paige of the year was produced on June 7.

However, more than manufacturing and sales records were being established by Graham-Paige. The powerful cars being shipped from Warren Avenue were being used the world over for successes in racing and rallying. This was especially so in Europe were the four-speed transmission was coveted for competitive purposes and the large American engine dwarfed most domestic makes.

In England, one D. M. K. Marendaz campaigned a Model 835 sedan at the famous Brooklands track. Classification of the straight eight sedan put it into the International Class B designation (from 5000 to 8000 cc). At 5274 cc the completely stock Graham-Paige[31] was one of the smaller motor cars to compete, and yet Marendaz placed first in the competition. In fact he broke the 200 km circuit by an average of 14 miles per hour and the 200-mile test by almost 16 miles per hour.[32] When the two records fell shortly afterwards,[33] Marendaz returned to the track to attempt recapturing the fastest designation. Unable to do so with the stock sedan body, he mounted a two-passenger boattailed racing body on the Model 835 and again triumphed. Britain's enthusiastic motoring press continued its praise of the Graham-Paige. *Motor* magazine said Marendaz's feat was "a particularly fine performance. The car ran with unfailing regular-

Surrounded by rally officials, supporters and well-wishers, Dr. Sprenger van Eijk (at the driver's side door) is shown aside his Model 621 sedan prior to the 1929 Monte Carlo Rally. The physician copped both first place in his class and in overall standings.

ity."[34] Early in November, G. N. Edwick entered an eight-cylinder model in a high-speed reliability trial on the same track and came away with a gold medal for his efforts.[35]

Attempting speed records of longer distance in England, Marendaz and his team piloted a Model 619 open car to victories in the 3000/4000/5000 mile and the 4000/5000 km races at Montlhery. Sprinting the last thousand miles in the later race, he averaged nearly 75 mph.[36] The motoring press covered the victories enthusiastically. Further enhancement of the Graham-Paige name included a series of Castrol Oil advertisements which proclaimed the speed records and featured a photograph of the special bodied racing car. The ads also noted in bold print that "13 records [were achieved] in 1929 by Graham-Paige using Castrol!" The annual speed trials sponsored by the Automobile Club of Belgium in Oostmalle also saw a Graham-Paige take first place in its class, averaging 74.3 miles per hour over a flying kilometer.

The combination of a powerful American-built engine and "twin top" gearbox proved to make the Graham-Paige successful in European rallies as well as speed races. In France, Graham-Paige placed first, third, fourth and seventh in the prestigious Deauville-LaBaule rally. The press said Graham-Paige "put up a remarkable exhibition of consistent running throughout the run." An even more prestigious victory in that country was the winning of the Challenge Trophy offered by the Automobile Club of Paris during the Tour de France. During June, a Graham-Paige cabriolet notched first place in its class and set a new record in the annual Automobile Club Of Marseilles hill climb at the famous Cote du Camp.[37] Later in the month the Automobile Club of Paris sponsored the 2,730-mile Tour de France, with a six-cylinder cabriolet taking three cups with Roberts (a well known French racing driver) at the wheel.

This German magazine advertisement displays the continental flair for design and presentation.

Later in the year, a Model 619 saloon, completely stock in every manner, was driven to victory in the 1929 Monte Carlo Rally. Dr. Sprenger van Eijk bested the other 92 entrants in the 1,851-mile rally, fighting not only a field of "the finest cars from all over Europe" but "weather conditions of appalling severity." Automotive enthusiasts throughout Europe had been very much impressed by the new American marque. This acclaim increased when a few weeks later a Graham-Paige posted a perfect score in the Paris-Nice Rally, taking first place in its class.

But the triumphs of Graham-Paige automobiles were not confined to Europe. In Brazil, a Model 614 captured first place in all four classes of the "Washington Luis Touring Test." The four-day 1200 kilometer rally ended with Roberto Thiry capturing the two amateur classes and Jose Armentano becoming champion of the professional classes.[38] An eight-cylinder Graham-Paige driven by Francisco Roig later won the Eight International Race at the Rabassada, near Barcelona, Spain. In Australia, a six-cylinder sedan driven by Jack Moran posted the best time of the day in the Mount Coo-tha hill climb. Australian dealer/driver Walter Whitbourn drove a stock Graham-Paige sedan in the Bendigo Motor Trial in June, achieving a perfect score. A similar event in Lilydale, Victoria, saw Whitbourn take not only first place in his class, but also in the open event.[39]

In the United States, the Post-Enquirer Challenge Cup was won in a Model 615 roadster. The 11.6-mile "road ascent" was achieved in record time by the Graham-Paige open car, and was further distinguished by the fact it was the only marque to win the cup on its first attempt.

Too, Robert Graham's desire to make Graham-Paige a well known entity outside of the United States was progressing as rapidly as domestic sales were.

By mid-year both European and American coachbuilders[40] had discovered the enticing possibilities concerning custom bodies using the Graham-Paige platform.

English custom body builder Mulliner of Birmingham created both a coupe and saloon (sedan), with a Weymann-type fabric body, for the Model 614 and 619 chassis,[41] and later on the Model 615 and 621 chassis.[42] Also available in Britain in 1929 was a "sportsman's saloon" by Hoyal Body Corporation. Of a more elegant design than the sporting Mulliner's type, these custom town sedans were constructed on the Model 621 and Model 827 platforms, and featured a rakishly slanted windshield, six wire wheels,[43] and non-integral trunks. Elegance, with an English accent, could be had in the Mother Country on a very American chassis.

The famed German custom body builder Erdmann & Rossi also created one-off versions of the Model 837. At least one elegant convertible coupe and convertible sedan were created on the long wheelbase eight-cylinder chassis.[44] Castagna, the prestigious Italian coach builder, also created a custom body for the large eight.[45]

In addition to the "custom bodies" available on the Model 837 chassis directly from the factory, Le Baron also created true custom bodies for at least two customers. Both examples created by the respected Detroit firm were of the dual cowl style.

When the accountants on Warren Avenue tallied the numbers for the first six months of 1929, a net profit of $1,341,711 was shown. It was quite an impressive amount for a company that showed over $4 million in losses for 1927. The interim balance sheet showed the liability of the firm was slightly more than $7 million, the total assets of the company were almost $22 million.[46]

Advertising commencing in August described the motor cars being produced by the Graham brothers as the "New 1930 Graham-Paige." An expanded advertising budget was predicated upon the record-breaking sales of the first half of the year.[47] However, with the exception of the Model 612, there was little real difference between these (1930 first series) cars and the cars built during the first six months of 1929.

These changes included the Model 615 now featuring a new engine mount,[48] chrome plated windshield frames, and an opaque glass visor in chrome bracketing. The Model 621 evidenced these same minor changes, as did the eight-cylinder offerings.[49] All models were now equipped with three-spoke steering wheels,[50] instrument gauges flush with the dashboard,[51] and adjustable seating[52] with improved upholstery materials.

The real changes were reserved for the "new" Model 612, one of the company's best sellers. The chassis was lengthened three inches, giving it the same platform as the Model 615. The Continental-based engine was bored out an additional 1/8 inch[53] boosting its horsepower from 62 to 66,[54] the gear ratio was reduced for faster getaway, and the tire size was increased for a more comfortable ride. The Model 612 now also shared the blue cloisonne radiator badge with the Model 615.

One feature which all the "new" models shared was another pioneering effort by the Graham-Paige engineers. Traditional industry practice was to have rubber matting covering the front floor boards. Graham-Paige was able to devise a system where floor board rubber, 1/8 inch thick, was molded directly onto the floor boards. Aluminum draft plates with live rubber inserts were also screwed to the boards to insure a draft-free front compartment.[55]

With these relatively minor changes, the assembly lines were able to quickly adjust and continue their record breaking pace. Prices were not raised on any models.

Spurred on by success in export sales, Robert Graham and his sales staff put additional effort into that realm. With distributors in over 70 countries, it was in their best interests to have the Graham-Paige name as well known around the world

Based on the Model 615 chassis, this Mulliner Weymann Sportsman Coupe was available in June of 1929 for £565. A four-door saloon version on this fabric-bodied automobile was also available for £20 less.

As Another Year Begins – 1929

as in the United States. Based on existing domestic versions, Graham-Paige International Corporation issued sales brochures and other print advertising in Spanish, Polish, Swedish, Norwegian, Dutch, and eight other languages.[56] For English-speaking nations, the advertising reflected cultural differences in body nomenclature and monetary units.

As they had done with the Graham Brothers truck, the brothers also attempted to target specific markets. A well-illustrated booklet featuring testimonials and specifications was produced specifically for railroad men as well as another for farmers.

The four-speed transmission continued to be emphasized in all forms of advertising for the remaining months of the year. During the second half of the year a program promoting a "Tachometer Test" was touted in advertising and available at all dealers. The stated intent was to:

> *...emphasize that the modern type four-speed transmission does much more than provide merely an additional gear ratio, but instead offers an entirely new range of motor car performance.*

Speedometer type tachometers, able to be quickly mounted by means of a flexible shaft connected to the distributor drive shaft, were shipped to all dealers for demonstration purposes.[57] "See Why 50 MPH Seems Like 38," was the tag line used on window posters, newspaper ads, sales brochures, and dealer helps. In addition to a "checkup list" given each prospective buyer, a sliding disc showing the difference between the speed and rpms of a three-speed automobile as compared with a four-speed Graham-Paige was provided.

Graham-Paige automobiles continued to be used in rallies, races, and publicity "stunts." One such example was the endurance run of Mr. and Mrs. Earl Williams of Salt Lake City. The two piloted a completely stock Model 621 sedan for a record 464 hours and seven minutes in October of 1929 at the Utah State Fairgrounds. Much publicized by the Warren Avenue firm, the sedan was said to be able to go on indefinitely but under the rules "governing such tests" the run ended when the car picked up a nail and the right rear tire went flat.[58]

October was also the month production exceeded the total number of vehicles produced during the entire year of 1928. This exceeded the 1927 total by more than three times.

Although the Graham brothers were experiencing unparalleled success and were a shining star in the automobile industry, they did not operate their business in a vacuum. As a part of the "Roaring Twenties" economy, they experienced all the variables any manufacturer necessarily encountered. There were plenty of variables for businessmen to be concerned with in 1928 and 1929.

The nature of the American economy during the 1920s was actually forged by World War I. During that first global conflict, the United States initially functioned as a supplier of goods and services to the Allied European countries. It was only in the latter part of the war that America became a participant. In its role as a supplier, the nation's economy profited and expanded: labor was in relatively short supply (raising wages considerably) and the manufacturers experienced little difficulty in the transition to providing war materiels. Agricultural exports skyrocketed, and farmers prospered as never before. The rush to fill government contracts also provided a terrific environment to develop technology and manufacturing techniques for America's part in the emerging global economy.

When Warren G. Harding was elected to the presidency of the United States in 1920, the American people had chosen a pro-business candidate who would cast the direction of governmental business policy for over a decade. Begun during Harding's administration—and continued even more emphatically during the tenure of Calvin Coolidge—was a policy known as "laissez-faire." Loosely translated from the French as "hands off," the policy gave almost free rein to businessmen pursuing increased production and profits. Very little in the way of business regulations or safeguards were made federal law, antitrust laws were routinely ignored,[59] and the government encouraged the expansion of business.

It was during this decade that automobiles[60] and other durable goods were first purchased on "time" or credit. The stock and bond market also came into the national consciousness for the first time. Investment banking,[61] construction, mass media, aviation, manufacturing, and agriculture all expanded rapidly. The automobile industry became a major economic indicator; substantially increased production was the expected norm each year of the decade. In 1926 the automobile industry produced 4.2 million motor cars, making it the largest industry in the nation. The advisability of even small investors to participate in stock offerings of the automobile industry was clearly demonstrated in 1927 when General Motors announced a $2.60 per share dividend totaling $65 million, the largest dividend in American history.

In addition to the availability of durable goods purchased on time, the lack of government controls on the economy—and especially on Wall Street—allowed the purchase of stocks and bonds without laying out the full purchase price. Known as purchasing "on margin," the practice allowed even the smallest investor to purchase stock with a minimum amount of cash.

As early as 1928 conservative economists cautioned that this practice was at best inadvisable and the increasingly wide price swings of an inordinately active stock market indicated fundamental problems with the nation's economic system. Too, the economists speculated that the infusion of new investors who knew little of the workings of the stock market were becoming dangerously overextended with margin buying. But to most Americans the economy appeared to be booming, there was little unemployment, and even a small-time investor could make a fortune in speculative investing. Besides, the tacit approval of the government for individuals to invest in stocks and bonds was instilled in the nation's collective mindset when it issued and promoted Liberty Bonds during the world war.

In 1928 the stock market began to swing wildly, fueling even more cautions from experienced economists. The fears were quelled for many Americans when President Herbert Hoover, elected in 1928 upon fellow Republican Coolidge's retirement from public service, announced the economy was in good shape and the end of poverty "was in sight."

In fact there were many conservatively managed, solidly based, and fiscally responsible firms doing a booming business. Companies like U. S. Steel, AT&T, General Motors, Radio Corporation of America, and Kennecott were corporate giants who provided thousands of jobs and manufactured products of value at a fair price.

Fabrication of roof assemblies are shown in one portion of the wood shop at the Wayne, Michigan, body plant of Graham-Paige.

As Another Year Begins – 1929

Workmen at the progressive assembly line at the Wayne plant are shown uniting cowls to doorless body frames.

As Another Year Begins – 1929

But by the summer of 1929, the fluctuations of the market had become so wild that even the most casual observers took pause.[62] On September 3 the number of shares traded on Wall Street rose to the unbelievable level of 4.4 million shares. With the accounting and tallying of these trades delayed by their sheer numbers,[63] uneasiness over the lack of control became ubiquitous. The warning signs were becoming even more pronounced. Buffeted by even more dramatic swings in stock prices, there were clear indications that the "bull market" was rapidly weakening. Some astute investors quietly sold their holdings, effectively getting out of the market.[64] But most investors were too busy trying to ascertain the status of their portfolio, devising strategies to conserve their paper fortunes.

On Wednesday, October 23, over 6 million shares were traded on Wall Street, and the ticker was well over an hour behind in reporting prices. The realization of how little control and how uninformed investors could find themselves was gradually becoming realized. The danger of purchasing on margin was becoming painfully evident to multitudes of investors when the wild price drops forced brokers to insist their holdings be "covered." Many times this loan—the purchase on margin—could not be met because of dramatically falling prices. The investor was then instantly, and heavily, indebted.

The slide on Wall Street quickly turned into a major breakdown. On the evening of Thursday, October 24, 1924, the ticker did not complete its recording of prices until more than four hours after the market closed. Trading that day started slowly, and a modest recovery of prices was noted early. However, by 11:00 a.m. the market floor was in chaos. The realization of how perilous their investments were and how little their stock's value was in cash sent corporate, institutional, and private investors into a selling frenzy. Huge blocks of stock were offered for whatever price was offered. By noon a total of 12,894,650 shares were traded.

Convinced the events of the preceding day were far from simply an "adjustment," investors panicked. The fevered pitch of trading was continued on Friday (October 25) as the president of the stock exchange and the heads of major investing firms tried to convince stockbrokers and the nation a frenzied sell-off was not in anyone's best interests.

Their efforts were in vain, as transactions on Tuesday, October 29—forever to be known as "Black Tuesday"—totaled 16,410,030 shares. The stock market had collapsed. In seven business days over 61,029,000 shares of stock had been traded. The house of cards had caved in.

Graham-Paige Motors Corporation common stock[65] had sold for as much as 54 in 1929. At year's end it could be had for 7 3/8.

Confident the crash was simply a severe "correction" by the economy, Joseph Graham—and most all manufacturers—anticipated a quick return to a prosperous economy and healthy sales. Employment stayed at its pre-crash level and plans were made for both long and short term business strategies. Executives attempted to continue "business as usual."

For the Graham brothers that meant constantly improved manufacturing techniques.

In the Wayne plant, a pioneering system of cleaning bodies prior to painting was installed. The "Deoxidine Process" was said to greatly enhance the metal surfaces to be enameled or lacquered by cutting soldering flux and otherwise cleaning the surface of dirt, grime, corrosion, and other foreign substances. Special cleaning booths were installed where workmen sprayed the liquid deoxidine on the assembled bodies. Following a 30-minute exposure in a drying oven, the resulting dried material was automatically brushed from the body, taking all manner of acids, dirt, and surface rust from the sheet metal.

At the Evansville body plant, the installation of modern butt welding stations facilitated the assembly of rear and side sections of closed bodies. Five skilled Graham-Paige welders were assigned to each buck, greatly decreasing assembly time.

Production at all the plants was continued at their previous, record-breaking pace. It was thought by the vast majority of American manufacturers that sales would rebound and continue to increase, as soon as the diversion of the crash faded.

As an indicator of that faith and optimism, the Graham brothers exhibited an example of their generosity and faith less than a fortnight after "Black Tuesday."

With a desire "to convey a token of their respectful devotion to the Pope, who had so kindly rewarded their activity on behalf of religious foundations," the Grahams presented Pope Pius XI (Sua Santita Pio XI) a custom-bodied Le Baron landaulet for his personal use. The motor car, its presentation, and principals are best described by the November 15, 1929, number of *L'Auto Italiana*:

> *The cars in the garages of the Vatican Palace have been recently increased in number following the gift of a Graham-Paige to his Holiness by the American Graham brothers, fervent Catholics and member of the Order of the Knights of St. Gregory. The gift is an act of deferential homage to the head of Christianity, and is a further inducement to the Holy Father to leave the Vatican, now that His Holiness' retirement behind the walls of the Vatican Palace is ended, and to circulate in this modern car, the fruit of the genius with which God has endowed humans.*
>
> *The magnificent ceremony during which the presentation was made took place in the Court of San Damaso on November 9, 1929. The event was characterized by the strictest privacy. The donors had given rigid instructions to their agents that no publicity whatever should be given the incident. It was desired that this should take the simple character of an act of religious devotion.*
>
> *The carriage-work, most appropriately, was made by the very famous American coachbuilder, Le Baron. The upholstery is in silk of havana brown and silver, with the metal parts in gold. All the accessories that the American manufacturers know so well how to select and construct are found on the car.*
>
> *Count Juiseppe and Rodolfo Lucidi who carried out the long and delicate negotiations which led to the acceptance of the magnificent gift by His Holiness, Pius XI, went to the Vatican City with lawyer Emilo Badini and Mr. Luigi Gallina, general agents of Graham-Paige for Italy. The presentation was in the presence of His Holiness.*

As Another Year Begins – 1929

According to records in the Vatican archives, this photograph was taken just prior to the first of many pleasureable rides by the Pope in the Le Baron bodied laudaulet.

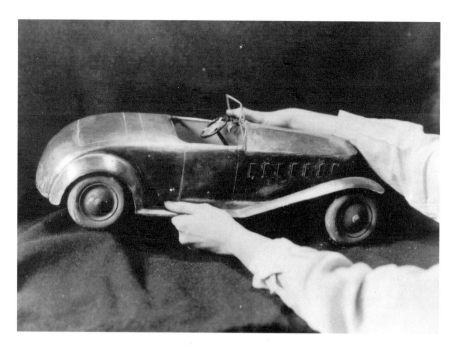

Photographed in New York City, these images reveal Norman Bel Geddes' idea of the "Ultimate Car." Commissioned by Ray Graham in 1929, the artist was given the task of creating and modeling the 1933 Graham. The brass and plaster model was amazingly similar to the actual motor car available for that model year. (Courtesy of the estate of Norman Bel Geddes, Edith Bel Geddes, Executrix/ University of Texas at Austin)

As Another Year Begins – 1929

The "retirement behind the walls of the Vatican Palace" refers to the Concordat Treaty of February 11, 1929. This treaty between Italy and Vatican City officially recognized each nation and allowed the head of the Roman Catholic Church to freely travel outside the walls of Vatican City, a privilege not previously accorded. Although the Pope had other impressive automobiles at his disposal,[66] it was soon evident that he very much preferred the Graham-Paige landaulet[67] over all others. The very first time the Pope left the Vatican he used the smooth-riding Graham-Paige to go to San Giovanni, and was said to often use it when he traveled to Castel Gandolfo.[68]

When his successor, Pope Pius XII (Sua Santita Pio XII), became the worldly head of the Roman Catholic Church, he, too, preferred the elegant landaulet over the other automobiles available to him. It was regularly used by Pope Pius XII whenever his duties took him outside of Vatican City.[69] In 1939 when the Pope went to Quirinale to visit the King of Italy, the Graham-Paige was his motor car of choice. Gravely ill during the last months of his life and suffering from permanent hiccups, Pope Pius XII asked that he be driven through the Vatican Gardens in the Graham-Paige: It was the smoothest riding car in the Vatican garages. Upon his death on February 10, 1939, the automobile was retired.[70]

* * * * * * *

Prior to the Crash it was announced that a "group of Detroit automobile millionaires" were planning on developing an elite oceanfront residential district near Miami Beach, Florida.[71] *MoToR* magazine reported that W. O. Briggs, the Fischer brothers, and the Graham brothers were planning a $10 million development in Florida. In addition to a dozen estates which would cost an average of $250,000 each, an airport, seaplane base, polo field, and large yacht basin were planned.[72] The debacle on Wall Street abruptly halted development on the already purchased land.

Too, there were immediate effects concerning the direction of the Graham-Paige Motors Corporation, specifically in the area of proposed future models.

The overwhelming success of the introductory Graham-Paige models had allowed the Graham brothers to be aggressive and progressive businessmen on more than one front. Although the Stickney and Pfau design used for the 1928 models was refreshing and pleasing, it was not one which Graham-Paige could afford to simply continue in the hectic automobile market of the late 1920s. The brothers looked forward and attempted to determine what the buying public might look for in the near future.

During late 1928, Ray Graham, directing the financial operations of Graham-Paige Motors Corporation from his office in New York City, initiated a social and business association with Norman Bel Geddes. Originally a performer in a small vaudeville troupe, Bel Geddes went on to become well known for his successfully designed stage sets on Broadway and his further artistic abilities for portraiture. Coupled with his good looks, quick wit, and engaging conversation, Bel Geddes became a habitue of the wealthier and more affluent circles in Gotham.

Although Ray Graham was always considered the "numbers man" of the three brothers, design was always of special interest to him and he followed closely the development of the initial Graham-Paige Motors Corporation offerings.

The success attributed to Bel Geddes stagecraft and other artistic endeavors allowed him to comment on the artistic and aesthetic value of contemporary manufactured products, including automobiles.

Bel Geddes was highly critical of the "square box" basis of production automobiles, and he freely shared his thoughts with the world.[73] Ray Graham's interest in streamlining could be traced all the way back to the enclosed engine compartment of the very first Graham Brothers tractor. As a proponent of streamlining, Bel Geddes developed sketches and models of futuristic designs in his newly created industrial design studio.

Perhaps it was inevitable the two like-minded men would meet and share their ideas. Subsequently, Ray Graham offered a design commission to Norman Bel Geddes. He hoped to be able to offer his brothers a fresh and exciting design for the next generation of Graham-Paige motor cars.

Acknowledging that the automobile market was surely not ready to embrace a totally streamlined model,[74] Ray Graham demonstrated his keen business sense when he asked Bel Geddes to project five years in the future—1933—and come up with a design which the company could possibly market at that time. Rather than simply submitting radical "pipe-dream" type renderings, Ray Graham asked for a design from which the company could work backwards from.[75] In other words, establishing a design, and then in 20% increments, work back to the starting point of 1928.

The theory included the thought that the company would not need to make radical, and expensive, body die changes every year or two.[76] Mass production could be made even more cost effective with the implementation of this "20%" plan.

The concept, although abstract, was embraced by the company and Bel Geddes was instructed to build models illustrating his proposed design. Two 1933 body styles, a roadster and a limousine, were developed and scale models built during 1929. Created from clay and sheet brass, the model did fairly accurately portray the eventual 1933 Graham design. The roadster, especially, was intriguing and presented futuristic features such as a rounded grill, a windshield which slid down into the cowl, an enclosed gas tank, disappearing top, driving lamps which turned with the front wheels, and a body totally devoid of molding.

The company gave serious though to embracing the Bel Geddes program, and allotted $8,000 for the development of a full size 1933 roadster prototype even though there was a strong mood of skepticism in some of the office on Warren Avenue. Bel Geddes and Ray Graham's quest for a 1933 prototype in 1929 was not to be. Following the stock market crash in October, the Ray Graham-financed commission was cancelled, and development of the prototype roadster was ended.[77]

As the year came to a close, optimistic businessmen—Joseph B. Graham included—came to realize that the stock market crash was going to impact their factories, careers, and fortunes in a profound way. Radical economic changes would soon affect all Americans for the rest of their lives.

Chapter Eight
End Notes

[1] Following a policy common in the automotive industry at the time, Graham-Paige offered two "series" of automobiles per year, or season. At the mid-year point of calendar 1928, minor changes were made in each of the models available. The most noticeable change made to the automobiles was the elimination of the vertical seams in the back of the body. This was enough of a change for the advertising department to consider these "new" models. Even though the Model 610 manufactured in August of 1928 was little different from the Model 610 manufactured in July of 1928, the automobiles produced in the latter half of the year were considered 1929 (first series) models. Thus the automobiles presented and produced in the first six months of calendar 1929—truly new models—were considered 1929 (second series). To the buying public, mechanics, and the engineering staff, a Model 612 was just that, a Model 612, regardless of what series the advertising staff might consider it. The policy was instituted to allow two "new" cars to be introduced each year, even though that was not, in truth, the case.

This disingenuous policy was continued until 1935. Prompted by the continuing effects of the Great Depression, the federal government mandated regulations not allowing new models to be introduced until October of the preceding year.

[2] The annual Chicago Auto Show was held the first week of February. Midwest dealers and distributors were hosted by Joseph and Robert Graham at the Red Lacquer Room of the Palmer House. Ray Graham was absent due to his recuperation in Florida from an ear infection brought on by a case of influenza. A telegram of congratulations and goodwill from the second eldest Graham brother was read at the meeting, as was a telegram from W. H. Neely, executive assistant to the president of Graham-Paige. Coincidentally, Neely was also recuperating from an illness and sent his regards from Florida as well.

[3] All the 1928 offerings of the Graham-Paige Motors Corporation used nickel plating on exterior brightwork—until the last quarter of the calendar year. During the last quarter of 1928 all models began to carry chromium plating, and all 1929 models carried it from the beginning of production.

[4] To 3 x 4 1/2 inches.

[5] The company went to lengths to explain that the engine was built in the Graham-Paige factories and was Graham-Paige engineered. One magazine advertisement, intended for the industry, noted that Graham-Paige motors were tested at 114 stations by 87 trained machinists during their assembly. It was pointed out that the machining of the cylinder block included 77 inspections and that 21 automatic machines were involved in its manufacture.

[6] The electrical system, as it was on all 1929 models, was positive ground.

[7] Graham-Paige offered, through its dealers, to retrofit 1928 models with the new electrical system.

[8] Within a month this price was "advanced" to $895.

[9] At the end of April, prices on the four-door sedan and coupe were "advanced" an additional $20, while the roadster and phaeton were increased by $35.

[10] To 3 1/4 x 4 1/2 inches.

[11] A Special Model 615 sedan finished in black lacquer with emerald reveals, a tan whipcord interior, and full option wheel treatment was shown at the Detroit Auto Show. A multitude of dealer requests prompted the factory to make this "Deluxe Sedan" available the second week of February. There was a $150 surcharge added to the list price for this Deluxe Sedan.

[12] At the time of its introduction, the phaeton was priced at $1,295. On February 18 that price was reduced to $1,195.

[13] Found on many larger and substantial automobiles of the day, Bijur lubrication was a full chassis lubrication system which was activated by a foot plunger. This act sent special chassis lubrication to all moving parts of the chassis. The system was a product of the Bijur Lubricating Corporation, 250 West 54th Street, New York City. A special display unit, a model of the system, was available to dealers after March 22 for $15.

[14] A two-door coach was not offered.

[15] Bore and stroke was 3 3/8 x 4 1/2 inches for the Continental Model 13K.

[16] This show car still exists and is in the possession of an Illinois collector. Reported cost for the construction of the phaeton in 1929 was $20,000. Joseph Graham subsequently gave the open car to his daughter, Virginia, who reportedly used the car regularly at the family's estate in Michigan. The vehicle has been considerably updated, according to Graham historian Karl Zahm. In 1936, Zahm reports, a 1934 supercharged engine was installed in conjunction with a standard three-speed transmission. Returned to Le Baron for "updating", the sidemounts were deleted, a lengthened aluminum hood installed, smaller 18-inch diameter wheels utilized, and many detail and trim items were changed from stock. The car became available in 1948 and passed through a number of collectors until becoming part of the Harrah Collection in 1960. Following its purchase in 1984 by the Illinois collector, a total restoration brought the phaeton back to its 1936 configuration. The car now features a polished aluminum body, black fenders, and red undercarriage. This is the only Le Baron custom bodied dual cowl phaeton known to exist.

Zahm also advises a special car robe was created for the sport phaeton's first showing at the New York show. The robe was stolen from the Graham-Paige stand and never recovered.

An oral interview in June of 1997 with Robert C. Graham, Jr. indicated that three examples of the custom Le Baron sport phaeton were created. The history and whereabouts of the other two examples is unknown.

[17] Following up their pioneering effort prior to the second dealers convention, the Grahams used "moving pictures" to extol the features of the four-speed transmission and other components. The majority of these films were for internal use, i.e. the service school; the public was exposed to these motion pictures through special showings at the factory and at dealer's showrooms. Louis Thoms, chief engineer of the Graham-Paige Motors Corporation, used a motion picture featuring the four-speed transmission when he addressed the Chicago sales convention during the last week of January 1929.

Later in the year, a motion picture entitled "Better Bodies" was produced for the general public. The 19-minute film details the building of Graham-Paige bodies, from the felling of the trees in the Graham Timberland in Florida to their delivery from the Wayne and Evansville plants to the Warren Avenue assembly plant. The strength of the bodies, their superior paint jobs, and overall construction were emphasized by showing actual factory scenes and demonstrations of the product.

[18] Radio ads were most appropriate since Graham-Paige automobiles could now be equipped with radios directly from the factory. Those radios were a product of the Automobile Radio Corporation of 4311-19 Third Place, Long Island, New York, and 1475 E. Grand Boulevard, Detroit, Michigan.

[19] Form 237 (1929, second series).

[20] It was common knowledge in southern Indiana that any former Graham Glass or Graham Brothers truck employee who was willing to relocate to Detroit or Wayne, Michigan, would be guaranteed a job. This later was to include any able-bodied man from southern Indiana. Many did indeed come to Detroit with the Graham brothers, and their descendants continue to inhabit the Detroit area.

[21] Secretary of Graham Paige Motors Corporation, E. A. Stone, announced on it was expected 1,000 men would be employed in Evansville. The 200 men that were then employed at Motor Bodies, Incorporated were transferred to the new plant upon its opening. Their former plant would remain in Graham-Paige ownership, but would be retained "for a sheet metal department." The first ten days of production at the new plant were limited to that of only touring cars; two- and four-door sedans would then follow. On May 4, 1929, roadsters were added to those body styles produced.

[22] On January 29, Graham-Paige purchased controlling interests in the Dalley-Jennings dealerships in Brooklyn and Newark. Later in the year, the Graham-Paige Company of Grand Rapids, Michigan, became a factory-owned branch, as did Graham-Paige of Louisville (serving 60 counties of southern Indiana and Kentucky).

[23] Robert Graham and his staff had increased the number of dealers from 201 to 503, and the number of distributors increased from 106 to 119. Announcements during April noted the addition of distributors in Manila, Philippines; San Juan, Puerto Rico; Caracas, Venezuela; and Bogota, Columbia.

[24] Not every body style was available immediately. For example, the two-door five-passenger sedans (Model 612 and 615) were not available for delivery until April 22.

[25] The total production during 1928 (72,956) was an increase of 233% over the 1927 production (21,881).

[26] *Motor Vehicle Monthly* did report in its June number that Servel, Incorporated, (the parent company of Hercules Products of Evansville, Indiana) had entered into a contract with Graham-Paige Motors Corporation to "supply the entire body needs for the new line of commercial cars it is to introduce." Joseph Graham's influence had prodded Col. Frank C. Smith, president of Servel, to build a new factory in Evansville. The new plant, dubbed Plant #3, was equipped to produce 400 bodies a day. That same announcement indicated, strangely enough, that the company had also entered into a contract with Chrysler to supply "a part" of their commercial car body requirements.

[27] Shipments to Canada, Cuba, and Hawaii were not included in the export totals.

[28] April alone had produced $407,890 of that profit.

[29] The stock was offered at $25 face value. Existing stockholders were first offered the stock, with an exchange of 15 shares of common stock for each 10 shares of 2nd preferred. The brothers had pledged to purchase any stock not obtained by investors. A total of 284,000 shares were offered.

[30] Production during June of 1929 showed an increase of 62% over the June 1928 level, which was also a record. The number of export shipments during May was described as "huge" by the company: that month accounted for 1,235 of the 6,262 motor cars exported to 70 countries during the first five months of year. This was three times the amount exported for the same period of 1928, putting Graham-Paige in eighth place in the industry for export production.

[31] The sedan was "straight off the road and with its full equipment of head lamps, bumpers, two spare wheels, trunk rack, etc."

[32] The existing records for the division were 62.57 mph for the 200km and 58.08 for the 200 miles. The Graham-Paige averages were 76.97 mph and 77.77 mph, respectively.

[33] By a six-liter Delage.

[34] E. M. Wright, automotive writer for the *London Sunday Pictorial*, wrote,

[Graham-Paige's]...performance was one of exceptional interest. This is, I understand, the first time a closed car has ever been used for record breaking of this kind at Brooklands, and the result indicates the performance obtainable today in ordinary private cars, such as the man in the street can buy."

The motor editor of *Sporting Life* magazine commenting on the 80.72 mph lap time said, "A remarkable performance, both as regards speed and consistency."

[35] The Graham-Paige bested 30 competitors with a Bentley and Armstrong-Siddeley taking the silver and bronze medals, respectively.

[36] Continuing to race the Graham-Paige nameplate, Marendaz returned to Montlhery in December of 1930. Again attempting to capture the International Class B category, he urged 101.848 kph from his American entry to insure victory. An attempt, in fog and generally bad weather, was made on the 200 km mark that month also. Unfortunately, a crash badly damaged the motor car and precluded another attempt.

[37] This fete was also accomplished at later hill climbs held at Montmarte and Montagne-Ste. Genevieve.

[38] The rally began in Sao Paulo, was routed to Rio de Janeiro and Petropolis and back to Sao Paulo. The route was approximately 745 miles.

[39] The hill climb, sponsored by the Royal Automobile Club, was held on Zi-Zag Hill, near Lilydale.

[40] In addition to coachbuilders of the carriage trade, the Graham-Paige chassis was used by a number of specialty body builders.

In 1929, Smith Brothers Motor Body Works of Toronto, Canada, built a special armored "Speed Car" on an eight-cylinder Graham-Paige chassis. A four-door sedan with disc wheels, the heavily armored body featured shields across the front fenders, a two-piece sliding bulletproof windshield and center opening doors. The sedan was put into service by the Toronto Police Department.

In March of 1929, the Curtiss Aerocar Corporation brought out a trailer, utilizing airplane-type construction, which was designed to be pulled by a modified Graham-Paige. The special Graham-Paige and the lightweight, streamlined trailer were connected by a pneumatic coupling designed by Glenn Curtiss, pioneer aviator, airplane manufacturer, and owner of the Curtiss Aerocar Corporation. In addition to self-contained family travel, the special units were also utilized at airports as "people movers." Later, a Graham Blue Streak model would also be used by Curtiss in conjunction with an updated trailer.

The H. O. McGee Manufacturing Company of Indianapolis, Indiana, used the Model 837 chassis as the foundation of at least 15 "sound cars." Employed by the Publix Theatre chain of Paramount Pictures, the vehicles were designed to look like a steam locomotive. Realistically done, the body effected each part of a real locomotive, down to the boiler, cow catcher, and smoke stack (which really did emit smoke). The rear of the chassis and special body was built to appear as a railroad car observation deck. These vehicles were paraded in all parts of the United States and later toured Europe. Intended as a publicity generating vehicle complete with public address system, they were truly distinctive. Three of these Model 837 "locomotives" are known to be in hands of collectors. The McGee firm had a history of producing these "locomotive" cars, having done so on a Dagmar chassis in 1917 and an Auburn chassis in 1924.

The J. T. Cantrell Company of Huntington, New York, used the six-cylinder Graham-Paige chassis for mounting its "Cantrell Suburban" station wagon. This "estate wagon" was a wooden creation from the cowl back and was quite popular on the East Coast. Other platforms were used for the "Suburban" but it was the Graham-Paige which was featured in the illustrated magazine advertising.

[41] Designated the Sportsman Coupe and Sportsman Saloon. The coupe was reported to be a three-window, four-passenger victoria with semi-integral trunk. Prices for these specially designed and constructed English bodies were between £70 and £90 above the stock price. Sales were handled by London distributor Eustace Watkins.

[42] It is believed a Model 612 or Model 615 with a British Weymann body was also produced.

[43] The wire wheel equipment was $250 over the cost of the custom body charges.

[44] The convertible coupe (or berline) was part of the Harrah Collection in Reno, Nevada, for many years. It was sold at auction to a private collector in the 1980s. A convertible sedan was also the personal car of Roy Margenau, Graham-Paige's European representative until late 1931.

[45] This custom-built convertible sedan was also used by representative Margenau.

[46] Liabilities were $7,058,855 and assets were $21,858,877, excluding current charges.

[47] The second quarter of 1929 saw 29,214 automobiles produced. This exceeded the previous quarterly record handily (the third quarter of 1928, at 26,741). Production for the first six months totalled 54,498, a 40% increase over the same period for 1928.

[48] The front motor mounts were rigid and of the two-point type. Steel brackets, part of the timing chain housing, were bolted directly to the frame. The rear of the engine was mounted in "tension type" rubber supports.

[49] The Model 837 featured the adoption of duplex seat cushions and, along with the Model 827, had the new type visor, softer cushions and new trim detail.

[50] It was explained that three spoke steering wheels, of solid rubber construction over a one-piece steel frame, were much safer for the driver in case of an accident. The center, upper spoke now pointed in the direction of the path of the motor car, with no steering wheel spoke pointed directly at the driver's abdomen.

[51] The decorative panel was discontinued, and the instrument gauges—flush with the dash—were outlined with a chrome bead.

[52] The individual front seats of the coach were mounted in steel runners which allowed their adjustment. The full cross seats of the other closed cars were adjustable with a self-locking crank handle.

[53] To 3 1/8 x 4 1/2 inches.

[54] The second series Model 612 was rated at 62 horsepower at 3200 rpm. The first series 1930 Model 612 was rated at 66 horsepower at 3000 rpm.

[55] The rear compartments continued to be carpeted.

[56] Newspaper advertising was printed in 22 languages.

[57] The largest single order for tachometers ever received by the North East Electric Corporation of Rochester, New York, was made by Graham-Paige in late June of 1929.

[58] The pair never left the automobile during the 19 day trial. The unpaved track at the fair grounds was lapped 18,232

times. The back portion of the seating area was curtained off and there they ate, slept, and bathed. The only modification made to the automobile was the locating of the battery on the running board, allowing the easy addition of distilled water. Refueling and lubrication were accomplished with the utilization of a tank truck which ran alongside the Model 612 when required. A technician then straddled the vehicles (using the sidemount as a brace) and filled the crankcase with oil. Gasoline was supplied in a similar manner.

[59] Although the anti-trust laws were still on the books, the government's "rule of reason" rendered them almost useless.

[60] A survey conducted in July of 1926 showed that one in six Americans owned an automobile. This was by far the highest ratio in the world. By 1927 it was estimated that Americans owned 39% of all automobiles on the globe.

[61] The expansion of investment banks was impressive. In 1912 there were 277 investment banks in the United States. By 1929 the number had grown to 1902. These banks fueled the unprecedented increase in corporate offerings and the resulting boom in corporate stock speculation.

[62] Examples of rapidly rising stocks included General Electric (from 268 to 391), U.S. Steel (from 165 to 258), AT&T (from 209 to 303), and Westinghouse (from 151 to 286).

[63] The stock ticker, used by every broker in America to monitor stock prices, was invented a few years earlier by Thomas Alva Edison. That day, those recording the transactions—as well as the mechanical ticker—were simply overwhelmed by the huge volume of trades.

[64] Joseph P. Kennedy, father of the future president of the United States, was one of those who secretly sold off his portfolio. One account, probably apocryphal, recounts that Kennedy decided to get out of the market when he heard his hotel shoeshine boy dispensing market advice.

[65] Calendar 1928 saw Graham-Paige stock peak at 61 1/4.

[66] The Pope's predecessor, Pius X, had motor cars at his disposal. However, he shunned them, preferring to take daily rides in the Vatican Gardens in horsedrawn carriages. In 1922 the Ladies of Milan presented Pius X with a Bianchi 15, and in 1926 he accepted—and likewise never used—a Bianchi 20.

The Graham-Paige was the third automobile accepted by the Pope in 1929. The first was a product of Italy, a

Fiat 525N limousine. The second motor car was also an Italian product, an Isotta Fraschini 8A.

[67] There is evidence of an unfortunate and embarrassing episode concerning the presentation of the landaulet, one which neither the Vatican nor the Graham-Paige Motors Corporation ever confirmed. Apparently the desire for an extremely private presentation with no attendant publicity was not understood by at least some of the brothers' representatives in Italy. The incident—no doubt predicated by an overzealous desire to please the Grahams—concerned a "recorder and film camera" which was concealed in the landaulet with the intention of filming the Pope without his knowledge. The evidence indicates that the Vatican, upon learning of the scheme, sent an envoy to the United States to recover the recording and film. When that mission was accomplished, the episode was officially closed forever. The fact that the automobile was accepted and no public mention was made of the incident indicates that the three Graham brothers were entirely ignorant of the incident. The desire of the Graham brothers to keep the gift private was strictly enforced: no mention of the gift was ever made in the U.S. motoring press and nothing concerning the custom car was ever mentioned in Graham advertising or literature.

[68] The car's chauffeurs included Giovanni Politi and Angelo Stoppa.

[69] Following the death of Pope Pius XII, the Graham-Paige was taken out of service and placed in the Papal Museum. One indicator of the favor the motor car curried during its tenure was the fact that, when retired, the odometer read 27,266 kilometers. A Citroen Italiana, presented to Pope Pius XI in 1930, had but 155 kilometers recorded when it was retired from service and placed in the same museum.

[70] The motor car is now housed in the Monumenti Musei at the Vatican. It has been painted a somber grey, and the wire wheels have been replaced by "modern" disc wheels. There are no current plans by the Vatican to restore the automobile to its 1929 grandeur.

[71] Bal Harbour lies north of Miami Beach, between Surfside and Sunny Isles.

[72] As the magnitude of the stock market crash and the ensuing Depression became evident, planning for the development ceased. The land lay idle until World War II when the marshy land was rented by the federal government for $1. During the

war it was used for a firing range, detention camp, and training site. Development of what was to become known as Bal Harbour, Florida, did not commence until after World War II.

[73] Bel Geddes' comments and thoughts on manufactured products and architecture were published widely in magazine and newspaper articles. Prior to being put under contract with Ray Graham, he had called the youngest Graham,

...one of the shrewdest and most far sighted executives in the industry...long realizing (that) a weak spot in car manufacture was body design.

Later, when under contract, Bel Geddes published Ray Graham's initial instructions to him:

Set a style...that is perfection in its own type of treatment. When that design is finished, we will call it 'the car of five years from now.' Then we will work backward step by step, year by year, over the five-year period, introducing certain details of the design into our yearly models until the fifth year we will be in production on the Ultimate Car. By that means we will educate the public gradually to our design.

In 1932 Bel Geddes published a book, *Horizons*, in which he put forth his thoughts on industrial design. In that book Bel Geddes states that it was Ray Graham who first encouraged him to get involved in the field.

[74] This wisdom was not exhibited by Walter P. Chrysler when he introduced the Airflow for the 1934 model year. Even at that late date, the automobile-buying public was not ready for a totally streamlined automobile.

[75] This concept of backwards design is explained in an excellent article by historian Michael Lamm in the May/June 1977 number of *Special Interest Autos*.

[76] That original thought was to continue for a second five-year period. A proposed 1938 automobile design was to be developed and the model line would evolve—backwards—from the projected 1938 Graham-Paige to the then-current 1933 model.

[77] It is important to note that Bel Geddes was not in the employ of the Graham-Paige Motors Corporation. Ray Gra-

ham—personally—contracted with the designer to formulate the five year plan and to produce the models of the projected body styles. Ray Graham underwrote the considerable expense involved and set up a separate corporation for the endeavor. The agreement between the two included a proviso that Graham-Paige had first opportunity to purchase the designs but, if they elected not to exercise this option, the designs could be sold to any interested automobile manufacturer. Following the declination of Graham-Paige, Ray Graham approached Alvan Macauley of Packard and was ultimately turned down as well.

An interesting aspect of the Bel Geddes association was his foray into non-traditional paint design. While under contract to Ray Graham, Bel Geddes experimented with a graduated paint job to be used on Graham-Paige automobiles. This graduated paint application, was in some ways similar to the graduated, but striped, paint job on the Ruxton sedan of 1929. When first approached with the idea and a rendering, the Grahams—especially Robert—thought the concept was impossible to achieve on production cars. Working with the Homer Binder Paint Company, Bel Geddes continued to work on the problem. Initially, Bel Geddes thought that hand stippling would achieve the desired effect. It was soon proven that this would be indeed impossible for production automobiles, and the end result was unsatisfactory regardless. Later experimentation with an air gun convinced Bel Geddes that the effect was indeed attainable, and satisfactory, on production cars. He did comment, however, that the application in the factory would need to be done by,

...men more intelligent than the average painter, and he would have to go through a period of training before he was put on the job.

The project was dropped when the commission was cancelled later in the year.

The cancellation of the Ray Graham contract did not end Bel Geddes' automotive career. Indeed, it was only a few years later that Joseph and Robert Graham contracted with the designer to create attractive new interiors for their motor cars. Bel Geddes later contracted with other automobile manufacturers, most notably General Motors. GM's "Futurama" exhibit at the 1939 New York World's Fair was primarily a Bel Geddes design. A huge scale model at the pavilion depicted American cities and transportation as the industrial designer imagined they would appear in 1960. Radically modern skyscrapers and "superhighways" were preeminent. The Futurama exhibit was easily the most popular and well attended display at the fair.

As Another Year Begins – 1929

Featured as a "display car" at this 1931 equestrian meet, the attractive Standard Six roadster was proffered to the sporting set for only $895.

Very Good Cars At Low Prices – 1930 And 1931

Very Good Cars At Low Prices
1930 And 1931

When the Graham brothers and their staff began planning the Graham automobiles to be available in January of 1930 (these models have been designed by later-day enthusiasts as 1930 second series Grahams), it was a time of great excitement and enthusiasm. Due to the unprecedented prosperity of the firm, the brothers would be able to present their most expanded offerings to date.

A number of developments pioneered by the firm and scheduled to be put into effect during 1930 would also certainly cement Graham-Paige's place as a major player in the industry.

First, a goal long held by the Graham brothers would come to fruition during the first week of 1930. Print advertising began to flood the market directly after the start of the new year proudly proclaiming,

From this time forward, the name Graham will stand alone on all the passenger cars manufactured by the Graham brothers.

A press release further commented:

The adoption of Graham alone signifies more than a mere change of name. It marks the final completion of a definite plan of the three Graham brothers, who, even before they entered the passenger car field, resolved that ultimately they should build automobiles that would be entirely Graham in design and in manufacture, both chassis and body.

Two and a half years of unparalleled success in the automobile industry allowed the three brothers to present their offerings unencumbered by any past bond.[1]

Additionally, the Grahams' long-time involvement in the glass industry[2] allowed them to be the first major manufacturer to offer their automobiles completely equipped with "non-shatterable" safety plate glass. Graham-built vehicles were the first in the industry to provide this safety feature[3] in all windows and doors, as well as windshields.[4]

Finally, the inauguration of the new decade was also when the Grahams would first offer a "commercial car," expanding their offerings to its widest range ever.

The excitement permeating the offices of Graham-Paige were tempered, however, by the uncertainty October's stock market crash had ushered in. The severity of the crash was becoming evident only as 1929 ended. Much to the chagrin of the industry, the anticipated recovery was neither prompt nor evident. Sales in all manufacturing sectors began to fall dramatically, especially in regard to new automobiles.

But the Graham brothers had been through this before. It was not difficult to recall when they not only survived, but prospered during a severe and sharp recession in 1921. While at the helm of the Graham Brothers Inc., production and sales of their trucks continued during that difficult time because they offered a quality product at fair prices, employed an excellent work force, and were directed by an able management team. With a guarded optimism, the Graham brothers were confident that with hard work and effort they could prosper during the present rocky economic environment. More than 6,000 employees prayed likewise.

Graham's most plenary range of vehicles ever was presented at the New York Auto Show in January 1930. The line consisted of four series of eights and two series of sixes. The eight-cylinder offerings included an entirely new automobile, one which the brothers had anticipated would be their sales leader.

The new Graham automobile was to be known as the Standard Eight in its basic guise, and the Special Eight[5] at the higher level of equipage. Both vehicles were powered by a Continental-based straight eight engine, featuring dimensions of 3 1/4 inches by 4 1/2 inches, garnering 100 horsepower at 3400 rpms, and utilizing five main bearings. Each was placed in a completely new 122-inch wheelbase chassis. As with all series beginning in January 1930, the new cars exhibited Graham's revamped styling. Modernization included a radiator shroud of fresh design. A sharper, more peaked radiator shell was used (replicated in the configuration of the headlamps as well), and the company's emblem no longer was affixed to the radiator assembly itself. A curved headlamp bar now centered the recently modified Graham emblem. Other changes evident on all series included door-type hood ventilators instead of louvers, fender-mounted parking lights, chrome-plated cowl bands on all models, new instrument panels, and a double belt molding on more rounded body panels.

The Standard Eight used a gear ratio of 4.43, and a newly revised three-speed transmission. Second gear was deemed a "silent" spiral type of gearing. Helical spur gears were used to ensure constant mesh, and much was made of this feature in the introductory literature and advertising. Vertical veined radiator shields were used on the Standard Eight, spring shackles were rubber bushed, and two-way hydraulic shocks were used. Inside sun visors were first used by Graham on the Standard Eight. For $1,445 a buyer could select either coupe with rumble seat or a four-door, five-passenger sedan. A seven-passenger sedan priced at $1,745 and a five-passenger convertible sedan listed at $1,985 were available later in spring.

The Special Eight was designed for those buyers who wanted more of an automobile on the 122-inch wheelbase. In addition to all the features exhibited by the lesser-priced version, this top end model featured a four-speed transmission and gear ratio of 3.91 for faster getaways. Radiator shutters were thermostatically controlled, and outside sun visors were used. The newly designed instrument panel featured a pressed-on wood facing, hassocks were used in the rear compartment

The Special Eight coupe was available for $1,595, as was the five-passenger sedan. A more sophisticated interior, a gear ratio of 3.91 and a four-speed transmission distinguished the series from the Standard Eight.

Offered at $2,085, this Special Eight convertible sedan was the most expensive body style available in the Special Eight configuration.

instead of foot rails, and an automatic dome light—generated by a switch in the doors—was standard. Again the price of the rumble seat coupe and four-door, five-passenger sedan was identical, at $1,595. Available later, the seven-passenger sedan was $1,845, and the convertible sedan was priced at $2,085.

The Custom Eight (127" W.B.) was the 1930 version of the former Model 827. It, too, featured all the improvements of the new season in addition to using a Johnson carburetor, Bijur lubrication, Houdaille shock absorbers, four-speed transmission, 3.92 gear ration, and cowl lamps on the surcingle as standard. The four-door sedan was the least expensive version of the Custom Eight 127 at $2,025, the coupe with rumble seat was $200 more, and the cabriolet and roadster (both with rumble seats) were $20 more than the coupe. The five-passenger phaeton was the highest-priced body style at $2,295.

This 100 horsepower Standard Eight sedan utilized the new 122-inch wheelbase chassis, as did the coupe. Both were priced at $1,445.

Very Good Cars At Low Prices – 1930 And 1931

The largest Graham automobile offered was again the 137-inch wheelbase model, now dubbed the Graham Custom Eight (137" Wheel Base).[6] Boasting a wheelbase ten inches longer than the Custom Eight (127" Wheel Base), this large automobile featured the same mechanical specifications as the smaller eight. As the most imposing of the four-eight cylinder models offered, it had the most impressive body styles available to the prospective customer. LeBaron supplied dignified seven-passenger sedans for $3,940, a town car for $4,255, and stately limousines for $4,505. Factory bodies for a four-door, five-passenger sedan and a five-passenger town sedan were a much more reasonable $2,455. A seven-passenger sedan from the factory was $2,525, and a limousine was $70 more. The seven-passenger phaeton was the least expensive factory offering at $2,295.

The six-cylinder models offered for 1930 were basically the improved and modernized Model 612 and Model 615. The former Model 612 was now called the Graham Standard Six. With a gear ratio of 4.7, seven main bearings, 66 horsepower at 3200 rpms, a powerplant of 207 cubic inches (3 1/8 x 4 1/2 inches), the 115-inch wheelbase chassis was a time-proven success. The sturdy three-speed transmission was used. Inside sun visors and a vertically veined radiator shield were standard. The body styles mirrored past successes with the base six-cylinder series. For only $895 one could purchase a rumble seat coupe, a two-door sedan, or a "Universal Sedan" which was a three-window, five-passenger sedan. The "Deluxe Sedan" was $995, as was the roadster. A Graham Standard Six phaeton was available for five dollars less than $1,000, and the rumble seat cabriolet was only $70 more[7] than the phaeton.

Custom Eight Cabriolet

Custom Eight Cabriolet

Custom Eight Cabriolet

Custom Eight Cabriolet

All cars featured above had a 127" Wheelbase and were equipped with Shatter-Proof Safety Plate Glass.

Very Good Cars At Low Prices – 1930 And 1931

Custom Eight Sedan with 137" Wheelbase and completely equipped with shatter-proof safety plate glass.

This sporty, Standard Six roadster with rumble seat was powered by a 207-cubic-inch engine, and had a 115-inch wheel base, and was offered at $995.

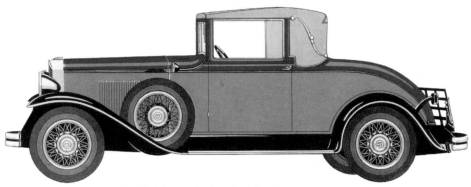

The cabriolet on the Standard Six chassis was the most expensive body style available. The list price was $1,065.

The Deluxe Standard Six town sedan was presented in April of 1930, priced at $845.

Very Good Cars At Low Prices – 1930 And 1931

The Graham Special Six for 1930 was actually the continuation of the former Model 615. As was past practice, this model had a slightly larger engine (224 cubic inches, 76 horsepower at 3400 rpm) and a faster gear ratio (3.916) than the smaller companion six. The traditional four-speed transmission was employed, and styling was identical to the remainder of the lineup.[8] Interestingly, the Special Six was offered in only three versions. The coupe was tabbed to be $1,195 (equipped with a rumble seat the price was advanced $30) and the four-door, five-passenger sedan was $1,225.

Little did the Graham management team realize when they put together the 1930 line that the lowly sixes, not the impressive eights, would top the tallies on the weekly sales reports.

For many companies the combined efforts of a name change, introduction of a revolutionary safety glass, and two completely new additions to its offerings—in addition to the restyling and modernization of their existing models—would have been challenge enough. Long ago, however, the Graham brothers proved they would be as progressive and innovative as possible to manufacture quality vehicles over the broadest possible scope.

On July 12, 1929, a confidential release was sent to all Graham dealers and distributors bringing them up to date on the development of the previously rumored commercial car.

Two major points were noted in the release: A) the anticipated entry into the commercial car field would be in October 1929 with a screen side and panel side commercial car, and B) "This announcement should not be construed as the entry of our company in the manufacture of motor trucks."

Due to manufacturing delays and other factory concerns, introduction of the new commercial cars took place on January 11, 1930.[9] Given the time-honored name "Paige," the commercial cars were afforded wide coverage in the motoring press. Remaining consistent in their intent and direction, the releases distributed to magazine editors began with the disclaimer that the new Paige Commercial Cars were indeed not trucks:

TO EDITORS—in connection with news stories of the Paige Commercial Car, we wish to call your attention to the fact that this is distinctly a commercial car in every respect, and not a truck: and we will appreciate your always referring to it as the Paige Commercial Car in headlines, captions, etc.

The integration of a commercial car into the Graham lineup appeared to be relatively easy. The company emphasized the fact that even though the new vehicle would be able to withstand all the hard use expected of a vehicle in the commercial class, it would have the refined appearance of a quality automobile. As was readily acknowledged by Graham-Paige, the new vehicle was based on the familiar Model 615 chassis and shared that model's sheet metal from the cowl forward. Available in two body styles, the panel side and the screen side, load capacity was 1,500 pounds. The commercial car offered a number of distinctive and innovative features which Graham engineers had based upon intended use. A new bumperette design was employed, making rear entry easier. Only a driver's side seat[10] was standard, allowing

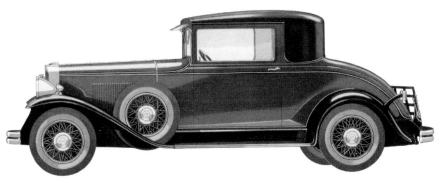

A 76 horsepower engine, coupled with a three-speed transmission, powered this $1,195 Special Six business coupe. A rumble seat advanced the price by $30.

At $1,225, the Special Six sedan was considered a good value by the buying public.

for materials up to nine feet long to be enclosed in the commercial car body. The exhaust pipe was vented to the side of the body rather than the end of the vehicle to insure no fumes would be drawn into the cargo area during loading or unloading. The introduction of gasoline was also made from the side of the commercial car for the same reason. The windshield was of two-piece design to insure good visibility, and the driver and passenger side doors were especially wide (33 1/2 inches) to facilitate easy side loading. The motor was virtually the same as used on the Model 615 except for the absence of the Lanchester dampener. Minor construction changes gave it a rating of 76 horsepower at 3200 rpm. The engineering department deemed a three-speed transmission the most appropriate for this type of commercial car.

The price for both the screen side and the panel body was $1095, and was available from stock, painted Graham-Paige Blue.[11] With the desire to put as many of these vehicles to work as possible, Graham-Paige also made the chassis available for $860.[12]

Print advertising distributed by the Graham-Paige Motors Corporation used tacit testimonials by a variety of businesses.

The record-breaking production of Graham-Paige automobiles during 1928 and most of 1929 did not lessen the emphasis and interest of the brothers concerning Graham Farms. Every effort was made to increase the productivity of the family homestead, even as it became the largest farm in the state. (Courtesy of David Graham)

Very Good Cars At Low Prices – 1930 And 1931

As was more than evident at the formal introductions at New York and Chicago, the Grahams had a comprehensive, well-balanced line of quality vehicles. They also had a large dealer and distributor network throughout the world, an enviable reputation gained from 2 1/2 years of record production and sales, and facilities to produce over 700 vehicles a day.

What they did not have were ready buyers for their product.

As the first few months of the year dragged on it was obvious the "correction" of the economy in late fall was much more serious than first thought. With the nation's economic health worsening each successive month, the buyers which the Grahams—and all other automobile manufacturers—anticipated to fill their showrooms were staying away in droves. Men who a scant few months prior may have been considered excellent prospects for a well-equipped eight-cylinder Graham automobile were now much more concerned about their ability to provide shelter and sustenance to their families than improving their livery.

In early February the annual report to the stockholders of the Graham-Paige Motors Corporation was made public. With the stunning and dramatic lack of sales for the new models fresh in everyone's consciousness, an incredibly surprising tale was told by the figures in the balance sheet. The company had again set a company record in 1929 by producing and selling more automobiles during the calendar year (77,007) than ever before. In almost everyone's mind the Graham-Paige Motors Corporation was considered a bright star in the automotive industry firmament. And yet, the company posted a loss of $1,463,587. With as much eloquence as he could muster, Joseph B. Graham explained to his stockholders that although the factory operations were "profitable," unanticipated and troubling losses with the subsidiary operations cost them dearly in 1929.

Had the company-owned dealerships and subsidiary operations been operated at full capacity, they would have indeed been profitable. However, with most of these operations located in metropolitan areas on "Automobile Row," high taxes and overhead wiped out any accrued profits prior to the stock market crash. This was also true with overseas dealerships, company-owned and otherwise, when the Depression became pandemic. Tremendous investment had been made since 1928 in the four Graham factories and operations in an attempt to keep up with the seemingly endless demand. When sales of automobiles slowed to a trickle, the company found itself with an extraordinary capacity for production, but precious little funds in reserve to ride out the lack of sales. The Graham-Paige Motors Corporation had a cash flow problem of the highest magnitude.

Sales for the first three months of 1930 were 6,496 units, as compared to 12,578 for the same period in 1929. The only comfort the Graham brothers could possibly take in these figures was every manufacturer in the industry was suffering as well. Graham-Paige was the 13th largest automobile manufacturer in the world during 1930. Even with production at nearly half of the previous year's tally, it was the same position the company held in 1929.

Evident to anyone with any past experience with the Graham brothers, this present challenge would not be meet with any lack of enthusiasm. To the contrary, these trying conditions were faced with renewed vigor.

At the end of January 1930, Joseph Graham, accompanied by John D. Biggers, visited the sprawling body plant in Evansville. An announcement made by the executives indicated the huge plant would henceforth be used exclusively for six-cylinder motor car bodies. Full-time employment of the 1,200 men and women would be continued as long as possible.

The Grahams' response to the rapidly changing market was multi-faceted. February saw a more pronounced effort concerning advertising and a more enthusiastic outreach for sales. A program of direct mail was instituted by Robert Graham to reach prospective buyers, and the sale of used Graham-Paige automobiles was encouraged by Warren Avenue for the first time. The advertising thrust was modified to stress the prices of the new offerings. The tag line "Very good cars at very good prices" was now commonly used in brochures and other manner of advertising. Beginning in April all magazine advertising carried the additional theme "Quality is the best policy" and stressed the high quality automobile provided by the Grahams for an entirely reasonable price.

In March, Joseph Graham announced the manner in which all Graham vehicles would be henceforth manufactured. Termed "Quality and Production Basis," the policy was described as,

> *...resulting from [their] ability as manufacturers acquired [by the Grahams] over the past 25 years. In complete charge of all the operations of their business, they have enabled to shape engineering, manufacturing, and sales policies to achieve the presentation of [their] low priced quality models. This achievement opens the way to a vastly larger market than the Company has hitherto reached, and consequently to a higher production volume. [With the introduction of new lower priced models] the company and its dealers will greatly extend the reputation and influence of the other higher priced models in the Graham-Paige line.*
>
> *...By shipping cars only as required for immediate wholesale and retail delivery and by regulating production during the off periods to build up a reasonable reserve stock to meet peak demand, it is hoped to provide steady employment for all Graham-Paige workers.*

More simply stated, the Grahams would now be producing—proportionately—even more of the lower-priced six-cylinder automobiles. And they would be manufactured only after dealers had ordered them. In reality, they had no other option and this new "policy" was simply an attempt to put an optimistic spin on their current predicament.

In a further attempt to reach more market prospects, the introduction of a number of new models were announced. A business coupe on the Standard Six chassis was made available to all dealers in April.[13] Designed to fit the needs of a commercial agent, the body was 1 1/2 inches wider than the standard coupe and featured additional storage. At the same time a five-passenger town sedan was introduced on the same chassis. Both body styles were quoted at a reasonable $845.[14] To spur sales in the eight-cylinder class, a new Special Eight seven passenger sedan was intro-

Very Good Cars At Low Prices – 1930 And 1931

duced in April on a special 134-inch wheelbase chassis. Available on the Standard Eight chassis[15] also, the sedan was extolled by the factory as a "very attractive motor car with a high class finish in every detail inside and out." Actually, the new model was simply a Special Eight on a longer wheelbase.[16] List price was $1,955 with six wire wheels and trunk rack. During July, a limousine ($2,155)[17] and five-passenger sedan ($1,905)[18] were added to the list of available eight-cylinder models on the 134-inch wheelbase chassis.

Although price was the dominating theme in all Graham advertising, the quality of the product was not forgotten. In that vein, the search for models which the public would readily embrace continued. At the end of March, Graham-Paige announced the Standard and Special Eight chassis would now be available with beautiful convertible sedan bodies by Locke & Company.[19] As the company was quick to note, "...the fine quality of bodies custom built by Locke is favorably known." Acknowledging these models would not ever get into volume production, Graham justified these loss leaders as "very desirable advertising for you" even though they

would be bought and "appreciated by [only] a few in every city served by our distributing organization." Although one might question why Graham pursued an attempt to sell semi-custom automobiles during a deep economic downturn, a look at the list prices would explain their strategy. The handsome and elegant convertible sedan bodies—true semi-customs-were attractively priced at $1,985 on the Standard Eight and only $100 more on the Special Eight chassis.[20]

Leaving no stone unturned in their attempt to garner sales, a confidential sales bulletin went out in May of 1930 reminding dealers and distributors the Custom Eight 137 chassis was ideal for custom body mounting by "undertakers." According to the bulletin,

An important field for the sale of Graham Chassis and Paige Commercial Chassis lies in the field of the Undertaker, or Funeral Director, and those special concerns organized for furnishing the above with extra and special equipment for funeral service. In this field there are 30,000 to 35,000 possible buyers. These are not confined to cities but are found in every town, large and small.

Referring to funeral coaches and hearses, the bulletin continued,

The Custom Eight 137" wheelbase chassis is admirably suited for this [type of custom] work.

In regard to service cars and flower cars,

...our Paige Commercial Car has all the requirements of high class combined with reasonable price.

Continuing to pursue all viable uses for the Paige Commercial Car, a special taxi sedan version was made available for trade during early March.

Only when the figures for the first six months of 1930 were made public was it realized how hard Graham-Paige had been hit by the staggering economy. In the first half of 1929, 54,500 vehicles had been produced and sold; total sales for the same period in 1930 totaled only 26,407. The 52% decrease in sales bode poorly for the firm and its employees.

Despite the optimistic forecast and predictions by Joseph Graham when he visited Evansville a few months earlier, employment figures at the body plant showed a decrease of almost 200 men by March. Following the year's second "vacation/inventory" shutdown[21] at the Indiana Graham plant in July, only 600 men returned to their jobs.

For Maximum Motoring Enjoyment in all Seasons and in all Climates

GRAHAM EIGHT CONVERTIBLE SEDAN
Custom Body by Locke
Completely Equipped with Shatter-Proof Safety Plate Glass

In March of 1930 Graham-Paige made available Standard and Special Eight chassis carrying limited production convertible sedan bodies by Locke. These prestigous, semi-custom motor cars were available for $1,985 and $2,085, respectively. (Courtesy of Karl Zahm)

Very Good Cars At Low Prices – 1930 And 1931

Following an address by former heavyweight champion Gene Tunney at the Woodward Avenue (Detroit) showroom and a tour of the Warren Avenue manufacturing plant, dealers from Iowa and Michigan participated in a driveaway of 67 Graham automobiles in July of 1930.

Layoffs at the three other Graham plants were proportionate in number. With sales at their lowest ebb ever, the luxury of introducing "improved" mid-year Graham automobiles was nixed. Advertising continued on a slightly modified scale, and value and price were overwhelmingly emphasized over style. The full page, black and white advertisement which appeared in the July 26 number of the *Saturday Evening Post* typified the manner of advertising. Headlined "Graham Values...leap still higher above the whole market," a Standard Six four-door town sedan was illustrated. It was no coincidence the $845 automobile was the least expensive model available from Graham-Paige. The side-bar featuring an illustration to accompany the shatter-proof safety glass features was prominent, as was the tag line "Quality is the best policy." Perhaps most telling, beyond the obvious, was the italicized line "—with no midseason model changes—."[22]

Changes were fast coming to the Graham-Paige Motors Corporation, and they were not always welcomed changes. The economic environment in which the Graham brothers were now attempting to sell automobiles and commercial cars could not have even been conceived of a scant 12 months prior.

* * * * * * *

As the traditionally busy spring and summer sales season weakly limped into early autumn, the dismal sales totals prompted the Graham brothers to continue the search for readily salable models.[23]

Encouraged by sales figures for the $845 Standard Six town sedan, it was thought perhaps a deluxe version would sell equally well. August saw the introduction of the deluxe town sedan with "special equipment." Although there were no mechanical improvements, this new model was equipped with chrome-plated rims, fender lamps, cowl band, tie rod, and headlamps. Furthering the visual upgrading of the six-cylinder sedan, the gear shift and emergency brake levers were chrome plated. The use of dome and corner lights, arm rests with ash trays, door pockets, loop-type toggle grips, walnut finish garnish molding, wood finish instrument board, and inside sun visors added to the effect. The availability of the new model prompted F. R. Valpey, general sales manager, to note:

The introduction of the deluxe town sedan is in keeping with our policy to work whole-heartedly with our dealers at all times. From all parts of the country our dealers advise that a sedan

body with deluxe equipment, mounted on the Standard Six chassis, would have a splendid appeal to the motor car-purchasing public and naturally we expect this model to prove one of the most popular cars in our line.

In a business move which would have been entirely unthinkable less than a year earlier, the Grahams made available several body styles of the 1929 Model 621. Manufactured for the previous season, these bodies had been in storage at the factory and were in white. Although they were not mentioned in any national advertising, the rumble seat roadster and similarly equipped coupe ($1,795), five-passenger phaeton ($1,865), and "victoria" coupe or five-passenger sedan ($1,595) were available to all dealers. It was obvious that the availability of these models was simply to utilize still existing stock. At this point, any sale added to Graham's tally was warmly welcomed. The list prices of these already introduced models remained the same.

Increased attention was also directed toward export sales. John D. Biggers, now president of Graham-Paige International Corporation, was optimistic concerning the automobile industry and Grahams' prospects abroad. When asked about the growing talk of protectionist tariffs enacted by the nation's trading partners, he said:

In nearly every country of Europe there is some talk of an organized effort to combat the increasing importation of American cars, but so far very little success has marked the endeavors of any organization backing these movements.

...The 1930 outlook is promising, not only for Europe but throughout the world. Manufacturers will export a larger percentage of their production than ever before. Figures for 1929 show that 11% of passenger cars built in this country have been exported. Although I expect no substantial gain in the number of units shipped during 1930, because of the slow start at the first of the year, I do believe that their valuation will be greater. Graham-Paige during the last year exported 14% of its total production and will exceed that ratio in 1930. We have obtained excellent results, especially in such markets as Europe, Argentina, Australia, New Zealand, Dutch East Indies, India, China, Japan, Mexico, and the Central American countries. It is my firm belief that in no more than two of these countries will we see even a slight decrease during 1930.

This was important not only to the management of the company, but to the employees as well. As Biggers noted,

It is generally recognized that, in mass production, low cost depends on maintaining capacity production at all times. And export business is a safeguard against seasonal fluctuations in production [due to the reversed seasons south of the border, the slack season in America was offset and balanced production could be attained].

Very Good Cars At Low Prices – 1930 And 1931

Throughout the stock market crash and the immediate adjustments it predicated, the Grahams remained optimistic. Their business sense, attitude toward both customers and employees, and competitive spirit were well known and admired. All three believed hard work, the manufacture of products of value, and a sincere faith in the economic system which spawned previous successes would serve them well.

The Grahams also had a revered sense of social obligation to their employees, evident as far back as the glass factory days in Loogootee. Even during the heady days of record-breaking Graham-Paige production, the Grahams respected and acted paternalistically toward their employees. An address by Joseph Graham on May 19, 1929, to the annual dinner of the Society of Automotive Engineers in Detroit dealt with his concern of the seasonal aspect of automobile manufacturing and its effect for the over 6,000 Graham-Paige employees. He said, in part,

The job that always has been hardest for me to do is to lay off any of my men because of the seasonal variation in demand and production, and I hope the time will come when this will no longer be necessary. A favorite expression of my brother Robert's is 'we progress through change.' I don't think there is a man here who could contradict the statement that the automotive engineers have brought about some [manufacturing] changes in the last few years.

I wonder if we consider sufficiently the human element in the factory in the making of these changes in our cars. No matter how well you engineer a job, competent men are needed along the assembly line and elsewhere in the making of the product.

In the production of a dependable automobile, to insure a steady job for these men is one of the utmost importance.

The one thing about the automobile business that differs from our other experiences is the tremendous effort that we have to make over a period of a few months in the year. I wonder whether...we appreciate the curve of employed and unemployed in our factories. I have a deep feeling for these men, and the job that always has been hardest for me to do is to lay off any of my men because of the seasonal variation...

Our company is not ambitious to be one of the largest concerns manufacturing automobiles—the greatest satisfaction we could desire would come from giving all our men a steady job through all the seasons of the year.

That is the feeling down in our hearts. The more we can develop our business to provide continuous employment for our men, for the happiness and satisfaction of their families, their wives, and their children, the better name we are going to build for our company, for our factory, and for our engineers.

Another indication of the Grahams' concern for their employees and dealers was noted in an address by Robert Graham at Chicago during a dealers' meeting in January 1929. He said,

As long as dealer balance sheets continue to improve nothing can stop the company's progress. Dealers can be assured of the factory's protection of their territories.

Regarding the factory employees he said,

No man who has been employed by the company in any capacity for the past one and one half years can quit without seeing Joe Graham personally.

Even when it became evident to all that the duration of the economic downturn would not come to a speedy conclusion, the Graham brothers continued to provide an annual company picnic at Walled Lake, just north of Novi, Michigan. The amusement park at that popular site was closed to the public for the day, and the families of all employees were treated to a day of company-provided revelry.[24]

As the president of the brothers' business concerns, it was Joseph Graham who was singled out for praise in regard to the Grahams' continued involvement in Evansville. The Grahams' faith in that community had been evident since 1913, and their enterprises had long been an integral part of Evansville's economy. Prior to an address to the Evansville Transportation Club on October 25, 1928, Joseph B. Graham was introduced by Lt. Governor F. H. Van Orman as "the one man who has done Evansville more good than any other single person."[25] The Graham Day parade was a magnificent example of the gratitude the entire community felt toward all three brothers.

Joseph B. Graham, president of Graham-Paige Motors Corporation.

Joseph B. Graham

Very Good Cars At Low Prices – 1930 And 1931

His concern for community involvement continued when he moved to Detroit, becoming a vice president at the Citizen's National Bank in Detroit, a director of the C & EI Railway, a director of the Natural Rivers and Harbors Congress, and the Detroit Community Fund.

At the same time, Joseph B. Graham was a manufacturing and automobile magnate of the highest order. Following the long held family tradition of the eldest son being in charge of business concerns, Joseph headed not only the glass concerns, truck business and Dodge Brothers involvement, he also assumed the presidency of the Paige-Detroit Motor Car Company upon its purchase. When the name of the corporation was later changed, he became president of the Graham-Paige Motors Corporation. Prior to the purchase of the Paige-Detroit Motor Car Company, Joseph Graham was additionally president of the Graham Brothers Investment Corporation.

He was also very much involved with the social implications of his business status. Joseph and Nell Graham lived in an impressive home at 8120 East Jefferson Avenue in Detroit and belonged to the Detroit Club, the Downtown Club, the Detroit Yacht Club, the Detroit Athletic Club, and the Detroit Golf Club. On a first name basis with virtually all the automobile and business tycoons in the Motor City, Joseph Graham was comfortable and at home in such a rarified environment. His many business trips to New York City to confer with Ray Graham prompted him to join the New York Athletic Club. Regular trips to Indiana allowed continued involvement in the Evansville Country Club and the Indianapolis Athletic Club. Summering in Florida gave him the opportunity to enjoy his membership in the Indian Creek Golf Club in Miami.

It should be pointed out, however, that regardless of titles, responsibilities or manner of business endeavor, the policy of "share and share alike" was in force from the very beginning. The trio had equal salaries and shares, regardless of the situation. This manner of management was so unique that the trade magazine *Automobile Topics*[26] commented on its singularity and success:

> *It has proved, all along, an excellent and natural distribution of talent, marked by a solidarity that [is] unique. Internal differences the brethren might have, but before the world they [are] invariably united.*
>
> *It has always been, from either of the three, 'My brothers and I' prefacing a conclusion or an announcement of any kind. None ever [makes] a decision until all have consulted together; outsiders never [sit] in the family councils. Moreover, each [is] an emissary of the other two; there [is] no approach to one through the others. The tribune [is] not only completely organized but thoroughly protected against invasion.*
>
> *Such fraternalism is seldom seen, but well worth seeing. As a family trait it probably explains the rapid attainments of the Grahams...*

Ray Graham, following the precedent of earlier family business endeavors, was the "numbers man" for the family. Operating from an office at the New York Central Building in New York City, Ray and Jean Graham maintained an estate at Roslyn on Long Island. New York City was the center of the financial world and a great deal of

A pensive Ray Graham in 1931.

Ray A Graham

effort was expended by Ray Graham to make the Graham interests prosperous in that world. His experience as manager of Graham Farms in the early days, coupled with his secretary/treasurer duties with the glass concerns, truck manufacturing business, the Graham Brothers Corporation, and the Graham Investment Corporation made him well suited to be the financial manager of the trio's business labors. It was the expertise of Ray Graham which allowed the automobile firm to grow as quickly as it did, making it a major manufacturer in the minds of important institutional investors.

Ray Graham, too, was a man of many interests and business concerns. While overseeing the finances of the Graham-controlled businesses, he also was a notable player in the glass industry. In 1928 he became chairman of the board of the Libbey-Owens Glass Company of Toledo and was later the president of the Libbey-Owens Securities Corporation.

Although he spent much time in New York City, Toledo, and Detroit, Ray Graham—like his brothers—never lost his love for Evansville and Washington, Indiana. One of his lifelong loves was his involvement in the early aviation industry. As early as 1919 Ray Graham owned airplanes, both land and amphibious types.[27] His involvement in the establishment of Evansville's first airport-Graham Field-and his establishment of the city's Aero Club were truly labors of love.[28]

Another of Ray Graham's interests had its beginnings during his early years in Indiana. From a young age Ray enjoyed hunting and shooting with his father, garnering Indiana's Junior Championship skeet shooting title as a teenager. During the early years of glass manufacture, Ray Graham established the Graham Gun Club—the first shooting club in Evansville.[29] The love of shooting never left him.[30] When the brothers joined the Dodge Brothers in Detroit, Ray joined the Detroit Trap Shooting Club and established the Dodge Gun Club. He was also instrumental in establishing the Shooting Club at the Graham-Paige Motors Corporation, created specifically for employees who shared his love of guns and trap/skeet shooting.[31]

Very Good Cars At Low Prices – 1930 And 1931

Although all three brothers were members, it was Ray Graham who exhibited the most enthusiasm for his membership in the Circus Fans Association. A lover of traditional American circus since his youth, Ray Graham attended numerous circus shows during adulthood and numbered among his friends Clyde Beatty. A friend later recalled Ray Graham always harboring the dream of owning a circus of his own. During one of his business trips to Evansville in 1928, he was elated to discover the Hagenbeck-Wallace Circus was in town. He promptly purchased 400 reserved seat tickets and distributed them to employees and their families. Later, when the circus was in Detroit, Ray made arrangements[32] for the employees of the Warren Avenue and Wayne factories to enjoy the spectacle, by his treat.[33]

As an equal member of the respected Graham triumvirate, Ray Graham also enjoyed the club and social status as a successful manufacturing executive. Memberships in Detroit included the exclusive Detroit Athletic Club and the Detroit Yacht Club. He was also a member of the Union League of Chicago. In New York City he maintained memberships in the Metropolitan Club, the Recess Club, and the New York Athletic Club. As an automobile manufacturer, he was a member of the Society of Automotive Engineers, and as a farmer he took pride in his membership in the American Society of Agricultural Engineers.

Several decades of success in the business world, however, did not exclude either Ray Graham or his brothers from normal human frailties. Beginning in the mid-1920s Ray Graham suffered a series of medical afflictions and was several times hospitalized. Stomach problems were not unknown to him, and several times so severe as to require hospitalization. A slightly cleft palate gave him almost continual concern and discomfort. Only extraordinary effort on Ray Graham's part allowed the Graham companies to grow as they did.

As his brothers did, Ray Graham held a special place in his heart for Evansville and Washington, Indiana. At the Graham Day parade in 1928, Ray was described by reporters as "quiet, extremely cordial, and friendly." Of the three, perhaps Ray was the most touched and awed by the community's gratitude regarding their business accomplishments.

Many years later, when business associates and children of the three brothers were interviewed, they spoke of how successful the three had been as a team. Each had specific talents and abilities, distinctly different, but complimentary and supplementary of each other. David Graham, one of Robert Graham's sons, reflected,

...one secret of their [the brothers'] success was that their abilities and temperaments balanced each other.

Of the three brothers, Robert Graham was the most outgoing and personable, serving the calling of family "salesman" very well. Robert Graham brought a wealth of sales experience from the farm, glass, and truck years to the Graham-Paige Motors Corporation. He reveled in the almost constant travel and contact with the front line salesmen who propelled Graham-Paige sales. David Graham also recalls,

Dad's chief stock-in-trade was his ability to sell you on an idea, make you think it was yours, and then subtly encourage you to develop it as fast as possible. No matter the idea, Dad had the

uncanny ability to make it seem important, and to make you feel important in doing it.

His son also recalled that Robert Graham was a pragmatist.

He was also wise enough to not try to oversell something. [A favorite saying was] 'never take a person fishing unless he likes to fish.'

David Graham said his father loved to fish and had a built-in competitive desire to catch them, [however] he knew that sometimes,

They simply won't bite so you might just as well relax and enjoy yourself on the water.

It was Robert Graham who also most exemplified the theme "To Sell Is To Serve." This twofold principle set forth that people have,

...basic needs which should be made known to them and, in addition, salesmen have a grave responsibility to their customers for complete satisfaction and product service.[34]

Robert Graham served as vice president of the glass concerns, truck firm, and Graham-Paige Motors Corporation. While at the helm of the Dodge Brothers organization, Robert Graham served as a vice president as well, while acting as sales manager for the entire corporation. His vice presidencies included the Graham Brothers Corporation and the Graham Investment Corporation, while his lone presidency (for a time) was that of the Graham-Paige International Corporation. Directorships included the C & EI Railway, Citizens Bank in Evansville, Peoples Bank in Washington, and the National Automotive Chamber of Commerce. Conceived when the family summered in Miami, the proposed Florida real estate

Robert C. Graham
"To Sell Is To Serve"

Robert C. Graham

Very Good Cars At Low Prices – 1930 And 1931

The sitting room and elevated study at the Robert C. Graham home on Jefferson Avenue, Detroit. The sitting room looked out over the Detroit River to Belle Isle.

investment was developed following World War II. When that investment was pursued Robert Graham served as president of the Miami Beach Heights, Inc. and Ocean Beach Heights Company, both based in Miami. He also served on the founding board of the Community National Bank in Bal Harbour and the first board of directors at St. Francis Hospital in Miami Beach.

Bertha and Robert Graham maintained homes at Washington, Indiana, Detroit, Miami Beach and Bal Harbour, Florida. Active in the business and social world at each location, Robert Graham's many memberships included the Washington Club, the Benevolent and Protective Order of the Elks, the Rotary Club, and the Knights of Columbus in Washington; the Bath Club, the Bal Harbour Club, and The Rod and Reel Club in Florida; the Detroit Yacht Club and many of the same clubs in Detroit to which his brothers belonged.

Ray Graham's love of hunting and shooting was equalled only by his brother Robert's love of boating. Beginning with adolescent navigation while summering with his family at the Graham compound at Conway, Michigan, Robert's devotion and enjoyment of sailing and boating only increased as he matured. While living in Detroit, his 83 1/2 foot yacht, *Atrebor* was used for both business and personal pleasure on Lake Erie, Lake Huron, and Lake St. Clair.[35]

Washington was always "home" to the Robert Graham family, however. It was the place he retired when business pressures, especially during the Depression, became overwhelming. Their custom-designed home was a showpiece in the small community of Washington and the Graham family enjoyed its comforts, while respecting and enjoying the company of the their fellow natives.[36]

The Graham brothers were major manufacturers, respected employers, socially accepted in Indiana, Michigan, and Florida, and millionaires many times over. At the same time, the stock market crash had radically altered everyday life for all Americans. Everyone, from millionaires to the recently impoverished, were looking earnestly for answers to those questions posed by the collapse of the economic system. For at least one weekend the trio was able to put those worries to the side and enjoy the simple pleasures of "home."

The three brothers again returned triumphant to Indiana in August 1930. This time, however, it was not to acclaim the brothers for their past successes in manufacturing. Rather, it was to give them their due for the agricultural successes they had garnered over the past two decades.

A three-day "Graham Farms Fair" was the occasion of their return. Although the brothers had gone on to success in the glass, truck and automobile industries, they had not forsaken their roots in the world of agriculture. On the contrary, they placed an emphasis on the Graham Farms while becoming major industrial manufacturers.

By 1928 Graham Farms had grown to include 5,000 acres of the best farmland in southern Indiana. The Graham Farms was the largest agricultural operation in the state.

Graham Farms was actually made up of several operations, in several locations. Farm #1 was primarily concerned with grain production, and was centered on the original acreage that Ziba had farmed before the turn of the century.[37] W. H. Chambers, longtime associate of all three brothers, was put in charge of all farming operations. Exceedingly prosperous for the day, the Graham Farms produced over

Very Good Cars At Low Prices – 1930 And 1931

Robert C. Graham's love of boating did not fade during his years in Detroit. Captain Joe Kenney commanded a crew of six on **Atrebor**, *Robert's 83 1/2-foot yacht. This impressive craft succeeded* **Margaret III**, *his 32-foot cruiser. (Courtesy of Willard Library)*

60,000 bushels of wheat and 50,000 bushels of corn annually.[38] In 1927 the state's three largest grain elevators were constructed on site to handle the large volume of grain.[39] Again, Graham tradition dictated the knowledge and success the Grahams were blessed to receive be shared with their neighbors. In addition to maintaining the already existing Graham model farms, Chambers was directed to conduct agricultural schools for local farmers, furnish profitable employment for residents of the area, loan farmers money on their crops, and to erect a community building.

East of the city of Washington was the grouping of operations designated as Farm #2. Described as the most up-to-date dairy operation in the nation, its 175 imported[40] prize-winning, purebred Jersey cattle were the pride of the farm. In 1929 the purchase of "Taxpayer," the national grand champion bull, was the talk of the agricultural world.[41] Originally established by Robert Graham, the dairy farm had been complemented by a cheese factory during the 1920s. The dairy was so successful that it supplied all the milk, cream, butter, and eggs consumed on the Baltimore and Ohio National Limited trains operating in the Midwest. The dairy operation was supervised by Swiss native Albert Steffen.[42]

Daviess County farmers found it advantageous and profitable to bring the Grahams their raw milk for processing. In 1928 over 20,000 pounds of milk were processed at the Graham dairy each day. Eventually, over 750 farmers brought their milk to the Graham Farms dairy operations for processing. Graham efforts to introduce pure bred cattle to local herds and their campaign to improve their neighbors' milk volume led to establishing branch operations in Loogootee, Petersburg, and Elnora.

Additional parcels of Graham-owned farm land served to raise hundreds of beef cattle, poultry and Poland hogs. Eggs were distributed "on a grand scale." A horticultural division was established with the establishment of huge greenhouses.

The bustling agricultural operations were the site of the "Graham Farm Fair" in August. The three-day exposition featured exhibits of the latest techniques in grain, dairy, and poultry production. The most up-to-date machinery was displayed, in addition to the Graham Farms themselves. Managers and supervisors gave lectures concerning production, and the overriding theme was education. But it was also a time for celebration and a "down-home good time." The Grahams, joined by thousands of their neighbors, watched harness races on the newly constructed Graham Farms track—the first in Indiana equipped for night racing. Dog races, headlined as "A Live Fox Chase," were also held at the new track.[44] Music was provided by local musicians throughout the festival, and delicious home-cooked meals were available to all. In conjunction with the fair, the Society Horse Show, the Wabash Valley Jersey Show and the St. Simeon Parish Fair were held. A "larger than average circus tent" was erected for the comfort of the fairgoers. A highlight of the fair, unparalleled by any other local exposition, was a visit by the Goodyear blimp.[45]

The celebration of agricultural success and hometown gratitude was great medicine for three industrialists whose manufacturing plants were being acutely affected by the crushing effects of an ever-deepening Depression. The three brothers' love of farming was evident throughout the three days. Their telling comments and obvious

To facilitate night-time competition at the annual Graham Days Farm Fair, the Graham brothers built the first illuminated race track in Indiana. (Courtesy of David Graham)

The Goodyear blimp Puritan at the 1930 Graham Days Farm Fair, near Washington, Indiana. (Courtesy of David Graham)

Very Good Cars At Low Prices – 1930 And 1931

enjoyment of "being back on the farm again" were obvious to all. Robert Graham, interviewed earlier, said,

> *I'd rather watch Albert Steffin make cheese than...anything else. Cattle and hogs, living things, are more interesting than motor cars.*

But it was the production and sales of motor cars which was to occupy the overwhelming majority of the three brothers' time. The poor economic situation the nation found itself in appeared to be an ideal time to exhibit those management, production, and sales skills for which the Grahams' were well known. The Graham-Paige Motors Corporation was in a position to prove to the industry and the public they were indeed a major independent force in the motor car business.

Recognition of the Grahams' status in the automobile trade was made evident when, once again, rumors of merger with various other manufacturers became commonplace. During the last week of September 1930, Joseph B. Graham returned from a business trip to southern states and found it necessary to announce to the motoring press,

> *There is no truth in reports concerning a merger of the Graham-Paige Motors Corporation and other automobile companies.*

Joseph Graham was able to flatly deny the rumors as both he and his brothers were supremely confident that the economic downturn would be of rather short duration. Concurring with most automobile manufacturers, the brothers anticipated they would be able to return to normal production and sales in a few months. When the financial figures to September 30 were made public, the brothers were able to confidently and truthfully announce that the company was in an overall strong financial condition. Even though there was a nagging cash flow problem due to a 50% drop in sales, they could point to the cash balance of $4,603,354 on hand with $1,351,364 in accounts receivable. Current assets were over 4 1/2 times over current liabilities and there was nearly twice as much cash on hand as current liabilities. The cash flow problem was perceived simply as a quandary which a financially strong company would weather and eventually profit from.

Robert Graham, acting in his capacity as executive sales manager, also remained optimistic. In a formal address he addressed the unique situation of the motor car industry:

> *When the public spending signal turns from yellow "caution" to the "go ahead" green, a tremendous purchasing power accumulated during months of curtailed buying will be released. The public will step on the business accelerator and spend.*
>
> *...There is today a great shortage in automobiles, the inevitable result of a long-continued restraint in buying. During this period millions of cars have worn out and other millions have been nursed along by their owners far beyond their normal life,*
> *while millions of potential first-car buyers have come into being but have held off from buying.*
>
> *...This total represents an actual shortage, a positive need rather than a merely potential market. Facing such a situation, the automobile industry is in an advantageous position as compared with many others. If the public, during any year, greatly reduces its expenditures for cigarettes, or soap, or potatoes, the lost sales will never be regained...With automobiles, however, conditions are better. If, for a whole year, people bought no automobiles at all, the consumption of automobiles would go on just the same, for millions of cars wear out every year.*
>
> *...And progressive motor car manufacturers and dealers are getting set now for quick get away when the light goes green, and those with the best sales pick-up will quickly get out in the lead.*

To reassure the stockholders the company's claims of financial stability were not so much positive positioning, a quarterly dividend of $1.75 per share of first preferred stock was issued in October.

To confront the loss of dealers resulting from the economic distress, Robert Graham also began a program of solicitation for new dealerships. Full page advertisements were taken out in the trade press extolling the virtue of a Graham dealership. These invitations emphasized the Graham policy which was in effect even during the days of booming sales:

> *It is part and parcel of the Graham principle and policy that the dealer shall be enabled, insofar as fair discount and fair handling on the part of the factory are concerned, to make money for himself. It [Graham policy] provides that he shall take cars only as he can readily digest them, and it protects him again by constantly improving the product but avoiding the radical changes which obsolete cars already sold.*

Manufacturing and design also geared up for changes in the way they formerly operated. Known throughout the industry for its state-of-the-art engineering facility and staff, Graham-Paige emphasized mechanical improvement even more so during the year. The brothers were dedicated to having their automobiles be the finest available in their price class. Experiments conducted during the summer of 1930 would result in a multitude of improvements to the chassis and power train for the next season.

The reputation the company garnered during its first three years of existence did not go unnoticed abroad. From its inception, the factory on Warren Avenue was continually toured by dealers, distributors, purchasers of new Graham automobiles, and delegations from other automobile manufacturers. More and more these visitors and delegations were foreign. One such delegation toured the factory during the summer of 1930, resulting in the sale of tooling and dies from recently retired models. It was the first of several contracts that Graham-Paige Motors Corporation had with the fledgling Japanese automobile industry.

Very Good Cars At Low Prices – 1930 And 1931

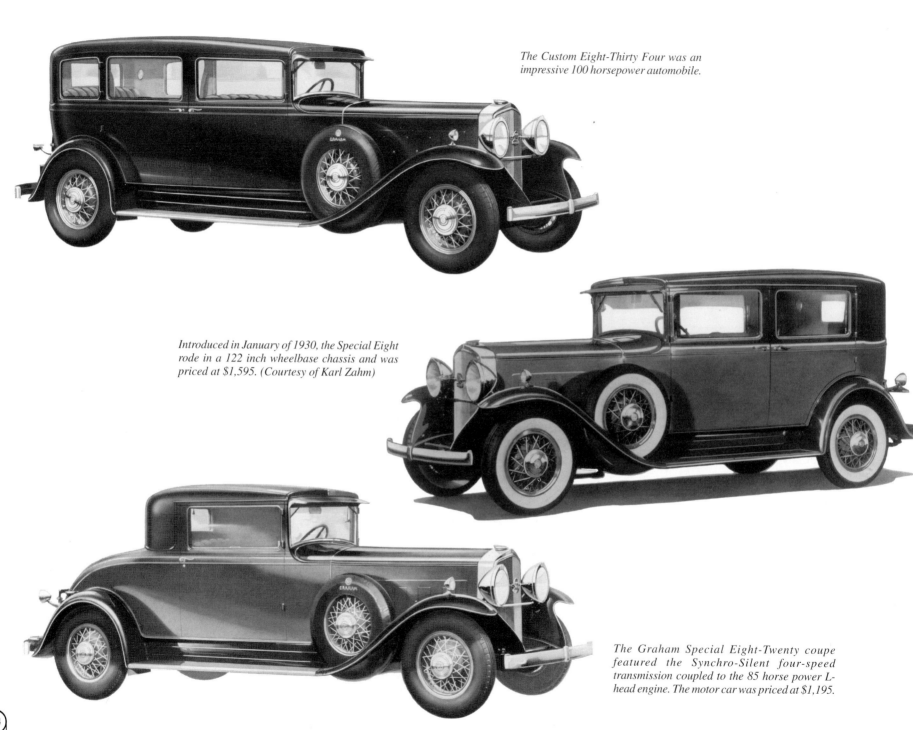

The Custom Eight-Thirty Four was an impressive 100 horsepower automobile.

Introduced in January of 1930, the Special Eight rode in a 122 inch wheelbase chassis and was priced at $1,595. (Courtesy of Karl Zahm)

The Graham Special Eight-Twenty coupe featured the Synchro-Silent four-speed transmission coupled to the 85 horse power L-head engine. The motor car was priced at $1,195.

Very Good Cars At Low Prices – 1930 And 1931

As layoffs began to spread in the motor car industry, qualified and valued men became available. Downsizing was evident at both the larger manufacturers and the custom body building firms. A direct effect of this was felt in the styling and design department on Warren Avenue. Raymond Dietrich, revered for years because of his elegant custom body designs, found himself without a position. Graham-Paige immediately offered him a commission and put him to work on the fine tuning of the proposed 1931 Graham models.

Another difficult but necessary decision was made during the fall of 1930. Graham-Paige had been associated with LeBaron from the start, and it was the three brothers' wish that the large eight-cylinder chassis of each series would catch on as a platform for custom bodies of the carriage trade. And indeed, there were quite a number of impressive and elegant automobiles created on both the eight- and larger six-cylinder chassis. However, the volume of this undertaking never justified the effort and expense afforded it, and the custom body program at Graham-Paige had been a financial drain since the company's inception. When the reasonably priced and beautiful Locke-bodied Graham Eights failed to sell even moderately in the summer of 1930, it was obvious that further effort in this direction would produce only a continuing hemorrhage of available funds. The association of LeBaron and Graham-Paige concluded at the end of 1930.

There were a multitude of changes occurring at Warren Avenue and the other Graham-Paige factories, entirely due to the lack of sales. But there was no lack of effort or desire by the Grahams. Everyone on staff was hard at work preparing the 1931 models for their January introduction. There was no doubt that these automobiles would be exactly what the market demanded and that regained prosperity would be "just around the corner."

* * * * * * *

When the 1931 Graham models (these models are known as 1931 second series models by enthusiasts) were announced at the New York Auto Show the first week of January,[46] the automobiles were very much improved from their immediate forerunners. Joseph B. Graham was able to announce the new models were,

> *...the finest products the Company has ever built. Not only are they more attractive than any of their predecessors, but they represent at their lower prices the greatest values in the history of the company.*

The reduction in list prices was most evident on the prestige model offered in the Graham line that month. The Custom Eight was the largest automobile the Graham brothers proffered during 1931. Using the same Graham-designed 100 horsepower engine (298.6 cubic inches, 3 1/4 x 4 1/2 inch bore and stroke) as was used in the previous Standard and Special Eights, this large automobile rode in the familiar 134-inch wheelbase chassis, featured a 4.09 to 1 gear ratio, and did not differ radically in appearance from the previous offering on the same wheelbase. Production was limited to five- and seven-passenger sedans ($1,845 and $1,895, respectively), and a seven-passenger limousine priced at $2,095. Graham wisely recognized the

obvious, that this Custom Eight would in all likelihood not be the largest selling model in the new line. A positive reflection was put on this fact when it was announced that these big eights would indeed be "factory built custom automobiles" and,

> *...trimmed to suit the wishes of the individual purchaser...the interior trim, upholstery, floor coverings, etc. will be fitted by hand and installed by a group of expert trim shop workers at the main plant in Detroit.*

The tenor of the times was evident when one realized that this "custom built" automobile was priced more than $2,000 less than its immediate predecessor.

The Graham-Paige Motors Corporation intended and desired that their smaller eight, the Special 820, would be their sales leader. Replacing the Standard and Special Eights of the previous season, the Special 820 had a wheelbase which was two inches shorter than those models, was powered by an 85 horsepower (245.4 cubic inches, 3 1/8 x 4 inch bore and stroke) motor of Graham design. Engineers at Graham-Paige were quoted in the announcements of the motor car's introduction that actual top speed would be "in the neighborhood" of 75 miles per hour. It was the smallest eight-cylinder motor car Graham had ever offered. A gear ratio of 4.09 to 1 was also used in this smaller eight. Special note was made of the bracing of the chassis by the engineers at Warren Avenue. The engineering department stated that they had found,

> *...that major frame deflections, reflected in fender wobble, lamp shimmy, etc., including body weave, occur usually between the kick-ups rather than at the kick-ups themselves. Therefore [we have] widened the lower flange of the frame side rails and have added a box type member below the frame side rail between the brackets carrying the rear end of the front and the front end of the rear springs. This reinforcement is riveted to the outside of the web, and to the lower side rail flange. This design not only stiffens the frame vertically, but [is] also responsible for a rather large increase in torsional rigidity.*

The stated intent of the Special 820 was to have it fit into the "quality car" market. Priced at $1,245 for the fully equipped five-passenger sedan, this smaller eight was indeed a good value. A five-passenger sport sedan and a rumble seat coupe were given a factory price of $1,195, and for only $1,155 one could purchase a Special 820 business coupe.

Rounding out the new lineup were the two six-cylinder models, the Standard Six and the Special Six. Both of these smaller Grahams featured a 115-inch wheelbase chassis and an improved 76 horsepower engine of Graham design. The automobile company was proud to point out that many of the features first available in 1930 on the eight-cylinder models were now featured on the smaller sixes. Following past practice, the smaller six featured a three-speed transmission while the Special Six featured a four-speed. Comparison of the two sixes were reflected in their listed prices: the five-passenger town sedan, coupe (with rumble seat), and roadster (with rumble seat) were offered for an eye opening $895 on the Standard Six offerings. The five-passenger sedan was $955, while a business coupe could be had for only $845. The Special Six had corresponding prices, with the five-passenger town sedan and coupe with rumble seat available for $975, the roadster equipped with a rumble seat at only ten dollars more, and five-passenger sedan for $1,035. For only $925, one could purchase a business coupe on the Special Six chassis.

It was obvious to those studying the offerings of the Graham brothers that the company was getting full use of the staff at the Engineering Building.

In addition to those refinements already mentioned, all models (excepting the Standard Six) featured a synchronizing mechanism for the engagement of high and third in their four-speed transmissions. Helical gears for quiet third-speed operation was an emphasized feature of the new mechanism. As explained to the motoring press, the "Synchro-Silent" transmission was a Graham breakthrough which provided silent and positive gear changing. "It does this by automatically equalizing the speeds of the rotating parts before the actual engagement of the gears takes place." The company was quick to point out that Graham was the only automobile utilizing four-speed transmissions which feature this synchronizing arrangement. A spiral gear drive was used in all ratios, except fourth which was direct drive. The mechanism was a self-contained unit, and was described as the "simplest means yet devised to insure positive and silent changes of gear ratio." In the transmission gearing itself, a higher proportion of nickel was used to insure longer life. In conjunction, the axle gears were 5/8 inch larger, and with the larger engines the ratio was dropped in each model. The result was an average of three more miles per hour to top speed and better fuel economy.

Attempting to make the Graham-designed engines the most powerful in their class, the Graham-Paige engineers also designed a new cylinder head (used on all models) which increased horsepower without changing the engine's dimensions or basic design. In the new cylinder head the Model C-5 spark plugs developed by Graham-Paige the year before were of special advantage. Those spark plugs, in conjunction with the new head design, essentially eliminated overheating. According to the engineering department,

> In the new cylinder head, these plugs set well down into the combustion chamber, so that the electrodes just clear the valves. Further details to be noted in the design include the reduction in the area of the low clearance space over the piston, eliminating missing.

Powerplant improvements also included a new intake manifold design, with rectangular cross-sections and intake ports. This was "a distinct departure from usual practice, giving new effectiveness in the distribution of fuel." A manifold heat control, operated from the instrument board, was utilized to "obtain the maximum efficiency of the engine through regulating the temperature of the intake mixture."

Mechanical improvements included Ross roller-mounted cam steering gears, crossmembers of the banjo type between flywheel housing and transmission, V-belt driven fan, vibration dampers on the crankshafts, and larger radiators. The Detroit

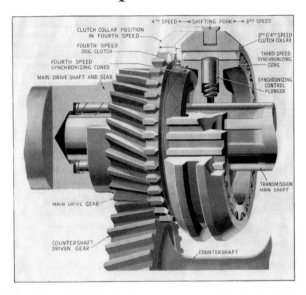

Graham Announces the Synchro-Silent Four-Speed Transmission

Lubricator carburetors featured a delayed-well type accelerating pump "effective in prolonging the period of enrichment following depression of the accelerator." Oilless spring shackles, with the shackle bolts supported in rubber compression blocks, were used on all models. It was claimed these newly designed shackles would insulate the body from road vibrations and eliminate the need for lubrication and adjustment.

Tire size was decreased on the Standard Six and Custom 834 to 18 inches, with 17 inch wheels on the Special Six and Custom 820.

Not all improvements, however, were mechanical. With Ray Dietrich's help, the appearance of the new models was modernized and refined without being radically different from the 1930 offerings.

To many observers the most striking changes were in the frontal appearance of the motor car. Although the radiator grill shape was not distinctly changed, it now featured fitted chrome plated vertical vanes. The headlight tie bar was likewise chrome-plated and a much larger emblem, featuring the familiar three profiles in shining bronze above and the name Graham below, was centered on it. An appealing single bar bumper was now used on all models as well. The two eights carried hood side panels with ventilating doors, while the six-cylinder models continued the use of louvers. The hood hinge was now covered by a chrome-plated molding, ending at

Very Good Cars At Low Prices – 1930 And 1931

Introduced in May of 1931, the Prosperity Six was the smallest automobile ever produced by the Graham-Paige Motors Corporation. In September prices on all body styles, including the Deluxe Sedan, were cut $100 to spur sales. (Courtesy of John Conde)

In 1931 one could purchase this 115 inch wheelbase, 76 horsepower Prosperity Six business coupe for $785. Compared to the motor cars and attendant prices offered by the firm since January of 1928, this was perhaps the greatest value the Graham brothers had ever offered the public.

the cowl ventilators, and the hood latch mechanism was concealed within the hood itself. Other noticeable changes to the motor car included the use of fender-mounted running lights on all series and a crank hole cover featuring a numeral indicating the number of cylinders in the power plant. With selected color combinations, fenders and other sheet metal were furnished in the body color. The running boards now carried a chrome-plated binding molding.

The interior of the motor cars was refined by the concealment of the windshield wiper motor in the header, the use of inside sun visors as standard equipment, deeper cushioning of the seats, and quarter tonneau lights on all models.

Production continued on the Paige Commercial Car, with virtually no changes made in design or detail. In an attempt to improve sales by making the Commercial Car appealing to a greater number of businesses, a pickup and sedan delivery were added to the two already available models.

Thus, as the financial condition of the country appeared to weaken on all fronts, the Graham brothers were able to present their most reasonably priced and feature-enhanced automobiles since 1928. The motor cars produced on Warren Avenue in 1931 offered everything a motorist would want in an automobile, including an attractive price. Unfortunately for the Grahams—and almost all other manufacturers—there were precious few people buying automobiles of any type. The shaky and uncertain economy was shrinking the "buying public" into a small and cautious group. Each Sunday evening the Graham-Paige Motors Corporation presented the nation with "The Graham Radio Hour", a program on the CBS network which featured the Detroit Symphony Orchestra and "America's beloved poet"—Edgar A. Guest.[47] The program was well received nationally, and Guest was henceforth associated with Graham-Paige for years. However, very few of the millions of listeners were in a position to purchase a new Graham automobile.

The overwhelming majority were much more interested in insuring their family's daily well-being.

When the annual report for 1930 was released by the Graham-Paige Motors Corporation in April of 1931, the optimistic verbiage used by President Graham to assuage the stockholders and employees was not enough to deflect their attention from the balance sheet. With total sales of only 33,560 for the calendar year, a 50% drop in production had been experienced. The company which burst upon the automobile industry with such promise only three years earlier, setting production records in the process, had lost nearly $5,000,000 during the year. Even the announcement that Mrs. Alfred G. Wilson, the former Mrs. John Dodge and longtime family friend of each of the brothers, had been elected to the board of directors did nothing to change the severity of the devastating economic report.[48]

Coming quickly upon the heels of this painful 1930 Annual Report was more bad news for the brothers. Wholly consumed with the bleak sales environment that was greeting their newly introduced line, the brothers were now rocked with legal problems dealing with past business activity.

These new concerns for the embattled motor car maker harkened back to 1925. It was during October of that year when the Dodge Brothers and the Grahams entered into a formal agreement where Dodge Brothers would continue to provide Graham Brothers power plants and other proprietary parts for the Graham Brothers trucks. At that time Dodge Brothers had already been supplying the components to Graham Brothers for over four years. In that agreement it was also set forth that Dodge Brothers was to continue to manufacture and sell,

...motor vehicles adapted to certain commercial uses but of an entirely distinct type and for entirely different uses from the trucks manufactured by the Graham Brothers....intended for lighter service only, such as parcels delivery, and consisting of an appropriate body for such uses placed upon the ordinary passenger car chassis.

The agreement was intended to formalize the existing gentlemen's agreement between the two companies that neither of them would "invade the field theretofore occupied by the other." In other words, Dodge was precluded from manufacturing heavy duty trucks and the Grahams were prevented from manufacturing commercial cars "as long as the operating agreement remained in force."

Since 1917 Dodge had been manufacturing light duty commercial cars (the 3/4 ton screen side and the panel). From the inception of the Graham Speed Truck in 1919, Graham had been concerned entirely with heavy duty trucks. The agreement, allowing both to continue their respective lines of vehicles, classified the Graham Brothers vehicles as,

...distinctly for heavier duty, placed upon a stronger frame than would suffice for a passenger car, and using a longer wheelbase.

Very Good Cars At Low Prices – 1930 And 1931

That same month, October of 1925, the three Graham brothers sold 51% of the common stock of their truck manufacturing firm to Dodge for $3 million. That contract also contained an option agreement concerning the remaining 49%. On April 30, 1926, Dodge Brothers exercised that option, paying an additional $3 million for the option and $10 million for the optioned stock. That sale included a stipulation that the three Graham brothers would be prohibited from manufacturing or selling trucks or buses for a period of five years. This was a standard restriction in a contract of this type, and the stipulation was never questioned by the Grahams. In July of 1928 the Chrysler Corporation acquired Dodge Brothers and all of its assets, including Graham Brothers Trucks.

The formal introduction of the Paige Commercial Car in January 1930 gave the rumor mills in the Motor City plenty of fodder. It was well known that the Grahams had agreed to not produce motor trucks for a period of five years, but few had actually read the agreement or knew what it specifically contained. It was with not a great deal of surprise or suspense when the Chrysler Corporation filed a lawsuit against Graham-Paige during the second week of 1931.

In that suit the Graham brothers were,

> *...enjoined perpetually from the use of the Graham name in the manufacture and sale of trucks and buses...and to make an accounting and payment for profits.*

The manufacture and sale of the Paige Commercial Car, direct competition to its own Dodge Commercial Car, had indeed garnered the attention of the industry giant. With Chrysler sales plummeting nearly proportionately with Graham-Paige, protection of its niche in any market was important. Too, a judgment in its favor would produce additional income for Chrysler during the current sales slump.

The response from Warren Avenue was quick and forceful. Joseph B. Graham, president of Graham-Paige, confidently proclaimed,

> *The filing of the suit by the Chrysler Corporation, while unexpected, is entirely welcomed to us. Everyone may be sure that neither the Graham-Paige Motors Corporation, Joseph B. Graham, Ray A. Graham, or Robert C. Graham have violated any right of the Chrysler Corporation or any other competitor and they may feel equally certain that the Graham-Paige Motors Corporation has never offered nor will it ever offer to the public, to any consumer, or to any of our dealers any product that we are not fully entitled to produce and sell. In due course we will answer whatever may have been filed against us by the Chrysler Corporation and its subsidiaries and I have no question but that whatever alleged complaint may have been embodied in its pleading by the Chrysler Corporation, it is entirely destitute of merit.*

The Graham brothers had never backed down from a challenge, and they were certainly going to fight the lawsuit with the same vigor and purpose exhibited in all business exigency.

The Grahams presented their answer to the suit at the end of March 1931. In that response, they freely acknowledged the restriction concerning the production and sale of trucks or buses for a period of five years (subsequent to April 30, 1926). They also brought to the court's attention the definition of the word truck.

The core of the Grahams' response dealt with the contention,

> *As the [Grahams]' business had never included the manufacture and sale of the lighter vehicles known as commercial cars, employing a passenger car chassis, they were not precluded from manufacturing such vehicles.*
>
> *The individual defendants never had any intention to restrict the right to use their own name in any business or in connection with any product other than trucks and buses which they then were manufacturing. They were not requested to surrender their name in relation to any product in the manufacture or sale of which they had not been engaged.*
>
> *Almost from the inception of the automotive industry the manufacturers of passenger cars have manufactured or assembled bodies adapted for commercial purposes on the regular standard passenger car chassis and sold them in the course of their regular business in passenger cars, and have likewise sold standard passenger car chassis without bodies with the intention and knowledge that the purchasers would install commercial bodies thereon, and the same has always been regarded by the trade and public in general as not being in the truck or bus business, and vehicles so equipped have been regarded as not being trucks or buses.*

In regard to the value of the Graham name and profits accrued from it, the response went on to say,

> *The Chrysler allegations as to the value of the name Graham to the plaintiffs are a gross exaggeration. The Chrysler Corporation, after acquiring the Dodge company, deliberately undertook to undermine and destroy the value of the name Graham, and substituted the name Dodge on the trucks and buses formerly known under the name Graham Brothers, types of vehicles that never had been manufactured by the Dodge company.*

The final page of the legal response included a statement of the Grahams' intent and attitude:

> *It is further asserted that the Grahams have not violated and do not intend in any way to violate their covenants made with the plaintiffs, and that the suit has be improvidently started by the Chrysler Corporation.*

Very Good Cars At Low Prices – 1930 And 1931

This was a challenge the brothers would not shrink from, especially since all legal precedence, and the facts, were on their side. Unfortunately, the lawsuit took away valuable time, effort, and funds which were sorely needed in the pursuit of their primary goal—the sale of Graham motor cars and Paige Commercial Cars.

Although it would be difficult to classify the terse announcement made by Graham-Paige Motors Corporation on October 5 as a resounding victory, it was a glimmer of success during a fall of disappointing economic and business news. Warren Avenue announced that the "suit instituted by the Chrysler Corporation last January...has been discontinued." The agreement to drop the legal action was described as "amicable," but no further details were divulged by either firm. It was easy, however, for the acute industry observed to surmise that the Chrysler Corporation saw that there were no real windfall profits to be garnered by the suit due to dismal actual sales of Paige Commercial Cars. In the same vein it was easy for the Grahams to concede the curtailing of further commercial car production for the same reason.[49]

It was with the backdrop of break sales projections and a continuing national economic crisis that the Grahams' brought out a "new" model. Always the optimists, this addition to the line was dubbed the "Prosperity Six." Aimed specifically at the low-priced, six-cylinder market, the motor car was introduced in mid-May and was the least expensive ever offered by the brothers. Described by the motor press as a "derivative of the present Graham Standard Six." A 70 horsepower (3 1/8 x 4 1/2 inch bore and stroke) engine was used in a two-inch shorter chassis (113-inches). Given the technical designation Model 56, most all other mechanical attributes were identical to the Graham Standard Six. Exceptions were the four-point rigid motor mounts, a fully automatic distributor and the use of a Schebler carburetor. In appearance the automobile was a clone of the Standard Six, with the exception of streamlined fender lamps. The motor car was an exceptional value, with the business coupe available for only $785, a two-window four-door sedan for $795, and a three-window sedan or rumble seat coupe for $825.

The expected surge in sales for this answer to the timbre of the times was not to be. Sales were much less than expected.

And yet the brothers remained enthusiastic, confident that an economic upturn was imminent, and that the automobile market would shortly and dramatically improve.

At the annual meeting of the stockholders of Graham-Paige, Joseph B. Graham emphasized,

> ...the effectiveness with which Graham-Paige Motors Corporation has carried out its program of whipping its production costs into line with current operations...As result of [these] plans the Company is in better position to carry on than at any time since its inception.
>
> Great advance[s] in the standardization of important chassis and body units and in the use of interchangeable parts has resulted in a substantial reduction in our production costs. We are today better prepared to carry on than at any other time since the inception of the Company.

The substance of this confident attitude was tempered, however, when details of the company's finances were explained. In a superlative example of positive thinking during adversity, President Graham also noted,

> During March, we produced and sold 2,447 cars and our net profits were $62,965.[50] The significance of this is apparent when the results of the first quarter of this year are compared with those of the similar a period of last year. During the first quarter of 1930, we produced and sold 9,669 cars and lost $489,480. During the first quarter of this year, while we produced and sold only 6,114 cars, **we lost only $178,523**. (Emphasis by the author)

Continuing their policy of no mid-year changes, there was no formal announcement made concerning the automobiles produced in the second half of the calendar year.[51] The Prosperity Six was the only model to exhibit any appreciable changes. Given the shortest wheelbase of any Graham-produced automobile, 110-inches,[52] the small six was still rated at 70 horsepower although it had a higher numerical rating at 224 cubic inches. In an attempt to move bodies on hand at the factory from the prior season, a Special 822 Graham was manufactured commencing in August. It was acknowledged that the two body styles available, a five-passenger sedan and a five-passenger convertible ($1,635), would not be big sellers but any sale was more than welcomed by Robert C. Graham and his staff.

The brothers' effort to bring the most fully equipped automobiles to the public at the most affordable price did not cease. Graham's version of freewheeling was made available on all chassis starting on June 21. A booklet entitled "Graham Improved Free Wheeling" was issued, detailing the company's involvement in improved power transmission.

> Free Wheeling, as originally introduced into this country, did not satisfy Graham engineers—either as to its practicality, simplicity, or dependability. Believing as they do, that progress in automobile design must simplify rather than complicate car operation, they sought for a type of Free Wheeling advantages which would retain all Free Wheeling advantages and be free from its earlier limitations and confusing features.
>
> Patiently and persistently, they continued to test and study all American and European Free Wheeling methods until, finally, they were able to place their approval on the Improved Free Wheeling now offered...

In August it was announced that freewheeling would be available to be retrofitted on all previous Graham models.

The effort to increase sales of their motor cars was all consuming for the Grahams and their administrative staffs. Following their best instincts, backed by sound business reasoning, they took another bold step to bolster sales. Considered for quite

Very Good Cars At Low Prices – 1930 And 1931

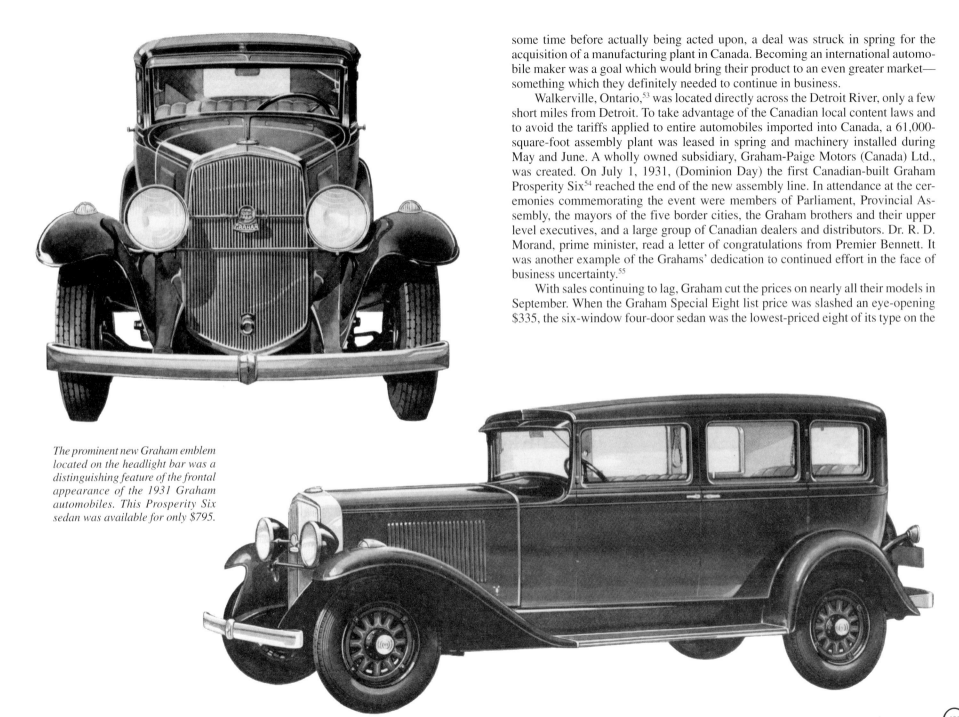

some time before actually being acted upon, a deal was struck in spring for the acquisition of a manufacturing plant in Canada. Becoming an international automobile maker was a goal which would bring their product to an even greater market—something which they definitely needed to continue in business.

Walkerville, Ontario,[53] was located directly across the Detroit River, only a few short miles from Detroit. To take advantage of the Canadian local content laws and to avoid the tariffs applied to entire automobiles imported into Canada, a 61,000-square-foot assembly plant was leased in spring and machinery installed during May and June. A wholly owned subsidiary, Graham-Paige Motors (Canada) Ltd., was created. On July 1, 1931, (Dominion Day) the first Canadian-built Graham Prosperity Six[54] reached the end of the new assembly line. In attendance at the ceremonies commemorating the event were members of Parliament, Provincial Assembly, the mayors of the five border cities, the Graham brothers and their upper level executives, and a large group of Canadian dealers and distributors. Dr. R. D. Morand, prime minister, read a letter of congratulations from Premier Bennett. It was another example of the Grahams' dedication to continued effort in the face of business uncertainty.[55]

With sales continuing to lag, Graham cut the prices on nearly all their models in September. When the Graham Special Eight list price was slashed an eye-opening $335, the six-window four-door sedan was the lowest-priced eight of its type on the

The prominent new Graham emblem located on the headlight bar was a distinguishing feature of the frontal appearance of the 1931 Graham automobiles. This Prosperity Six sedan was available for only $795.

On July 31, 1931 (Dominion Day), the first Graham automobile produced in Canada was driven from the assembly line. The Prosperity Six sedan was later used by Graham-Paige Motors (Canada) Ltd. as a courtesy vehicle at the Canadian National Exhibition in August. (Courtesy of AAMA)

market. The Prosperity Six, already the lowest-priced automobile ever produced by the Graham-Paige Motors Corporation, was reduced by $100. The Standard Six and Special Six were reduced by $185 and the Paige Commercial Car was cut by $200.

The anticipated spate of sales failed to materialize, and the monthly financial reports continued to be highlighted with red ink. On the New York Stock Exchange, common stock of the Graham-Paige Motors Corporation fell at one point to an almost unbelievable price of 3.[56]

As the year came to an end, the much anticipated end of the nation's economic malaise did not appear to be forthcoming. Although not reported in the press,[57] the Graham brothers were again approached by a syndicate of bankers. Even though the company had lost a great deal of money during the year, the financial wizards had devised a plan whereas the assets of the company would be sold off and three brothers would not only recoup their losses but profit handsomely. Joseph, Ray, and Robert Graham declined the offer, terming it legal but by no means ethical. Their gains through such a scheme would come at the expense

of the stockholders and employees, a valued trust which they would not breach. The leitmotif of integrity and honesty continued for the brothers, even when it became very expensive.

While all the automobile industry suffered mightily from the dearth of sales, it was the smaller independent firms such as Graham-Paige which felt the effects of the slump at their fullest. Many firms reacted just as the Grahams did, by improving their product and reducing the prices on existing models. But the vision and wisdom of the three Grahams went far beyond that initial response. Beginning at mid-year there was an unprecedented flurry of activity in all the departments and offices on Warren Avenue. Preparations for the introduction of the 1932 Graham motor cars was proceeding at a frenzied pace. The three Grahams—brothers, friends, and business associates for over two decades—were confident that the 1932 Graham motor cars would be so impressive and inspiring the industry and the buying public would be overwhelmed by their style, grace, and value.

That is exactly what happened.

Very Good Cars At Low Prices – 1930 And 1931

Chapter Nine
End Notes

[1] Only the name of the vehicles produced was changed. The firm continued with the nomen Graham-Paige Motors Corporation until April 4, 1962. At that time, reflecting its then contemporary interests, the name was changed to the Madison Square Garden Corporation.

[2] On December 10, 1928, Ray A. Graham was elected as both a director of Libbey-Owens Sheet Glass Company and was shortly afterwards elected to Chairman of the Board. The laminated safety glass used in the 1930 Grahams was developed "in association with Libbey Owens Sheet Glass Company."

[3] Studies done by the Graham-Paige Motors Corporation indicated that 70% to 75% of all injuries caused by automobile accidents were due to broken glass.

[4] Each full page magazine ad issued by Graham-Paige during 1930 included a sidebar highlighting the now standard shatterproof plate glass. In March a full page advertisement in the *Saturday Evening Post* was entitled "The Grahams gladly insure their public against the hazards of glass." Two sales brochures were issued: "Protected from flying glass" (Form No. 334) and "Protected."

[5] The engineering department did not identify all the individual models by the names assigned by the advertising department. Communication between the various departments of the factory, the engineers, and the dealers and mechanics in the field used model numbers. For the First Series 1931 automobiles the Standard Six was Model 44, the Special Six was Model 45, the Special Eight was Model 42, and the Paige Commercial Car was Model 46. For the Second Series 1931 vehicles the Standard Six was either the Model 46 or 53, the Special Six was the Model 54, the Special 820 was the Model 49, the Custom 834 was Model 42.

In the same sense, the Second Series 1930 automobiles were likewise identified: the Standard Six was the Model 44, the Special Six the Model 45, the Special Eight was the Model 42, and the Paige Commercial Car was Model 46.

The model numbers were also noted on the respective owner's manuals.

The 1931 First Series models were similarly designated and assigned identification numbers by the engineering department. The Custom 834 was Model 42, the Standard Six was Model 46/53, the Special 820 was Model 49, and the Special Six was Model 54.

[6] This nomenclature was used by Graham-Paige in its technical identification and advertising.

[7] Deluxe versions of the coupe with rumble seat ($945) and without rumble seat ($895), in addition to a deluxe five-passenger town sedan ($945), were available later in spring.

[8] The Special Six used vertically veined radiator shields, rubber bushed front spring bolts and an outside sun visor.

[9] Information was released to the trade press on January 11, but formal introduction to the public—via newspapers—was one week later.

[10] The seat was covered in genuine leather. In March, predicated upon requests by dealers, the passenger side seat was made optional for an additional $30.

[11] Realizing that companies may want to coordinate their vehicles with company colors, the factory would ship the commercial cars with only a sealer coat (primer) and deduct $15 from list. By February the name of the paint code was changed to Graham Blue on all factory bulletins.

[12] Bumpers were an additional $15.

[13] Some sources indicate that introduction of the business coupe was accomplished in June of 1930. The model was available in April; however, poor sales induced Graham to continue submitting data to the trade papers. Several articles appeared months after its "formal" introduction.

[14] Actual production of the previously announced $895 four-door six-window sedan was begun at this time also.

[15] A three-speed transmission was used. The price on the Standard Eight chassis was $1,745 with four painted wood wheels, $1,755 with four natural wood wheels, and $1,855 with six wire wheels and trunk rack. The same bumper, advertising, and glass charges were effected as in the Special Eight.

[16] This new model was priced at $1,845 with four painted wood wheels, $1,855 with four natural wood wheels, and $1,955 with six wire wheels, side mountings and trunk rack. Bumpers were $30, shatterproof glass was $32.50, and advertising was $30.

[17] Price with four painted wheels was $2,045 and four natural wood wheels was $2,055. The same charges applied for safety glass, bumpers, and advertising as the other 134 inch wheelbase models.

[18] The price with four painted wood wheels was $1,795 and with four natural wood wheels it was $1,805. The charges for bumpers, safety glass, and advertising were identical to the initial model.

[19] J. Vinton Locke founded Locke & Company in New York City in 1902, following his graduation from Hamilton College and an apprenticeship at the Healy coach building firm. With financial backing from the Fleischmann family, a modern and spacious factory was established at East 56th Street and York Avenue. In addition to custom body work, Locke & Company also sold the French Hotchkiss automobile following World War I. From the beginning, Locke & Company was known for its distinctive and high quality town cars. Many of these unique automobiles featured French type cane work; an art at which Locke & Company excelled. In 1925 the firm received its first order for a "series" or run of semi-custom bodies to be fitted on Franklin chassis. This manner of business continued when it was awarded similar contracts to body the current Chrysler "80" and several models of Lincoln. The Graham contract was in the same vein. In 1926 the company moved to expanded facilities in Rochester, New York. The New York facilities were maintained mostly for repair and repainting work. A victim of the Depression, Locke & Company ceased operations in 1932.

[20] As with the recently available 134-inch wheelbase Special and Standard Eight, base price included painted wood wheels. Natural wood wheels, six wire wheels with truck rack, advertising, bumpers, and safety glass were extra. By the end of the next month, requests from dealers induced the factory to make the model available in several additional color combinations.

[21] The first "down" period was in January.

[22] Technically, the Graham-Paige Motors Corporation continued to produce two distinct models during each calendar year. Although the advertising did not note this fact in any manner, there were indeed changes in these series and the engineering department made sure that the dealers, salesmen, and service departments realized the differentiation. Two series each year, acknowledged by present day enthusiasts as a handy method of identification, continued at Graham-Paige until 1935.

[23] There were only very slight changes from the models available during the first six months of the year. Enthusiasts have, however, dubbed those models produced during the last six months of 1930 as First Series 1931 models.

[24] A home movie" of the 1936 company picnic at Walled Lake, taken by Richard Kishline-son of chief engineer Floyd Kishline-is still extant. The film features Robert Graham, Cannonball Baker, Floyd Kishline and family, and the environs of Walled Lake.

[25] It was noted that in 1923 there was not a single Evansville company listed on the New York Stock Exchange. The tremendous progress and prosperity of the Grahams' Evansville enterprises since that time had helped propel six firms, including the Grahams', to that prestigious exchange. Joseph Graham returned the platitudes by saying, "Labor in Evansville is the most productive and loyal that I have ever come in contact with."

[26] The August 20, 1932, issue, which detailed Ray Graham's tragic death.

[27] A boyhood "chum," Roderick Wright, was Ray Graham's pilot.
The Aero Club, led by Ray Graham and Karl Kae Knecht, brought aviation pioneer Sir Anthony Brown to Evansville for a lecture and honorary dinner in 1919. The Englishman was one of the first two aviators to cross the Atlantic.

[28] This love of aviation continued for Ray Graham. He was instrumental in the establishment of an airport for Washington in June of 1930. The "municipal" airport for the city was on land donated by Graham Farms, adjacent to the site of the Graham Farm Fair and Parish Fair. It was the first time planes had landed in Daviess County, and the appearance of the Goodyear blimp, Puritan, at the Farm and Parish Farm was considered quite an event.

[29] In 1913, under the direction of Ray Graham, Evansville hosted a state championship shoot. Ray Graham was involved both as an organizer and a participant. A somewhat friendly rivalry broke out as his specially invited guest and he were put into direct competition. His invited guest, also a crack shot, was his father-in-law John L. Winston. Graham family folklore indicates that it was John L. Winston who taught Annie Oakley to shoot.
Ray Graham had also established an earlier gun club at the Graham Farms in Washington.

[30] The Graham brothers established a private shooting preserve near Washington, Indiana, during the 1920s. "Quail's Roost" featured a rustic log construction lodge situated on abundant acreage. In a brochure entitled "Washington-A Real Home Town" it is reported that Ray Graham, while in Canada for a goose hunt, was invited to hunt with and share the lodge of the Prince of Wales. Subsequently, he was invited to visit the prince in England. Ray returned the favor by inviting the prince to Quail's Roost.

[31] The shooting range was located at the Wayne plant site. A photograph in the author's collection, shows a tidy club house and gun racks directly alongside the main factory.

[32] The arrangement details were handled by the Graham-Paige Legion organization. Executive Secretary was Hubert A. McNally.

[33] A film of the event was made by the company, and exists in the hands of several collectors. The author showed a video copy of the film at the 1997 Graham Owners Club, International Meet in Ludlow, Vermont. In addition to the circus acts and clowns, Robert Graham and his children and Joseph Graham and his children are featured. Ray Graham and his family were in New York at this time of company "treat."

[34] David Graham also relates his father harbored a real concern, later in his life, about the effects television was having on the nation. "He compared them [television commercials] to the original "drummers" or salesmen who went from door to door in town after town because he felt these salesmen were greatly responsible for the fast development of America, since they told people about the new things which were available. He was fearful that TV was so powerful that it was overselling and causing people to overextend their budget by buying things they didn't need."

[35] The raised deck vessel was a wooden craft powered by twin Speedway six-cylinder engines (7 x 8 1/2 bore and stroke). Built in the teens, the craft was previously named the Pamila, and the Hiawatha. Captain Joe Kenney commanded a crew of six for the vessel. Prior to owning the Atrebor, Robert Graham enjoyed his 32-foot cruiser, named *Margaret III*.
Robert Graham's love of boating can be traced back to his childhood summers at the Graham family compound at Conway, Michigan. All the brothers sailed and raced motor boats in their youth, although Robert was the only brother to own a yacht as an adult.

[36] The home was designed in the style of the Frank Lloyd Wright's famous "prairie school" of architecture. Originally commissioned by wealthy railroad man M. D. Kelly in 1912, Keith Architecture designed the two-story home. Constructed of glazed red brick, the home features a large porch with mosaic tile floors, hip roof with wide overhanging eaves, a green Spanish tile roof, and wrought-iron grillwork over the windows and front entrance. The side entrance marquee, replete with leaded glass borders, was custom built by the Winslow Brothers Company. The interior of the palatial home was designed by Marshall Field and Company of Chicago. The design is highlighted by custom-made Honduran mahogany cabinetwork and panels, beamed ceilings, marble fireplaces, French windows with crystal glass panes, parquet flooring, a skylight in the central hall, and mahogany paneling. An upper level was used as servants' quarters. The basement level contains a billiard room in addition to chauffeur's room. The brick home is complemented by a two-story garage. In 1983 the home was placed on the National Register of Historic Places by the United States Department of the Interior. Locally, the home was known as "Mimi's Place," as it was the home of Bertha "Mimi" Graham until her death in 1970.

[37] A privately printed history of Graham Farms indicated that there were parts of the acreage which had never been owned by anyone but a Graham. "Some was purchased directly from the U. S. Government, some from the State of Indiana, and some from the old Wabash and Erie Canal Company."

[38] The volume was so great that a special railroad siding was built to facilitate loading from the large elevators. A small community sprung up near this siding and was officially known as "Graham."

[39] The Grahams also erected the largest corn crib in the state.

[40] The cattle were imported directly from the Isle of Jersey, England, by Col. E. H. Bull of Toronto, Canada.

[41] The grand national champion cost "several thousands of dollars."

[42] While in Switzerland, the Swiss government sent Steffen to Russia and China to study their dairy industries. The Graham brothers met Steffen while he was studying the American dairy industry, and immediately hired him.

[43] In Indianapolis.

[44] Mayor McCarty of Washington was the official starter for the races.

[45] The airship was the Puritan NC-7A.

Very Good Cars At Low Prices – 1930 And 1931

[46] The formal introduction of the 1931 Graham automobiles was in stark contrast to that of the 1928 and 1929 models. An elaborate and expensive extravaganza was out of the question for the beleaguered motor car manufacturer. A simple open house was held at the C. H. Jennings Corporation, the New York distributor for Graham automobiles, on Tuesday, January 6. A buffet luncheon was provided from noon until 3:00 p.m. The new Graham models were displayed not only at the sales branch, but also on the first and third floors of the Grand Central Palace, site of the automobile show.

[47] A series of these poems, suitable for framing and including appropriate etchings, were available in Graham-Paige showrooms.

[48] The election of Mrs. Wilson to the board of directors on April 20, 1931, was noted in the motoring press to be the first time a woman had served on "the board of a leading car producing company." The association of the Grahams and the Dodge family began with the early use of Dodge components in Graham Brothers trucks. Even when the Graham brothers resigned from Dodge Brothers in 1926, their social relationship continued. The children of the three Graham brothers fondly remember playing with the Dodge children on the lawn at Meadowbrook Hall.

The 1930 Standard Six cabriolet.

Mrs. Dodge was a multimillionaire and perhaps the richest woman in the nation. Although the press pointed out her active involvement in Detroit businesses since her first husband's death, the election to the board was for the most part symbolic. Indeed, she had bankrolled the Wilson Theater and was for a time the president of the Fidelity Bank in Detroit. However, both ventures were ultimate business failures. Her presence on the Graham board was obviously not for her abilities or finesse in automobile manufacturing.

It is interesting to note that the Chrysler Corporation had introduced its own "commercial car" in the fall of 1928. Promoted under the name Fargo, the commercial vehicle was available in both a half-ton four-cylinder model (Packet) and a three-quarter-ton six-cylinder model (the Clipper). The Packet was powered by a 45 horsepower engine and had an overall length of 169 inches, while the Clipper carried a 65 horsepower engine with an overall length of 175 inches. As reported in The Standard Catalog of American Cars, 1805-1945, Chrysler advertising explained,

Passenger car lines of the most modern accepted standards are characteristic throughout the Fargo line. Belt mouldings, passenger car type radiator shells, color scheme, general body streamlining, rounded rear body corners, and fenders all contribute to that end.

The Fargo was available only during the 1929 model year, as sales were disappointing. During the year, however, the Packet and Clipper chassis were available with automobile bodies. The Standard Catalog notes that these vehicles were simply called sedans or, more properly, station wagons.

[49] Although there technically was a 1932 model of the Paige Commercial Car, and it was available through the spring of 1932, it was simply the assembly of existing parts and supplies. There was no difference between it and the 1931 models.

[50] That computes to a profit of $25.73 per automobile.

[51] However, two distinct models per year—regardless of how small these changes might be—were created and acknowledged by the engineering department. Enthusiasts consider these automobiles as First Series 1932 models.

[52] The 1928 Graham-Paige Model 610 utilized a 110-1/2 inch wheelbase chassis.

[53] Walkerville, Ontario, is now part of the city of Windsor.

[54] The Prosperity Six was the only Canadian assembled model to have Canadian serial numbers.

[55] The first fleet sale of Grahams was made in late August to the Bowes Dollar Taxi Company of Toronto. A driveaway of 20 Graham Prosperity Sixes added to the company's livery of 20 1928 Graham-Paige sedans. Many of those first sedans achieved a total of more than 100,000 miles of service. The company commented "...their record of dependability and economy resulted in the purchase of the second fleet of twenty." The fleet was used on the grounds of the Canadian National Exhibition (August 28-September 12). The first assembled Canadian Graham, serial number 1, was used for passenger transportation on the exhibition grounds. This same sedan was used as lead car in the procession to Toronto when the fleet was delivered to Bowes by Automobile and Supply Ltd., the Graham representative in Toronto.

[56] That figure was the lowest price during the year; 13 was the highest price the stock attained during calendar 1931.

[57] No mention of the overtures were ever published. David Graham, youngest son of Robert C. Graham, related details of the offer to members of the Graham Owners Club, International, during a lecture at its annual meet in 1996.

Very Good Cars At Low Prices – 1930 And 1931

A 1928 Graham-Paige Model 614 Four Passenger Coupe

Appendix

A. Graham Genealogy

B. The Field And Track Records Of Harry Mulford Jewett

C. Paige-Detroit Motor Car Company Annual Production, 1910-1927

D. Graham Brothers Truck Production And Identification

E. Serial Numbers And Mechanical Specifications

F. Paige/Jewett And Graham-Paige Body Makers, 1916-1932

G. Graham-Paige Motors Corporation Annual Production, 1928-1941

H. The Advertising And Promotion Of Graham-Built Trucks, Tractors, And Automobiles

I. Graham-Paige International Distributors Throughout World

A. Graham Genealogy

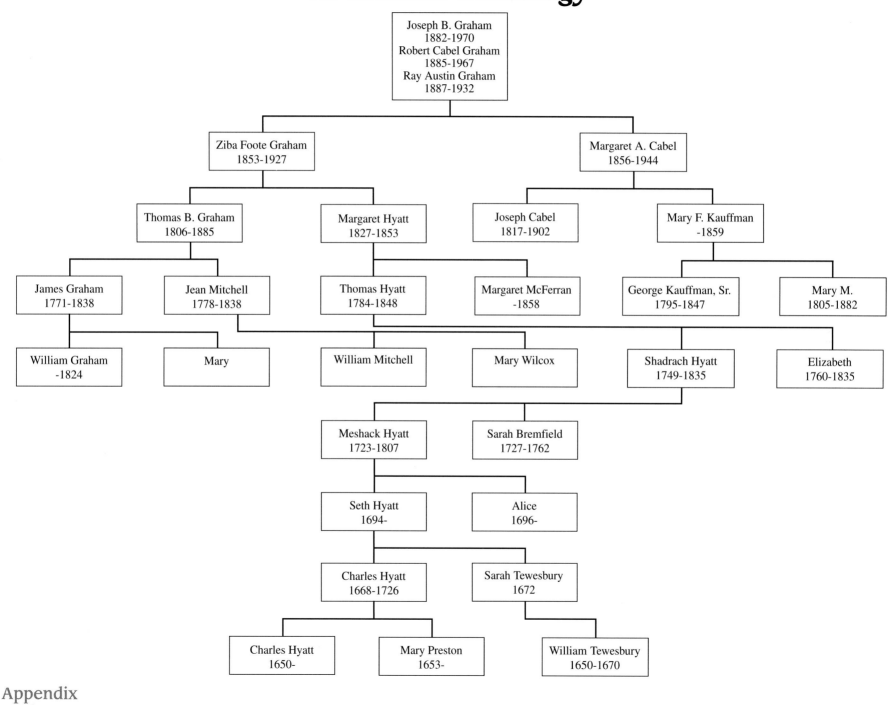

B. The Field And Track Records Of Harry Mulford Jewett

Although no little fame was accrued by Harry M. Jewett during his years with the University of Notre Dame and the Detroit Athletic Club, he was personally reticent concerning these honors and never doted upon them. A sportsman his entire life, he continued in equestrian and other more gentile sports following his collegiate successes in rowing, on the baseball and football fields, and the cinder oval.

The Detroit Athletic Club was important to Jewett throughout his entire life, first representing them as a world class athlete and later as a leader and officer of that prestigious organization. Following his retirement from active competition, a display was established at the Detroit Athletic Club featuring his many medals and awards. Those laurels are now lost to history.

Due to Jewett's disregard for personal adulation, the following compilation of Jewett's track and field accomplishments is necessarily incomplete. A study of news accounts and periodicals of the day reveal but a fraction of his victories. They are presented here only as a glimpse at his track and field career, with the hope that further documentation may be forthcoming.

MAY 1889
Ann Arbor, Michigan.
Hop, skip, and jump: 44' 8".
Jewett joined the Detroit Athletic Club in May of 1889. Because the absence of an official judge, this effort was not certified as a record.

OCTOBER 14, 1899
South Bend, Indiana

100 yard dash	10 seconds	school record/gold medal
16 pound shot	38' 10"	school record
Hop/skip/jump	41' 10"	school record
Standing jump		2nd place
High jump	5' 10"	school record
Running Jump	20' 5"	
	21' 3 3/4"	gold medal

Jewett was awarded the school's Gold Medal for "Champion General Athlete" three years in a row. The official university newspaper said "...general opinion is that he is the greatest general athlete ever seen at Notre Dame, and the college should be proud of the records he has made." Jewett also attained "Scholastic Roll Of Honor."

AUGUST 16, 1890

100 yard dash		bested a field of 8 runners
Hop/step/jump	44' 5"	broke US amateur record
	44' 1/2"	later established new record in same meet

AUGUST 30, 1890

100 dash	10.2 seconds

JUNE 14, 1890
Won Western Championship by defeating defending champion John Owen

AUGUST 21, 1890
Defeated Mortimer Remington, champion of Manhattan Athletic Club in dash. It was noted in the report of this track meet that Jewett was 6' 1" tall, weighed 169 1/2 pounds, and had 39 1/2 inch chest measurement.

MAY 16, 1891
Detroit, Michigan "Challenge Medal Race"
150 yard dash   16 seconds, won the race by three yards.
Notre Dame described the winner of this race as "Our Hal" and the "Defender of the Blue and Gold."

JUNE 6, 1891
Allegheny Athletic Association Meet at Pittsburgh, Pennsylvania

100 yard dash	10.6 seconds (on a slow, wet track)
	10.2 in final heat
220 yard dash	25.4 seconds, winner
broad jump	20' , winner

1891
Buffalo, New York

100 yard dash	winner
220 yard dash	winner

A newspaper account of this meet declared, "...one of the best all-around athletes of his age this country has ever produced."

1891
Canadian Championship at Toronto
220 yard dash   21.6 seconds, **World's Record**

SEPTEMBER 1892
100 Yard dash   9.8 seconds, **World's Record**, broke record of John Owen.

The Larchmont II Six-Sixty-Six Four Passenger

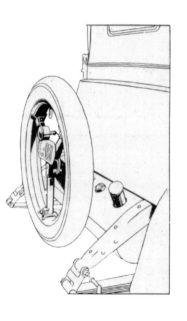

Appendix

C. Paige-Detroit Motor Car Company
Annual Production
1910-1927

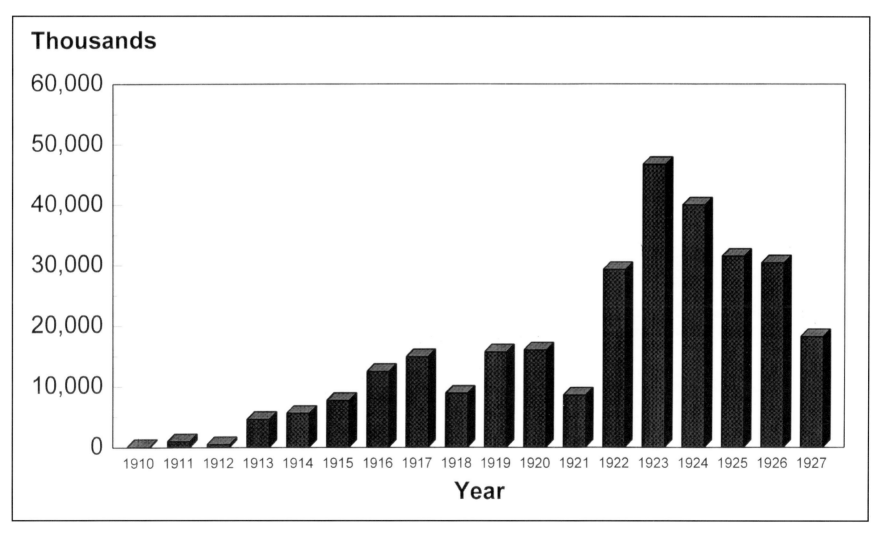

D. Graham Brothers Truck Production And Identification

Historians endeavoring to document the wide variety of truck and bus models manufactured by the Graham brothers are presented with a daunting task. When a serious study is made of known variations in chassis, engine, and body configurations available, it becomes evident the Grahams' produced a plethora of chassis\engine variations and a myriad of body styles. Factoring into this study is the lack of extant factory archives. Data compiled from private collections, libraries, and other historical archives present a fairly accurate representation of Graham Brothers truck production, but the data available is by no means comprehensive. A complete presentation of serial and engine numbers, model codes, and production totals and dates may not be possible. However, given the material presently available to the serious researcher – coupled with the dedicated effort of Graham enthusiasts – an honest attempt can be made to sort out and identify the vehicles produced.

Pioneering work in this area was done by truck historian David Chambers. The following production numbers, in addition to the production dates data, is from an article published in *Antique Automobile* magazine in 1968.

Graham Brothers Truck And Bus Production Total

1921	1,086
1922	3,401
1923	6,971
1924	10,743
1925	24,298
1926	37,463

As a note to the table on the facing page, Mr. Chambers commented: It should be remembered all Dodge Brothers serial numbers after December 12, 1923, began with the prefix "A". At the same time the Graham brothers were assigning frame serial numbers to their trucks and buses, Dodge Brothers also were assigning serial numbers to the same vehicles. In line with Dodge policy, these numbers ran concurrent with Dodge passenger car serial numbers. On Graham Brothers trucks and buses, the Dodge number was found in the usual place, viz, die-cut on an aluminum plate on the upper right toeboard. On vehicles built from 1923-1926, this number also was die cut into the chassis under the right front fender, at the rear of the rear, right front spring shackle.

Beginning in May 1925, the Graham Brothers frame serial numbers carried a "D" "E" or "S" prefix denoting where the truck was assembled. The Graham Brothers numbers were die-cut into the chassis under the left front fender and near the spring horn. The Graham Brothers chassis number was in no way coded or assigned to denote the vehicle size, wheelbase, or capacity.

A great deal of additional, in-depth research has been made by John C. Bittence, editor of the *Dodge Brothers Club News*, the official publication of the Dodge Brothers Club.

The following information is adapted from articles by Mr. Bittence in that publication. The author is grateful for his permission to reproduce it here.

Graham Brothers Chassis Identification

One logical approach to identifying a truck from the confusing array of varieties offered by Graham Brothers is to consider only the chassis/engine base. Many truck bodies and cabs came and went over the years to install on these chassis, but the basic progress in Graham Brothers truck development is reflected in the dozen or so chassis that were available at any one time.

The Grahams standardized on three or four wheelbases, two or three load-carrying capacities, and then offered practically every possible combination on these chassis. Later, with the addition of chassis with steel wheels to those with the usual wood artillery wheels, the number of combinations increased. With the six cylinder engines, the combinations increased even further.

Over the years the most popular chassis were continued, sometimes with adjustments in specifications. Others were introduced and deleted in one year.

Graham Brothers did not hold to any yearly model change over the years. From 1922 on, however, we see a great deal of positioning of models in the market with a

Graham Brothers Truck Chassis Identification

Capacity	Wheel Base	Year 20-22	Year 22-23	Year 23-24	Year 24-26	Year 26-27	Year 27-28
1/2 ton	108						SD
3/4 ton	116					DCT	DDT
1 ton	118		D	DAT			
1 ton	126	-	-	-	-	BC	BD
1 ton	130	-	-	-	BB		
1 ton	137					IC	ID
1 ton	140		G				
1 ton	140	1000	B	BA			
1 ton	140			HA	HB		
1 1/2 ton	118		E	EA			
1 1/2 ton	118		H*				
1 1/2 ton	124				EB		
1 1/2 ton	137					MC	MD
1 1/2 ton	137	-	-	-	-	CC	-
1 1/2 ton	140				MB		
1 1/2 ton	140				LB		
1 1/2 ton	140	2000	C	CA	CB		
1 1/2 ton	158	3000	F	FA	FB		
1 1/2 ton	162					LC	LD
1 1/2 ton	162	-	-	-	-	FC	-
2 ton	114						ED**
2 ton	137					OC	OD**
2 ton	162					TC	TD**

* Also listed as 2000-lb. capacity (not "1-ton") in some literature.
** These came with the new Senior Six engine.

Graham Brothers Truck
Production Dates By Frame Numbers

At Detroit

Graham Bros. No		Date
1922		
50000		April 15
51000		October 25
1923		
52000	(87000)	March 20
	Corresponding Dodge Bros. No.	
53000		May 28
60000		August 7
61000		November 6
1924		
62000		January 12
63000		March 2
64000		April 28
65000		July 7
66000		August 13
70000		September 25
71000		November 28
1925		
72000	(A232500)	January 2
73000		February 27
74000	(A290000)	March 25
75000		April 23
75392		May 5
1925 New Series		
D100001		May 1
D101001	(A360000)	June 15
D102001		July 16
D103001		August 17
D104001		September 16
D105001	(A 450000)	October 10
D106001		November 5
D107001	(A 480000)	December 3
D108001		December 22
1926		
D109001		January 25
D110001	(A530000)	February 11
D111001	(A550000)	March 2
D112001	(A570000)	March 17
D113001		April 1
D114001		April 16
D115001	(A63000)	May 4
D116001		May 15
D117001	(A660000)	May 27
D118001	(A680000)	June 11
D119001		June 24
D120001	(A720000)	July 23
D121001		August 10
D122001		August 23
D123001	(A770000)	September 9
D124001		September 23
D125001		October 8
D126001	(A810000)	October 28
D127001		November 16
1927		
D130000	(A842000)	January 16
D135000	(A860000)	February 12
D140000	(A881000)	April 7
D145000		May 19
D150000		June 27
D155000		September 12
D160000		October 27
D165000		December 5
1928		
D170000		January 24
D175000		April 11
D180000		June 13
D185000		July 18

At Evansville, Indiana

Graham Bros. No		Date
1921		
17000		February 21
18000		May 8
18960		November 9
19000		November 19
1922		
20000		April 28
21000		October 30
1923		
22000		April 12
30000		August 3
31000		October 17
1924		
32000	(A30000)	February 5
	Corresponding Dodge Bros. No.	
33000		April 23
34000		July 30
35000		October 10
36000		December 2
1925		
37000		January 5
38000	(A260000)	February 17
39000		March 24
40000		April 13
40830		May 5
1925 New Series		
E100001		May 4
E101001	(A360000)	June 15
E102001	(A390000)	July 21
E103001	(A420000)	August 26
E104001		September 16
E105001		October 29
E106001		November 25
E107001		December 28
1926		
E108001		January 30
E109001	(A540000)	February 19
E110001		March 15
E111001	(A600000)	April 12
E112001		April 30
E113001	(A650000)	May 20
E114001		June 10
E115001		July 9
E116001		August 12
E117001	(A760000)	August 31
E118001		September 4
E119001	(A810000)	October 29
E120001		December 10
1927		
E121001		January 19
E122001		February 17
E123001	(A810000)	March 18
E125000		May 14
E130000		November 2
1928		
E135000		July 9

At Stockton, California

Graham Bros. No		Date
1925 New Series		
S100001		June 24
S101001		December 4
1926		
S102001		April 22
S103001		July 27
S103501		September 14
S104001		November 8
1927		
S104501		January 19
S105001		February 21
1928		
S110000		July 2

Please note, on coinciding dates when even numbered, corresponding Dodge Brothers frame serial numbers were reached, they are so recorded in parenthesis.

variety of wheelbases and capacities coming and going over the years. Chassis of a particular wheel base were revised, one by one, until over a period of months a whole new "series" had been introduced.

During 1923, to indicate the first major wave of redesign, the letter "A" was added to the previous single-letter model designations as each chassis was improved or changed to fit certain marketing plans. By the end of 1924 we find a line of Graham Brothers truck chassis Models BA through HA, collectively known as the "A Series." From then on the model changes were signaled by an advance of the second letter in the designation. Beginning in 1924, continuing through 1926 models, BB through YB, were introduced as the "B Series." These included three buses, JB, YB, CLB, the latter being an adaptation of the truck CB chassis.

The "B Series" data provides a good example of how the Graham Brothers designation system worked through the 1925-26 period.

The presence of a third letter in the model designation specifies a variation. Understanding this third-letter code involves some speculation. "L" or "M" seem to indicate a lowered chassis, often used for buses or trucks requiring a lowered deck for loading. "L" could also signal a lengthened chassis. An "X" indicates smaller wheel sizes, sometimes with duals at the rear. An "R" usually means dual wheels at the rear, in some cases disc wheels as well. Later on, third letters would signal choices among steel-disc; steel-spoke; and wood spoke wheels; size and location of gas tank; running board size; and other details.

Starting around June 1, 1925, new "C Series" models designated BC through YC were introduced. By far the best seller in this series was the one-ton BC. Available with many popular body styles, this was the famous "G-Boy."

The big news for the "C Series", however, were the new two-ton trucks. Models OC and TC were powered by the conventional Dodge Brothers four cylinder engine, rated at two tons, on 137 and 162 inch wheelbases. One can imagine the rear reduction needed to get that dependable Dodge Brothers four cylinder ingine to haul a 3,615 chassis, plus two tons of load. Top speed was said to be 22 mph. However, these workhorses were available well into the spring of 1927, so they evidently worked. The "C Series" of Graham Brothers chassis continued into 1927 before they were replaced.

Calendar year 1927 revealed several of the most significant changes in the Graham Brothers truck line since the beginning, represented by the "D Series." Perhaps the most important development was the introduction of the 2249 first Senior Six engine, May 1927, which was quickly placed in service in a trio of 2-ton chassis. On June 23, the ED, 114 inch "Roadbuilder" chassis was the first to use the Senior engine. The old EB 1 1/2 ton roadbuilder was discontinued in October 1926 without ever going into a "C Series", apparently. In July, 1927, Senior-powered OD and TD chassis with 137 and 162 inch wheel bases appeared. The six-cylinder engine must have added real pep to these two ton chassis.

The new four cylinder 124 passenger car engine introduced this year eventually went into the 3/4, 1, and 1 1/2 ton trucks, but not immediately. Early August 1927 saw the introduction of the 124-powered BD, ID, and IDX chassis. Two weeks later the MD, MDX, LD, and LDX got their 124 engines. By the end of 1927 the newly renamed Truck Division of Dodge Brothers was marketing at least 17 possible load/wheel base configurations on thirteen chassis—all with new engines.

"For Carrying loads up to 3 and 4 tons Graham Brothers standard 124-inch and 140-inch wheelbase chassis may be used with semi-trailers, giving a greater length loading space. A distinct advantage of semi-trailer operation lies in the fact that several trailers may be used with each truck or tractor, reducing to a great extent its idle time," as stated in the catalogue.

Appendix

Graham Brothers Truck Chassis And Body Designations

Body #	Type	Chassis used	Inside Length•	Inside Width•	Height•	Capcity cu yd or *Flareboard•	Other
206	Open cab on chassis						
205SV	Semi-closed cab						
205V	Closed cab						
253	Express truck (pickup bed)	BB	97	46	15	*6	
453	Express truck (pickup bed)	BB	96	49-1/2	55	*7-1/2	
251	Canopy	BB	97	46	54-1/4	*6	
451	Canopy	BB	96	49-1/4	55	*7-1/2	
252	Screen canopy	BB	97	46	54-1/4	*6	
452	Screen canopy	BB	96	49-1/4	55	*7-1/2	
250	Panel	BB	97	44-3/16	54-1/4	none	
450	Panel	BB	96	49-1/4	55		
254	Stake	BB	92	66-1/2	25	*none	
ST- I	Coal truck, shovel type	BB			1-2/3		No dump, fixed bed; 12-in. shovel board
457V	Carry-all trucks	BB	76	51	15-1/4	*7-1/2	Two seats on each side
214	Hydraulic dump	CB, MB, MBM				1-1/2	Full length running boards, rear fenders
416	Express truck (pickup bed)	CB, MB, MBM	108	51	15-1/4	*6	Full length running boards, rear fenders
408	Canopy	CB, MB, MBM	108	51	49-1/2	*6	Full length running boards, rear fenders
409	Canopy screen	CB, MB, MBM	108	51	49-1/2	*6	Full length running boards, rear fenders
410	Canopy screen w/ lengthwise seats	CB, MB, MBM	108	51	49-1/2	*6	Full length running boards, rear fenders
225	Panel, hinged side door & shelves	CB, MB, MBM	111	50-1/8	51-1/2	*none	Full length running boards, rear fenders
438	Panel, plain	CB, MB, MBM	108	51	55	*none	Full length running boards, rear fenders
220	Panel, arched windows	CB, MB, MBM	111	51	58		Full length running boards, rear fenders
221	Stake	CB, MB, MBM	108	66-1/2	30		
	Body sub frame for hydraulic dump	CB, MB, MBM					
J-1 Special	All-purpose	CB, MB, MBM				2-2/3	Converts to dump or platform w/hydraulic
L-5 Special	Fuel, hydraulic dump	CB, MB, MBM				2-2/3	For coal, hydraulic dump
ST-2	Coal truck, shovel type	CB, MB, MBM				2-2/3	No dump, fixed bed; 12-in. shovel board
B-503 special	Ice truck, with top	CB, MBM		62		1-1/2	Canopy top, side curtains
B-502 special	Ice truck open	CB, MBM				1-1/2	Open
221	Stake truck	CB, MBM	108			1-1/2	
217	G-Boy farm truck	CB, MBM	108	66-1/2	26	1-1/2	
438	Panel truck	CB, MBM	108	49-1/2	55	1-1/2	Fully enclosed body
223	Stock rack tnick	CB, MBM	108	66-1/2	44	1-1/2	A high stake type truck body
416	Express truck (pickup bed)	CB, MBM	108	51		1-1/2	
410	Carryall (Bus)	CB, MBM					14018 children, open body

• Denotes measurements in inches

Graham Brothers Truck Chassis And Body Designations (continued)

Body #	Type	Chassis used	Inside Length·	Inside Width·	Height·	Capcity cu yd or *Flareboard·	Other
B-418	Milk truck	CB, MB, MBM				1-1/2	Capacity 70 cases, 210 gallons in quarts. Partitions rear side door access
525	Panel truck	CB, MBM	108	49-1/4	55	1-1/2	
211	Gravity dump	EB				1-1/2	
213	Hydraulic dump	EB				1-1/2	
(none)	Semi-tractor	EB					Dual rear wheels available
L-3 Special	Coal truck, hydraulic dump	EB				2-2/3	
429	Express (pickup bed)	FB, LB, LBM	144	51	15-1/4	*7-1/2	Full length running boards, rear fenders
428	Canopy	FB, LB, LBM	144	51	55	*7-1/2	Full length running boards, rear fenders
436	Canopy screen	FB, LB, LBM	144	51	55	*7-1/2	Full length running boards, rear fenders
440	Canopy screen w/ length wise seats	FB, LB, LBM	144	51	55	*7-1/2	Also called "carry all"
222	Stake	FB, LB, LBM	144	66-1/2	30	*none	
439	Panel truck	FB, LBM	144	49-1/4	55	1-1/2	
427	Schoolbus	FB, LBM					26-34 children, long side sitting benches
B-423	Special Furniture truck	FB, LB, LBM	144	72	78	1-1/2	Description same as B-472 except "for furniture"; 27-in. tailgate
B-472	Special Van	FB, LB, LBM	144	72	78	1-1/2	Description same as B-423 except no " furniture"; 27-in. tailgate
B-432	Linemans truck	FB, LB, LBM	144	52	72		Racks for ladder, pikeman pole, coil, wire
222	Stake	FB, LB, LBM	144	66-1/2	1-1/2		
553 food	G-Boy express (pick-up bed)	BC	96	51		1	Full length runningboards, rear fenders. For
552	G-Boy screen truck	BC	96	51	49-3/4	1	
554	G-Boy Stake truck	BC	94	66-1/2		1	
551	G-Boy canopy	BC	96	51	53-1/2	1	
550	G-Boy panel truck	BC	96	49	53-1/2	1	
551	G-Boy Canopy truck	BC				1	
658	G-Boy farm truck	BC	92	72		1	Full width body over rear wheels
654	Stake truck with adjustable top	BC					Canvas all weather top
650	Panel truck	BC	96	49	53-1/2	1	

· Denotes measurements in inches

Appendix

E. Serial Numbers And Mechanical Specifications

This specification chart, as well as the body supplier chart in Appendix F, was compiled for this volume by Graham historian Karl S. Zahm. I am indebted for his contribution.

Paige-Detroit Motor Car Company

Year/Model	Cyls	Engine Make/Type	Displ	(SAE HP) BHP@RPM	WHB	Serial #	Prod. Start	Price Range
1915 Paige								
Model 36	4		251.3	(25.6)	116	14000-20000		
Model 46	6	Cont. 7N	303.1	(29.4)	124	55000-59999		
Model 36	6		212.0	(21.6)	112	80000-81500		
1916 Paige								
Model 38	6	Ruten. 25	230.1	(23.5)	117	85000-89923		$1050
Model 46	6	Cont. 7N	303.1	(29.4)	124	60000-65599		$1295-$2250
1917 Paige								
Model 39	6	Ruten. 25	230.1	(23.4)	117	89924-101999		$1175-$1775
Model 51	6	Cont. 7N	303.1	(29.4)	127	70000-74999		$1295-$2250
1918 Paige								
Model 39	6	Ruten. 25	230.1	(23.5)	117	102001-112000		$1330
Model 55	6	Cont. 7N	303.1	(29.4)	127	75000-79500		$1775-$2250
1919 Paige								
Model 39	6	Ruten. 25	230.1	(23.5)	117	112001-114999		$1595-$1885
Model 55	6	Cont. 9N	303.1	(29.4)	127	82001-84999		$2150-$3330
1920 Paige								
Model 42	6	Ruten. 25	230.1	(23.5)	119	200001-209999		$1555
Model 55	6	Cont. 9N	303.1	51@2200	127	115001-124999		$2060-$3330
1921 Paige								
Model 44	6	OWN	248.9	43@1800	119	210000-217500	1/21	$1770-$2645
Model 66	6	Cont. 8A	331.4	70@2300	131	125002-131090	1/21	$2795-$3750
1922 Paige								
Model 44	6	OWN	248.9	49@2400	119	217501-221000	1/22	$1465-$2245
Model 66	6	Cont. 9A	331.4	70@2200	131	131091-139999	1/22	$2195-$3350
1923 Paige								
Model 70	6	Cont. 9A	331.4	70@2200	131	140000-143114	1/23	$2450-$3435
1924 Paige								
Model 70	6	Cont. 9A	331.4	73@2400	131	143115-149896	1/24	$1895-$2895

Serial Numbers And Mechanical Specifications (continued)

Year/Model	Cyls	Engine Make/Type	Displ	(SAE HP) BHP@RPM	WHB	Serial #	Prod. Start	Price Range
1925 Paige								
Model 70	6	Cont. 10A	331.4	73@2400	131	151546-157416	7/24	$2165-$2840
1926 Paige								
Model 70	6	Cont. 10A	331.4	73@2400	131	157417-159999	7/25	$2165-$2840
Model 72	6	OWN	248.9	63(d2800	115	160001-163596	1/26	$1295
Model 72	6	OWN	248.9	63@2800	125	400001-410829	1/26	$1495-$2295
1927 Paige								
Model 65	6	OWN	248.9	63@2800	115	163597-168621	8/26	$1395-$1495
Model 75	6	OWN	268.4	68@3000	125	410830-418999	9/26	$1655-$2145
Model 45	6	Cont. 19L	185.0	43@2600	109	313923-325345	1/27	$1095-$1295
Model 85	8	Lyc. 4H	298.6	80@3000	131 1/2	500001-501400	1/27	$2295-$2795
1928 Paige								
Model 45	6	Cont. 19L	185.6	43@2600	109	325501- finis	8/27	$1095-$1195
Model 45A	6	Cont. 19L	185.6	43@2600	109	325501- finis	8/27	$995-$1095
Model 65	6	OWN	248.9	64@2800	115	169001- finis	8/27	$1395-$1495
Model 75	6	OWN	268.4	68@3000	125	419001- finis	8/27	$1655-$2145
Model 85	8	Lyc. 4H	298.6	80@3000	131 1/2	501401- finis	8/27	$2145-$2665
1922 Jewett								
Model 50	6	OWN	248.9	50@2400	112	10000-28517		
1923 Jewett								
Model 50	6	OWN	248.9	50@2400	112	28518-55432		$1065-$1695
1924 Jewett								$1135-$1745
Model 50	6	OWN	248.9	50@2400	112	55433-102594		
1925 Jewett								
Model 50	6	OWN	248.9	50@2400	112	102595-259990	7/24	$1260-$1780
1926 Jewett								
Model 50	6	OWN	248.9	50@2400	115	260000-299999	7/25	$1245-$1680
Model 40	6	Cont. 9U	169.2	40@2400	109	300000-315500	1/26	$995-$1095
1927 Jewett								
Model 45	6	Cont. 19L	185.0	43@2600	109	?	9/26	$1150-$1295

Appendix

Graham-Paige Motors Corporation

Year/Model	Cyls	Engine Make/Type	Displ	(SAE HP) BHP@RPM	WHB	Serial #	Prod. Start	Price Range
1928 Graham-Paige								
Model 610	6	OWN	175.2	52@3100	111	800001-821423	1/28	$860-$875
Model 614	6	OWN	207.0	71@3200	114	700001-707559	2/28	$1275-$1295
Model 619	6	OWN	288.6	97@3200	119	600001-605754	1/28	$1575-$1725
Model 629	6	OWN	288.6	97@3200	129	550001-552643	1/28	$1985-$2185
Model 835	8	Lyc. 4H	298.6	86@3000	135	503001-504299	(pre-prod./showcars)	
Model 835	8	Con. 14K	322.0	120@3200	135	503001-504299	2/28	$2285-$2485
1929 Graham-Paige **First Series**								
Model 610	6	OWN	175.2	52@3100	111	821424-847527	8/28	$860-$875
Model 614	6	OWN	207.0	71@3200	114	707560-712028	7/28	$1275-$1295
Model 619	6	OWN	288.6	97@3200	119	605755-607368	7/28	$1575-$1595
Model 629	6	OWN	288.6	97@3200	129	552644-553661	8/28	$1985-$2185
Model 835	8	Con. 14K	322.0	120@3200	135	504300-505145	7/28	$2285-$2485
1929 Graham-Paige **Second Series**								
Model 612	6	OWN	190.8	62@3200	112	848001-881229	1/29	$885-$1025
Model 615	6	OWN	223.9	76@3200	115	713001-727999	1/29	$1155-$1295
Model 621	6	OWN	288.6	97@3200	121	608001-612049	1/29	$1595-$1865
Model 827	8	Con. 14K	322.0	120@3200	127	555001-557179	1/29	$1925-$2195
Model 837	8	Con. 14K	322.0	120@3200	137	506001-507014	1/29	$2195-$4430
1930 Graham-Paige **First Series**								
Model 612	6	OWN	207.0	66@3200	115	881230-897036	7/29	$855-$1025
Model 615	6	OWN	223.9	76@3200	115	728000-733608	7/29	$1155-$1295
Model 621	6	OWN	288.6	97@3200	121	612050-614300	7/29	$1595-$1890
Model 827	8	Con. 14K	322.0	120@3200	127	557180-557535	7/29	$1925-$2195
Model 837	8	Con. 14K	322.0	120@3200	137	507015-507395	7/29	$2195-$4430
1930 Graham **Second Series**								
Model (Std. Six) 46	6	OWN	207.0	66@3200	115	900001-918000	1/30	$895-$1065
Model (Spcl. Six) 45	6	OWN	223.9	76@3400	115	735001-738600	1/30	$1195-$1225
Model (Std. Eight) 822	8	OWN	298.6	100@3400	122/	660001-660925	1/30	$1445-$1985
					134	670001-670015	1/30	$1745
Model (Spcl. Eight) 822	8	OWN	298.6	100@3400	122/	615001-617025	1/30	$1595-$2085
					134	625001-625100	1/30	$1845

Serial Numbers And Mechanical Specifications (continued)

Engine Year/Model	Cyls	(SAE HP) Make/Type	Displ	BHP@RPM	Prod. WHB	Price Serial #	Start	Range
Model (Custom Eight) 127	8	Con. 14K	322.0	120@3200	127	558001-558250	1/30	$2025-$2295
Model (Custom Eight) 137	8	Con. 14K	322.0	120@3200	137	508001-508325	1/30	$ 2455 - $4505
1931 Graham **First Series**								
Model (Std. Six) 46	6	OWN	207.0	66@3200	115	918001-926896	8/30	$845-$1045
Model (Spcl. Six) 45	6	OWN	223.9	76@3400	115	738601-740265	8/30	$1195-$1225
Model (Spcl. Six) 621	6	OWN	288.6	97@3200	121	614301-614397	8/30	$1595-$1865
Model (Std. Eight) 822	8	OWN	298.6	100@3400	122/	660926-661138	8/30	$1445-$1985
					134	670016-670036	8/30	$1695-$1945
Model (Spcl. Eight) 822	8	OWN	298.6	100@3400	122/	617026-617769	8/30	$1595-$2085
					134	625101-625476	8/30	$1795-$2045
Model (Custom Eight) 127	8	Con. 14K	322 . 0	120@3200	127	558251-558308	8/30	$2025-$2295
Model (Custom Eight) 137	8	Con. 14K	3 22 . 0	120@3200	137	508326-508460	8/30	$2455-$4505
1931 Graham **Second Series**								
Model (Prosp. Six) 56	6	OWN	207.0	70@3200	113	1515001-1516000	5/31	$785-$825
Model (Std. Six) 53	6	OWN	223.9	76@3400	115	1500001-1511600	1/31	$845-$955
Model (Spcl. Six) 54	6	OWN	223.9	76@3400	115	1200001-1202000	1/31	$925 -$1035
Model (Spcl. Eight) 820	8	OWN	245.4	85@3400	120	1000001-1002800	1/31	$1155-$1245
(Cust. Eight) 834	8	OWN	298.6	100@3400	134	626001-626200	1/31	$ 1845-$2095
1932 Graham **First Series**								
Model (Prosp. Six) 56	6	OWN	207.0	70@3200	113	1516001-1523162	8/31	$785-$825
Model (Std. Six) 53	6	OWN	223.9	76@3400	115	1511601-1511776	8/31	$945-$995
Model (Spcl. Six) 54	6	OWN	223.9	76@3400	115	1202001-1203699	8/31	$985 -$1035
Model (Spcl. Eight) 820	8	OWN	245.4	85@3400	120	1002801-1004212	8/31	$1185-$ 1285
Model (Spcl. Eight) 822	8	OWN	298.6	100@3400	122	618151-618229	8/31	$1635
Model (Custom Eight) 834	8	OWN	298.6	100@3400	134	626201-626336	8/31	$1895-$2145
1932 Graham **Second Series**								
Model (Graham Six) 56	6	OWN	207.0	70@3200	113	1525001-1525700	1/32	$765-795
Model (Blue Streak) 57	8	OWN	245.4	90@3400	123	1010001-1015000	1/32	$1095-$1270
1933 Graham **First Series**								
Model (Graham Six) 56	6	OWN	207.0	70@3200	113	1525701-1526611	6/32	$680-$710
Model (Six) 58	6	OWN	223.9	80@3400	118	1600001-1602940	6/32	$825-$895
Model (Eight) 57	8	OWN	245.4	90@3400	123	1015001-1019714	6/32	$925-$1070

Appendix

Engine Year/Model	Cyls	(SAE HP) Make/Type	Displ	BHP@RPM	Prod. WHB	Price Serial #	Start	Range
1933 Graham **Second Series**								
Model (Std. Six) 65	6	OWN	223.9	85@3400	113	1605001-1609000	1/33	$745-$835
Model (Std. Eight) 64	8	OWN	245.4	90@3400	119	1800001-1802000	1/33	$825-$935
Model (Cust. Eight) 57A	8	OWN	245.4	95@3400	123	1020001-1021000	1/33	$1045-$1095
1934 Graham **First Series**								
Model (Std. Six) 65	6	OWN	223.9	85@3400	113	1609001-1611900	7/33	$745-$835
Model (Std. Eight) 64	8	OWN	245.4	90@3400	119	1802001-1803200	7/33	$845-$935
Model (Cust. Eight) 57A	8	OWN	245.4	95@3400	123	1021001-1021730	7/33	$1045-$1095
1934 Graham **Second Series**								
Model (Std. Six) 68	6	OWN	223.9	85@3400	116	1615001-1620320	1/34	$695-$780
Model (Deluxe Six) 68	6	OWN	223.9	85@3400	116	1615001-1620320	1/34	$805-$890
Model (Std. Six) 68	6	OWN	223.9	85@3400	116	1620321-1623500	4/34	$745-$845
Model (Spcl. Eight) 67	8	OWN	245.4	95@3400	123	1805001-1805914	1/34	$875-$960
Model (Std. Eight) 67	8	OWN	245.4	95@3400	123	1805001-1805914	1/34	$995-$1050
Model (Cust. Eight) 69	8s	OWN	265.4	135@4000	123	1025001-1025088	1/34	$1245-$1330
Model (Cust. Eight) 71	8s	OWN	265.4	135@4000	138	1025001-1025088	1/34	$1695-$1730
1935 Graham **First Series**								
Model (Std. Six) 68	6	OWN	223.9	85@3400	116	1623501-1627520	6/34	$695-$845
Model (Spcl. Eight) 67	8	OWN	245.4	95@3400	123	1805915-1807575	6/34	$875-$960
Model (Std. Eight) 67	8	OWN	245.4	95@3400	123	1805915-1807575	6/34	$965-$1050
Model (Spcl. Eight) 69	8s	OWN	265.4	135@4000	123	1025646-1027517	6/34	$1045-$1165
Model (Cost. Eight) 69	8s	OWN	265.4	135@4000	123	1025089-1027517	6/34	$1245-$1330
1935 Graham **Second Series**								
Model (Six) 74	6	Con. C600	169.6	70@3500	111	1700001-1711470	1/35	$595-$635
Model (Spcl. Six) 73	6	OWN	223.9	85@3400	116	1635001-1639903	1/35	$795-$915
Model (Eight) 72	8	OWN	245.4	95@3400	123	1810001-1811020	1/35	$925-$1045
Model (Supgd. Eight) 75	8s	OWN	265.4	140@4000	123	1035001-1036252	1/35	$1095-$1215
1936 Graham								
Model (Crusader) 80	6	Con.C600	169.6	70@3500	111	300001-308220	11/35	$635-$695
Model (Crusader) 80A	6	Con.C600	169.6	70@3500	111	300001-308220	3/36	$595-$655
Model (Cavalier) 90	6	OWN	217.8	85@3300	115	200001-202755	11/35	$765-$825
Model (Cavalier) 90A	6	OWN	199.1	80@3300	115	210001-212750	3/36	$695-$775
Model (Supercharger) 110	6s	OWN	217.8	112@4000	115	100001-105500	11/35	$865-$925

Serial Numbers And Mechanical Specifications (continued)

Engine Year/Model	Cyls	(SAE HP) Make/Type	Displ	BHP@RPM	Prod. WHB	Price Serial #	Start	Range
1937 Graham								
Model (Crusader) 85	6	Con.C 600	169.6	70@3500	111	315001-319318	10/36	$690-$795
Model (Cavalier) 95	6	OWN	199.1	80@3300	116	215001-223250	10/36	$850-$945
Model (Supercharger) 116	6s	OWN	199.1	106@4000	116	130001-135551	10/36	$1015-$1080
Model (Cust. Super.) 120 Cp/Cv	6s	OWN	217.8	116@4000	116	120001-120199	10/36	$1105-$1170
Model (Cust. Super.) 120 Sed.	6s	OWN	217.8	116@4000	120	110001-113022	10/36	$1160-$1190
1938 Graham								
Model (Standard) 96	6	OWN	217.8	90@3600	120	225000-227610	10/37	$1025
Model (Special) 96	6	OWN	217.8	90@3600	120	225000-227610	10/37	$1075
Model (Supercharger) 97	6s	OWN	217.8	116@4000	120	140000-142410	10/37	$1198
Model(Cust. Super.) 97	6s	OWN	217.8	116@4000	120	140000-142410	10/37	$1320
1939 Graham								
Model (Special) 96	6	OWN	217.8	90@3600	120	600001-602913	10/38	$940-$965
Model (Cost. Spcl.) 96	6	OWN	217.8	90@3600	120	600001-602913	10/38	$1070-$1095
Model (Superchgr.) 97	6s*	OWN	217.8	116@4000	120	500001-502479	10/38	$1070-$1095
Model (CusL. Superchgr.) 97	6s	OWN	217.8	116@4000	120	500001-502479	10/38	$1200 - $1225
1940 Graham								
Model (Deluxe)108	6	OWN	217.8	93@3800	120	605001-605661	10/39	$995 -$1020
Model (Custom)108	6	OWN	217.8	93@3800	120	605001-605661	10/39	$1135-$1160
Model (Del. Superch.)107	6s	OWN	217.8	120@4000	120	505001-505358	10/39	$1135-$1160
Model (Cust. Superch.) 107	6s	OWN	217.8	120@4000	120	505001-505358	10/39	$1265-$1295
Model (Hollywood Super) 109	6s	OWN	217.8	120@4000	115	700001-700145	5/40	$1250
1941 Graham								
Model (Hollywood Cust) 113	6	OWN	217.8	93@3800	115	900001 & Up	7/40	$968
Model (Hollywood Super) 109	6s	OWN	217.8	124@4000	115	700146 & Up	7/40	$1065

* = An "s" adjacent to cylinder number denotes supercharged.

NOTE: This listing compiled from such contemporary sources as *Automobile Trade Journal*, *MoToR*, *NADA Used Car Guides* and Graham-Paige factory literature. In such instances where conflicts arose, the most reasonable data was used.

F. Paige/Jewett And Graham-Paige Body Makers
1916-1932

Paige

1916	Springfield Body Company
1917-1924	C. R. Wilson
1925	Wilson, Murray, Robbins, Griswold
1926	Robbins, Murray, Griswold
1927	Briggs, Murray, Central, Robbins

Jewett

| 1922/1923 | Wilson, Widman |
| 1924/1925 | Wilson, Widman, Gotfredson |

Graham-Paige

1928 All by Briggs, except Model 835 coupe and cabriolet (Robbins); Model 610 coupe and sedan (own)

1929 1st Series All by Briggs, except Model 835 coupe and cabriolet (Robbins) Model 610 coupe and sedan (own); Model 614 phaeton Griswold); Model 619 phaeton (Griswold); Model 629 coupe and cabriolet (Robbins)

1929 2nd Series All by Briggs, except Model 612 touring, roadster, and sedan (own); Model 615 touring, roadster and sedans (own); Model 621 roadster, coupe, cabriolet (Robbins); Model 827 roadster, coupe, cabriolet (Robbins); Model 837 limousine, town car, sedan-limousine (LeBaron)

Graham

1930 1st Series Data not published in *MoToR* or *Automobile Trade Journal*

1930 2nd Series All by Briggs, except Model 45 sedan (own); Model 46 phaeton, roadster, sedan (own); Model 822 Special and Standard (own), except convertible sedan (Locke); Model 127 roadster, coupe, cabriolet (Robbins); Model 137 coupe and cabriolet (Robbins); Model 137 limousine, town car, sedan-limousine (LeBaron)

1931 1st Series Model 822 Special and Standard convertible sedans (Locke); Model 137 limousine (LeBaron)

1932 1st Series Special Model 822 convertible sedan (Locke)

(Courtesy of Robert C. Graham, Jr.)

G. Graham Paige Motors Corporation
Annual Production
1928-1941

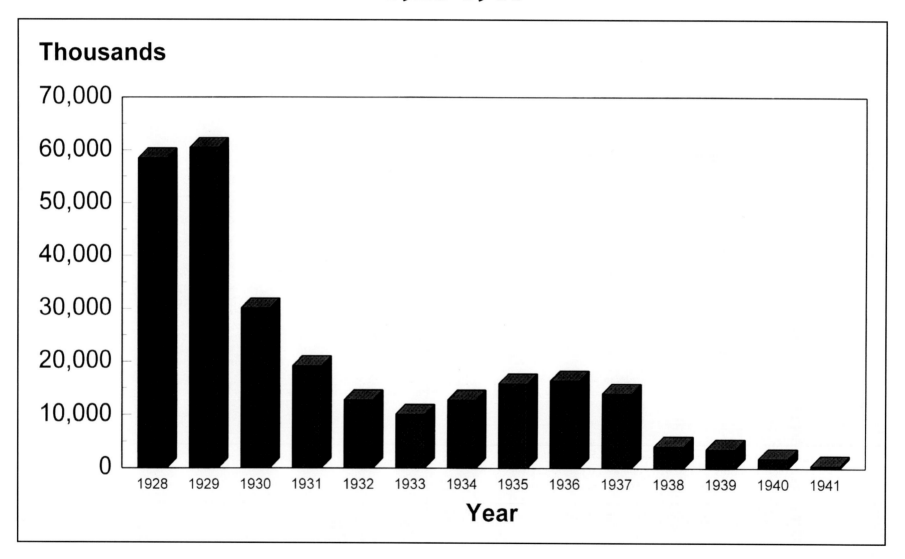

Appendix

H. The Advertising And Promotion Of Graham-Built Trucks, Tractors, And Automobiles

The following compilation relates details concerning all pieces of Graham-related sales literature known to the author. Numerous archives, libraries, universities, institutions and personal collections were consulted; however, it is certainly not a complete listing of all the sales literature produced by the Grahams to make their products known. A study of advertising and reference numbers utilized by the Graham companies reveal conspicuous gaps in some series listed below. Each year dedicated and diligent collectors of Graham ephemera discover a previously unseen piece. Readers who are able to document any sales or technical literature not listed here are urged and encouraged to contact the author.

Graham Brothers Trucks

1917

PC folder, 8-1/4 X 11", "Graham Brothers offer you all of this for $350", Model T Ford conversion to stake truck shown

PC catalog, 12 pages, 8-1/2 X 11, "Graham Brothers Truck-Builder and a Motor Car make a Complete Truck"

PC catalog, 16 pages including covers, 9 X 6", "Graham Brothers Truck-Builder Makes A One Ton Truck With A Ford"

1919

PC folder, 9 x 11 3/8", "Announcing A Truck That Hauls More At Higher Speed— Graham Brothers Speed Truck"

1920

PC Booklet, 16 pages plus black/gold/blue covers, "Graham Brothers 1 1/2 Ton Speed Truck"

1923

B&W booklet, 19 pages, 5-1/2 X 8", "Graham Brothers Truck"

B&W catalog (file folder), 12 pages plus part color covers, "Trucks for Laundries - Cleaners -Dryers"

B&W catalog, 71 pages, 8-1/2 X 11", "Trucks for Professional Hauling and Warehousing Industries"

1924

B&W catalog (file folder), 24 pages plus part color covers, "Trucks for the Road Builder & Contractor"

B&W catalog (file folder), 24 pages plus color covers, "Trucks for the Bottler"

B&W catalog (file folder), 24 pages plus color covers, "Trucks for the Baker"

B&W catalog (file folder), 24 pages plus color covers, "Trucks for the Milk Products Industries"

B&W catalog (file folder), 24 pages plus color covers, "Trucks for Petroleum Products"

B&W catalog (file folder), 24 pages plus color covers, "Trucks for Department Stores"

B&W catalog (file folder), 24 pages plus color covers, "Trucks for General Hauling"

B&W catalog (file folder), 24 pages plus color covers, "Trucks for the Ice Industry"

B&W catalog (file folder), 24 pages plus color covers, "School Buses"

PC catalog 16 pages including covers, 7 x 10", "Graham Brothers Truck", standard bodies and chassis

1925

PC mailer, 10 X 6-1/2", "One Ton — Lighter, Sturdier, Lower in Price. Standard Bodies for Every Business"

PC catalog, 48 pages, 7 X 10", "Graham Brothers Trucks/1 and 1-1/2 Ton"

B&W book, 52 pages with brown covers, 5 1/2" x 8 1/2", "Operating Record For Motor Trucks and Passenger Buses, Graham Brothers, Canada."

B&W catalog (file folder), 24 pages plus color covers, "Trucks for the Paper Industry"

B&W catalog (file folder), 24 pages plus color covers, "Trucks for the Lumber Industry"

B&W catalog (file folder), 24 pages plus color covers, "Trucks for the Furniture Industry"

B&W catalog (file folder), 24 pages plus color covers, "Trucks for the Produce Industry"

B&W catalog (file folder), 24 pages plus color covers, "Trucks for the Hardware Industry"

B&W catalog (file folder), 24 pages plus color covers, "Trucks for the Feed Industry"

B&W catalog (file folder), 24 pages plus color covers, "Trucks for the Grocer"

B&W catalog (file folder), 24 pages plus color covers, "Trucks for the Confectionary Industry"

B&W catalog (file folder), 24 pages plus color covers, "Trucks for the Chemical Industry"

B&W catalog (file folder), 24 pages plus color covers, "Trucks for Public Utilities"

B&W catalog (file folder), 24 pages plus color covers, "Trucks for the Oil Industry"

PC catalog, 32 pages, plus black/yellow/blue covers, 7 X 10", "Graham Brothers Trucks" No. 75

PC Sheets (7), 3 /4 x 6 3/4" "Graham Brothers Prices, Standard Models", May 15, 1925

PC mailer, 8-1/2 X 5-1/4", "Speed — To Save Your Time & Increase Your Earnings" V-5

B&W catalog, 19 pages, 3 3/4 x 6 3/4", "Graham Brothers-Special Equipment/Steel Dump Bodies and Hydraulic Hoists"

1926

PC catalog, 26 pages including covers, 4 X 6-3/4", "Graham Brothers Trucks, Commercial Cars and Motor Coaches", C-404-6N

B&W catalog (file folder), 24 pages plus maize colored covers, "Trucks for the Farmer"

1927

B&W card, 7 x5", "An Important Announcement of Real Value", second annual transportation show at Convention Hall, Detroit

B&W folder, 8 X 9-1/2", "Hughes-Keenan Steel Truck Bodies for Graham Bros. G-boy and 1-1/2 ton trucks", Form 112G

PC folder, 10 X 6 1/2", "A New Truck!", features one-ton models

PC folder, 11 X 7', "When Profits Depend On Trips Per Day"

PC booklet, 5 X 7-1/2", 20 pages including covers, (dealer's) Sales Ammunition Service #17, "Truck Performance"

PC booklet, 5 X 7-1/2", 24 pages including covers, (dealer's) Sales Ammunition Service #18, "Price and Improvements"

PC booklet, 5 X 7-1/2", 16 pages including covers, (dealer's) Sales Ammunition Service #19, "Graham Brothers 1927 Sales Plan"

PC booklet, 5 X 7-1/2", 24 pages including covers, (dealer's) Sales Ammunition Service #20, "The New Engine in Graham Brothers Trucks"

PC booklet, 5 X 7-1/2", 24 pages including covers, (dealer's) Sales Ammunition Service #21, "Competitive Trucks"

PC booklet, 5 X 7-1/2", 24 pages including covers, (dealer's) Sales Ammunition Service #22, "The Two Ton Truck"

PC booklet, 5 X 7-1/2", 24 pages including covers, (dealer's) Sales Ammunition Service #23, "Selling Commercial Vehicles"

PC booklet, 5 X 7-1/2", 36 pages including covers, (dealer's) Sales Ammunition Service #24, "Graham Brothers/Standard Body Types"

PC folder, 10 x5 1/2", "Six 4-4" (Six cylinder, four speed transmission, and four wheel brakes

1928

PC booklet, 5 X 7-1/2", 24 pages including covers, (dealer's) Sales Ammunition Service #28, "Taking the Children to School"

PC booklet, 5 X 7-1/2", 26 pages including covers, (dealer's) Sales Ammunition Service #30, "Brakes, Safety, and Profits"

PC booklet, 5 X 7-1/2", 24 pages including covers, (dealer's) Sales Ammunition Service #31, "Breaking into a New Field - 3 Ton"

FC mailer, 10 X 6-1/4", "Built Complete"

B&W book, 7 X 10", 77 pages with black covers, "Graham Brothers Commercial Truck Operation and Care"

PC folder, 9 X 6", "More Earning Power for YOUR Business"

PC folder, 9 X 6", "Give Your Driver A Good Job"

B&W catalog, 24 pages plus blue covers, 8 1/2 x 11", "Trucks for the Farmer"

Paige Automobiles (Graham Built)

1928

PC catalog, 20 pages including covers, 5-3/4 X 8-3/4", "A Complete line of Sixes & Eights"

Graham-Paige Automobiles
1928

Dealer's three-ring binder (black leatherette), 4 X 7", "Graham-Paige Sales Manual"

Dealer's three-ring binder, B&W, 8-1/2 X 12-1/4", 21 pages, Models shown are: 610, 614, 619, 629 & 835, padded covers with embossed emblem

PC catalog, 8 pages including covers, 9 X 12", "My Studio Has Designed....Graham-Paige", includes individual sheets (six), 11 X 8", Model 610: four-door sedan: Model 619:, four-passenger coupe and five-passenger sedan, Model 629: sedan, town sedan, seven-passenger sedan

B&W folder, 4 pages including covers, 4 X 6", "My Studio has Designed....Graham-Paige", prices shown on back cover, no cars shown

B&W photograph album, embossed black leatherette (Fabrikoid), 11 X 8", 16 glossy photos on linen backing, intended for sales room use

B&W photograph album, embossed black leatherette (Fabrikoid), 7 X 4", 16 glossy photos on linen backing, pocket size for salesman's personal use

PC catalog, 16 pages including covers, 10 X 6-1/2", "A New Line of Motorcars"

PC catalog, 16 pages including covers, 10-1/2 X 6-1/2", "A New Line of Motorcars" Imprinted by Danish Importer, Danish Text

PC catalog, 16 pages plus covers, "Graham-Paige", first page states "This book illustrates the Graham-Paige line of motor cars. Some of these cars will be introduced at the automobile shows, other later..."

B&W book, 32 pages plus brown covers, 3 1/2 x 6 1/2", "Graham-Paige Model 610-Brief Specifications/Selling Points/Complete Structural Information"

B&W book, 32 pages plus green covers, 3 1/2 x 6 1/2", "Graham-Paige Model 614-Brief Specifications/Selling Points/Complete Structural Information"

B&W book, 32 pages plus covers, 3 1/2 x 6 1/2", "Graham-Paige Model 619-Brief Specifications/Selling Points/Complete Structural Information"

B&W book, 32 pages plus covers, 3 1/2 x 6 1/2", "Graham-Paige Model 629-Brief Specifications/Selling Points/Complete Structural Information"

B&W book, 32 pages plus covers, 3 1/2 x 6 1/2", "Graham-Paige Model 835-Brief Specifications/Selling Points/Complete Structural Information"

B&W folder, 3 1/2 X 6", "Graham-Paige Price List—January 10, 1928—Salesman's Pocket Reference"

B&W folder, 3 1/2 X 6", "Graham-Paige Price List—April 21, 1928—Salesman's Pocket Reference"

B&W letter/folder, 8 1/2 x 11", "To All Distributors and Dealers: Electrotypes [of company logos] in varying sizes for local printed matter.

PC booklet, 4 X 9", 8 pages including covers, "A Gift of Life Insurance to Graham-Paige Salesmen"

B&W book, 3-1/2 X 6", 32 pages plus grey covers, "Graham-Paige Model 610", specifications

B&W book, 3 1/2 X 6", 36 pages with grey covers, "Graham-Paige Model 629"

Rotograuvre, Detroit Free Press, 8 pages Newspaper Supplement

B&W folder, 6 X 10", "Now on Display - The Complete Line of Graham-Paige Motor Cars", 5 Six-cylinder sedans and 1 eight-cylinder sedan shown, Printed by an Australian importer (dealer)

B&W folder, 8 1/2 X 11", "Announcing the First Showing of Passenger Cars by the Three Graham Brothers", printed by an Australian Importer (dealer)

PC catalog, 4 pages, 8 X 10-1/2", "The Graham-Paige Eight", Model 835 shown

Full color folder, 10 X 13", "The Eight by Graham-Paige", 835 sedan shown, Adv. Form No. 102

Full color folder, 10 X 13", "The Eight by Graham-Paige", 835 sedan shown, Adv. Form No. 102A

Full color folder, 10 X 13", "The Eight by Graham-Paige", 835 sedan shown, Ref. No. 102C, Canadian

Full color folder, 10 x 12", "The Eight—A New Motor Car by Graham-Paige" Canadian

PC catalog, 24 pages, 11 X 6", "A Complete Line of Motor Cars", Adv. Form 110

B&W catalog, 16 pages, 5 3/8 x 7 7/8", "Four Speeds Forward/Standard Shift", Ref. No. 116

PC folder, 8 X 10-1/2", Model 610, five passenger sedan shown, Canadian

B&W folder, 8 X 10-1/2", Model 610, five passenger sedan shown

PC folder, 8 X 10-1/2", Model 614, coupe & sedan shown, Adv. Form 112

PC folder, 8 X 10-1/2", Model 619, coupe & sedan shown, Canadian

PC folder, 8 X 10-1/2", Model 619, coupe & sedan shown

B&W folder, 8 X 10-1/2", Model 629, five and seven passenger sedan shown

PC folder, 11 X 8", Model 610 coupe, Adv. Form 179

PC folder, 8-1/2 X 11", "A Complete Line of Motor Cars", Adv. Form 212

Full color folder, 9 X 12, Model 610, two models shown, Adv. Form No. 215

Full color folder, 9 X 12", Model 614, two models shown, Adv. Form No. 216

Full color folder, 9 X 12", Model 619, two models shown, Adv. Form No. 217

Full color folder, 9 X 12", Model 629, four models shown, Adv. Form No.218

Full color folder, 9 x 12", Model 614, sedan and coupe shown, Adv. Form No. 220

PC folder, 9 X 4", "Within Reach of Millions", Model 610, coupe and sedan, Adv. Form No.224

PC folder, 9 X 4", "Distinguished by its Performance", Model 629, Adv. Form No. 224

B&W booklet, 20 pages, 4 x 9", "Expert Testimony", from English trade journals

PC book, 44 pages plus full color covers, 6 x9", "Motor Cars for Farmers", 11-28FI

PC folder, 9 X 12", Spanish text

PC mailer, 9 X 6", "Drive With Four Speeds Forward", Model 614 featured

B&W folder, 4 X 6", "Integrity and Unity of Purpose", Model 610, 619, 629

PC folder, 8 X 4", "A New Coupe for Business Use", Model 610 shown, Adv. Form No. 184

B&W folder, 6 x 3 1/2" "Graham-Paige Price List, Effective August 20, 1928"

PC folders, 8 1/2 X 11", set of three folders which dealers sent to prospects during May 1928 Direct Mail Campaign. Model 619 five-passenger sedan, 629 five-passenger sedan, 619 four-passenger coupe are featured. Includes cover letter dated April 27, 1928, order form, and mailing list form.

Folder, 12 pages, 5-1/2" x 10-1/2", "A Profitable Enterprise"

PC loose bound catalog, 80 pages plus covers, 10-1/2 X 14", "Graham-Paige Dealer Helps"

PC folder (to dealers), 8 1/2 X 11", "Announcing the New Graham-Paige Electric Signs", includes cover letter and order blank.

B&W catalog, 6 X 7-1/4", "Specifications - Models 610, 614, 619, 629 & 835"

PC booklet, 12 pages plus covers, 4 3/4 X 7 3/4", "About The Ride You Sell—For Graham-Paige Salesmen"

B&W folder, 3 1/2 x 9", "Retail Plan—C.I.T Corporation" June 10, 1928

PC folders, 8 1/2 X 11", set of three folders which dealers sent to prospects during September 1928 Direct Mail Campaign. Model 614 is featured. Includes cover letter dated August 16, 1928, order form, and mailing list form.

B&W sheet, 8 1/2 X 11", "Graham-Paige Luggage Equipment—The Morrison Trunk Adds Greater Convenience and Beauty"

B&W sheet on tan paper, 8 1/2 X 11", "Graham-Paige Motor Luggage—Designed and Manufactured by Berg Auto Trunk and Specialty Company, Inc., includes cover letter

PC card 8 x 3 5/8", F-K Trunks and Racks for Latest Graham-Paige Models—F-K Specialties and Supply Company. Model 610 shown.

PC sheet, 9 1/4 X 12", "Graham-Paige Road Sign"

B&W folder, 4 x 7 1/2", Graham-Paige Motor Company-Facts of Interest To Our Employees

B&W folder, 8 1/2 X 11", 4 pages, "Graham-Paige Showroom Lighting Fixture", illustrated and includes order form

B&W folder, 8 1/2 X 11", 4 pages plus order form, "The Spirit Of The Graham-Paige Legion", features a Legion banner, plaque, and framed illustration of the Knight for showroom decoration; also ID badges, files, and Graham-Paige Legion March records.

PC folder, 8 1/2 X 11", "To Know You Better...A Christmas Bonus For Fighters!", includes sales report form entitled "A Contest for Fighters"

B&W catalog, 9 1/2 X 12", 8 pages including covers, "Graham-Paige", an Amsterdam dealer's reprint of an article in the magazine De Auto November 28, 1928, includes prices, Dutch text

PC Christmas Card, 5 5/8 X 7 1/2", imprinted with logo and dealer's name inside

Lantern slides (theater slide), glass, 4 X 3", set of 8 (featuring six cylinder models)

1929

Blue and silver stamp, 2 X 2 1/2", Come to Detroit—National Graham-Paige Dealer Meeting, January 3-4, 1929. The stamp features the medieval knight image.

B&W folder, 5-1/2" X 7", "An Invitation to a Pre-showing", automobiles were shown at the factory's new 1st series engineering building January 5-6, 1929

B&W cards on blue paper, 3 x 5", Registration, Hotel, and Train reservation cards for attendees of the January 3-4 Dealer's meeting, cover letter.

B&W catalog, 16 pages, 5-3/8 X 7-7/8", "Four Speeds Forward/Standard Shift", Ref. No. 116

Color catalog, 24 pages, embossed emblem with end papers, 9-1/4 X 12-1/2", Models 619, 629 & 835

PC folder, 9 X 12", "The New Sixes and Eights", full line, Form No. 236

PC folder, 9 X 12", "The New Sixes and Eights", full line, Form No. 236, Canadian

PC catalog, 6-7/8 X 11", 12 pages including covers, 15 models shown including 612, 615, 827 & 837, Form No. 237 (also distributed in Australia, the phaetons are termed "tourer" in this piece)

PC catalog, 16 pages including covers, 6-7/8 X 11", 14 models shown on 612, 615, 621, 827 & 837 chassis, distributed by importer (dealer) in the Netherlands (text in Dutch)

PC catalog, 16 pages including covers, 6-7/8 X 11", 14 models shown on 612, 615, 621, 827 & 837 chassis, distributed by importer (dealer) in Spain (text in Spanish)

B&W folder, 6 X 8-1/2", "You Are Invited to a Showing", Mechanical and Automobile showing held at Graham-Paige's main show room on Woodward Avenue, April 13-23, 1929

B&W sheets, 8 1/2 x 11", Order Form For Graham-Paige Dealers Helps-1929"

B&W dealer handout sheet, 8 1/2 X 11", "Graham-Paige News—United States Bureau of Roads purchase of 1929 Model 612 sedans"

2nd series

B&W catalog, 8 pages including covers, 5-1/2 X 8-1/2", "Specifications", Model 615 sedan shown, all other model specs given

PC catalog, 20 pages including blue covers, 5-1/4 X 6-1/2", "Four Speed Advantages", Ref No. 240, no cars shown

PC folder, 4 X 9", Model 612 shown, Ref no. 241

PC folder, 4 X 9", Model 615 shown, Ref. No. 242

B&W plastic enclosed perspective slide, 8-1/4 X 3", rendering shows operation of four speed transmission

PC catalog, 20 pages including green covers, 6-1/2 X 6-1/2", "Four Speed Advantages"

Color folder, 9 X 12", "As Another Year Begins", Models 615 & 827

PC catalog, 12 pages, 11 X 6-1/2", "As Another Year Begins"

Full color catalog, 12 X 9", "Aktieselskabet Cyclone" (As Another Year Begins), Models 615 and 827, Danish Text

B&W catalog, 7 pages, 5-1/2 X 8-1/2", "Brief Chassis Specifications", full line, Adv.Form No. 246

B&W catalog, 8 pages including covers, 7 X 4", "Body Details of Graham-Paige Model 612"

B&W catalog, 8 pages including covers, 7 X 4", "Body Details of Graham-Paige Model 615"

PC folder, 9 X 12", Models 612/615, blue sedan on cover, Adv. Form No. 250

PC folder, 10-1/2 X 5", "An Unusually Attractive & Practical Two-door Sedan", Models 612/615 sedans shown, Ref No. 253

PC folder, 9 X 12", "The New Graham-Paige Sixes & Eights/ Open Models", Ref. No. 254

PC folder, 8 X 10", "The Thrill of Two High Speeds", Model 621

PC folder, 8 X 10", "The Thrill of Two High Speeds", Model 621, Canadian

PC folder, 8 X 10", "The Thrill of Two High Speeds", Model 621, Spanish Text

Full color folder, 13 X 10", "The New Eights"

Full color folder, 13 X 10", "The New Eights", Canadian

B&W folder, 9 X 12", "A Sound Body on a Sound Chassis", Adv. Form 250

Book, pc (with full color covers) 44 pages plus covers, 6 X 9", "Motor Cars for Railroad Men", 3-29 RI

Book, B&W with black Fabrikoid embossed cover, 4 1/2 X 7", 180 pages, "Graham-Paige Sales Manual-1929", (two versions: "Issue A" and "Issue B")

Magazine, "Graham-Paige Progress", 10 1/2 X 14", March 1929, Volume III Number 5

Magazine, "Graham-Paige Progress", 10 1/2 X 14", April 5, 1929, Volume III Number 7

Magazine, "Graham-Paige Progress", 10-1/2 X 14", May 13, 1929, Volume III Number 8

Magazine, "Graham-Paige Progress", 10-1/2 X 14", June 21, 1929, Volume III Number 9

Magazine, "Graham-Paige Progress", 10-1/2 X 14", July 31, 1929, Volume III Number 10

Magazine, "Graham-Paige Progress", 10-1/2 X 14", August 14, 1929, Volume III, Number 11

Magazine, "Graham-Paige Progress", 10-1/2 X 14", October 10, 1929 Volume III Number 7

PC catalog, 7-1/2 X 10-1/2", 4 pages plus covers, Reprint of an article in De Auto (Netherlands). Printed by importer (dealer), Dutch text. November 28, 1928

Full color folder, 9 X 12", "New Sixes and Eights/Abreast of the Times", Models 615, 621, 827

Full color folder, 9 X 12", "New Sixes and Eights/Abreast of the Times", Models 615, 621, 827, Canadian

PC folder, 4 X 9", full line

PC folder, 4 X 9", Model 615

PC single sheets (eight, in envelope) 8-1/2 X 11", "Approved Accessories for the Graham-Paige Owner"

B&W book, 16 b&w pages plus white embossed covers, 4 X 8", "One Year of Progress"

Rotograuvre, Detroit Free Press, sepia, "As Another Year Begins", 1929

PC catalog, 10 pages, 7 X 11", "A New Line of Sixes & Eights", Ref. No. 237

PC folder, 10 X 7-1/2", "Introducing the Tachometer Test", Adv. 258

PC sliding disc, 4-1/2" diameter, "Try the Tachometer Test"

B&W card, 3 1/2 X 7 1/2", "Check Up Card—Graham-Paige Tachometer Test"

B&W book (with red covers), 33 pages plus covers, 3-1/2 X 6-1/2", "A Reference Book Featuring Model 612 For Use by Graham-Paige Salesmen", Detailed Mechanical Specifications, also Second Edition, March 1, 1929

B&W book (with red covers), 33 pages plus covers, 3-1/2 X 6-1/2", "A Reference Book Featuring Model 615 For Use by Graham-Paige Salesmen", Detailed Mechanical Specifications, also Second Edition, March 1, 1929

B&W book (two versions: grey cover and brown cover), 32 pages plus covers, 3-1/2 X 6-1/2", "A Reference Book Featuring Model 621 For Use by Graham-Paige Salesmen", Detailed specifications (Also Second Edition, March 1, 1929

B&W book (with red covers), 33 pages plus covers, 3-1/2 X 6-1/2", "A Reference Book Featuring Model 827 For Use by Graham-Paige Salesmen", Detailed mechanical specifications

B&W book (with yellow covers), 33 pages plus covers, 3-1/2 X 6-1/2", "A Reference Book Featuring Model 837 For Use by Graham-Paige Salesmen", Detailed mechanical specifications

PC Christmas Card, 7 x 10", imprinted with message and signatures of the Graham brothers

1930
First Series

PC catalog, 5 1/2 x 8 3/8", 8 pages, "Chassis Specifications for the 1930 Graham-Paige Sixes and Eights", Adv. No. 261

Full color mailer, 11-1/2 X 8-1/2", "The New Model 612"

Full color folder, 11 1/2 x 8 1/2", "La Nouvelle 612—Une Voiture de Valeur Exceptionelle", French text

Full color catalog, 20 pages including covers, 9 X 5-3/4", "The New 1930 Graham-Paige Model 612", Ref. No. 269

Full color catalog, 20 pages including covers, 9 X 6", "Modelo Para 1930 — Graham-Paige 612" (The New 1930 Graham-Paige 612), text in Spanish

Full color catalog, 20 page including covers, 9 X 6", "The New 1930 Graham-Paige 615", No. 270

Full color mailer, 9 X 5-1/2", "Your 1930 Car", features 612 and 615 models, Form No. 273, also catalog (non-mailer)

Folder, Model 612, two-door sedan shown, Adv. 253

PC folder, 8-1/2 X 11", "Don't Keep Graham-Paige Customer Records Buried", Vis-u-All records for dealers

Full Color catalog, 9 X 8", 16 pages including covers, "The Finer 621—1930 Series", Form No. 286

PC folder, 5 x 8", 8 pages plus covers, "Life Insurance Plan for Employees of Graham-Paige Motors Corporation" (Aetna)

B&W book, brown covers with yellow pages, 84 pages, "Graham-Paige Standardized Service, 5th Edition" (flat rate book)

Paige Commercial Cars
1930

Color folder, 8-1/2 X 9", "The Paige - A Commercial Car", (1500 lb. commercial car)

PC folder, 7 X 10", "The Paige Commercial Car - Built by Graham-Paige Motors Corporation", Form No. 330

1931

PC folder, 7-1/2 X 10", "Business Accepts"

Graham Automobiles
1930

B&W book with brown leatherette covers, 149 pages, 4 X 7", "Salesman's Reference Handbook: A Compilation of Facts Concerning Graham Motor Cars For Use By Retail Salesmen", First Edition 1930, Second Edition 1930

Full color folder, 9 X 12", "The Graham Story - Human Values, U.S. Motor Car Values", models shown: Standard and Special Eight, Ref No. 302

Full color folder, 7-1/2 X 9", "Very Good Cars at Low Prices", Standard and Special Sixes shown, Ref. No. 303

PC folder, 8-1/2 X 6-1/2", "The Graham Story - Human Values vs. Motor Car Values", Special and Standard Eights shown, Ref. No. 312

B&W dealer wall poster, 33 X 15 1/2", featuring three upcoming Saturday Evening Post advertisements, January 25, 1930.

PC folder, 11 x 9", "Convertible Sedan by Locke", Ref No. 326

Magazine, "Graham-Paige Progress", 10-1/2 X 14", May 1930, Volume IV, Number 2

Full color catalog, 16 pages with red covers, 9-1/2 X 6-1/2", "The Graham Sixes", Ref. No. 328 (two versions: wood wheels on Special Six Sedan, also wire wheels shown on same model)

Full color folder, 7 X 10-1/2", "Quality is the Best Policy", Special and Standard Sixes shown, Ref. No. 329

Full color catalog, 12 pages with blue cover, 8 X 11-1/2", "The Eights", Ref. No. 331

Full color catalog, 8 pages with red and white covers, 11 X 5", "The New Graham Eights", Ref. No. 332

Full color catalog, 8 pages with yellow and black covers, 9 X 4", "The New Graham Sixes", Ref. No. 333

PC folder, 3-14/ X 6-1/4", "Protected From Flying Glass", Form No. 334

PC folder, 4-5/8 X 7-3/4", "Protected"

Full color folder, 10 3/4 X 5 1/2", "Now You Can Make Your Dollar Go Farther", Form 339.

B&W folder, 4-1/4 X 6-1/2", "Insuring The Public Against The Hazards of Glass"

PC folder (with color plate), 12 X 9", Models shown: Custom Eights, with blue/black sedan on plate

PC catalog, 8 pages plus covers, 7 X 9-1/2", "Now the Grahams Build Their Own Bodies"

B&W catalog, 5-1/2 X 9", 44 pages plus covers, "The Graham Line - 6's & 8's"

PC catalog, 12 pages, 6 X 9", "For the Woman"

B&W booklet, 12 pages, 4 X 9", full line chassis specifications

B&W folder, 4 X 6", "Shatter-Proof Glass"

B&W folder, 3-1/4 X 5-3/4", "The Best Way to Start Your Graham in Zero Weather"

PC folder, 8-1/2 X 11, "Outstanding Features of Interest"

PC folder, 9 X 7", "Three New Sedans"

PC catalog, 20 pages, 6 X 9", "Four Speed Advantages" (testimonial letters)

PC catalog, 6 pages including covers, 10-1/2 X 13-3/4", "Graham-Paige Legion March", Sheet Music. Custom Eight sedan and phaeton shown on back cover, Imprinted by importer (dealer) in Netherlands. Dutch covers, English lyrics.

B&W folder, 6 X 7-1/2", "Directory of Graham Exhibits at the National Automobile Show, New York - January 4 to January 11, 1930"

PC folder, 4-1/2 X 5-5/8", "Lista de Precio's No. 12" Price list, text in Spanish

PC folder, 6-1/4 X 3-1/2", "Always Far in Advance", Sixes and Eights shown

1931

B&W dealers prospectus, 41 pages plus padded covers, 10-1/2 X 11-1/4", 14 models shown

Sepia catalog, 16 pages including covers, 5-1/2 X 10-1/2", "New Beauty", Ref. No. 340 (two versions)

PC catalog, 16 pages including green covers, 5-3/8 X 8-3/8", "The New Graham Syncro-Silent Four Speed Transmission", Form No. 341

PC folder, 3-1/2 X 6-1/4", "Why is the Syncro-Silent Four Speed Transmission So Important to You?"

Color catalog, 16 pages including gold covers, 8 X 12", "Graham Eights", Ref. No. 343, Models: 820 & 834

Color catalog, 16 pages including silver covers, 8 X 12", Graham Sixes", Ref. No. 344, Models shown: Standard and special sixes

B&W cataog, 31 pages, 5-1/2 X 8", "How to Sell Graham Sixes and Eights", Form No. 345

PC catalog, 8 pages plus covers, 6 X 8", "Beauty, Comfort, and Driving Ease for the Woman"

B&W folder, 8 pages , 10 1/4 x 14", "Graham Progress", Volume 5 Number 1, January 13, 1931

B&W folder, 8 pages, 10-1/4 X 14", "Graham Progress", Volume 5 Number 9, June 1, 1931

PC folder, 8-1/2 X 3-1/2", "The New Graham Six", sedan and town sedan shown

B&W folder, 5-3/8 X 8-1/2", "You are Cordially Invited to Attend the Opening of Our New Downtown Showroom", August 22, 1931

Full color catalog, 16 pages including silver covers, 12 X 8 ", "Special Sixes", Ref. No. 347

Full color folder, 8-1/2 X 8", "Very Good Cars at Low Prices - Graham Sixes", Adv. Form 393

PC catalog, 16 pages including red covers, 4-1/2 X 6-3/4", "Graham Improved Free Wheeling", Form No. 104

B&W catalog, 16 pages including covers, 7-1/2 X 9-1/4", "Approved Graham Accessories", one car shown

PC catalog, 8 pages, 8-1/2 X 11", "Distinctive Accessories for your Graham"

PC folder, 3-1/2 X 6-3/8", "Enduring Charm for Graham Interiors" Graham-Fry seat covers

Color catalog, 16 pages including red covers, 8 X 12", "Prosperity Six Built by Graham", full line

Color catalog, 16 pages including red covers, 8 X 12", "Prosperity Six Built by Graham", Full line: Canada

Full color folders (four), 8-1/2 X 11", "Prosperity Six - Most Everybody Can Afford It" Town sedan, coupe, four door sedan shown. Back of each folder consecutively list 54 reasons (12, 14, 14, 14) why the Prosperity Six is better. Imprinted with name of Pittsburg dealer.

PC folder, 11 X 8-1/2", "Why the Prosperity Six is a Better Six"

PC folder, 8-1/2 X 11", "Why the Prosperity Six is a Better Six", Walkerville, Ontario

Dealer's three-ring binder (black Fabrikoid), 4-1/2 X 7", "Comparative Data", 100 pages

PC folder, 8-1/2 X 11", "Comparisons", (with Prosperity Six) Ref. no. 101-5M. No cars shown

PC folder, 8-1/2 X 11" "Comparisons" (with Standard Six)

Color folder, 3-1/2 X 8-1/2", "Prosperity Six"

Color folder, 8-1/2 X 11", "Reasons for Owning the Graham Prosperity SIx", letter format with one model shown

B&W data book, 8-1/4 X 10-3/4", 32 pages, "Charts", No cars shown, statistical sales information for dealers

B&W folder with seperate sheets, 8-1/2 X 11", "Dealer Sales Helps", April 1931

B&W Graham Selling Course folder includes ad mat, cards, sheets and miscellaneous selling aids. No cars shown

PC folder, 4 pages, 8-1/4 X 11", "Why are Graham Cars Better Cars?", green, 8 cylinder, 4 window sedan shown

PC folder, 4 pages, 11 x 8 1/4", "Why Is The Prosperity Six A Better Six"

PC folder (plus individual sheet with etching of Edgar Guest), 12-1/2 X 10-1/4", folder has Knute Rockne on cover, Text of Guest's eulogy for Rockne during Graham Radio Hour, April 5, 1931. In imprinted envelope

B&W etching, 12 1/2 X 10 1/4", Edgar Guest poem "The Little Clothes Line", in imprinted envelope

B&W etching, 12 1/2 X 10 1/4", Edgar Guest poem, "Children and the Car", in imprinted envelope

PC etching, 12 1//2 X 10 1/4", Edgar Guest poem, "Easter", in imprinted envelope

B&W sheet (etching) in imprinted envelope 12 X 10", text of Edgar Guest poem "Don't Touch"

B&W etching, 12 1/2 x 10 1/4", Edgar Guest poem, "The Good Little Boy", in imprinted envelope

B&W etching, 12 1/2 x 10 1/4", Edgar Guest poem, "Fly a Clean Flag"

B&W catalog, 20 pages plus covers, 4 X 8-1/2", "Shooting Speed by Cannon-Ball Baker"

1932
First Series

PC string-bound program, 4 pages plus silver covers, 4-1/2 X 7-1/2", "Strong Hearted Men", from "America at Work" luncheon sponsored by the Graham Legion, January 15, 1932, New York, New York

PC folder, 3 1/2 x 6 1/2", "The Magic of Motors-A Special Exhibition/January 15, 1932, New York, New York

PC catalog, 10 pages including covers, 4 X 6, "After Four Years"

Full color catalog, 9-1/2 X 11-3/4", 4 pages, "The Graham 822-100 Horsepower", Model shown: Special 822 convertible sedan

2nd Series

PC folder, 3-1/2 X 8-1/2", "The New Graham Eight-New Lower Price, New Modern Features", blue sedan shown, Standard and Deluxe prices and features, Ref. No. 107

Full color catalog 13 X 11", 8 pages including covers, "A Truly Modern Motor Car - Graham Built in Canada", Form 108 (printed in Canada)

Full color folder, 3-3/4 X 8-1/2", "The New Graham 8", Ref. No. 109. Model shown is Blue Streak Eight (Two versions, involving specifications and placement of illustrations.)

Full color folder, 3-3/4 X 8-1/2", "The New Graham 8—A Truly Modern Motor Car", Ref. No. 109. Blue Streak Eight shown. Graham 8 compared with 15 competitive makes

Full color folder, 8-1/2 X 3-1/2", The New Graham 8—A Truly Modern Motor Car" three Eights shown, Ref. No. 109A

Full color folder, 8-1/2 X 3-1/2", "The New Graham Six", Ref. No. 110

PC folder, 8-1/2 X 11", "The Graham Six - 1932", Ref. No. 111, Model: 56, full line

PC catalog, 16 pages, 8 X 5", "Truly Modern", mechanical details of Eight, Ref. No. 112

PC mailer, 9 X 4", "Beauty Backed by Value", four-door sedan shown, Ref. No. 113

Color folder, 13 X 10", "Tomorrows Car at Today's Prices", four plates of Blue Streak models, Ref. No. 114, (two cover versions)

Color folder, 10-1/4 X 13", "A Truly Modern Motorcar", model Blue Streak Eight shown

B&W booklet, 8 pages, 8 3/4 x 11 3/4", "Graham Blue Streak Eight Is Truly Modern", dealer handout reprinted from December 19, 1931 *Automobile Topics*.

B&W book, 29 pages, 3 X 5-1/2", "Facts", data book for Model 57

Leatherette bound book, 3 x 5 1/4", 72 pages, "Graham Facts—1932 Graham Eight"

B&W newspaper, 10-1/4 X 13-3/4", 8 pages, "Graham Progress", Vol. 6 No. 1 (February 13, 1932) Model: Blue Streak coupe shown

B&W newspaper, 10 1/4 X 13 3/4", 8 pages, "Graham Progress", Volume 6 No. 2, April 9, 1932)

B&W newspaper, 10 1/4 X 13 3/4", 8 pages, "Graham Progress", Volume 6 No. 3, (June 16, 1932,)

B&W newspaper, 10 1/4 X 13 3/4", 8 pages, "Graham Progress", Volume 6 No. 5, (October 15, 1932)

B&W newspaper, 10 1/4 X 13 3/4", 8 pages, "Graham Progress" Volume 6 No. 6, (December 6, 1932)

PC catalog, 8 pages, 5 X 7", "Master of Mountains", Model: Blue Streak Eight Convertible, stripped down version shown

1933

PC folder, 8-1/2 X 3-1/2", "1933 Great Graham Sixes and Eights", Form No. 115

PC catalog, 8 pages, 11 X 16", "Styles of the Year - Chicago Edition", full line

PC catalog, 8 pages, 11 X 16", "Styles of the Year - Denver Edition", full line

PC catalog, 8 pages, 11 X 16", "Styles of the Year - New York Edition", full line

PC catalog, 8 pages, 11 X 16", "Styles of the Year - Seattle Edition", full line

PC catalog, 8 pages, 11 X 16", "Styles of the Year - Rochester Edition", full line

PC catalog, 8 pages, 11 X 16", "Styles of the Year - Los Angeles Edition", full line

PC catalog, 8 pages, 11 X 16", "Styles of the Year-Portland Edition", full line

PC catalog, 8 pages, 11 X 16", "Styles of the Year", factory issue, (no city indicated) full line

Color catalog, 20 pages, 9-1/2 X 11-1/2", "Graham, The Most Imitated Car on the Road", full line

PC (red) newspaper, "Graham Progress—Starting 1933 With a Bang", February 10, 1933

B&W newspaper, "Graham Progress", May 19, 1933

Color catalog, 20 pages, 9 X 11", "Graham, The Most Imitated Car on the Road", full line, Canadian

PC folder, 8-1/2 X 11", "The Graham Six", 1933 Model 56 is shown, Ref. No. 111A

PC folder, 10-1/2 X 8", "1933 Graham Six" head-on view of six with straight bumper, Ref. No. 120

PC folder, 3-1/2 X 6", "1933 Graham Six/Companion to the Great Graham 8", shows six cylinder models, Ref. No. 121

B&W book, 8 1/2 X 11", 28 pages, "25 Reasons Why You Should Own A Graham—The Most Imitated Car On The Road", testimonials.

PC folder, 8 1/4 X 10 3/4", "Drive-A-Graham Week", issued by Richmond, Virginia dealer during week of July 21st-28th, $50 certificate for each adult who test drove the "Safest Car On The Road." This factory issued folder illustrates a sedan with the caption, "Truly A Little Chariot from Heaven."

2nd series

PC folder, 4 X 7", "The Most Imitated Car on the Road", Ref. No. 122

PC folder, 4 X 7", "The Most Imitated Car on the Road", Ref. No. 122 (Canadian)

PC folder, 3-1/2 X 6-1/2", "Graham Eight — Second Series 1933/ Compared with 14 Competitive Makes" Canadian Issue

PC catalog, 7 X 4", "The Most Imitated Car on the Road", Ref. No. 123

B&W salesman's brief (typewritten) 9 pages, 8-1/2 X 11", "Questions and Answers - The New Graham", March 30, 1933

B&W book, 3 X 5-1/2" "Graham Facts - 1933", 68 pages with red covers

B&W booklet, 16 pages, 4 X 8-1/2", "High Compression Vitalized Power"

B&W folder, 3-1/2 X 6-1/2", "Graham Safety Ride Demonstration"

1934
First Series

FC catalog, 20 pages including covers, 11 X 10-1/2", "Graham" Ref. No. 34-1, full line

PC catalog, 20 pages including covers, 10 X 11", Ref. No. 34-1, Canadian

Green sepia newspaper, 8 pages, 12 X 17", "Graham News", Ref. No. 34-2, full line (with Supercharged Special 8)

Brown sepia newspaper, 8 pages, 12 X 17", "Graham News", Ref. No. 34-2 full line (with Six, Deluxe Six, Standard Eight, Custom Eight)

Brown sepia newspaper, 8 pages, 12 X 17", "Graham News" Ref. No. 34-2 full line. Text in Spanish

PC catalog, 16 pages including covers, 4 X 7", "Bring Up-to-date Your Knowledge of Motorcar Performance", Ref. No. 34-3

2nd series

B&W catalog, 12 pages, 4 X 6-1/2", "The Graham Supercharger - What it Does, What It Is, and Why", Ref. No. 34-9

B&W dealer handout sheet, reprinted from newspaper article in *Anderson Herald* (Indiana), 17 1/2 X 23", "22 New Grahams Sold in 29 Days", May 3, 1934

PC catalog, 9 1/2 X 6 3/4", "The Car With Character of It's Own", Ref. No. 34-12

PC sheet, 8-1/2 X 11", Supercharger Eight shown, Ref. No. 34-12, Supp.

PC folder, 6 x 9-1/2", "A Car With Character of It's Own - Made in Canada", Form 34-12C

PC folder, 12 X 9", "Graham Standard Six", Ref. No. 34-13 (blue print)

PC folder, 12 X 9", "Graham Standard Six", Ref. No. 34-13 Int. (orange print)

PC folder, 12 X 9", "Graham Special Eight", Ref. no. 34-14 (green print, shows mid-year change)

PC folder, 12 X 9", "Graham Special Eight", Ref. no. 34-14 Int (Belgian edition, Dutch text)

PC folder, 12 X 9", "Graham Custom Eight", revised hood, blue print, Ref. No. 34-15

PC folder, 12 X 9", "Graham Custom Eight", Ref. No. 34-15 Int (Belgian edition, Dutch text)

PC folder, 5-1/2 X 9", "De Nieuwe Graham Custom Eight met Compressor" Dutch text, supercharger unit featured on cover

B&W cardboard folder, 4 X 8", "Graham Prices—1934 Second Series—January 9, 1934- for Salesmen's Use Only"

PC folder, 3 1/2 XC 8 1/4", "Graham Directional Signal-An Effective Safegard Against Costly and Dangerous Accidents"

B&W price sheet, 6-3/4 X 9-7/8", March 1934, French text

B&W book with green covers, 125 pages, 3-1/2 X 5", "Graham Facts - 1934"

1935
First Series

PC folder, 4 X 7-1/2", Prices - January 2, 1935

PC folder, 10-1/4 X -1/2", "What did they say at the Auto Shows?"

B&W book, 192 pages, 3 X 6", "Graham Facts - 1935, First Edition" (also Second Edition)

PC portfolio, 12 X 9", full line, "Graham" 12 page catalog with color plates A-K (also AA), correction note, and budget plan certificate/NY prices, Ref. No. 35-1

PC catalog, 9 X 12", "Graham $595—& Up", Ref. No. 35-2

PC folder, 5 1/2 X 8 1/2, "A New Graham in the Lowest Price Range"

2nd Series

PC folder/mailer, 3-3/4 X 8-1/2", "Graham/Complete Line", Ref. No. 35-3 (two versions known: open and closed rumble seat)

Full color folder, 11 X 8-1/2", Deluxe Six, Ref. No. 35-4

PC folder, 9 X 6", "1935 Graham Sixes and Eights", Ref. No. 34-12B (orange trim)

PC folder, 8-1/2 X 11", "Added Refinements", Ref. No. 35-8

PC sheet, 11-1/4 X 8-1/2", Graham In-Built Luggage Compartments" 35-K

PC folder, 9 X 12", "The Latest Graham - Special Six, Eight, and Supercharged Eight"

PC folder, 12 X 9", "The Latest Graham Standard Six"

PC booklet, 12 pages, 4-1/2 X 5", "Let's Take Another Look"

PC folder, 8 1/8 x 10", "The Graham Six/The Aristocrat at a Democratic Price", distributed by Walter Whitbourn PTY. LTD., Melbourne, Australia

B&W folder, 3-3/16 X 5", "Price List — Graham Cars — Effective May 10, 1935" Printed by Australian (Melbourne) Distributor. Six cylinder sedan and couple shown.

Sepia folder, 9 X 12", "The Latest Graham", full line

PC catalog, 12 pages, 9 X 11", "Hidden Values"

PC catalog, 12 pages, 12 X 9", "Hidden Values", Canadian edition

PC mailer, 12 X 6", "A Message from Graham to the Independent Service Station", Graham Six touring shown, $595

B&W dealer handout, 8 1/2 X 11", "Glendale Party Makes Trip to Phoenix—Graham Claims Economy Mark", Model 74 shown, reprinted from *Glendale News Press*, August 1, 1935

PC mailer, 12 X 6", "10 Times as Many Prospects", Graham Six shown

PC mailer, 12 X 6", "You Have Heard A Lot of Rumors - Here Are the Facts", Graham Six shown

FC folder, 10 X 12", "Deluxe Graham Six Touring Sedan", two and four door Model 74 sedans shown, Walkerville, Ontario, Canada

PC folder, 3-3/4 X 6-1/2", "Graham Leads Again With Supercharger", Walkerville, Ontario, Canada

Folder, 10 X 16-1/2", "It's a Graham - Here's the Car We've Always Wanted", Model 74 shown

PC portfolio, 13 1/4 X 9", "Some Opinions on the New GRAHAM Cars", issued by the London agents of Graham-Paige, Cleverly's. Cover letter, testimonials, price list, motor road test, and sales folder, eleven coachwork styles illustrated.

PC folder, 9 X 12", 8 pages, "Graham News", Ref. No. 35-2 (four known color and print variations, with same text: "Most Imitated Car on the Road", all versions shows side view of Model 74 sedan on cover)

PC folder, 9 X 12", 8 pages, "Graham News", Ref. No. 35-2 "The Most Imitated Car On The Road", yellow and black with woman beside Model 74 on cover

PC folder, 9 x 12", 8 pages, "Graham News", Ref No. 35-2C, text is headlined "Lasting Satisfaction" Canadian edition

PC folder, "Accessories"

B&W cataog, 24 pages, 8-1/2 X 11", "What Owners Say About the Graham Supercharger Eight", Ref. No. 35-7, engine and three models shown

PC folder, 8-1/2 X 11", "All These Extra Values In The Deluxe Graham Six", 35-9

B&W book with grey covers, 196 pages, 3 X 6", "Graham Facts - 1935, Second Edition"

B&W folder, 12-1/2 X 8-1/2", "Graham Six - $595"

Full color folder, 10 X 15-1/2", "Here's The Car", Six shown

1936

Full color folder, 9 X 12", "The Style Award Goes to Graham", Ref. No. 1-36, full line

Full color folder, 9 X 12", "The Style Award Goes to Graham", Ref. No. 1-36 5mc (Canadian)

Full color folder, 9 X 12", "The Style Award Goes to Graham", Ref. No. 1-36, Spanish text

Full color folder, 8 X 10-1/4", "The Style Award Goes to Graham", Series 80, full line

Full color folder, 8 X 10-1/4", "The Style Award Goes to Graham", Series 80, full line, Canadian, 2-36-2MC

Full color folder, 8 X 10-1/4", "The Style Award Goes to Graham", Series 90, Form 3-36

Full color folder, 8 X 10-3/4", "The Style Award Goes to Graham", Series 90-A, full line, Form 11-36

Full color folder, 8 X 10-1/4", "The Style Award Goes to Graham", Series 110, Form 4-36

Full color folder, 8 X 10-1/4", "The Style Award Goes to Graham", Series 110, Form 4-36, Canadian 4-36-2500C

B&W salesman's presentation aid, 8 1/2 X 11", 3 pages, "High Points in Presenting theGraham Cavalier"

B&W book, 44 pages, 4-1/2 X 7-1/2", Sales data, Series 80-90-110, Ref. No. 5-36

Sepia catalog, 12 pages, 5 X 6-1/2", "Magic of the Supercharger", Ref. No. 6-36, no cars shown (two back cover versions)

PC folder, 8 1/2 X 11", 6 pages, "6% New Car Plan—C.I.T. Corporation in Cooperation with Graham-Paige Motors Corporation"

Color mailer, 8-1/2 X 11", full line, Ref. No. 8B-36

FC mailer, 8 1/2 X 11", "The Whole Country Is Talking", Form 8C-36, Portland issue, several Model 110s shown.

Color catalog, 16 pages, 16 X 12", "The Style Award Goes to Graham", Ref. No. 9-36, full line

PC folder, 4 X 8", "Graham Economy", Form 12-36-25M

PC folder, 5-3/4 X 7-1/2", "Big News for Boat Owners", Graham Supercharger Marine Engine, Form 13-36-3M, (two variations: Hacker Gold Cup boat shown on latter issue)

PC folder, 7 1/2 X 10 1/2", 4 pages, "Timken—A Sign of Extra Value In Any Automobile/Graham-Timken Equipped"

PC catalog, 12 pages, 13 X 15-3/4", "Here They Are - Three Great New Grahams for 1936", dealer oriented

B&W dealer's window poster on heavy paper, 30 X 20", "Graham Proves Economy From East to West", two sided with many illustrations

Wire bound full color book, 12 X 9", 40 pages including covers, "3 Great New Grahams for 1936"

PC catalog, 17 pages including covers, 8-1/4 X 4", "That Which Endures"

PC folder, 3-1/2 X 7-1/2", "Drive the Car That Beat Them All", 5-16-36

B&W folder, 4 X 8", "1936 Prices, Terms and Accessories", Effective November 2, 1935, Form 7-36-10M

PC catalog, 12 pages, 10-1/2 X 14-1/2", "How Good is Your Arithmetic?"

PC postcard, 5 1/2 X 3 1/2", "The Graham Supercharger...inaugurates a New Era of Super Performance in automobiles"

PC postcard, 5 1/2 X 3 1/2", "The Graham Body Plant at Wayne, Michigan, which carries on the Graham reputation for high quality and distinctive style"

Full color Players Cigarette Card, 2-5/8 X 1-3/8", "Lammas Graham Foursome Drop Head Coupe"

1937

B&W folder, 4 X 9", "Prices - January 1, 1937"

Sepia catalog, 8 pages, 11-1/2 X 15-1/2", full line

Color folder, 8-1/2 X 11", "Graham Crusader for 1937"

Color folder, 8-1/2 X 11", "Graham Crusader for 1937" (text in Swedish)

Color folder, 8-1/2 X 11", "Graham Crusader for 1937" (text in Spanish)

B&W book, 132+ pages, 4 X 6-1/2, "Facts book"

B&W catalog, 8 1/2 X 11", 4 pages, "Graham-Paige Custom Built Radio for Models 86, 87,   88, 89—Installation and Operating Instructions"

B&W Sales Brief, 8 pages, 8-1/2 X 11", "The Graham Supercharger - The Greatest Automotive Achievement of the Decade"

FC mailer, 8 1/2 X 11", 4 pages, "This Year As Always—You're Years Ahead In A Graham", Portland dealer issue

B&W catalog, 7 1/2 X 11", "Nisson Model 70", Japanese issued catalog showing 1937 Graham Crusader presented as Nisson Model 70

Dealer's newspaper, 11 X 14-3/4", 6 pages, "Graham Supercharger News", January 1937,   Volume 1 #2

Dealer's Newspaper, 11-3/4 X 15-1/2", 4 pages, "Graham Supercharger News — Extra!" Supplement to Volume 1, #2, covers Economy Run, imprinted by Portland dealer.

Dealer's newspaper, 11 X 14-3/4", 6 pages, "Graham Supercharger News", March 1937, Volume 1 #3

Dealer's newspaper, 11 X 14-3/4", 6 pages, "Graham Supercharger News", April 1937, Volume 1 #4

Dealer's Newspaper, 6 pages, 11 x 14 3/4", "Graham Supercharger News" October 28, 1937, Volume 1, #9

Dealer's Newspaper, 6 pages, 11 X 14-3/4", "Graham Supercharger News" December 15, 1937, Volume 1, #9.

FC mailer, 8 1/2 X 11", "The Aristocrat of the Low Priced Field"

FC mailer, 8 1/2 X 11","Delightful to Look At..."

B&W card, 4 X 2", "The New 1937 Supercharger, The World's Greatest Gas Saver"

B&W card, 3 3/4 X 2 1/4", "Farther And Faster On A Gallon Of Gasoline Than Any Car In The World..."

Color folder, 8-1/2 X 7", Supercharger & Cavalier

Spiral bound book, 7-1/2 X 4", "Colors For 1937 Graham", color chips with overlay

Full color mailer, 8-1/2 X 5-1/2", "All Three in Advance"

Full color mailer, 8-1/2 X 5-1/2", "Again America's Champion"

Full color mailer, 8-1/2 X 5-1/2", "A Marvel to Own"

Full color mailer, 8-1/2 X 5-1/2", "Four Great Features"

PC folder, 3-1/2 X 8-1/2", "Graham Philco Radio"

PC folder, 3-1/2 X 8-1/2", "3-Way heaters"

PC folder, 9-1/2 X 6", "A New Supercharger Convertible by Graham"

Color folder, 8-1/2 X 7-1/4", "The Graham Supercharger for 1937 - America's Economy Champion", full line

Full color folder, 5-1/2 X 8-1/2", "Only Graham Gives Supercharger Economy - Performance - Power", Imprinted by Milwaukee dealership

Full color folder, 8-1/2 X 11", "An Invitation", imprinted by Portland dealership, Supercharger, Cavalier, Crusader sedans shown

Color catalog, 28 pages, 12 X 9", "Graham Supercharger for 1937", full line

PC catalog, 12 pages including covers, 6-3/8 X 9-3/8", "More Power for Less Gasoline -The Supercharger Story in a Nutshell", two black and white sedans shown

PC catalog, 16 pages including covers, 5-1/2 X 8-1/2", "Graham Approved Accessories"

Sepia newspaper, 22-1/2 X 16", "Graham - Supercharged for Super Performance and Super Economy"

Sheet (red print), 8 1/8 X 10", Graham 1937 Models and Prices" distributed by Jack Olding and Company, London

B&W folder, 4-1/2 X 9-1/4", 1937 prices

PC showroom display, 15-1/2 X 23-1/2" sheets, 24 pages, mounted on metal stand

Graham-Bradley Tractor
1938

PC folder, 11 X 14", Ref. no. 97291-1-3-38
PC catalog, 12 pages including covers, 8-1/2 X 11", Ref. No. Rf97611-4-38

Graham Automobiles
1938

Color catalog (also folder version), 16 pages, 7-1/2 X 12", "Graham for 1938", full line
Color catalog, 16 pages, 7-1/2 X 12, "Graham for 1938", as above, text in Dutch, white covers
PC folder, 11 X 8-1/2", "Graham for 1938"
FC loose leaf book, 5 3/4 X 3 3/4", ten plastic pages plus PC covers, "Graham Colors for 1938"
B&W newspaper, 10 3/4 X 14 3/4", 4 pages, "Graham Supercharger News", Volume 1, No. 9. Issued in New York City October 28, 1937 as a special New York Auto Show supplement issue.
PC folder, 11 X 8-1/2", "Graham for 1938", Spanish Text
PC mailer, 8 pages, 10-3/4 X 8", "The Spirit of Motion", coupe and four door sedan illustrated
B&W folder with cover letter, 8-1/2 X 11", a dealer issued piece (Netherlands) showing Pennock custom job, Dutch text
B&W folder, 8 1/2 X 11", "Lammas-A Car Built To A New Ideal", three Lammas-Graham models shown with specifications, printed and issued in Britain.
PC album with stand, 32 pages, 17 X 23", hardbound, "Graham Value-Scope", full line, comparisons and specifications, dealer sales aid
PC mailer, 8-1/2 X 7-1/2", "Take My Tip About the 1938 Graham"
PC postcard, 8 X 5", "1939 Graham" sedan shown (two versions of text: one is directed to the dealer from the factory, the other is directed to the prospective customer from the dealer)
PC catalog, 36 pages, 8-5/8 X 5-3/4", "Graham Approved Accessories"
PC catalog, 36 pages, 8-5/8 x 5-3/4", "Graham Approved Accessories", Canadian
B&W folder, 4 X 9", Prices - November 22, 1937
B&W folder, 4 X 9", Prices - October 27, 1937
B&W folder, 4 X 9", Prices - April 12, 1938
B&W catalog, 8 1/2 X 11", 4 pages, "Graham-Philco Custom Built Radio—Model 96 and 97 Installation and Operating Instructions"
Book, 104 pages with brown covers, 4-1/2 X 7", "1938 Graham Facts Book"
PC slide card, 8 X 4", "1938 Graham Value Comparisons"
PC sheet, 8-1/2 X 11", Preferential delivery order

1939

PC newspaper, 8 pages, 11 X 16", "Graham for 1939", full line
PC catalog, 8 pages, 11 X 16", "Graham for 1939", Canadian
PC folder, 5-1/2 X 8-1/2", "Spirit of Motion", Three models shown
PC catalog, 7 X 9 1/2", 5 pages, "1939 Graham", British issue (female model on fender of car, two models shown, prices in pounds.)

FC spiral bound book, 5 3/4 X 3 3/4", ten plastic pages plus PC covers, "Graham Colors for 1939", includes both regular and custom colors.
B&W folder, 8 1/2 X 11","1938 Annual Report of Graham-Paige Motors Corporation"
B&W book, 44 pages, 8-1/2 X 11", "Training School for Graham Retail Salesmen"
PC catalog, 8 1/2 X 5 1/2", 16 pages including covers, "An Important Message about Graham for 1939", directed to prospective dealers
PC folder, 4 X 8-1/2", chrome trim equipment
B&W folder, 3-1/2 X 5-1/2", Michigan dealers
B&W booklet, 3 1/2 X 5 1/2", "Canadian Retail Prices/May 18, 1939"
PC booklet, 4 X 8", Prices - October 1, 1938
B&W sheets, yellow cover, 8 1/2 X 11", "Dealer Addendum 'A'", October 2, 1939
PC booklet, 4 X 8", Prices - December 19, 1938
Yellow booklet, 3-1/8 X 6-1/4", "Canadian Retail Prices - May 18, 1939"
Salesman's data book, 64 pages, 4 X 5-1/2", 11-38
Spiral bound book, 6 X 4", "Graham Colors 1939",
B&W newspaper, 11 X 15", "Supercharger News", Volume 1 #10, February 1939
B&W newspaper, 11 X 15", "Supercharger News", Volume 1 #11, May 1939 (30th Anniversary Issue)
PC folder, 8-1/2 X 11", French text, two models shown
PC folder, 8-1/2 X 11, Dutch text, two models shown
PC commemorative stamp, 2 X 1 1/2", "Celebrating 30 Years of Engineering Leadership-Graham-Paige 1909-1939"
B&W folder, 4 X 5-5/8", "See the 1939 Graham At Your Nearest Graham Dealer", Michigan dealers listed

1940

Full color catalog, 24 pages, 6 X 9", "Graham" full line, (two versions of text: specification differences, 110 & 120 hp)
PC folder, 6 X 9", "Graham...for 1940", full line
B&W folder, 6 X 9", "Graham...for 1940" full line
B&W card, 5-1/2 X 8-1/2", "Graham for 1940" (Spirit of Motion sedan)
B&W (on yellow paper) price booklet, 12 pages including covers, 4 X 8", "1940 prices", includes accessories, colors and options, (4-1-40)
B&W data book, 120 pages with cream colored covers and green binding, 4-1/2X 6-3/4", "Graham Facts Book", full line
B&W newspaper, 8 pages, 10-1/4X 13", insert of the Dearborn (Michigan) Press for July 18, 1940

1941

PC postcard, 5-1/2 X 3-1/2", "Flash! The Excitingly Swank 1941 Graham Hollywood Is On Display"
Sepia Postcard, 5-1/2 X 3-1/2, "Flash! Miss Laraine Day, M.G.M. star is shown here with the New Graham Hollywood, which is fast becoming one of the most popular cars with the California Motion Picture colony."
Sepia postcard, 5-1/2 X 3-1/2", "Let's Go Hollywood With Graham/We Invite you to Drive the Glamor-Car of 1941"
B&W Dealer handout. Single sheet, 8-3/4 X 6", "Let's Go Ho!!ywood with Graham/We Invite You To Drive The Glamor-Car of 1941"

B&W folder, 8 x 3-1/2", "Important News for You" Ralph Hamlin (dealer) issued.

1942-1946

B&W catalog, 24 pages, 8-1/2 X 11", Parts catalog for Graham owners. No cars shown (year of issue has not been documented), also Canadian version
B&W mailer, 4 X 8-3/4", "Parts Service Letter" (year of issue has not been documented)

1945

Graham-Paige Annual Report
B&W sheets, 8 1/2 X 11", "An Important Announcement To The Stockholders of Graham-Paige Motors Corporation" October 1945

1946

Dealer's Franchise Agreement for Farm Equipment, 4 pages, 8-1/2 X 11", April 18, 1946
B&W folder, 8 1/2 X 11", "Graham-Paige Motors Corporation Balance Sheets"

Frazer
1947

PC folder, 5 1/2 X 8 1/2", "Welcome to Willow Run", Kaiser-Frazer Corporation/Graham-Paige Motors Corporation
Full color folder, 9-1/2 X 12", full line, Ref. No. 1946
Full color catalog, 20 pages including covers, 9-1/2 X 12", "The 1947 Frazer", Ref. no. 1946

Graham-Paige Factory Service Department (Auburn, IN)
1945

B&W mailer, 8 1/2 X 4", "Many Facts of Interest to You, Mr. Graham Owner

Graham-Paige Motors Corporation (York, PA)
1948

Sepia folder, 8-1/2 X 5-1/2", "Rototiller, Power Tiller of a Hundred Uses"

Graham Factory Service (Auburn, IN)
1960s

B&W mailer, 8 1/2 X 11", 4 pages,"Graham Factory Service", advises of "factory overhaul of your Graham engine, and availability of NOS parts.

I. Graham-Paige International Distributors Throughout World

Algeria	Algiers	Anglo-American Automobile Co. Ltd.
Arabia	Aden	Ahmed Yusuf Khan
Argentine	Buenos Aires	Victor Irureta
Austria	Vienna	Duhan & Co.
Australia	Adelaide	Maughan Thiem & Co.
	Brisbane	Moxon Motors, Ltd.
	Melbourne	Walter Whitbourn Pty. Ltd.
	Perth	Arthur Bales, Ltd.
	Sydney	W. H. Lober Motor Co.
Balearic Islands	Palma de Majorca	Antonio Bibiloni
Belgium	Antwerp	S. A. Graham-Paige Belgium
	Brussels	Establissements De Clercq
Belgian Congo	Boma	Nunes & Freitas
Brazil	Bahia	Souza Teixeira Cia.
	Pernambuco	Dantas Bastos & Cia.
	Porto Alegre	Weiss Santerre & Cia., Ltd.
	Rio de Janeiro	J. Gentil Filho
	São Paulo	G. Corbisicr & Co. Ltd.
British Honduras	Belize	Mr. Rocky Batty
Bulgaria	Sofia	N. Schopoff
B. W. I., Jamaica	Kingston	Dr. G. W. Scotland
Canary Islands	Las Palmas	Felip Gonzales
	Santa Cruz de Tenerife	Jacob Ahlers
Ceylon	Colombo	Freudenberg & Co.
Chile	Santiago	Huidobro & Ocampo
China	Mukden	To Shio & Co.
	Shanghai	Auto Palace Co. Ltd.
	Tientsin	Robertson-Evans Motors
Colombia	Bogota	Antonio Puerto
Czechoslovakia	Prague	Dietrich & Dubsky
Free State of Danzig		Finance & Auto Sales Co.
Denmark	Copenhagen	Aktieselskabet Cyclon
D. E. I. Suniatra	Medan	Lian Tiong & Co.
	Padang	Gob Soen Hien
	Palembang	Behn Meyer
Dutch West Indies	Curacao	Abady & Cardoze
Ecuador	Guayaquil	Fabrica de Calzado
Egypt	Cairo	J. Attard & Co.
England	London	Graliani-Paige Motors Ltd.
Estonia	Tallinn, Reval	Friedrich John
Fiji	Suva	Walter Horne & Co.
Finland	Helsingfors	Autola Oy
France	Paris	Etabts. A. d'Andiran
French Morocco	Casablanca	S. A. V. A.
French Indo-China	Saigon	Société Nouvelle Des Rizeries Meridionales
Germany	Berlin	Graham-Paige Automobil, G. m. b. H.
Gibraltar		Joseph Cazes & Co.
Greece	Athens	C. P. Cosmetalos
	Salonica	W. Smithson & Co.
Guatemala	Guatemala City	G. Kepler
Holland	Utrecht	N. V. Gcbr. Ncfkcns' Automobiel-Maatschappij
Hungary	Budapest	Apart Automobil & Accessary Corp.
Iceland	Reykjavik	Gislason Brothers
India	Bombay	Bombay Motor Car Co. Ltd.
	Delhi	Pearey Lal Sons
	Karachi	Toleram & Co.
	Lucknow	Eduljee Co.
	Peshawar	Afghan Motor House
	Quetta	P. N. Maira & Sons
	Rangoon	Indian Motors
Italy	Milan	Emilio Badini
Japan	Tokyo	Mitsui Bussan Kaisha, Ltd.
Java	Banjoewangi	J. K. Van Lesuswarden
	Soerabaja	L'Auto
Jugoslavia	Belgrade	Lazar L. Milichevich & LjubomerCrnogorats
Latvia	Riga	Handels Unternehmen E. Daniels
Manchuria	Dairen	S. Mimoto
	Harbin	J. J. Fegelbom
Mexico	Guadalajara	Schnaider and Cortina
	Leon	Guanajuato Automotriz
	Mexico City	DeLuxe Motors, S. A.
	San Luis Potosi	Potosi Motors
	Torreon	Laguna Motors, S. A.
New Foundland	St. Johns	Joseph Cocker
New Zealand	Wellington	Wright, Stephenson & Co. Ltd.
Norway	Oslo	Mathiesen & Hesselberg-Meyer
Palestine	Jerusalem	Halaby & Co.
Panama	Ancon	Isthmian Motor Co. Inc.
Peru	Lima	E. M. Pozzi & Cia.
Persia	Teheran	A. Nassif
Philippines	Manila	French Motor Co.
Porto Rico	San Juan	Insular Motor Corp.
Portugal	Lisbon	J. Coelho Pacheco
Portuguese Africa	Benguela	Leandro Ramos, Coelho, Ltd.
Romania	Bucharest	Branceni-Iliescu G.
Repub. of Salvador	San Salvador	C. Sansur & Hnos.
Siam	Bangkok	B. Grimm & Co.
South Africa	Cape Town	Wilson & Perkins, Ltd.
	Durban	Barlow's Motor Co. Ltd.
	East London	Atkinson's Motor Garages, Ltd.
	Johannesburg	S. T. Richards Motor Co. Ltd.
	Kimberley	Weatherby Motors
Southern Rhodesia	Bulawayo	Southern Motors
Spain	Albacete	Estanislao Ibanez, Martinez
	Badajoz	Luis Pla Alvarez
	Barcelona	Automoviles Sociedad Espanola, S. A.
	Bilbao	Rotaeche y Elorduy
	Granada	José Rubio Marquez
	La Coruna	Labarta Vaamonde, S. L.
	Madrid	Automovilcs Sociedad Espanola, S. A.
	Oviedo	D. Prospero Blanco
	Seville	Joaquin Mauri

Appendix

	Valencia	José Serratosa
	Zaragoza	Otama
Spanish Morocco	Ceuta	Romani Lopez y Compania
	Melilla	José Parres e Hijo, S. L.
Straits Settlements	Singapore	Eastern Auto Co.
Sweden	Göteborg	Aktiebolaget Gradur
	Malmo	And. Skog Malmo A. B.
	Stockholm	N. Y. A. Automobile Firma Holmer A. B.
Switzerland	Lausanne	Garage de Georgette, Société Anonyme
	Zurich	Automobilewerke Franz A. G.

Syria	Beyrouth	Michel Andraos
Tahiti	Papeete	Mr. E. Laguesse
Tasmania	Hobart	Twintop Motors Pty. Ltd.
Trinidad	Port-of-Spain	Nothnagel Brothers
Tunisia	Tunis	Guglielmo Calo & Co.
Turkey	Istanbul-Taksim	Otomobil ve Levazimi Ltd. Sirketi
Uruguay	Montevideo	Frugoni Hermanos
Venezuela	Caracas	C. H. Machado & Cia.
	Maracaibo	Lares Y Rincon
Yugoslavia	Zagreb	Arthur Kauders

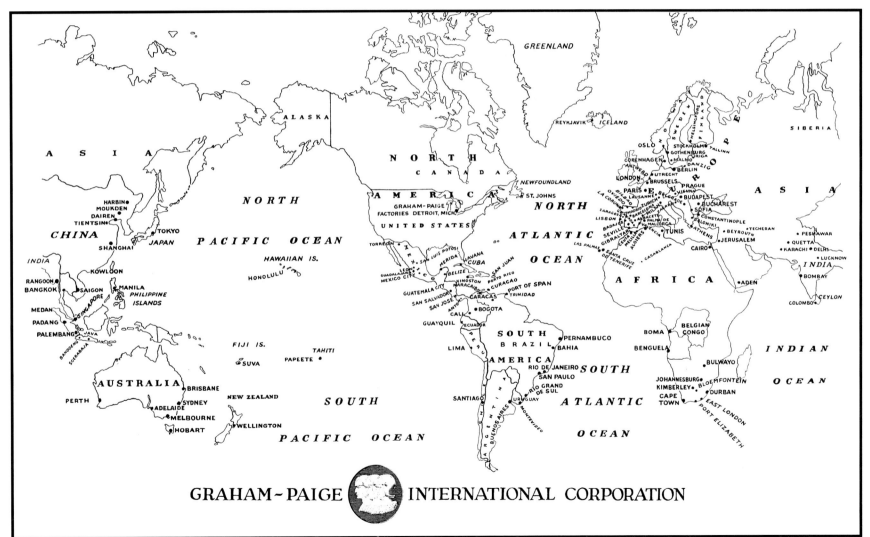

GRAHAM~PAIGE INTERNATIONAL CORPORATION

Appendix

The 1928 Graham-Paige Model 629 seven passenger sedan.

Appendix

Bibliography

Books

Aiken, William E., *The Roots Grow Deep*, Lezius-Hiles Publishing Company, Cleveland, Ohio, 1957

The American Car Since 1775, Automobile Quarterly Books, E.P. Dutton and Company, New York, 1971

Baillie, Luareen (editor), *American Biographical Index*, K.B. Sauer, New York

Bel Geddes, Norman, *Horizons*, Boston, Little, Brown, and Company, 1932

Bennett's Evanville (IN) City Directories, various years

Bigham, Darrel E., *An Evansville Album*, Indiana University Press, undated, Bloomington, Indiana

Blackburn, Tom, *Evansville, Indiana/1812-1962*, undated

Boyd's Philadelphia City Directory, 1910 through 1914, published by C. E. Howe Company

Brigham, Grace, *Serial Numbers of the First Fifty Years*, Brigham Press, Marietta, Georgia, 1974

Broderick, Robert, *The Catholic Encyclopedia*, 1975

Clark, Charles F., *Annual City Directory of the City of Detroit 1867-1868*

Collins, Lewis, *Historical Sketches of Kentucky*, 1848

Collins, Lewis, and Collins, Richard, *History of Kentucky* (1874), reprinted by the Kentucky Historical Society, Frankfort, Kentucky, 1966

Crabb, Richard, *The Birth of a Giant, The Men and Incidents That Gave America The Motor Car*, Chilton Book Company 1969

Crowther, Bruce and Penfold, Mike, *The Big Band Years*, Facts on File Publications

Daviess County, Indiana, Sponsored by Indiana State Library, Indianapolis, Indiana, 1938

Daviess County—Interim Report, Historic Landmarks Foundation of Indiana, September 1987

Daviess County Profile, Washington Chamber of Commerce, undated

Davis, Donald Finlay, *Conspicuous Production—Automobiles and Elites In Detroit, 1899-1933*, Temple University Press, Philadelphia, Pennsylvania, 1988

Detroit Athletic Club—Fiftieth Anniversary, privately printed, Detroit, Michigan, 1963

Dew, Lee A., *Owensboro, The City of the Yellow Banks*, Rivendell Publications, Bowling Green, Kentucky, 1988

Durnford, Hugh and Baechler, Glenn, *Cars of Canada*, McClellan and Stewart Limited, Toronto, Canada, 1973

Elwart, Joan Potter and Pitrone, J. M., *The John Dodge Story*, Meadow Brook Hall Publications, Oakland University, Rochester, Michigan, undated

Elwart, Joan Potter and Pitrone, J. M., *The Dodges—The Auto Family Fortune and Misfortune*, Icarus Press, South Bend, Indiana, 1981

Fairfield, E. William, Fire and Sand, *The History of the Libbey Owens Sheet Glass Company*, Lezius-Hiles Company, Cleveland, Ohio 1960

Forbes, B.C. and Foster, O.D. *Automotive Giants of America-Men Who Are Making Our Motor Industry*, B.C. Forbes Publishing Company, New York, New York, 1926

Fulkerson, A. O., (Editor), *History of Daviess County, Indiana*, B.F. Bowen and Company, 1915

Garvey, Timothy J., *Public Sculptor: Lorado Taft and the Beautification of Chicago*, University of Illinois Press, Urbana and Chicago, 1988

Gilbert, Frank, *The History of the City of Evansville and Vanderburg County, Indiana*, 1910

Glover and Cornell, *Census of Manufacturers and Development of American Industries*

Green River Road: From Cornfields to Concrete, Windmill Publications, Mt. Vernon, Indiana 1993

Gustin, Lawrence R., *Billy Durant-Creator of General Motors*, Craneshaw Publishers, Flushing, Michigan, 1973 and 1984

Hamm, Charles, *Yesterday's Popular Song In America*, W. M. Norton and Company, New York and London

Heasley, Jerry, *The Production Figure Book for U.S. Cars*, 1977

Hendry, Maurice D., *Cadillac-Standard of the World/The Complete History*, Princeton Publishing, Inc. 1979

History of Daviess County, Kentucky, 1883

History of Knox and Daviess Counties, Indiana, The Goodspeed Publishing Company, Chicago, Illinois, 1886

History of Okmulgee County, Oklahoma, Historical Enterprises, Inc. Tulsa, Oklahoma

Hoffman's Okmulgee City Directory

Holt, Harry Q. *History of Martin County*, Volumes One and Two

Indiana—From Frontier to Industrial Commonwealth, Volume 4, 1954

Inglehart, J. E., *History of Vanderburgh County*, Dayton, Ohio, 1923

Jewett, Harry Mulford, *The Idea Behind Grousehaven*, privately printed, 1928

Klinger, Ed, *How A City Founded To Make Money Made It: The Economic and Business History of Evansville, Indiana*, undated

Langworth, Richard and Norbye, Jan, *The Complete History of Chrysler Corporation*

Latham, Caroline and Agresta, *David Dodge Dynasty, The Car And The Family That Rocked Detroit*, Harcourt Brace Jovanovich, Publishers 1989

Marks, Geoffrey and Beatty, William K., *Epidemics*, Charles Scribner's Son, New York, New York, 1976.

Marquis, Albert Nelson (Editor), *The Book of Detroiters*, published by A. N. Marquis & Company, Chicago, Illinois. Both the 1908 and 1914 editions were used.

Martin, Baird, *Historical, Industrial, and Civic Survey of Okmulgee and Okmulgee County*, WPA Writer's Project, 1936

Marvin, Robert B., *Packard, A Chronology of the Company, The Cars, and the People*, R-Mac Publications, Inc., Jasper, Florida, 1994

McCutchan, Kenneth A., *At The Bend In the River: The Story of Evansville*, 1982

McPherson, Thomas A. *The Dodge Story*, Crestline Publishing, 1975

Meigh, Edward, *The Story Of The Glass Bottle*, published by C.E. Ramsden & Company, Ltd.

Moody Manual of Investments

Moretti, Valerio (Editor), *Le Auto Dei Papi/Settant'anni di Automobilismo Vaticano (Pontiff's Cars/Seventy Years of Vatican Motoring*, Rome, Italy, November 1981

Morlock, James E., *The Evansville Story*, Evansville College, 1956

National Cyclopedia of American Biography, New York, New York, 1975

Okmulgee, Oklahoma, written by and published by Okmulgee, Oklahoma Chamber of Commerce, undated but believed to be 1919.

Peter, Robert, *History of Bourbon, Scott, Harrison, and Nicolas Counties (Kentucky)*, O. L. Baskin and Company, Chicago, Illinois, 1882

Pitrone, Jean Maddern, *Tangled Web, The Legacy of Auto Pioneer John F. Dodge*, Avenue Publishing Company, Hamtramck, Michigan, 1989

Potter, Hugh O., *A History of Owensboro and Daviess County County, Kentucky*, Herff Jones-Paragon Publishing, Montgomery, Alabama and Louisville, Kentucky, 1974

Schockel, B.H., *Manufactural Evansville 1820-1933*, 1947

Scoville, Warren G., *Revolution in Glass Making*, Harvard University Press, 1948

Sloan, Alfred P. *Adventures of A White Collar Man*, Doubleday, Doran, and Company, Inc., 1941, New York, New York

Sparks, C. *Tractor Directory and Operating Book*, published by Clarke, Madison, Wisconsin, 1919

Standard Catalog of American Cars 1805-1942, edited by Beverly Rae Kimes and Henry Austin Clark, Jr., Krause Publications, Iola, Wisconsin, both the 1985 and 1988 editions were used.

Standard Catalog of Light Duty Trucks 1896-1986, Krause Publications, Iola, Wisconsin

Story of the Graham Farms, privately printed, July 25, 1961

Taft, Ada Bartlett, *Lorado Taft-Sculptor and Citizen*, privately printed, Greensboro, North Carolina 1946

Taft, Lorado, *The Blind*, University of Illinois Press, Urbana, Illinois, 1988.

Taylor, Robert, Jr. Indiana—*A New Historical Guide*, Indiana Historical Society 1989

Toulouse, Julian Harrison, *Bottle Makers and Their Marks*

Tractor and Implement Blue Book, Midland Publishing Company, St. Louis, Missouri, 1927

Velliky, John R. and Pitrone, J.M., *Dodge Brothers/Budd Company Historical Photo Album*, Harlo Press, Detroit, Michigan 1992

Washington (Indiana) City Directory, various years

Who's Who In America 1930-1931

Whorrall, Bill, *A Photographic History of Martin County*, Indiana Arts Commission, 1993

Weisberger, Bernard, *Dreammaker-William C. Durant-Founder of General Motors*, Little, Brown, and Company, Boston and Toronto, 1979

Williams' Cincinnati City Directory, City Guide and Business Mirror, 1861 through 1865, Williams & Company, Cincinnati

Williams, Michael, *Ford and Fordson Tractor*, Blanford Press, 1985

World Book Encyclopedia, 1975

WJR-AM 760 Fiftieth Anniversary Booklet, privately printed, Detroit, Michigan, 1972

Newspapers

Anderson Herald (Indiana), Arizona Republican (Phoenix), Chicago Tribune, Claire Sentinal (Michigan), Cleveland Leader, Dearborn Press, Detroit Free Press, Detroit News, Detroit This Week, Evanville Courier, Evansville Courier-Journal, Evansville Journal, Evansville Press, Glendale News Press, Horseless Age, Indianapolis Star, Jersey Journal, Jersey Observer, L'Auto Italiana, Lincoln (Nebraska) Journal, Los Angles Times, Loogootee Enterprize, Loogootee Tribune, New York Sun, New York Times, New York World, North Woods Call (Michigan), Martin County Tribune, Okmulgee Chieftan, Okmulgee Daily Times, Rose City News (Michigan), Shoals News (Indiana), South Bend Times, Standish Independent (Michigan), Stockon Record, Toledo Blade, Valley Advance, Wall Street Journal, Washington (Indiana) Democrat

Archives And Libraries

American Automobile Manufacturers Association, Detroit, Michigan

Archives of the University of Notre Dame, Notre Dame, Indiana

Automobile Hall of Fame

Bank of Stockton Archives

Checotah (Oklahoma) Chamber of Commerce

Chicago Historical Society

Corning Museum of Glass, The Rakow Library

Department of Commerce\Patent and Trademark Office, Washington, D.C.

Detroit Public Library

Dossin Great Lakes Museum Archives, Detroit, Michigan

Evansville (Indiana) Police Department

Family History Library, Salt Lake City, Nevada

Haggen Museum, Stockton, California

Hercules Center, Hercules Corporation, Henderson, Kentucky

Indiana State Library

International Geneological Index, Family History Library

Joseph Hamilton Daveiss Papers, Filson Club, Louisville, Kentucky

Kentucky Department for Libraries and Archives, Frankfort, Kentucky

Libbey-Owens-Ford Corporate Library

Loogootee Public Library

Michigan Department of Natural Resources, Lansing, Michigan

Michigan Department of State, Lansing, Michigan

Monumenti Musei Gallerie Pontificie, The Vatican

Oklahoma Historical Society, Oklahoma City, Oklahoma

Okmulgee Public Library

Owensboro-Daviess County Public Library

Owens-Illinois Glass Company (Owens Bottle Company minutes, 1915-1916)

Register of Deeds Office, Okmulgee County Court House, Okmulgee, Oklahoma

Rifle River Recreation Area Archives, Lupton, Michigan

Rose City Area Historical Society Archives, Rose City, Michigan

San Joaquin County Historical Museum

State Historical Society of Wisconsin

State of Indiana, Bureau of Mines and Mine Safety

State Library, Hartford, Connecticutt

Stockton-San Joaquin County Public Library

Lorado Taft Papers, Archives of the University of Illinois, at Urbana

Toledo-Lucas County Public Library

University of Michigan, University Library, Ann Arbor

University of the Pacific Libraries, Stockton, California

University of Southern Indiana, Library Services, Special Collections Department, Evansville, Indiana

University of Texas, Theatre Arts Collection, Harry Ransom Humanities Research Center, Austin, Texas

Willard Library, Evansville, Indiana

Census Reports

The Reconstructed (from tax lists) 1790 Census of Delaware (First Census), Delaware Geneological Society, Washington, Delaware, 1983

Marriage Records and Bonds, Bourbon County (Kentucky) County Clerk 1786-1930. Marriage Bonds, Drawer 3, Part 1. Salt Lake City Geneological Society of Utah, 1954-59

1850 United States Census, Daviess County, Indiana

1860 United States Census, Daviess County, Indiana

1870 United States Census, Wayne County, Michigan

1880 United States Census, Wayne County, Michigan

1900 United States Census, Wayne County, Michigan

1910 United States Census, Wayne County, Michigan

1920 United States Census, New York County, New York

Fifteenth Census of the United States (1930) Manufacture 1929, III, Washington, DC, 1933

Tax List, Bourbon County, Kentucky, 1791

Unpublished Accounts

Dare, John, oral history of Grousehaven (typewritten manuscript), August 27, 1970

Gazlay, Francis Pershing, typewritten biography of his father Henry J. Gazlay, 1988

Graham, Eliza C., typescript with handwritten annotations, 1938

Kishline, F. Richard, typewritten biography of his father, Floyd F. Kishline, 1994

Klinger, Ed typewritten correspondence to R.B. Brigham, 1960

Songer Family Geneology, 1993

Wolter, Mrs. U.W., typewritten manuscript, undated, Willard Library, Evansville, Indiana

Nye, Vern typewritten manuscript, 1956

Magazines

Accessory and Garage Journal, American Glass Review, Australian Motorist, Automobile Dealer and Repairer, Automobile History Review, Society of Automotive Historians, Automobile Industries, Automobile Journal, Automobile Manufacturer, Automobile News Almanac, 1937, Fourth Edition, Automobile Topics, Automobile Trade Journal, Chicago History, Colliers, Commercial Car Journal, Cycle and Automobile Trade Journal, Detroit Athletic Club News, Fruit Jar Newsletter, Glass Industry, Glass Container, Heritage, Horseless Carriage Gazette, Michigan Journal S-O, MoToR, Motor Age, Motor Life, Motor Record, Motor Transport, Motor Truck, Motor Vehicle Monthly, Motor West, Motor World, National Bottler's Gazette, 1912-1913, National Glass Budget, National Glass Budget/Glass Factory Directory, National Used Car Market Report/Suppliments, New York Times Magazine, Notre Dame Scholastic, Power Wagon Magazine, The Forks (Daviess County Geneological Society publication), Smithsonian, Time

Brochures

"Why Go To Scotland For Your Shooting When Good Or Better Can Be Had In Michigan", 1932, published by the Grousehaven Shooting Reserve, authored by H. M. Jewett

"Rifle River Recreation Area", Michigan Department of Natural Resources, Parks and Recreation Division, 1995

Doctoral Papers

Holscher, Harry, "The Historical Development of Lids, Stoppers, and Closures and Their Effect Upon The Design of the Container", 1970

Williams, Lewis W., "Lorado Taft: American Sculptor and Art Missionary", University of Chicago, 1958

Interviews

Hazel Russell

Irma Kuhn

Ruth Schnepper

Edgar Kolb

Richard Kishline

Scott McKibben

Barbara Graham Pierce

Robert C. Graham, Jr.

David Graham

Photo Credits

All illustrations in this volume are from the Michael E. Keller Collection, with the exception of the following:

Willard Library (Pages 14, 15, 26, 40, 41, 43, 181)
Martin County Historical Society (Page 18)
Robert C. Graham, Jr. (Pages 16, 55, 119, 138, 213)
David Graham (Pages 117, 135, 139, 172, 182, 227)
Karl Zahm (Pages 90, 114, 115, 132, 174, 184)
Holt-Atherton Department of Special Collections/University of Pacific (Page 52)
San Joaquin County Historical Museum (Page 51)
University of Notre Dame Archives (Page 64)
Henry Austin Clark, Jr. (Page 62)
AAMA (Page 192)
Albert Kahn Associates (Pages 86, 91)
John Conde (Pages 95, 137, 187)
Ken Dunsire (Page 134)
Musei Vatican/Archivic Fotografico (Page 159)
Estate of Norman Bel Geddes/University of Texas at Austin (Page 160)
Frederick P. Williams (Page 131)
Bank of Stockton Archives (Page 51)

*The distinguished and celebrated Tyrone Power, Sr. portrayed **The Spirit of the Legion** for the Graham-Paige Motors Corporation. (Courtesy of David Graham)*

INDEX

Index

Index

Index

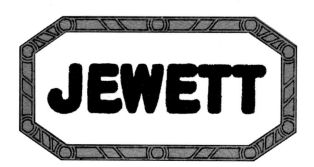

JEWETT

Robert C. Graham

GRAHAM BROTHERS
EVANSVILLE, INDIANA, U.S.A.

Graham Brothers

PAIGE
COMMERCIAL
CAR

Ray A. Graham

PAIGE JEWETT

GRAHAM BROTHERS
CANADA

GRA
A.

PAIGE-DETROIT MOTOR CAR CO.
PAIGE
DETROIT

GRAHAM BROTHERS
GB
DETROIT

The
Most Beautiful
Car in
America

The Most Serviceable

PAI
MOTOR